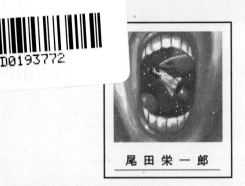

尾田栄一郎

I hear that yawning is the body's way of saying it wants oxygen. I think the reason yawns are so contagious is that whenever one person yawns, the oxygen on the face of the earth decreases significantly. It's the law of conservation of mass. Speaking of which, one time I did such a big yawn that the space shuttle, that dream of mankind, went up into space. Well, that's only half true. Time for volume 55!

  –Eiichiro Oda, 2009

iichiro Oda began his manga career at the age of 17, when his one-shot cowboy manga **Wanted!** won second place in the coveted Tezuka manga awards. Oda went on to work as an assistant to some of the biggest manga artists in the industry, including Nobuhiro Watsuki, before winning the Hop Step Award for new artists. His pirate adventure **One Piece**, which debuted in **Weekly Shonen Jump** in 1997, quickly became one of the most popular manga in Japan.

ONE PIECE VOL. 55
IMPEL DOWN PART 2

SHONEN JUMP Manga Edition

This graphic novel contains material that was originally published in English in SHONEN JUMP #87–89. Artwork in the magazine may have been slightly altered from that presented here.

STORY AND ART BY EIICHIRO ODA

English Adaptation/Lance Caselman
Translation/Laabaman, HC Language Solutions, Inc.
Touch-up Art & Lettering/Vanessa Satone
Design/Sean Lee
Editors/Alexis Kirsch, Yuki Murashige

Printed in the U.S.A.

Published by VIZ Media, LLC
P.O. Box 77010
San Francisco, CA 94107

10 9 8 7
First printing, October 2010
Seventh printing, December 2016

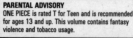

www.viz.com

THE WORLD'S MOST POPULAR MANGA
www.shonenjump.com

SHONEN JUMP MANGA

ONE PIECE

Vol. 55
A RAY OF HOPE

STORY AND ART BY
EIICHIRO ODA

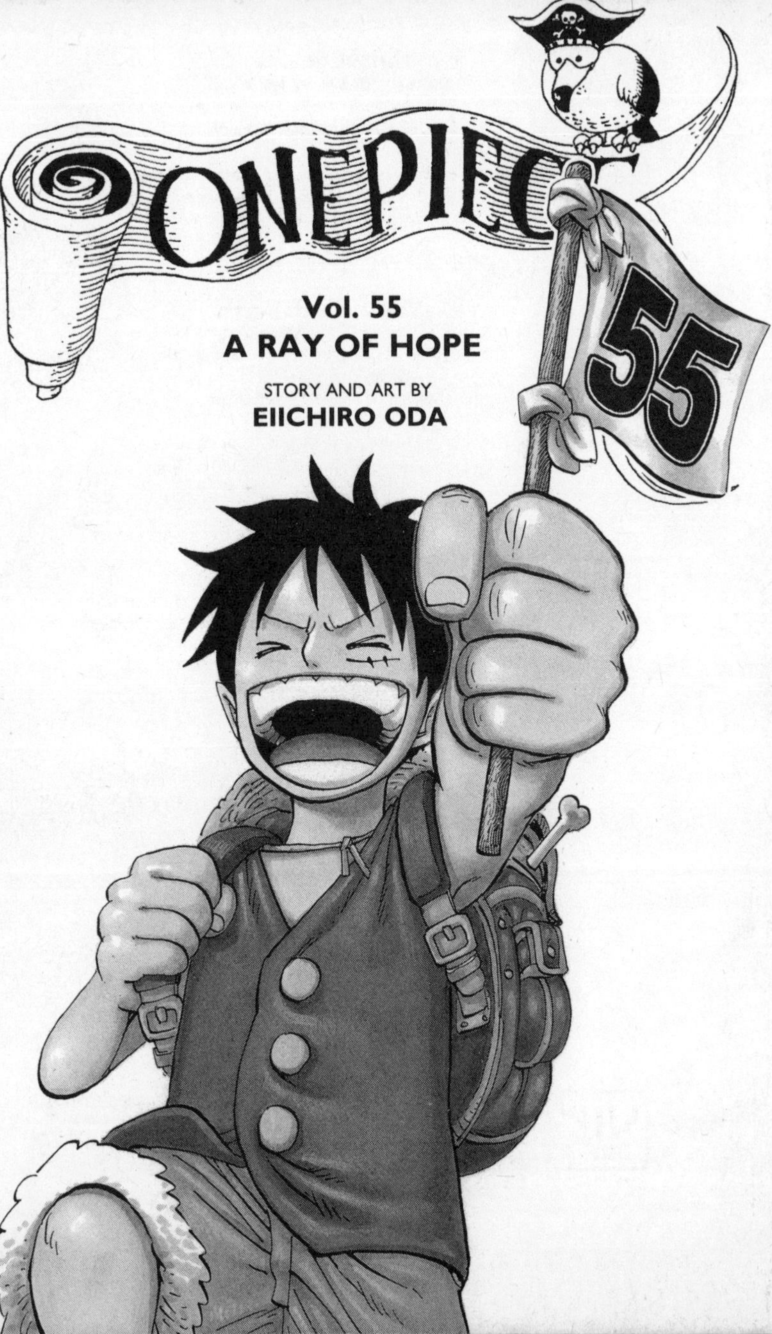

55

Underwater Prison Impel Down

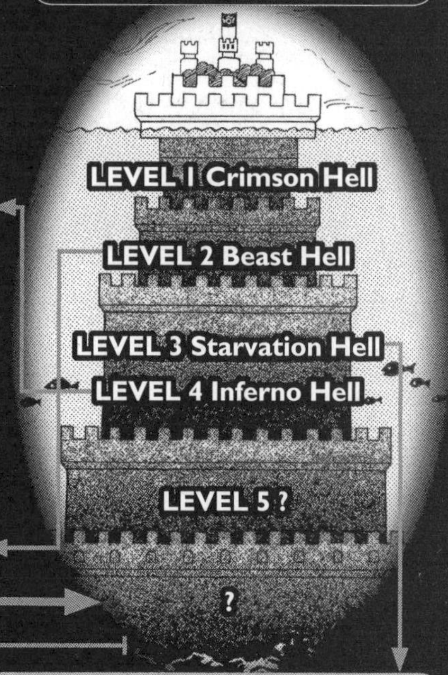

LEVEL 1 Crimson Hell
LEVEL 2 Beast Hell
LEVEL 3 Starvation Hell
LEVEL 4 Inferno Hell
LEVEL 5 ?
?

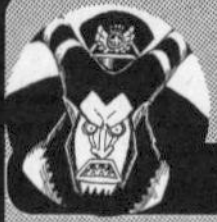

The warden of Impel Down. He possesses the powers of the Vemon-Venom Fruit.

Magellan

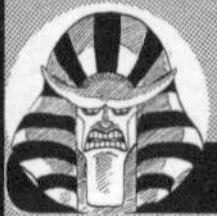

The under warden of Impel Down.

Hannyabal

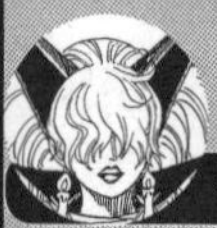

The security chief of Impel Down and the commander of the Jailer Beasts.

Sadie

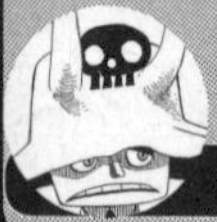

Commander of the Blugori.

Saldeath

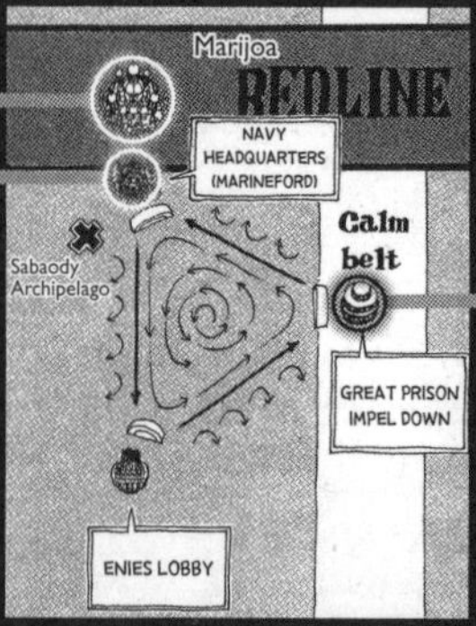

Marijoa
REDLINE
NAVY HEADQUARTERS (MARINEFORD)
Calm belt
Sabaody Archipelago
GREAT PRISON IMPEL DOWN
ENIES LOBBY

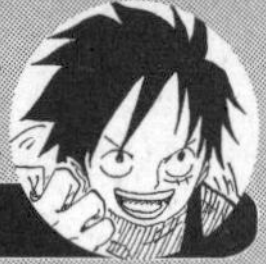

Captain of the Straw Hat pirates. He's currently on Level 3 of Impel Down trying to save his brother, Ace.

Monkey D. Luffy

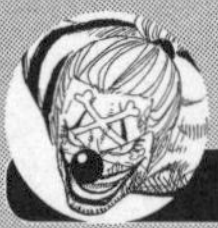

He was trying to escape from the prison when he encountered Luffy.

Buggy the Clown

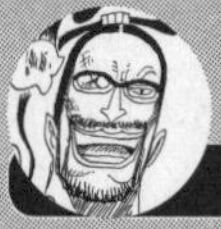

This former Baroque Works agent was imprisoned on Level 2. He was freed by Buggy, and they hit it off.

Mr. 3

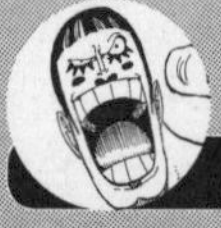

He went with Luffy in search of a mysterious person he calls "Iva."

Mr. 2 Bon Clay

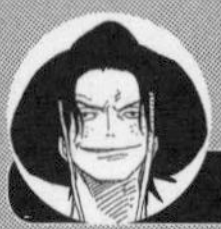

The second division commander of the Whitebeard pirates and Luffy's older brother. He was defeated by Blackbeard Teech and is currently imprisoned in Impel Down.

Portgaz D. Ace

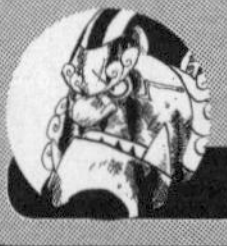

One of the Seven Warlords of the Sea. He is currently imprisoned in Impel Down as punishment for refusing the summons of the World Government.

Jimbei

THE STORY OF ONE PIECE

Volume 55

The Four Emperors

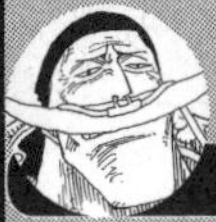

Captain of the Whitebeard pirates. He is on the way to rescue Ace.

Edward Newgate

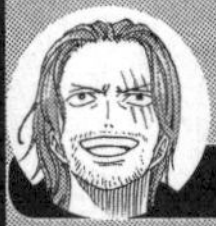

Captain of the Red-Haired pirates. Nobody knows what he will do in this war.

"Red-Haired" Shanks

Monkey D. Luffy started out as just a kid with a dream—to become the greatest pirate in history! Stirred by the tales of pirate "Red-Haired" Shanks, Luffy vowed to become a pirate himself. That was before the enchanted Devil Fruit gave Luffy the power to stretch like rubber, at the cost of being unable to swim—a serious handicap for an aspiring sea dog. Undeterred, Luffy set out to sea and recruited some crewmates—master swordsman Zolo; treasure-hunting thief Nami; lying sharpshooter Usopp; the high-kicking chef Sanji; Chopper, the walkin' talkin' reindeer doctor; mysterious archaeologist Robin; cyborg shipwright Franky; and Brook, a musical skeleton!

After their defeat in the battle of the Sabaody Archipelago, the Straw Hat pirates find themselves scattered to various islands. Luffy ends up on the Island of Women, where he wins the heart of Boa Hancock. When he learns that Ace is soon to be executed, he recruits the empress to help him break into the impregnable underwater prison Impel Down. But as he searches for his brother, Luffy encounters his old enemy Buggy the Clown and becomes embroiled in the battles between Buggy and his jailers, thereby revealing his presence to the enemy. With an army of guards and monsters hot on their heels, the fugitives pass through Crimson Hell and Beast Hell and continue downward. On the way, they free Mr. 3 and Mr. 2 Bon Clay. But as the outlaws continue their descent, the forces of the entire prison gather on Level 4 to capture Luffy.

Warlords of the Sea

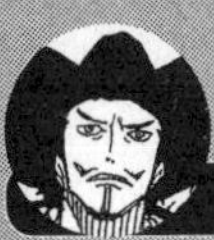

The world's most powerful swordsman. He has shown an interest in Luffy's crew.

Dracule Mihawk

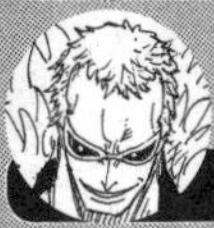

A mysterious man who believes that power is everything.

Don Quixote Doflamingo

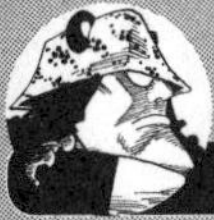

Also known as "the Tyrant," he scattered Luffy and his crew all over the Grand Line.

Bartholomew Kuma

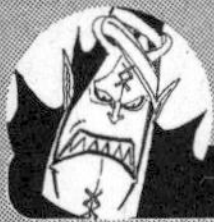

Although he already lost to Luffy once, he answers the call of battle.

Gecko Moria

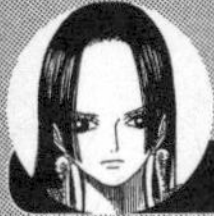

The empress of Amazon Lily and captain of the Kuja pirates.

Boa Hancock

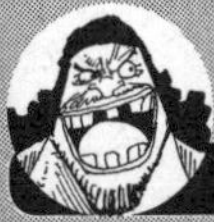

Captain of the Blackbeard pirates. He caused Ace's capture.

Marshall D. Teech

The Navy

Currently assembled at Navy Headquarters in Marineford.

Fleet Admiral	Sengoku
Admiral	Aokiji
	Kizaru
Vice Admiral	Garp
	Momonga
Commodore	Smoker
Captain	"Black Cage" Hina
	T-Bone
Ensign	Tashigi

Vol. 55
A Ray of Hope

CONTENTS

Chapter 533: Level 4: Inferno Hell	7
Chapter 534: Warden Magellen vs. Pirate Luffy	27
Chapter 535: Friend	47
Chapter 536: Level 5: Frozen Hell	67
Chapter 537: A Ray of Hope	86
Chapter 538: Level 5.5: New Kama Land	107
Chapter 539: Emporio Energy Hormone	127
Chapter 540: Level 6: Infinite Hell	146
Chapter 541: The Greatest Ever	167

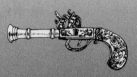

Chapter 533:
LEVEL 4: INFERNO HELL

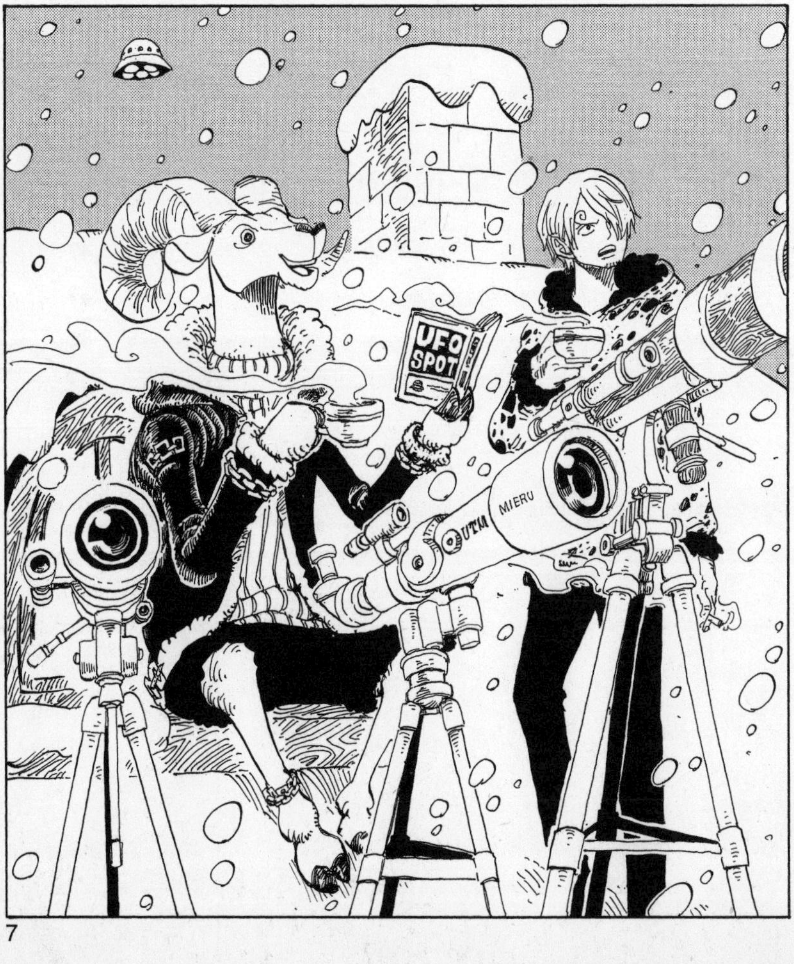
UFO SPOT
UTTA MIERU

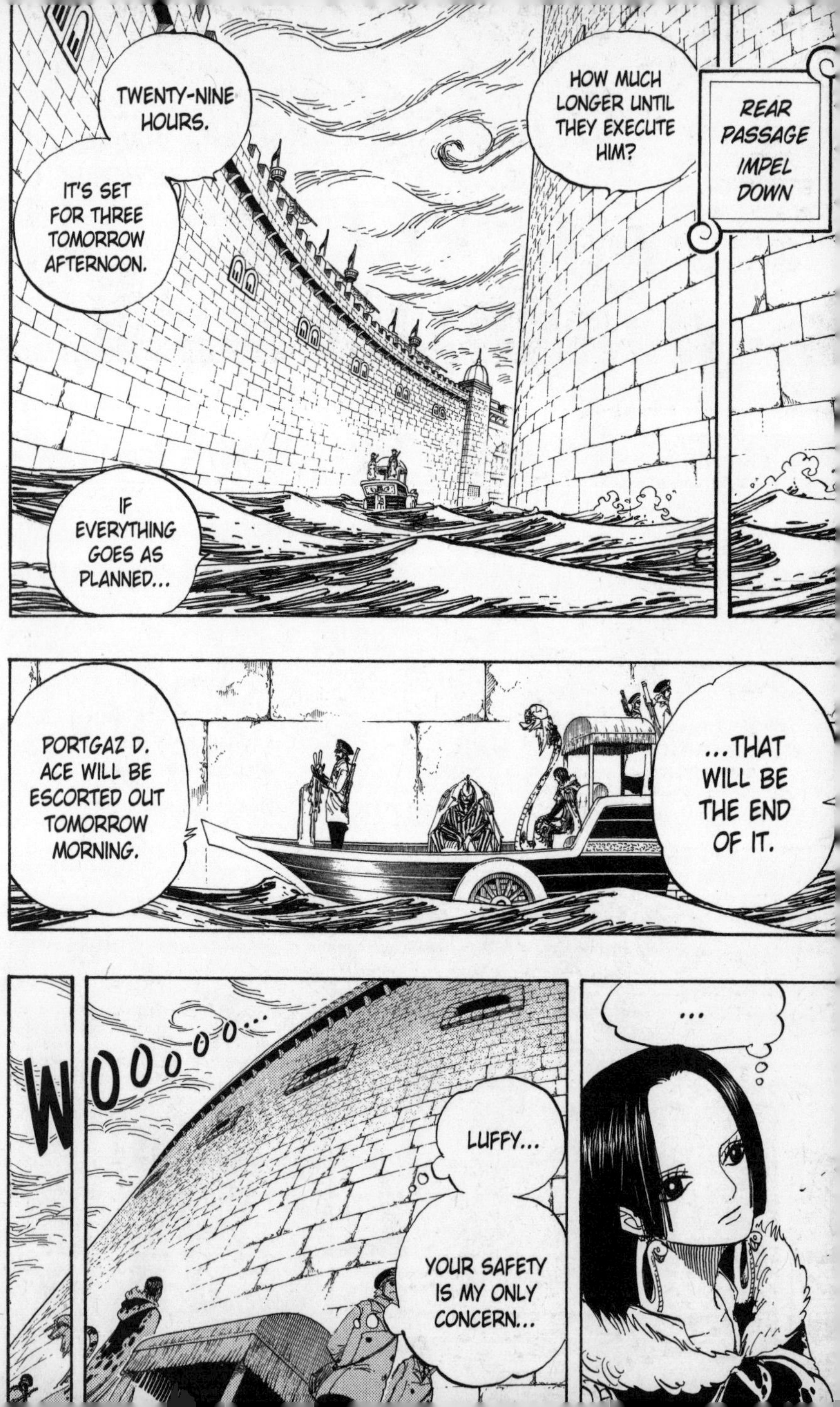
REAR PASSAGE IMPEL DOWN
HOW MUCH LONGER UNTIL THEY EXECUTE HIM?
TWENTY-NINE HOURS.
IT'S SET FOR THREE TOMORROW AFTERNOON.
IF EVERYTHING GOES AS PLANNED...
...THAT WILL BE THE END OF IT.
PORTGAZ D. ACE WILL BE ESCORTED OUT TOMORROW MORNING.
...
LUFFY...
YOUR SAFETY IS MY ONLY CONCERN...
WOOOOO...

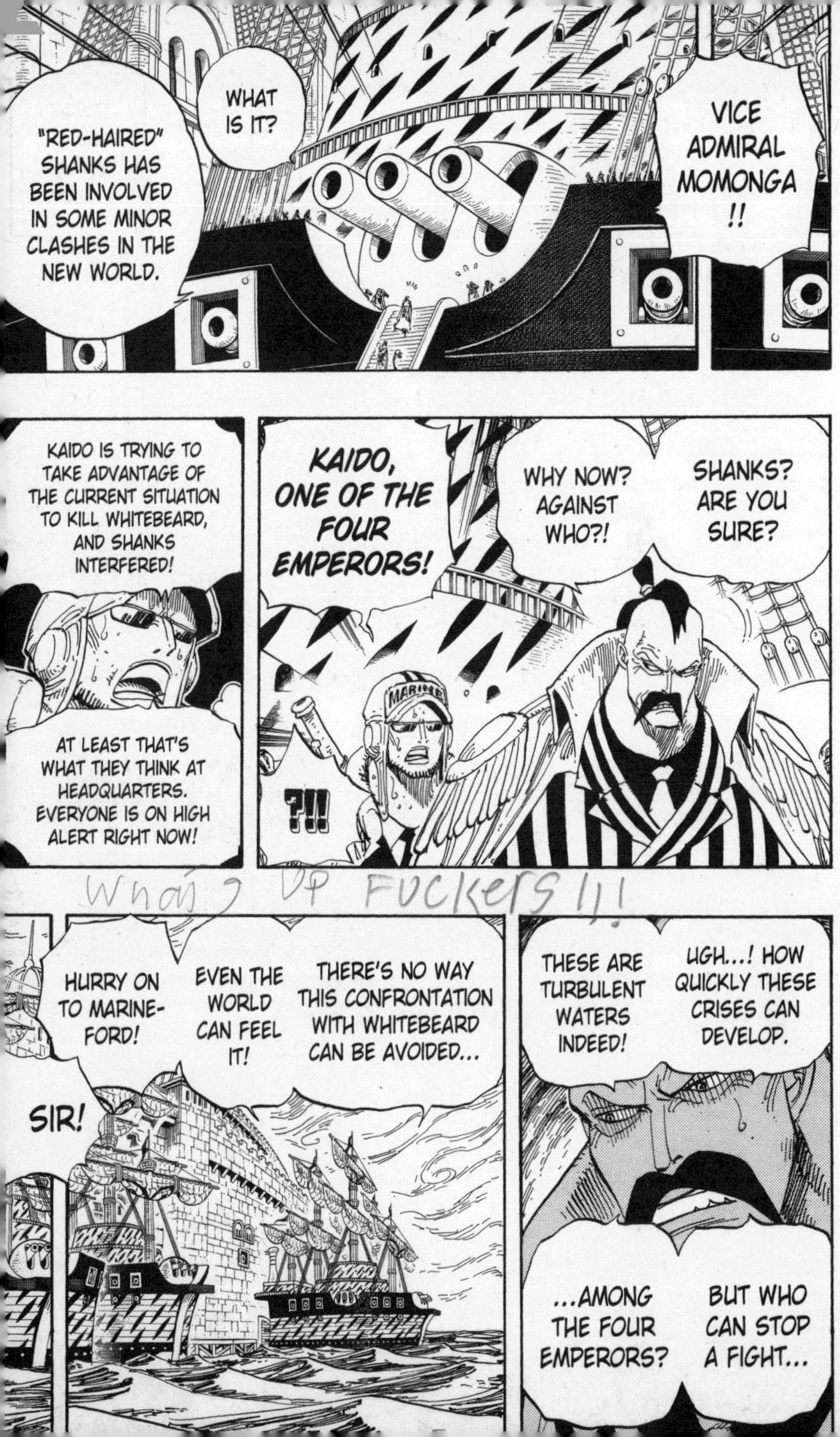
VICE ADMIRAL MOMONGA!!
WHAT IS IT?
"RED-HAIRED" SHANKS HAS BEEN INVOLVED IN SOME MINOR CLASHES IN THE NEW WORLD.
SHANKS? ARE YOU SURE?
WHY NOW? AGAINST WHO?!
KAIDO, ONE OF THE FOUR EMPERORS!
?!!
KAIDO IS TRYING TO TAKE ADVANTAGE OF THE CURRENT SITUATION TO KILL WHITEBEARD, AND SHANKS INTERFERED!
AT LEAST THAT'S WHAT THEY THINK AT HEADQUARTERS. EVERYONE IS ON HIGH ALERT RIGHT NOW!
Whats up Fuckers!!!
UGH...! HOW QUICKLY THESE CRISES CAN DEVELOP.
THESE ARE TURBULENT WATERS INDEED!
BUT WHO CAN STOP A FIGHT...
...AMONG THE FOUR EMPERORS?
THERE'S NO WAY THIS CONFRONTATION WITH WHITEBEARD CAN BE AVOIDED...
EVEN THE WORLD CAN FEEL IT!
HURRY ON TO MARINE-FORD!
SIR!

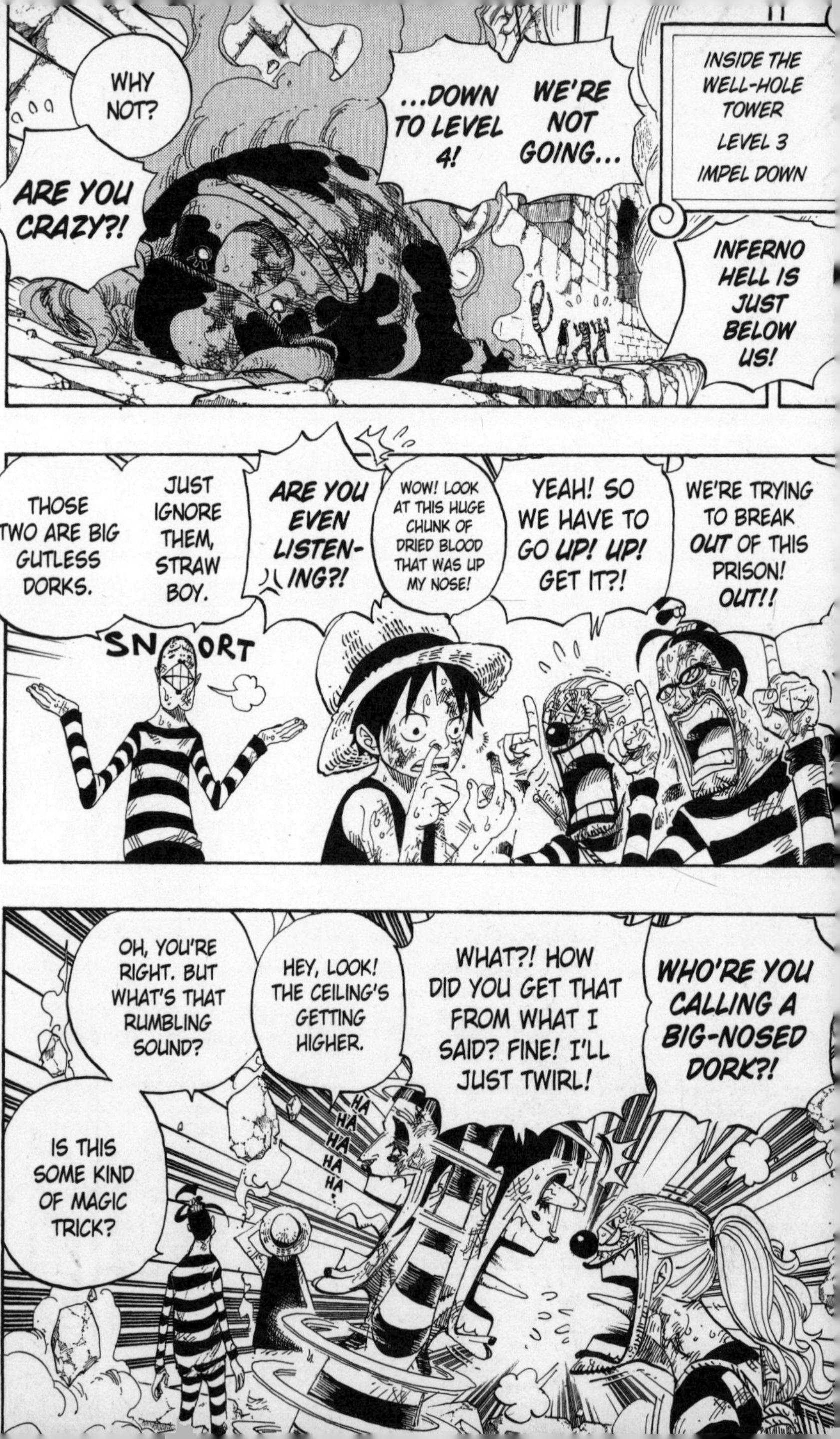

INSIDE THE WELL-HOLE TOWER LEVEL 3 IMPEL DOWN
INFERNO HELL IS JUST BELOW US!
WE'RE NOT GOING...
...DOWN TO LEVEL 4!
WHY NOT?
ARE YOU CRAZY?!
WE'RE TRYING TO BREAK OUT OF THIS PRISON! OUT!!
YEAH! SO WE HAVE TO GO UP! UP! GET IT?!
WOW! LOOK AT THIS HUGE CHUNK OF DRIED BLOOD THAT WAS UP MY NOSE!
ARE YOU EVEN LISTENING?!
JUST IGNORE THEM, STRAW BOY.
THOSE TWO ARE BIG GUTLESS DORKS.
SNORT
WHO'RE YOU CALLING A BIG-NOSED DORK?!
WHAT?! HOW DID YOU GET THAT FROM WHAT I SAID? FINE! I'LL JUST TWIRL!
HA HA HA HA HA
HEY, LOOK! THE CEILING'S GETTING HIGHER.
OH, YOU'RE RIGHT. BUT WHAT'S THAT RUMBLING SOUND?
IS THIS SOME KIND OF MAGIC TRICK?

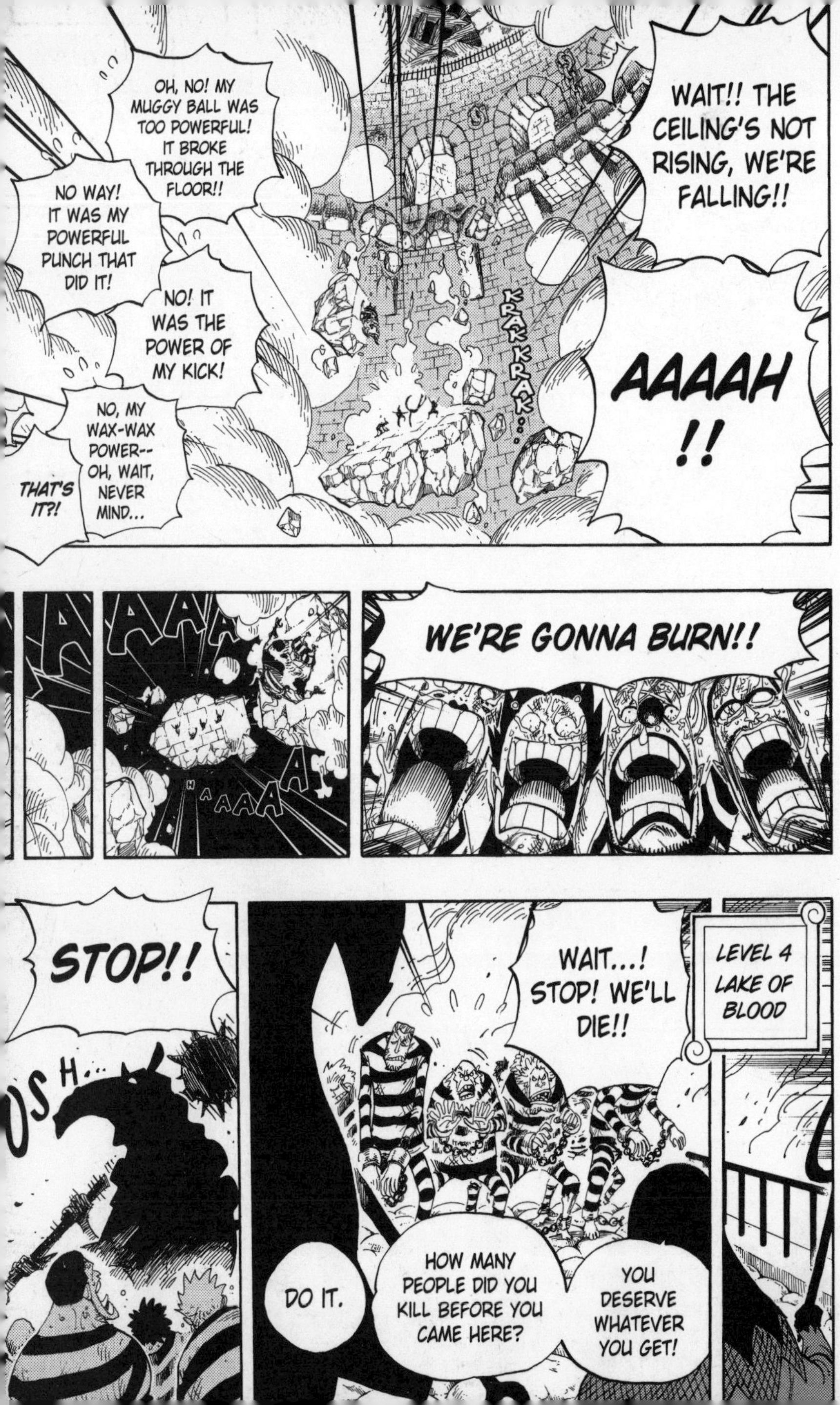
WAIT!! THE CEILING'S NOT RISING, WE'RE FALLING!!
AAAAH !!
KRAKKRAK...
OH, NO! MY MUGGY BALL WAS TOO POWERFUL! IT BROKE THROUGH THE FLOOR!!
NO WAY! IT WAS MY POWERFUL PUNCH THAT DID IT!
NO! IT WAS THE POWER OF MY KICK!
NO, MY WAX-WAX POWER-- OH, WAIT, NEVER MIND...
THAT'S IT?!
WE'RE GONNA BURN!!
LEVEL 4 LAKE OF BLOOD
WAIT...! STOP! WE'LL DIE!!
YOU DESERVE WHATEVER YOU GET!
HOW MANY PEOPLE DID YOU KILL BEFORE YOU CAME HERE?
DO IT.
STOP!!

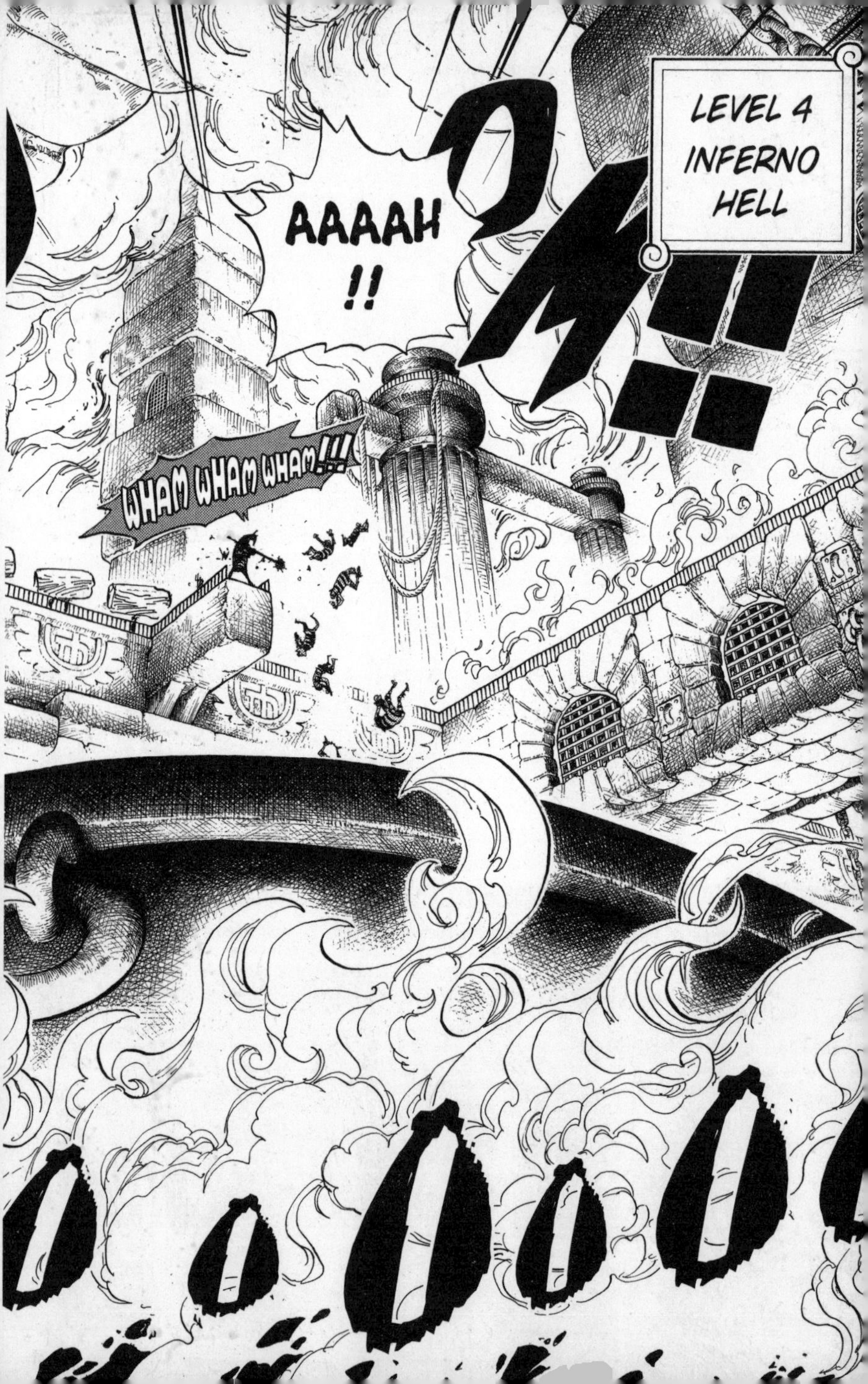
LEVEL 4 INFERNO HELL
AAAAH!!
WHAM WHAM WHAM!!!

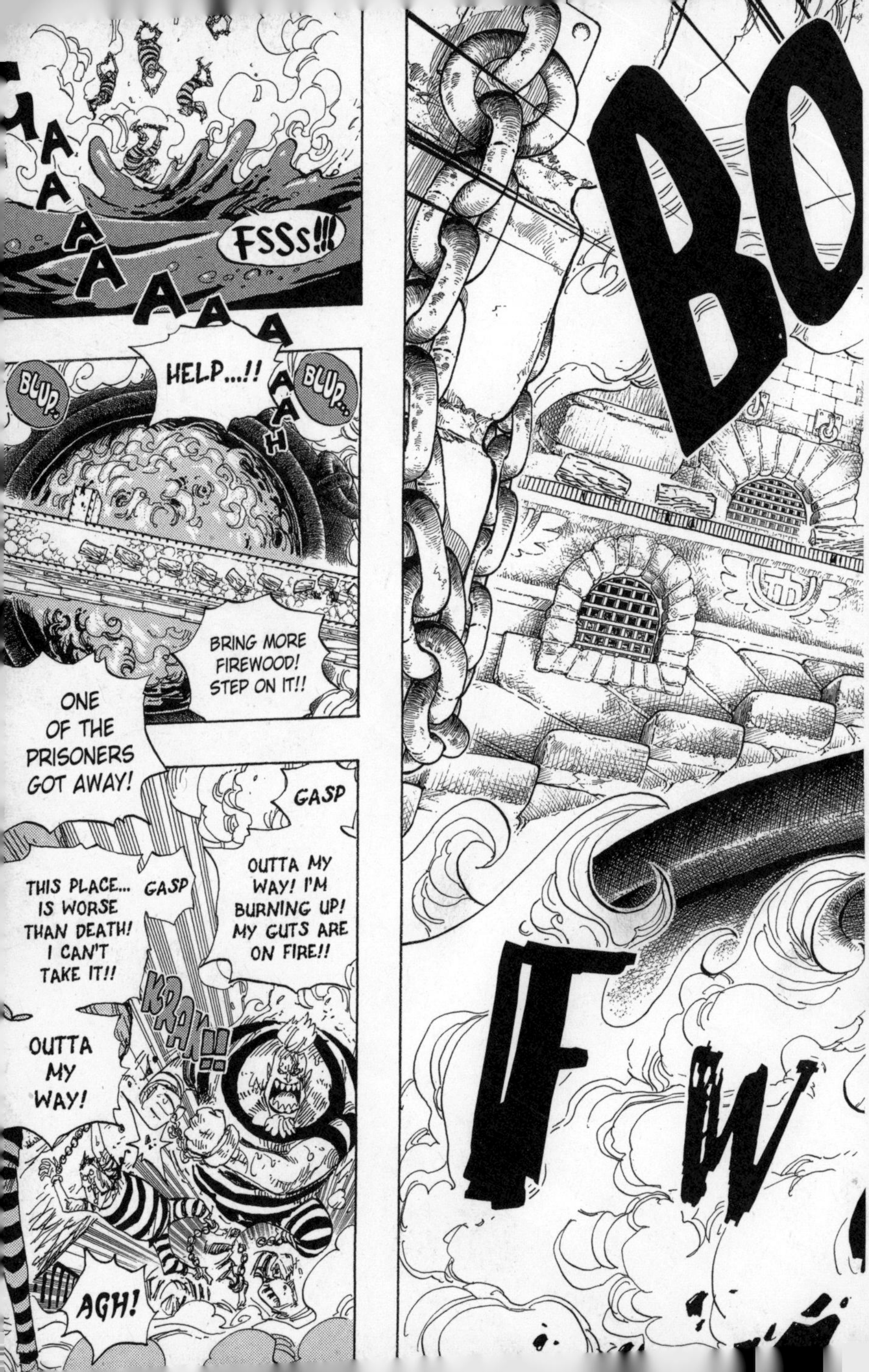
BO
FW
AAAAAAAAAAAH
FSSS!!!
HELP...!!
BLUP...
BLUP...
BRING MORE FIREWOOD! STEP ON IT!!
ONE OF THE PRISONERS GOT AWAY!
GASP
OUTTA MY WAY! I'M BURNING UP! MY GUTS ARE ON FIRE!!
GASP
THIS PLACE... IS WORSE THAN DEATH! I CAN'T TAKE IT!!
KRAK!!
OUTTA MY WAY!
AGH!

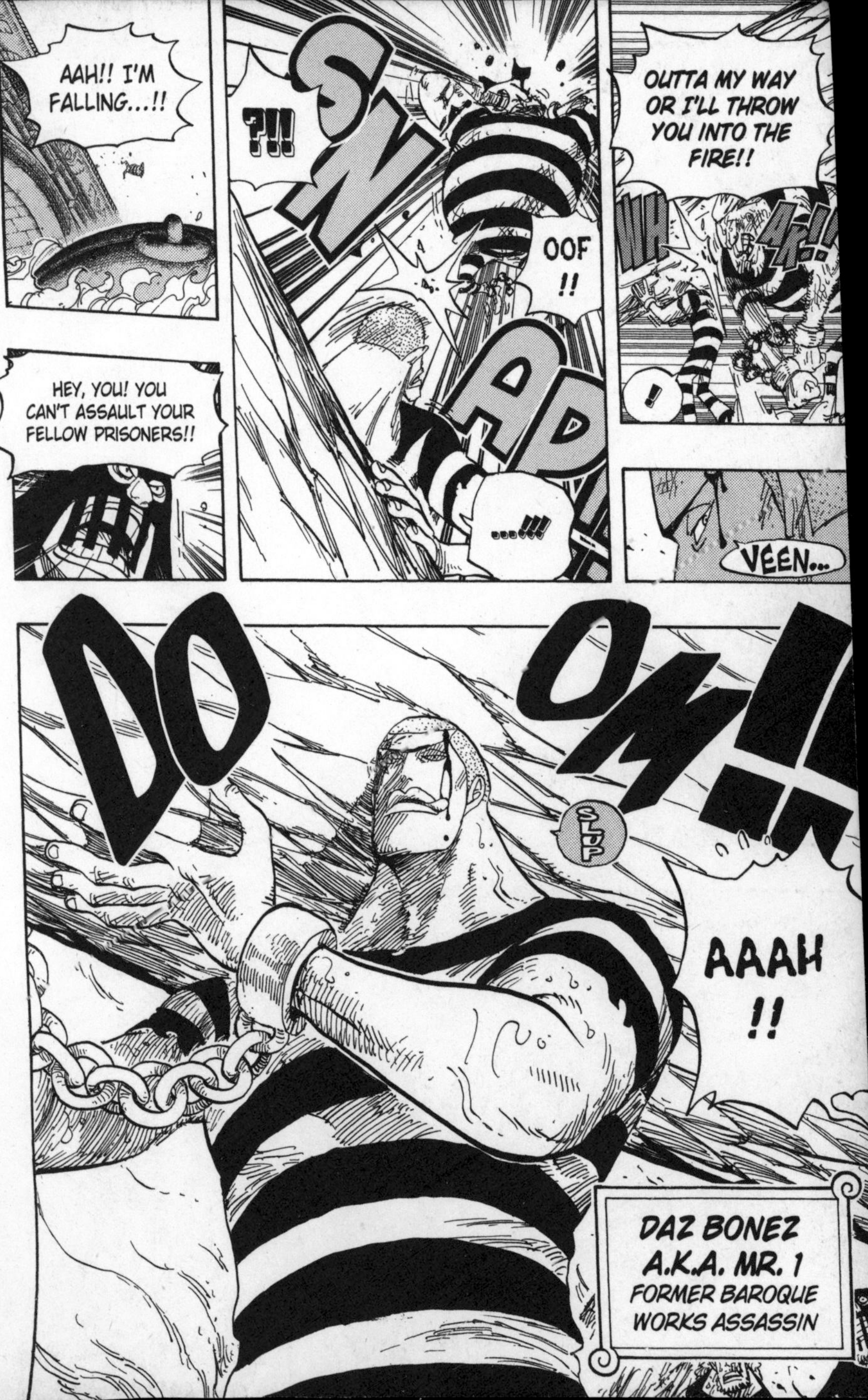
OUTTA MY WAY OR I'LL THROW YOU INTO THE FIRE!!
WH
AA!!
!
VEEN...
?!!
SN
AP
OOF !!
...!!!
AAH!! I'M FALLING...!!
HEY, YOU! YOU CAN'T ASSAULT YOUR FELLOW PRISONERS!!
DO
OM!!
SLUP
AAAH !!
DAZ BONEZ A.K.A. MR. 1
FORMER BAROQUE WORKS ASSASSIN

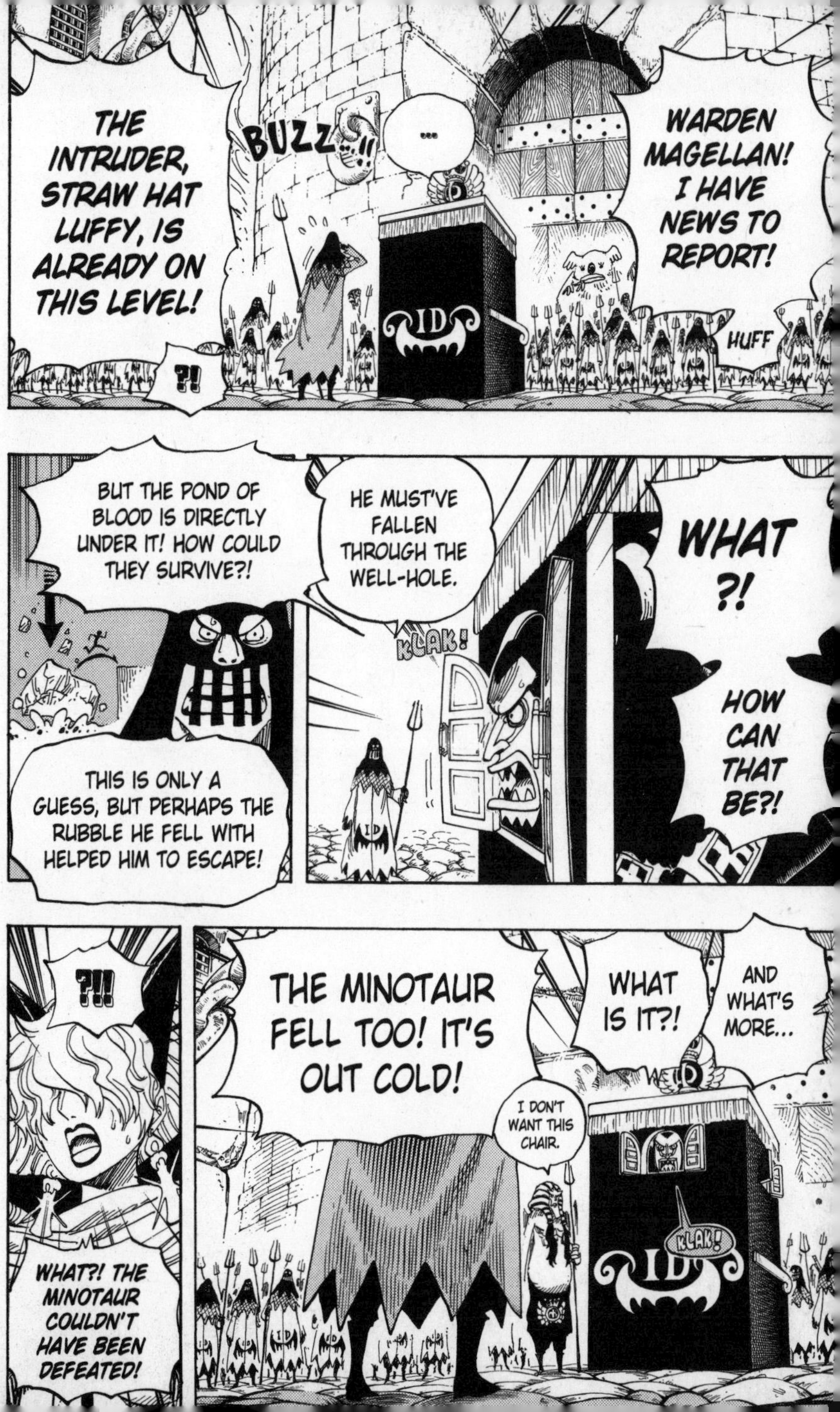
WARDEN MAGELLAN! I HAVE NEWS TO REPORT!
HUFF
...
BUZZ...!!
THE INTRUDER, STRAW HAT LUFFY, IS ALREADY ON THIS LEVEL!
?!
WHAT?!
HOW CAN THAT BE?!
HE MUST'VE FALLEN THROUGH THE WELL-HOLE.
KLAK!
BUT THE POND OF BLOOD IS DIRECTLY UNDER IT! HOW COULD THEY SURVIVE?!
THIS IS ONLY A GUESS, BUT PERHAPS THE RUBBLE HE FELL WITH HELPED HIM TO ESCAPE!
AND WHAT'S MORE...
WHAT IS IT?!
THE MINOTAUR FELL TOO! IT'S OUT COLD!
I DON'T WANT THIS CHAIR.
KLAK!
?!!
WHAT?! THE MINOTAUR COULDN'T HAVE BEEN DEFEATED!

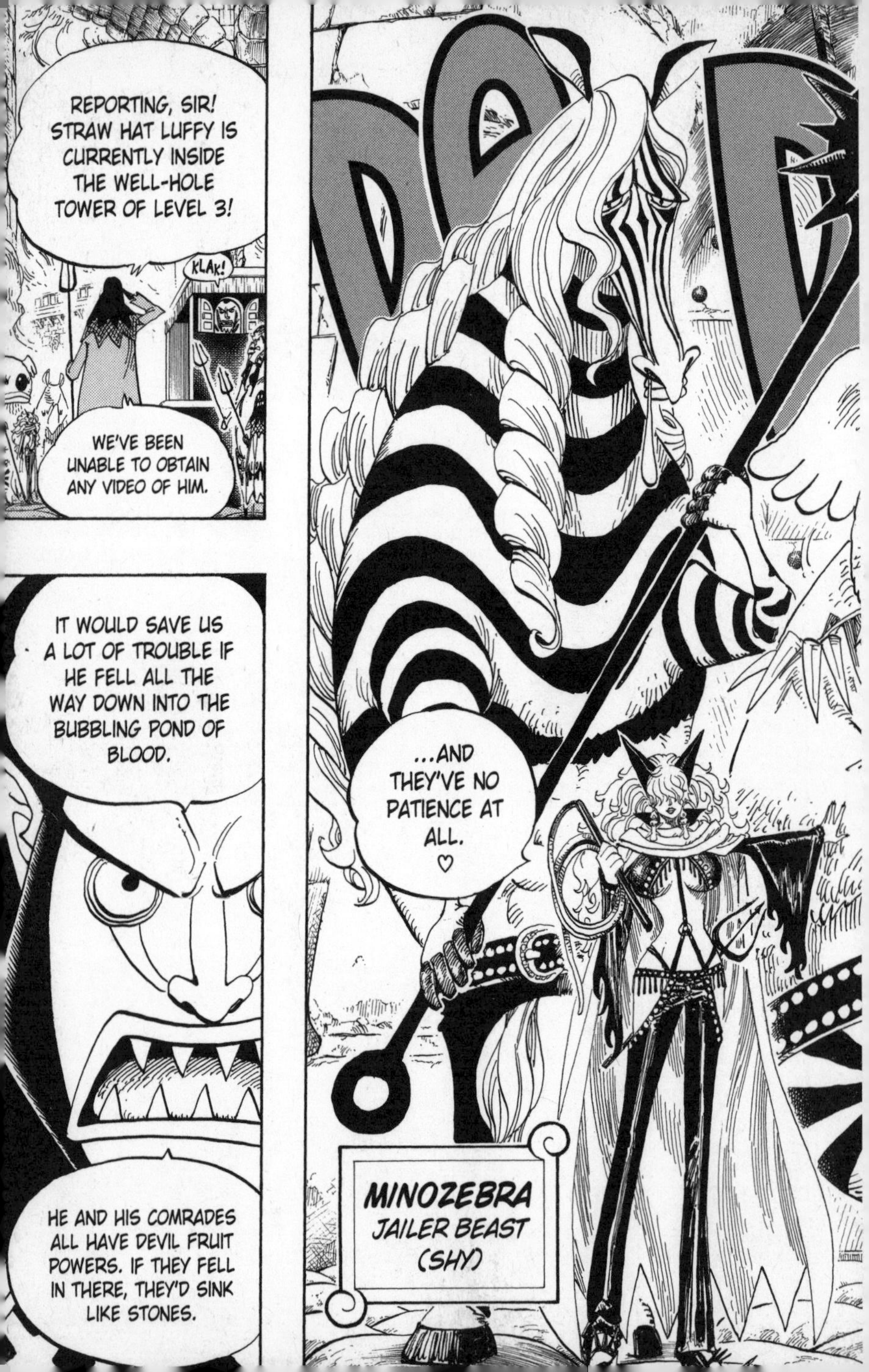
DOOM
...AND THEY'VE NO PATIENCE AT ALL. ♡
MINOZEBRA
JAILER BEAST
(SHY)
REPORTING, SIR! STRAW HAT LUFFY IS CURRENTLY INSIDE THE WELL-HOLE TOWER OF LEVEL 3!
KLAK!
WE'VE BEEN UNABLE TO OBTAIN ANY VIDEO OF HIM.
IT WOULD SAVE US A LOT OF TROUBLE IF HE FELL ALL THE WAY DOWN INTO THE BUBBLING POND OF BLOOD.
HE AND HIS COMRADES ALL HAVE DEVIL FRUIT POWERS. IF THEY FELL IN THERE, THEY'D SINK LIKE STONES.

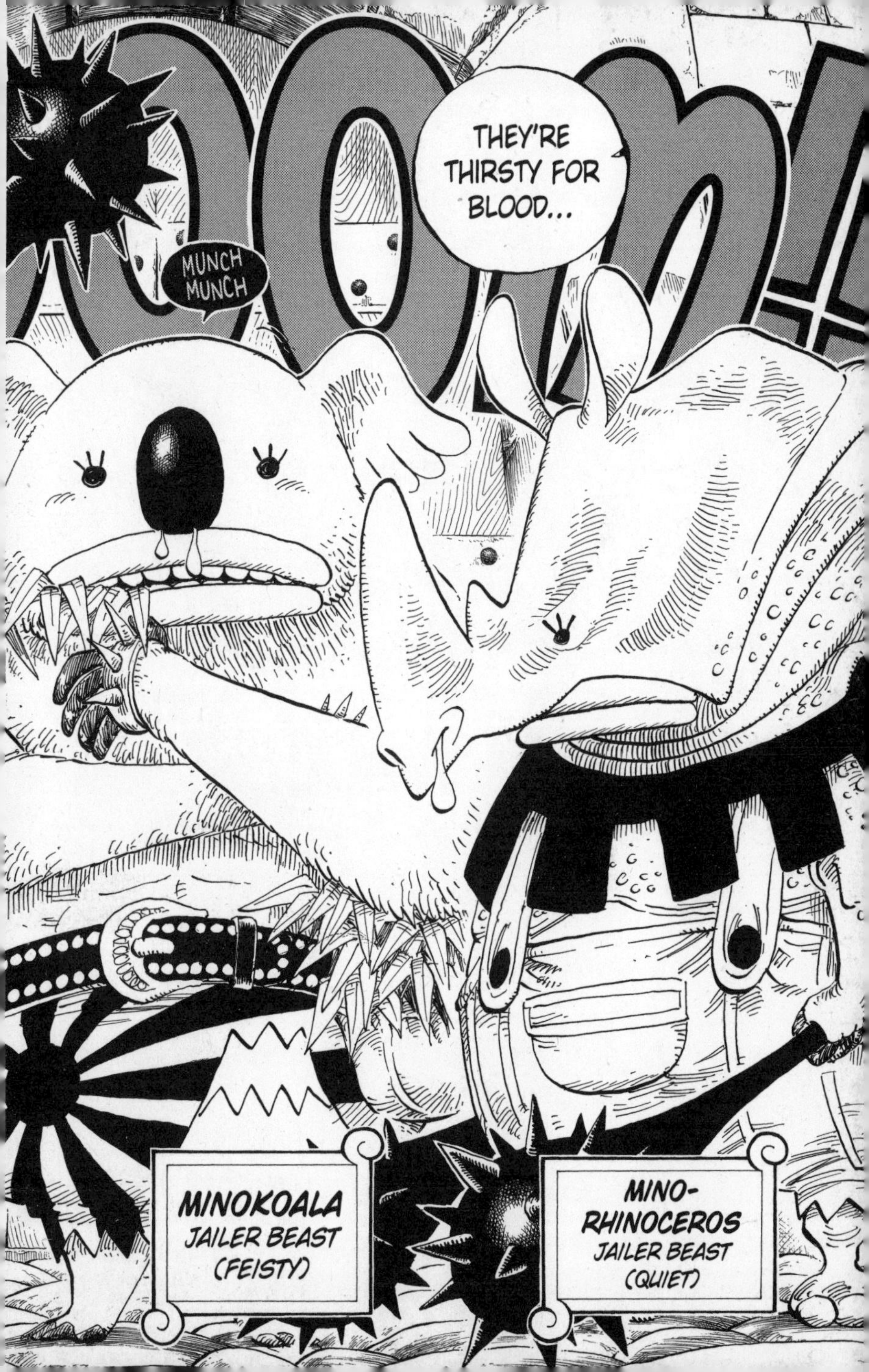
THEY'RE THIRSTY FOR BLOOD...
MUNCH MUNCH
MINO-RHINOCEROS JAILER BEAST (QUIET)
MINOKOALA JAILER BEAST (FEISTY)

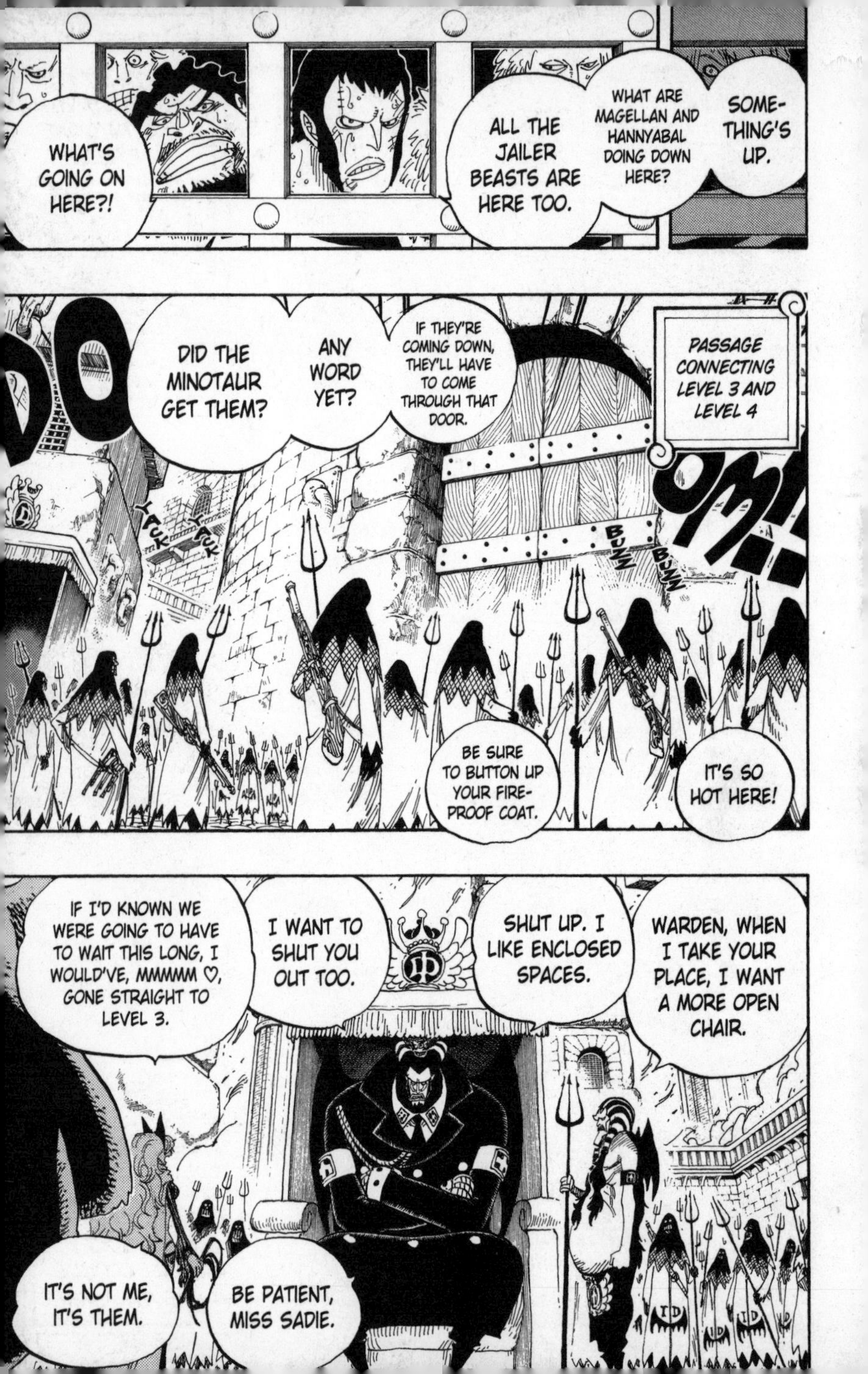
SOME-THING'S UP.
WHAT ARE MAGELLAN AND HANNYABAL DOING DOWN HERE?
ALL THE JAILER BEASTS ARE HERE TOO.
WHAT'S GOING ON HERE?!
PASSAGE CONNECTING LEVEL 3 AND LEVEL 4
DOOM!!
IF THEY'RE COMING DOWN, THEY'LL HAVE TO COME THROUGH THAT DOOR.
ANY WORD YET?
DID THE MINOTAUR GET THEM?
BUZZ BUZZ
YACK YACK
IT'S SO HOT HERE!
BE SURE TO BUTTON UP YOUR FIRE-PROOF COAT.
WARDEN, WHEN I TAKE YOUR PLACE, I WANT A MORE OPEN CHAIR.
SHUT UP. I LIKE ENCLOSED SPACES.
I WANT TO SHUT YOU OUT TOO.
IF I'D KNOWN WE WERE GOING TO HAVE TO WAIT THIS LONG, I WOULD'VE, MMMMM ♡, GONE STRAIGHT TO LEVEL 3.
BE PATIENT, MISS SADIE.
IT'S NOT ME, IT'S THEM.

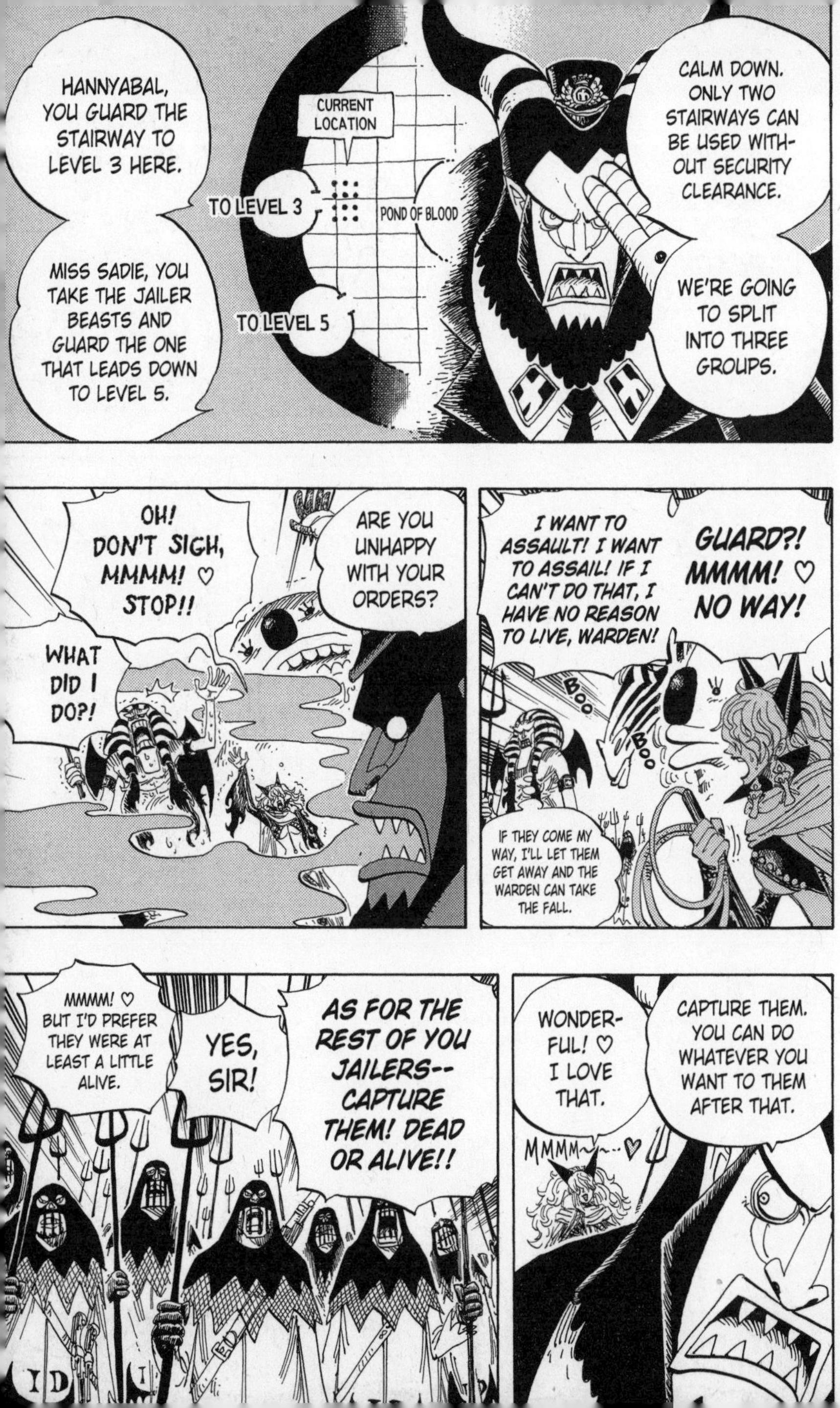
CALM DOWN. ONLY TWO STAIRWAYS CAN BE USED WITH-OUT SECURITY CLEARANCE.
WE'RE GOING TO SPLIT INTO THREE GROUPS.
CURRENT LOCATION
POND OF BLOOD
TO LEVEL 3
TO LEVEL 5
HANNYABAL, YOU GUARD THE STAIRWAY TO LEVEL 3 HERE.
MISS SADIE, YOU TAKE THE JAILER BEASTS AND GUARD THE ONE THAT LEADS DOWN TO LEVEL 5.
GUARD?! MMMM! ♡ NO WAY!
I WANT TO ASSAULT! I WANT TO ASSAIL! IF I CAN'T DO THAT, I HAVE NO REASON TO LIVE, WARDEN!
BOO
BOO
IF THEY COME MY WAY, I'LL LET THEM GET AWAY AND THE WARDEN CAN TAKE THE FALL.
ARE YOU UNHAPPY WITH YOUR ORDERS?
OH! DON'T SIGH, MMMM! ♡ STOP!!
WHAT DID I DO?!
CAPTURE THEM. YOU CAN DO WHATEVER YOU WANT TO THEM AFTER THAT.
WONDER-FUL! ♡ I LOVE THAT.
MMMM~~~♥
AS FOR THE REST OF YOU JAILERS-- CAPTURE THEM! DEAD OR ALIVE!!
YES, SIR!
MMMM! ♡ BUT I'D PREFER THEY WERE AT LEAST A LITTLE ALIVE.

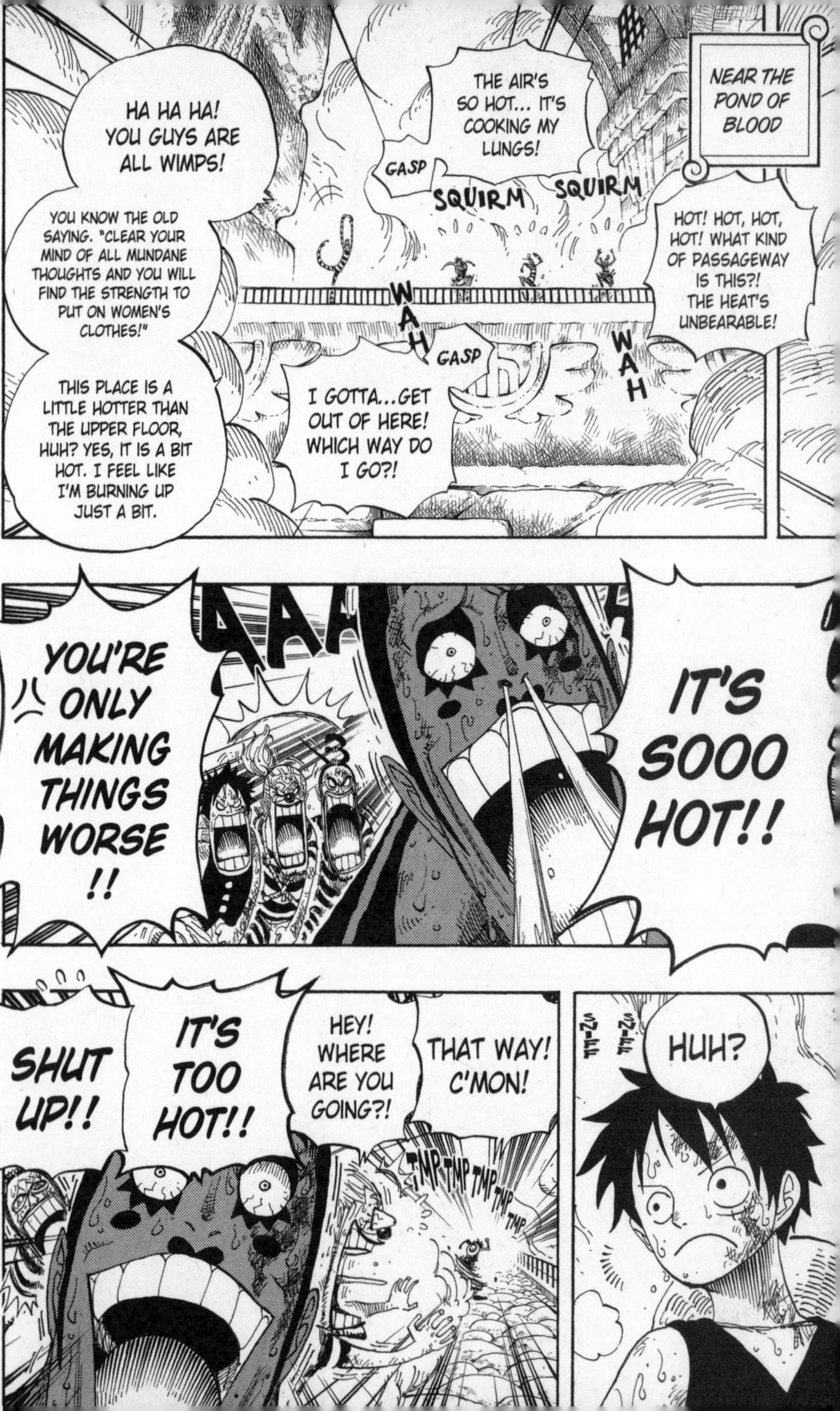
NEAR THE POND OF BLOOD
HOT! HOT, HOT, HOT! WHAT KIND OF PASSAGEWAY IS THIS?! THE HEAT'S UNBEARABLE!
THE AIR'S SO HOT... IT'S COOKING MY LUNGS!
GASP
SQUIRM
SQUIRM
WAH
WAH
GASP
I GOTTA...GET OUT OF HERE! WHICH WAY DO I GO?!
HA HA HA! YOU GUYS ARE ALL WIMPS!
YOU KNOW THE OLD SAYING. "CLEAR YOUR MIND OF ALL MUNDANE THOUGHTS AND YOU WILL FIND THE STRENGTH TO PUT ON WOMEN'S CLOTHES!"
THIS PLACE IS A LITTLE HOTTER THAN THE UPPER FLOOR, HUH? YES, IT IS A BIT HOT. I FEEL LIKE I'M BURNING UP JUST A BIT.
IT'S SOOO HOT!!
YOU'RE ONLY MAKING THINGS WORSE!!
SNIFF
SNIFF
HUH?
THAT WAY! C'MON!
HEY! WHERE ARE YOU GOING?!
TMP TMP TMP TMP TMP TMP
IT'S TOO HOT!!
SHUT UP!!

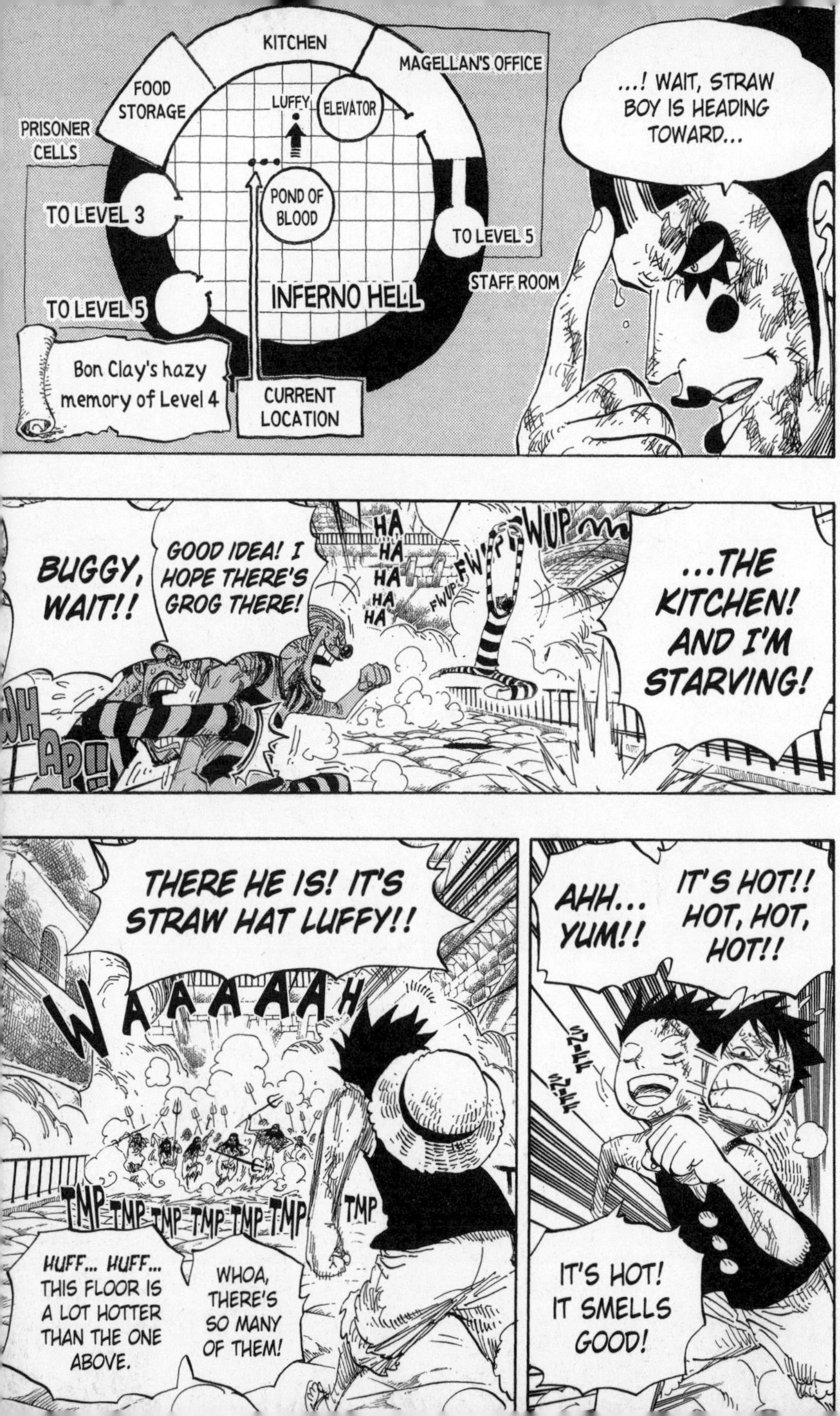
...! WAIT, STRAW BOY IS HEADING TOWARD...
KITCHEN
MAGELLAN'S OFFICE
FOOD STORAGE
PRISONER CELLS
LUFFY
ELEVATOR
TO LEVEL 3
POND OF BLOOD
TO LEVEL 5
STAFF ROOM
TO LEVEL 5
INFERNO HELL
Bon Clay's hazy memory of Level 4
CURRENT LOCATION
...THE KITCHEN! AND I'M STARVING!
FWUP
FWUP
FWUP
HA HA HA HA HA
GOOD IDEA! I HOPE THERE'S GROG THERE!
BUGGY, WAIT!!
WHAP!!
IT'S HOT!! HOT, HOT, HOT!!
AHH... YUM!!
SNIFF
SNIFF
IT'S HOT! IT SMELLS GOOD!
THERE HE IS! IT'S STRAW HAT LUFFY!!
WAAAAAH
TMP TMP TMP TMP TMP TMP TMP
WHOA, THERE'S SO MANY OF THEM!
HUFF... HUFF... THIS FLOOR IS A LOT HOTTER THAN THE ONE ABOVE.

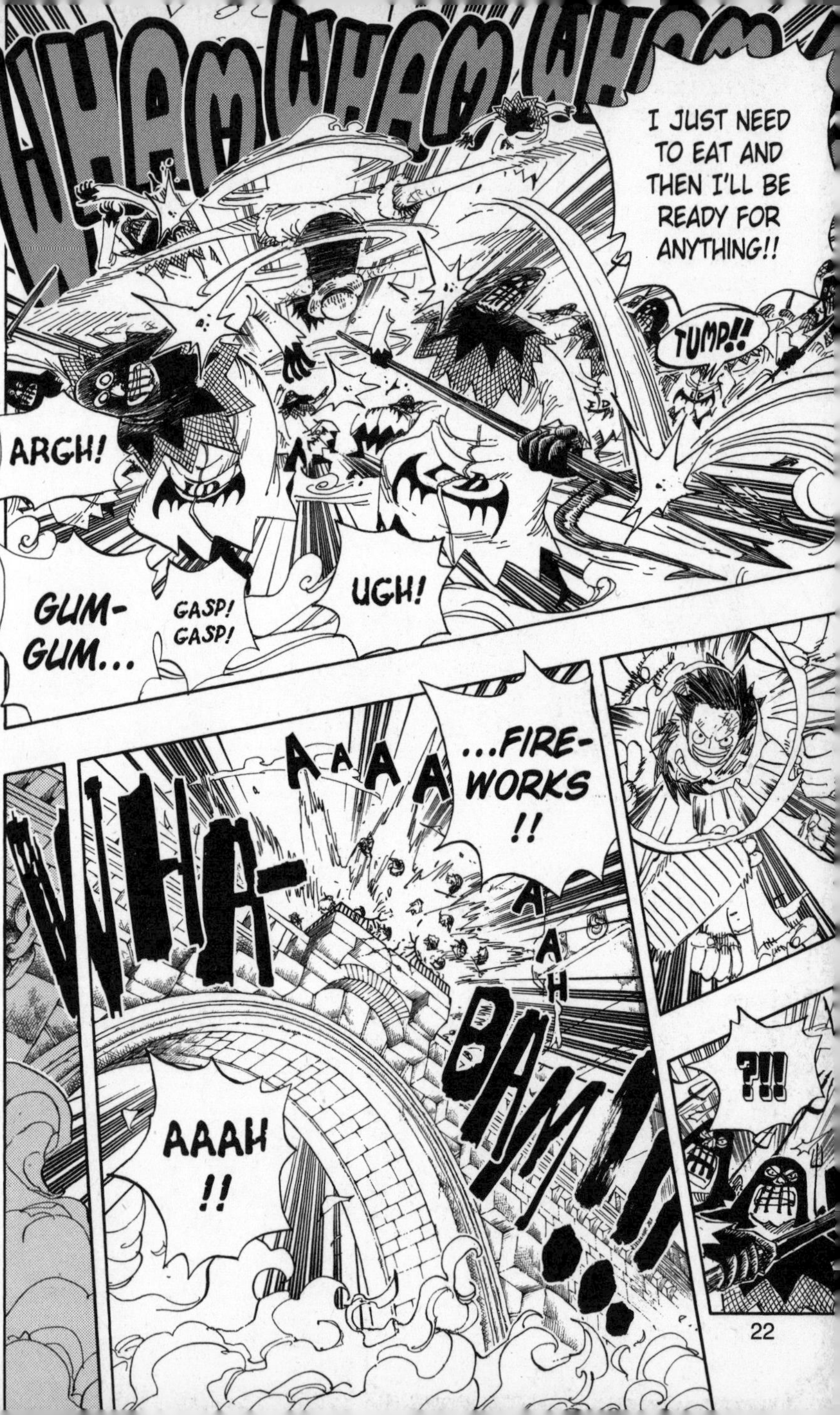
I JUST NEED TO EAT AND THEN I'LL BE READY FOR ANYTHING!!
WHAM WHAM WHAM
TUMP!!
ARGH!
UGH!
GASP! GASP!
GUM-GUM...
...FIRE-WORKS!!
?!!
AAAAAAH
WHA-
BAM
AAAH!!

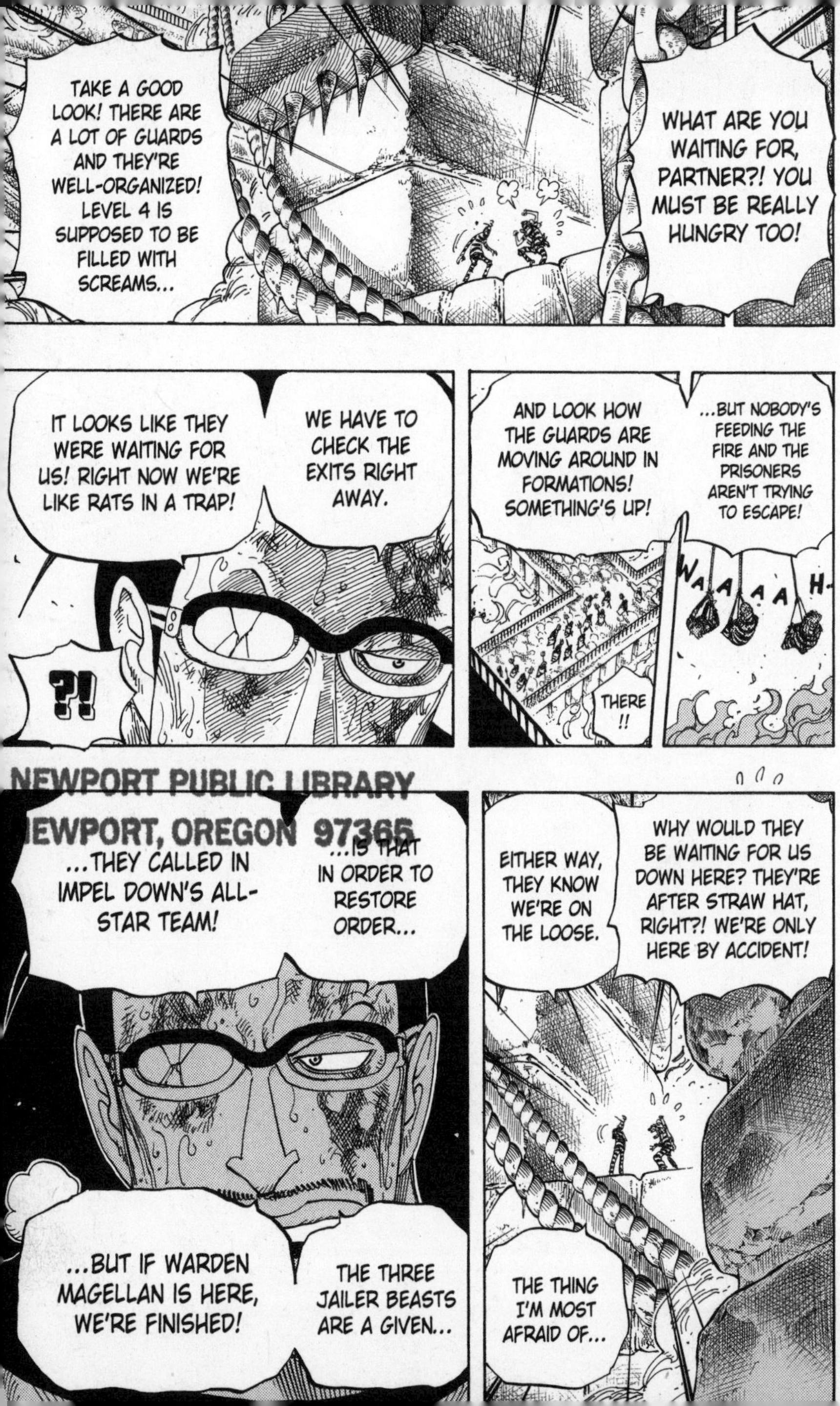
WHAT ARE YOU WAITING FOR, PARTNER?! YOU MUST BE REALLY HUNGRY TOO!
TAKE A GOOD LOOK! THERE ARE A LOT OF GUARDS AND THEY'RE WELL-ORGANIZED! LEVEL 4 IS SUPPOSED TO BE FILLED WITH SCREAMS...
...BUT NOBODY'S FEEDING THE FIRE AND THE PRISONERS AREN'T TRYING TO ESCAPE!
AND LOOK HOW THE GUARDS ARE MOVING AROUND IN FORMATIONS! SOMETHING'S UP!
WAAAAH-
THERE!!
WE HAVE TO CHECK THE EXITS RIGHT AWAY.
IT LOOKS LIKE THEY WERE WAITING FOR US! RIGHT NOW WE'RE LIKE RATS IN A TRAP!
?!
WHY WOULD THEY BE WAITING FOR US DOWN HERE? THEY'RE AFTER STRAW HAT, RIGHT?! WE'RE ONLY HERE BY ACCIDENT!
EITHER WAY, THEY KNOW WE'RE ON THE LOOSE.
THE THING I'M MOST AFRAID OF...
...IS THAT IN ORDER TO RESTORE ORDER...
...THEY CALLED IN IMPEL DOWN'S ALL-STAR TEAM!
THE THREE JAILER BEASTS ARE A GIVEN...
...BUT IF WARDEN MAGELLAN IS HERE, WE'RE FINISHED!

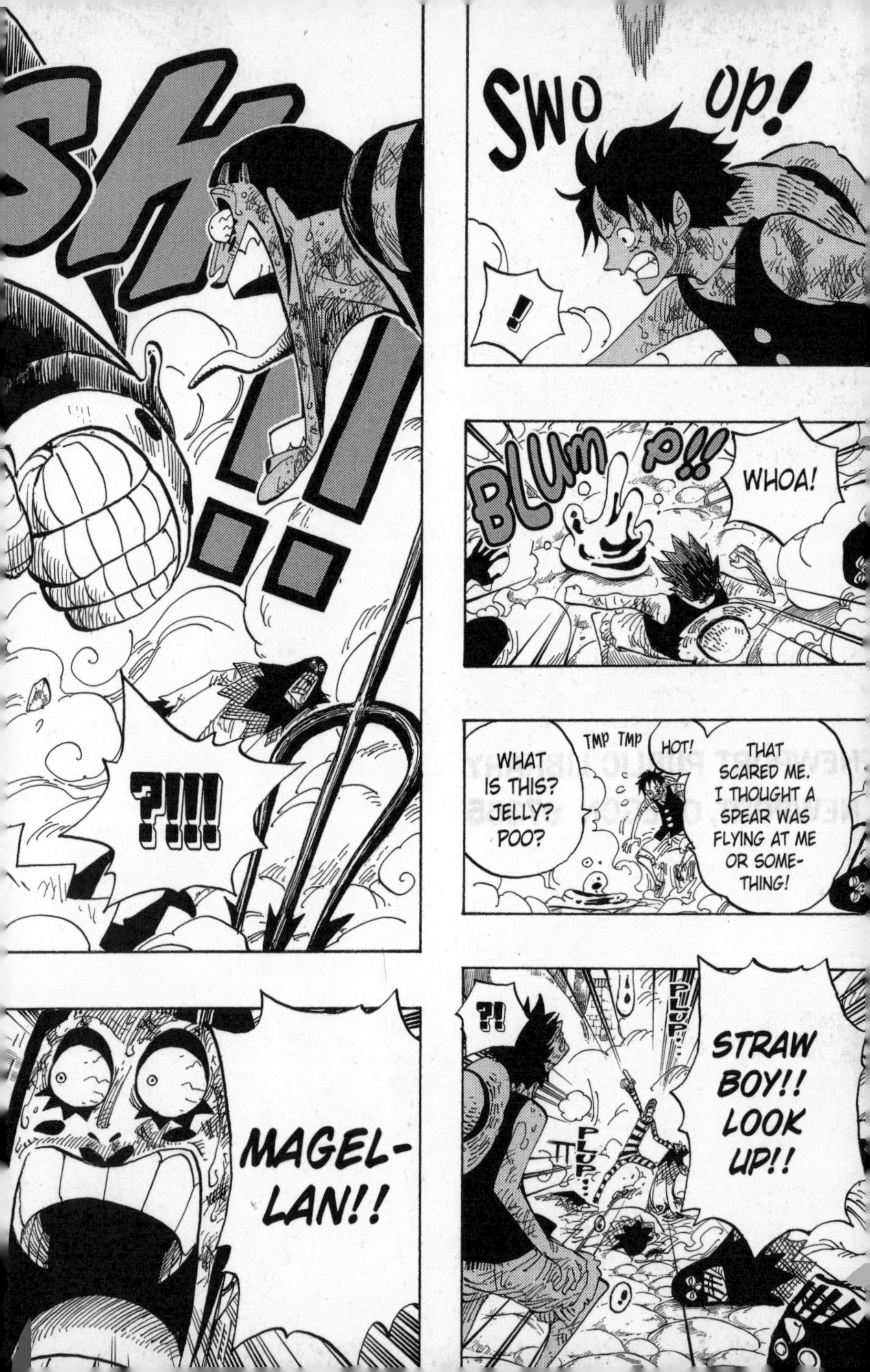
SWOOP!
!
WHOA!
BLUMP!!
THAT SCARED ME. I THOUGHT A SPEAR WAS FLYING AT ME OR SOMETHING!
HOT!
TMP TMP
WHAT IS THIS? JELLY? POO?
SH!!
!!
?!!!
STRAW BOY!! LOOK UP!!
PLUP...
?!
PLUP...
MAGEL-LAN!!

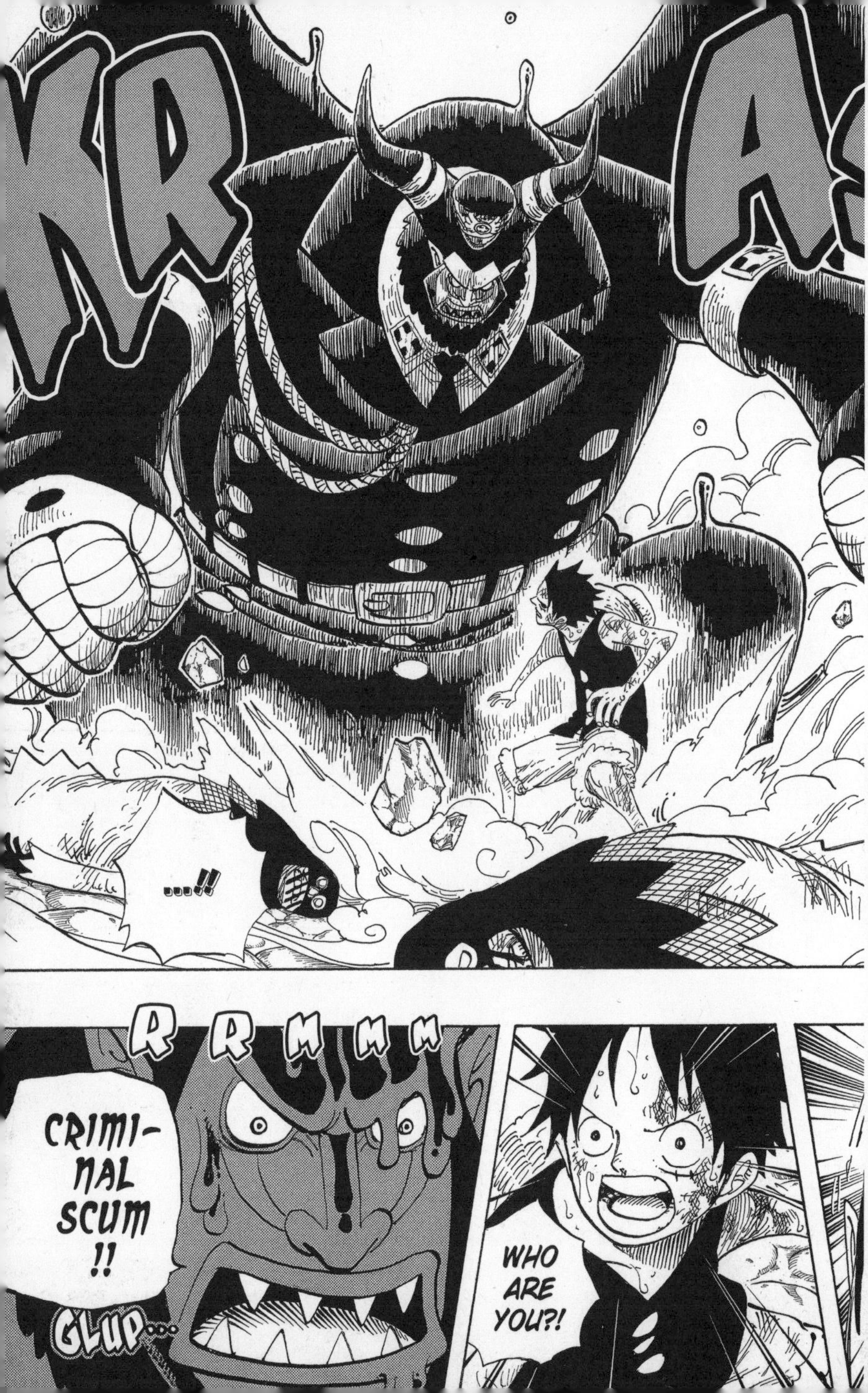
KR
A
...!!
WHO ARE YOU?!
R R M M M M
CRIMI-NAL SCUM!!
GLUP...

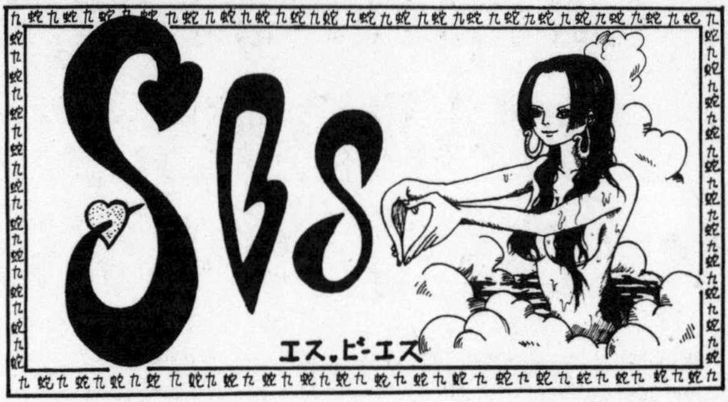
SBS
エス.ビ-エス
(Kan of Taiwan)

Reader(Q): Hello, Odacchi! I wanted to write you a letter so here it is!

--Koeda, Hyogo Prefecture

Oda(A): Right. Thank you. Moving on.

Q: I spotted Captain T-Bone on page 42, panel 6, of volume 54. But how did he survive his battle with Zolo?

--Manticore, Age 16

A: Wow! You're right. That's him all right. That's definitely Captain T-Bone who lost the fight in the Water Seven story arc. He must've done something really desperate to survive. Yeah, that must be it.

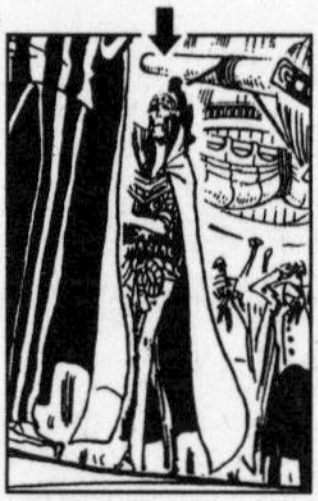

Q: Godfather! I have a question! In volume 52, chapter 508, page 110, Capone's stomach opens up and starts playing a tune. I can't get it out of my head that it's the song they used to play in *Ultraman* whenever the Space Patrol would fly out of the base in their fighter jet.

--From: I used to watch it on video back then

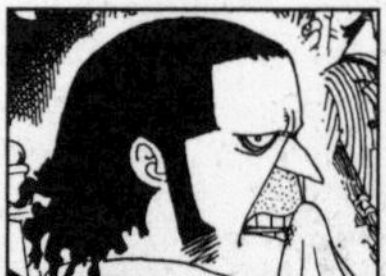

A: Ah-hah! I see. Well, I've received similar letters from a lot of people, so if so many people say it, I guess it must be right. I did have a tune playing in my head when I wrote it. I knew it was from my childhood, but I couldn't remember exactly where it was from. Ha ha! By the way, I used the same tune when the Groggy Monsters appeared in volume 33.

Chapter 534:
WARDEN MAGELLAN VS. PIRATE LUFFY

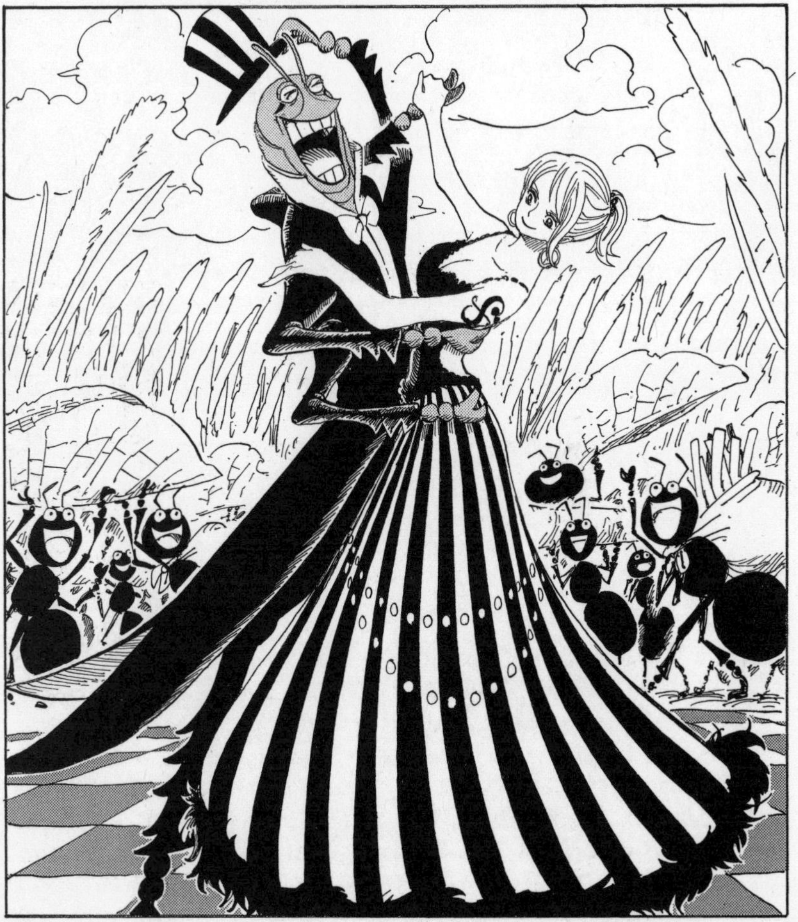

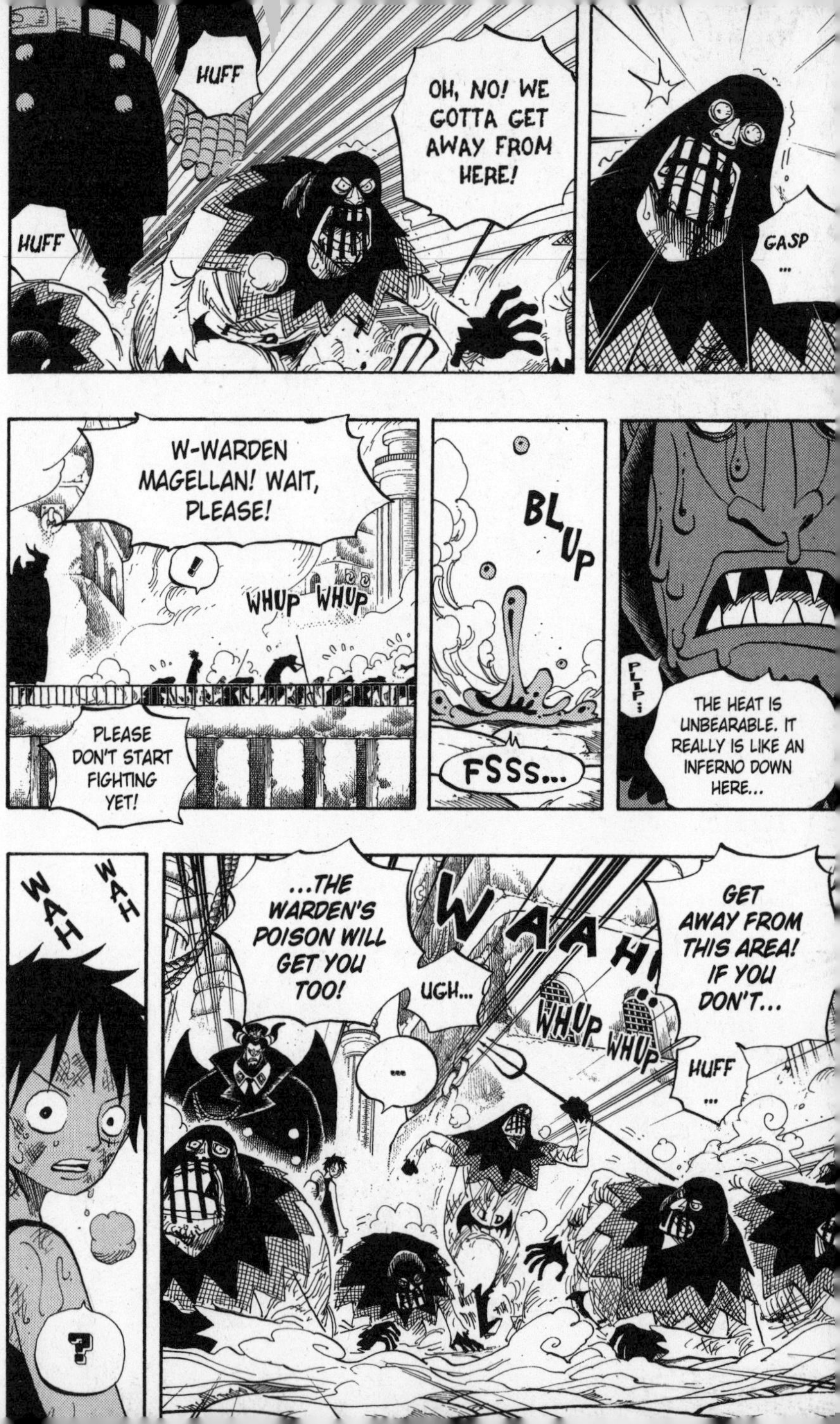
GASP ...
OH, NO! WE GOTTA GET AWAY FROM HERE!
HUFF
HUFF
PLIP
THE HEAT IS UNBEARABLE. IT REALLY IS LIKE AN INFERNO DOWN HERE...
BLUP
FSSS...
W-WARDEN MAGELLAN! WAIT, PLEASE!
!
WHUP WHUP
PLEASE DON'T START FIGHTING YET!
GET AWAY FROM THIS AREA! IF YOU DON'T...
WAAH
...THE WARDEN'S POISON WILL GET YOU TOO!
UGH...
WHUP WHUP
HUFF ...
...
WAH WAH
?

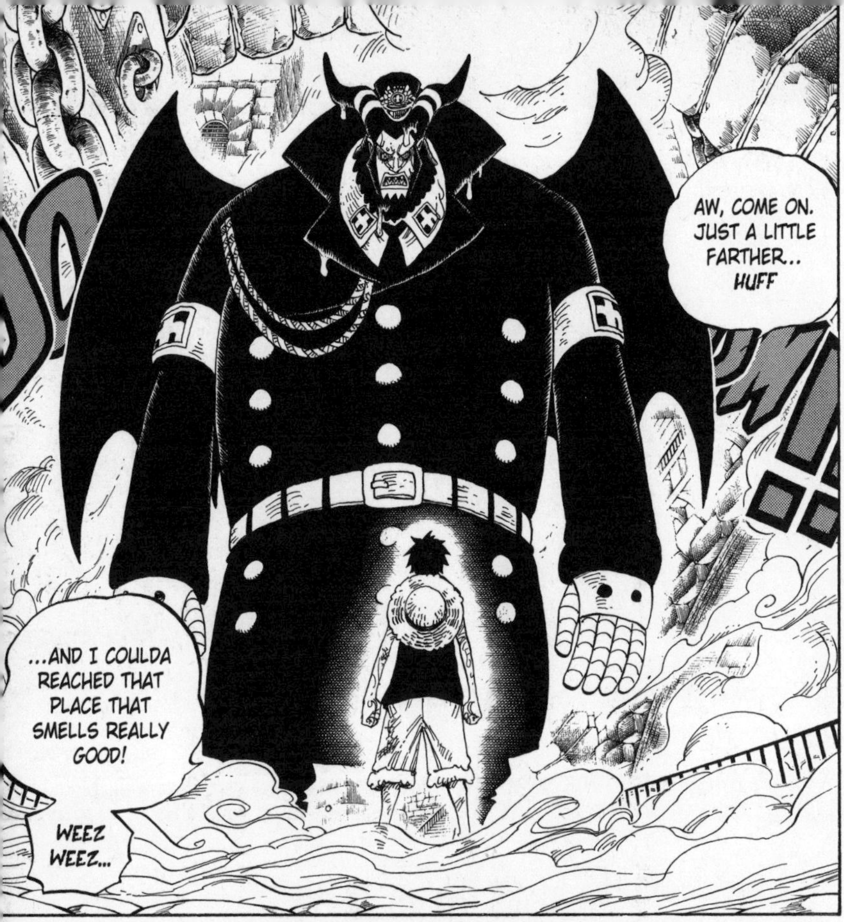
AW, COME ON. JUST A LITTLE FARTHER... HUFF
...AND I COULDA REACHED THAT PLACE THAT SMELLS REALLY GOOD!
WEEZ WEEZ...

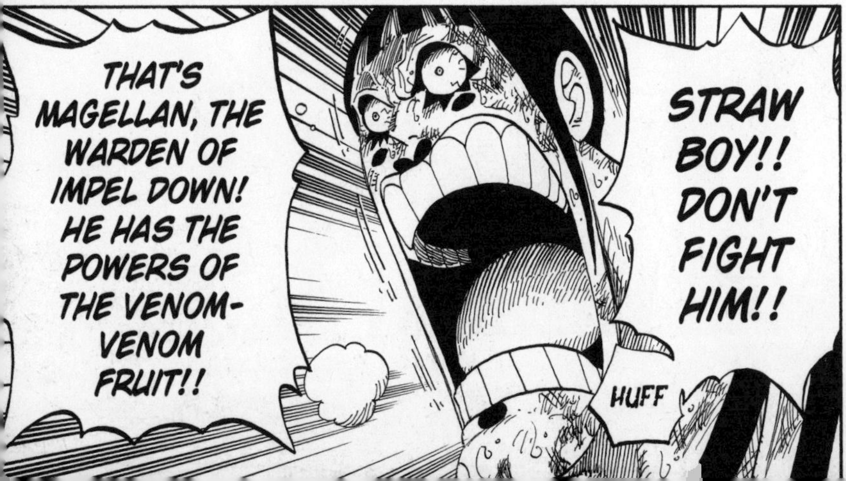
STRAW BOY!! DON'T FIGHT HIM!!
HUFF
THAT'S MAGELLAN, THE WARDEN OF IMPEL DOWN! HE HAS THE POWERS OF THE VENOM-VENOM FRUIT!!

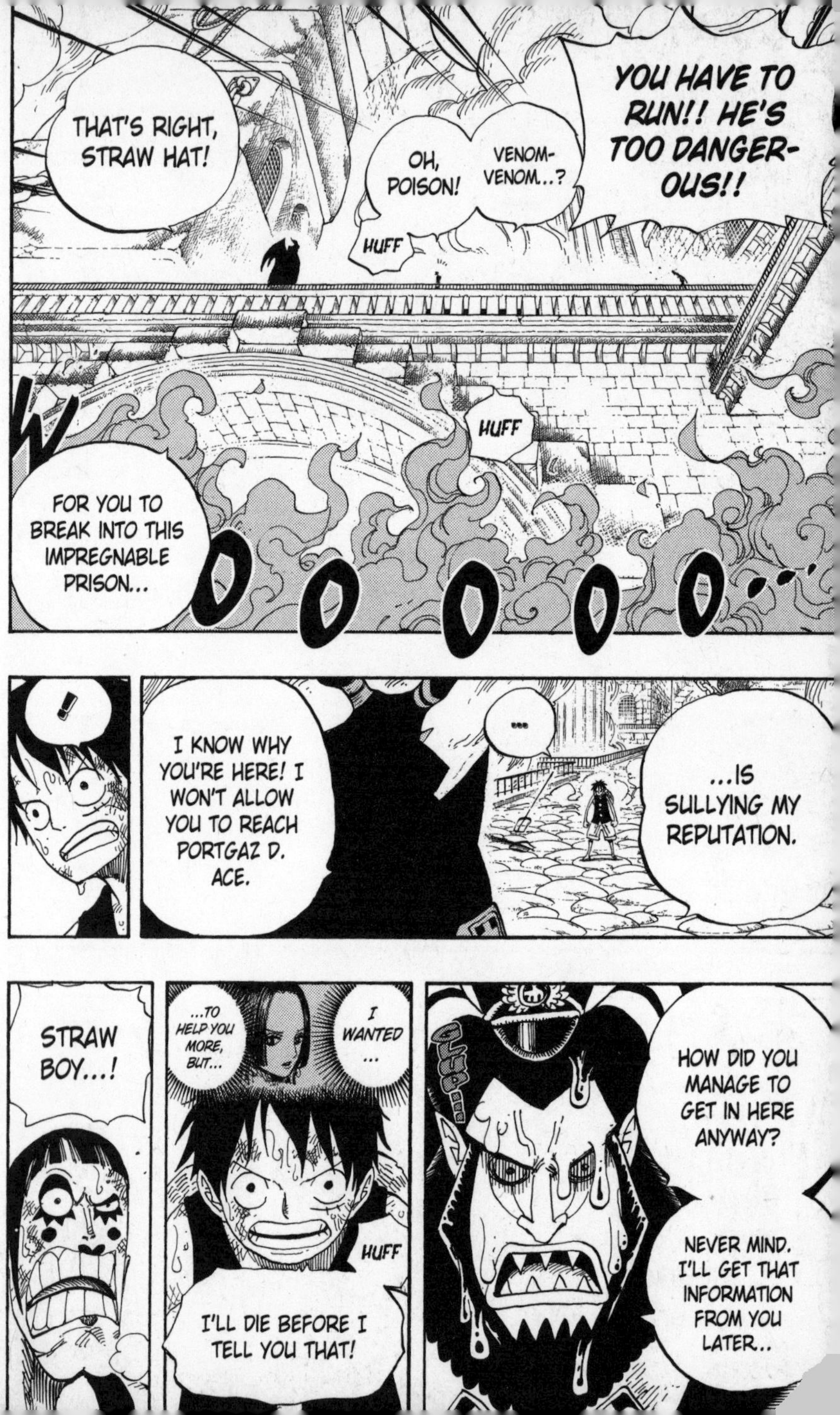
YOU HAVE TO RUN!! HE'S TOO DANGER-OUS!!
VENOM-VENOM...?
OH, POISON!
HUFF
THAT'S RIGHT, STRAW HAT!
HUFF
FOR YOU TO BREAK INTO THIS IMPREGNABLE PRISON...
WOOOOO...
...IS SULLYING MY REPUTATION.
...
I KNOW WHY YOU'RE HERE! I WON'T ALLOW YOU TO REACH PORTGAZ D. ACE.
!
HOW DID YOU MANAGE TO GET IN HERE ANYWAY?
NEVER MIND. I'LL GET THAT INFORMATION FROM YOU LATER..
I WANTED...
...TO HELP YOU MORE, BUT...
HUFF
I'LL DIE BEFORE I TELL YOU THAT!
STRAW BOY...!

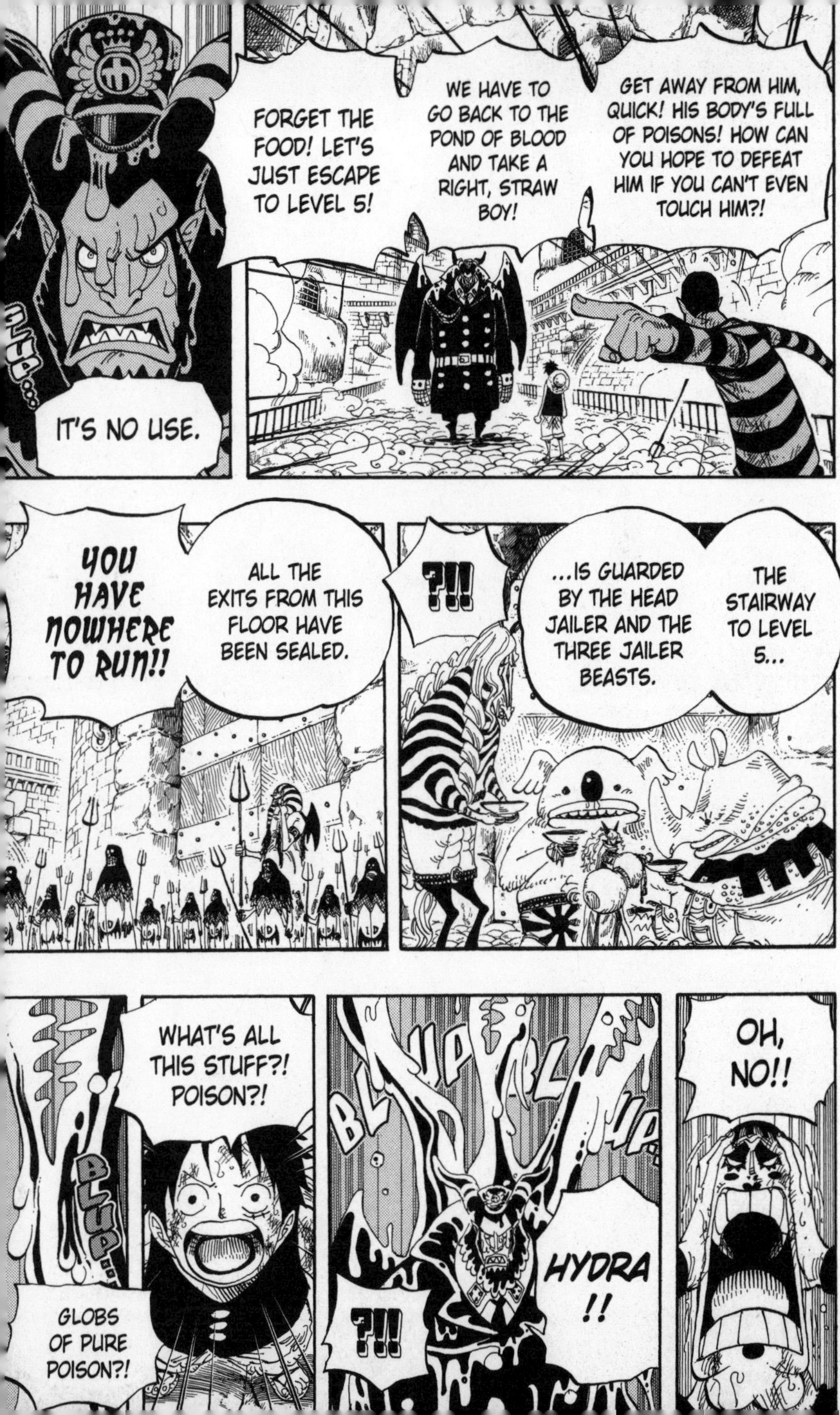
GET AWAY FROM HIM, QUICK! HIS BODY'S FULL OF POISONS! HOW CAN YOU HOPE TO DEFEAT HIM IF YOU CAN'T EVEN TOUCH HIM?!
WE HAVE TO GO BACK TO THE POND OF BLOOD AND TAKE A RIGHT, STRAW BOY!
FORGET THE FOOD! LET'S JUST ESCAPE TO LEVEL 5!
BLUP...
IT'S NO USE.
THE STAIRWAY TO LEVEL 5...
...IS GUARDED BY THE HEAD JAILER AND THE THREE JAILER BEASTS.
?!!
ALL THE EXITS FROM THIS FLOOR HAVE BEEN SEALED.
YOU HAVE NOWHERE TO RUN!!
OH, NO!!
BLUP
BLUP
HYDRA !!
?!!
WHAT'S ALL THIS STUFF?! POISON?!
BLUP...
GLOBS OF PURE POISON?!

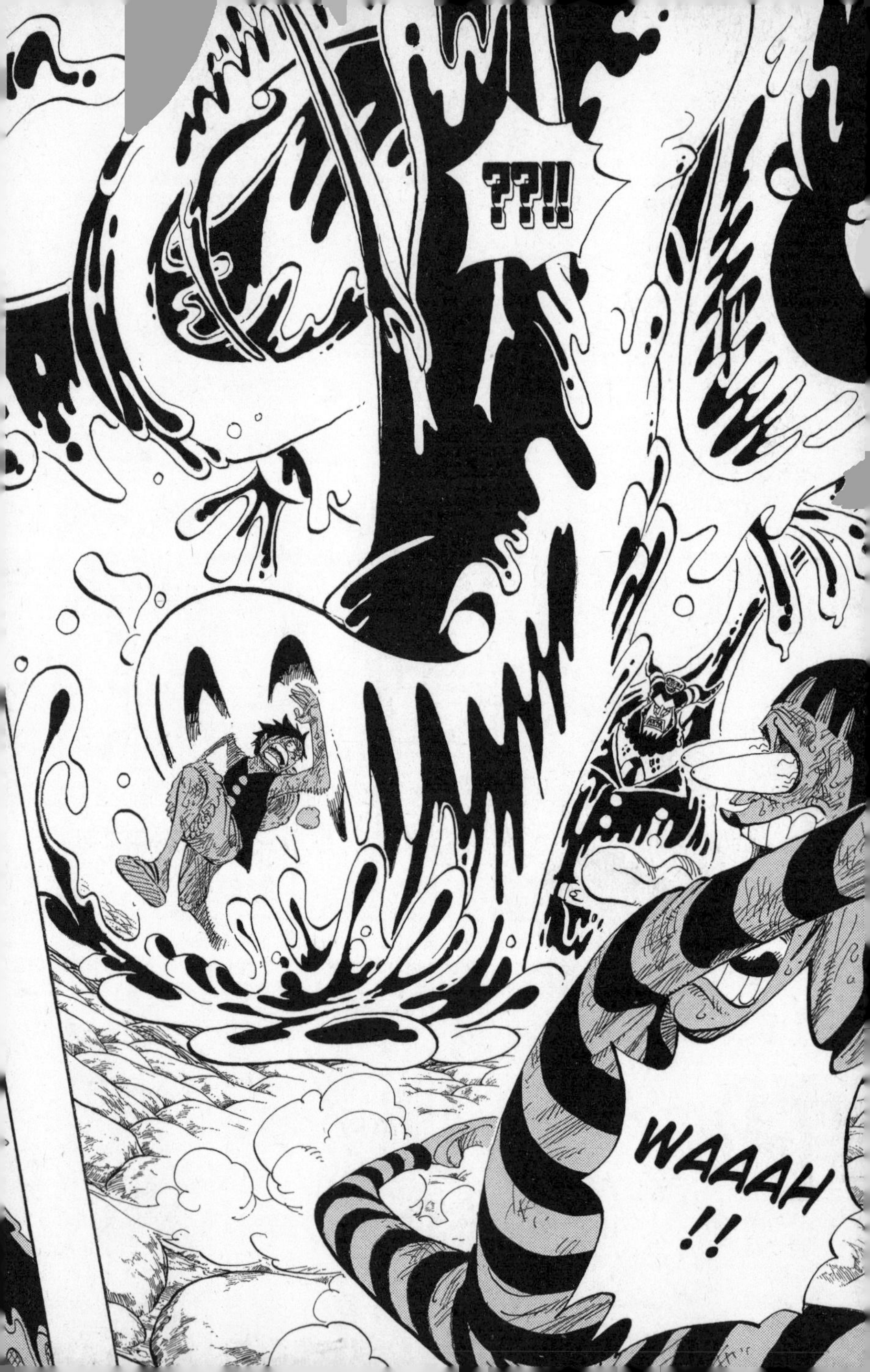
??!!
WAAAH !!

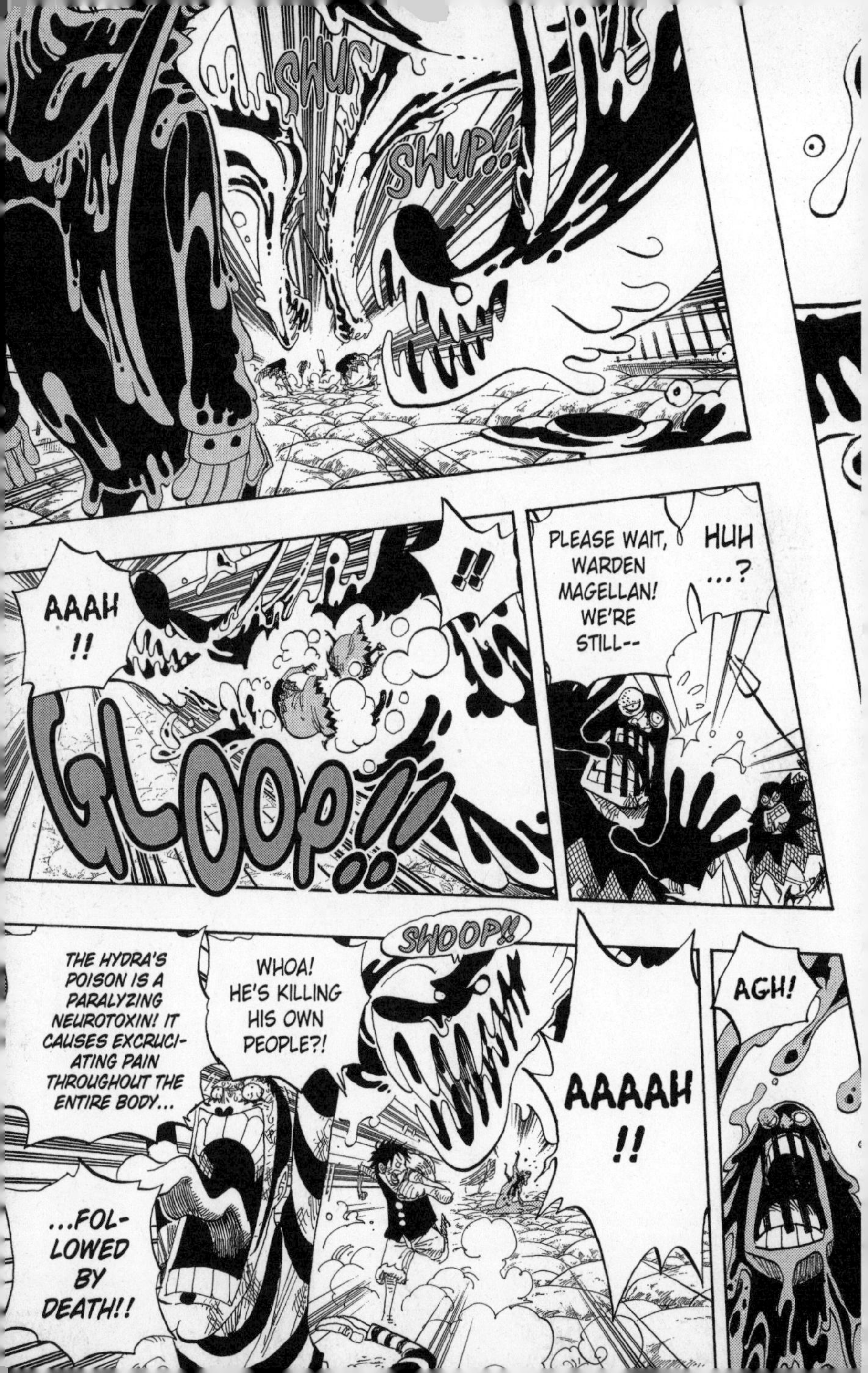
SHUP!!
SHUS
HUH ...?
PLEASE WAIT, WARDEN MAGELLAN! WE'RE STILL--
!!
AAAH !!
GLOOP!!
AGH!
SHOOP!!
AAAAH !!
WHOA! HE'S KILLING HIS OWN PEOPLE?!
THE HYDRA'S POISON IS A PARALYZING NEUROTOXIN! IT CAUSES EXCRUCI-ATING PAIN THROUGHOUT THE ENTIRE BODY...
...FOL-LOWED BY DEATH!!

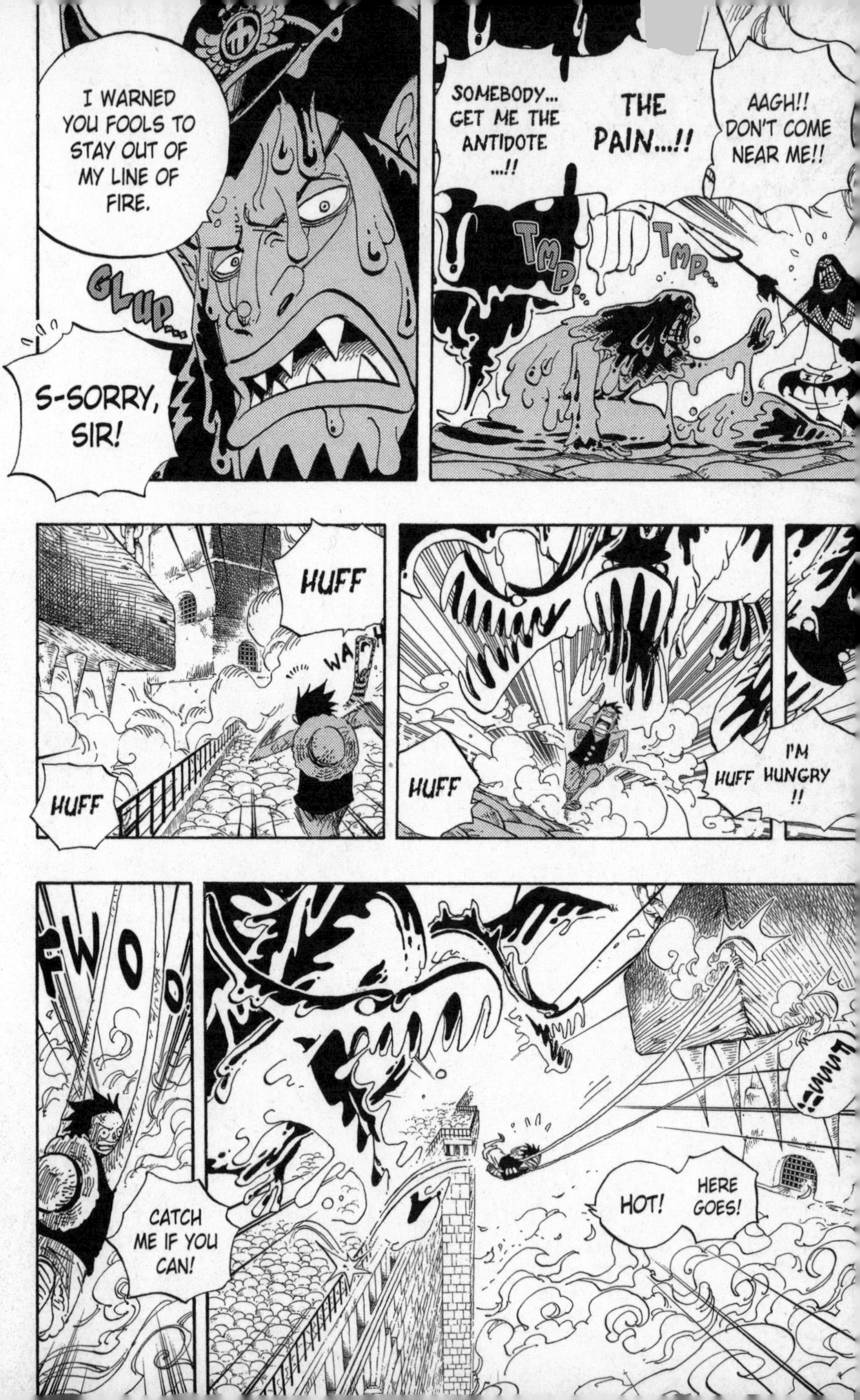
AAGH!! DON'T COME NEAR ME!!
THE PAIN...!!
SOMEBODY... GET ME THE ANTIDOTE ...!!
TMP...
TMP...
I WARNED YOU FOOLS TO STAY OUT OF MY LINE OF FIRE.
GLUP...
S-SORRY, SIR!
I'M HUNGRY !!
HUFF
HUFF
HUFF
HUFF
HERE GOES!
HOT!
CATCH ME IF YOU CAN!
FWOO

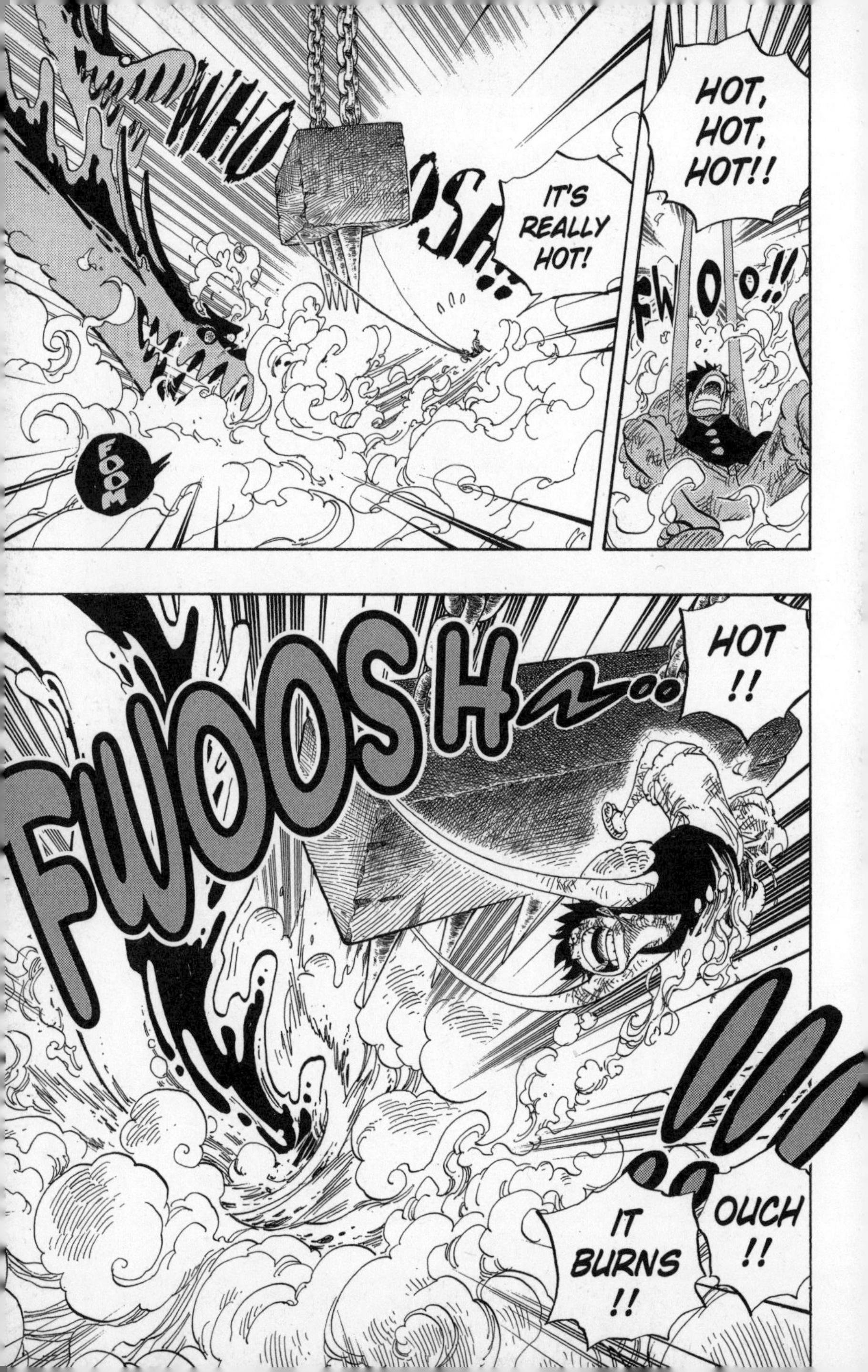
HOT, HOT, HOT!!
FWOOO!!
IT'S REALLY HOT!
WHO
OSH
FOOM
HOT !!
FWOOSH
OUCH !!
IT BURNS !!

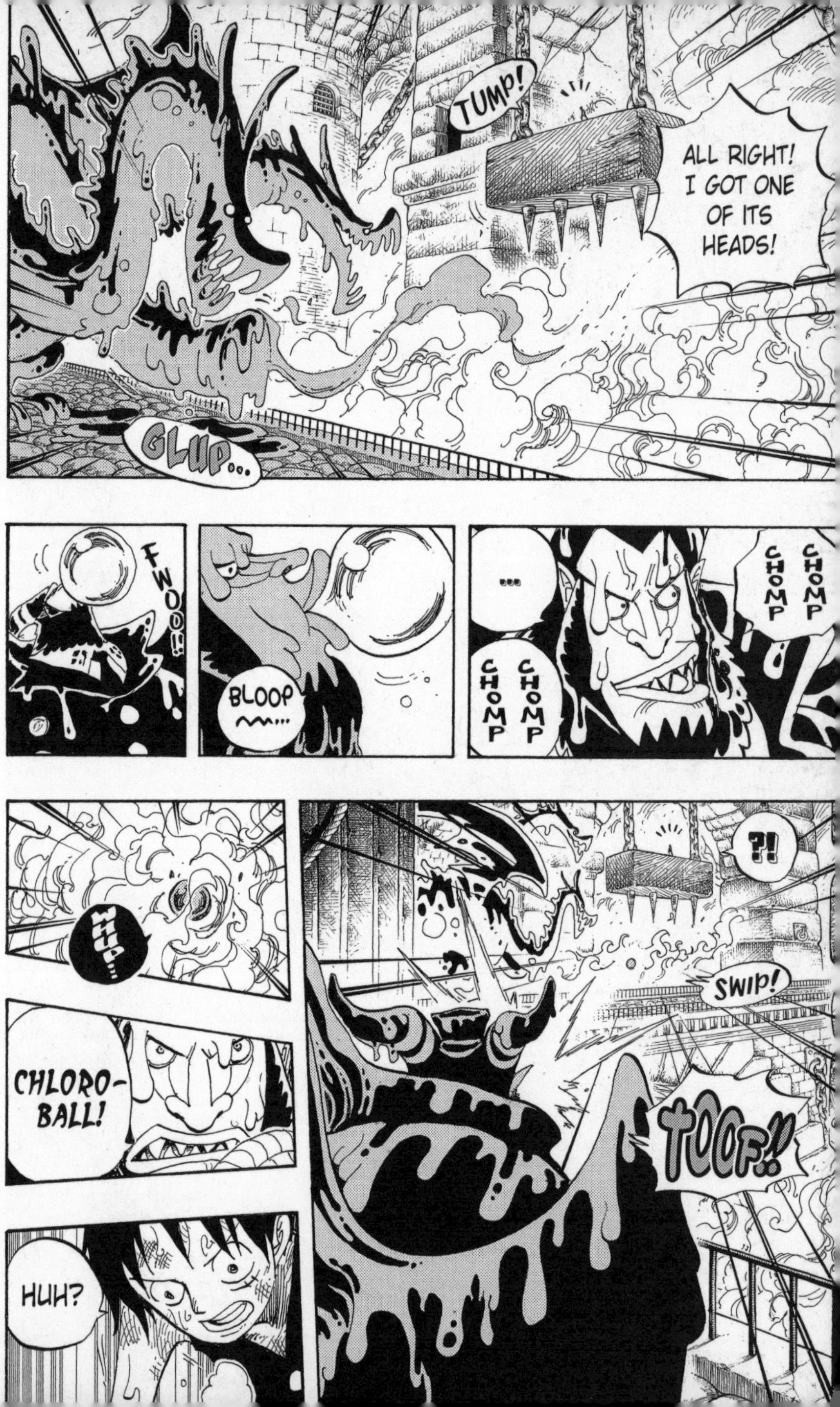
ALL RIGHT! I GOT ONE OF ITS HEADS!
TUMP!
GLUP...
CHOMP CHOMP
...
CHOMP CHOMP
BLOOP~...
FWOOO!!
?!
SWIP!
TOOF!!
CHLORO-BALL!
HUH?

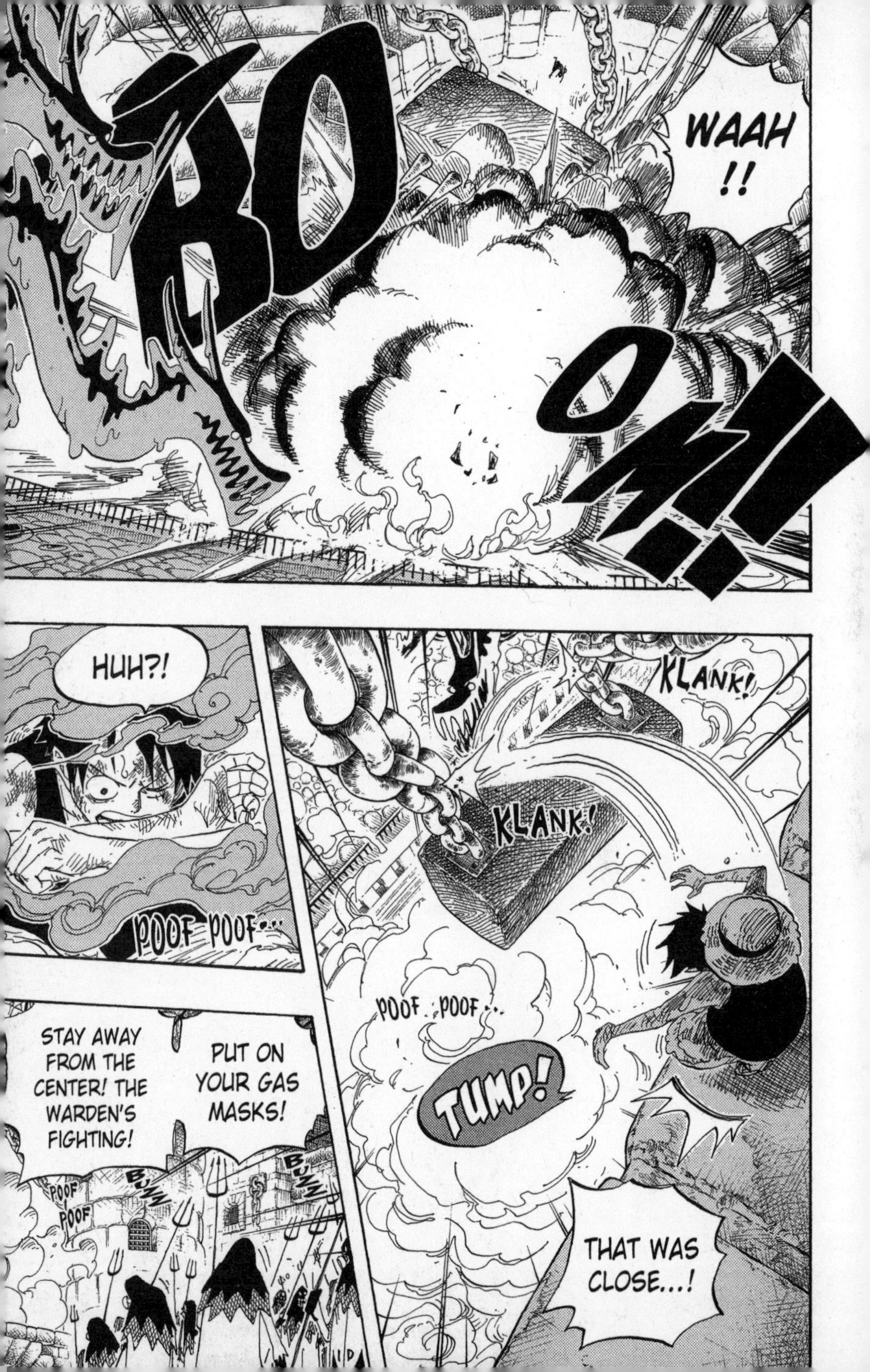
WAAH!!
BOOM!!
KLANK!
KLANK!
POOF POOF...
TUMP!
THAT WAS CLOSE...!
HUH?!
POOF POOF...
PUT ON YOUR GAS MASKS!
STAY AWAY FROM THE CENTER! THE WARDEN'S FIGHTING!
BUZZ
BUZZ
POOF POOF

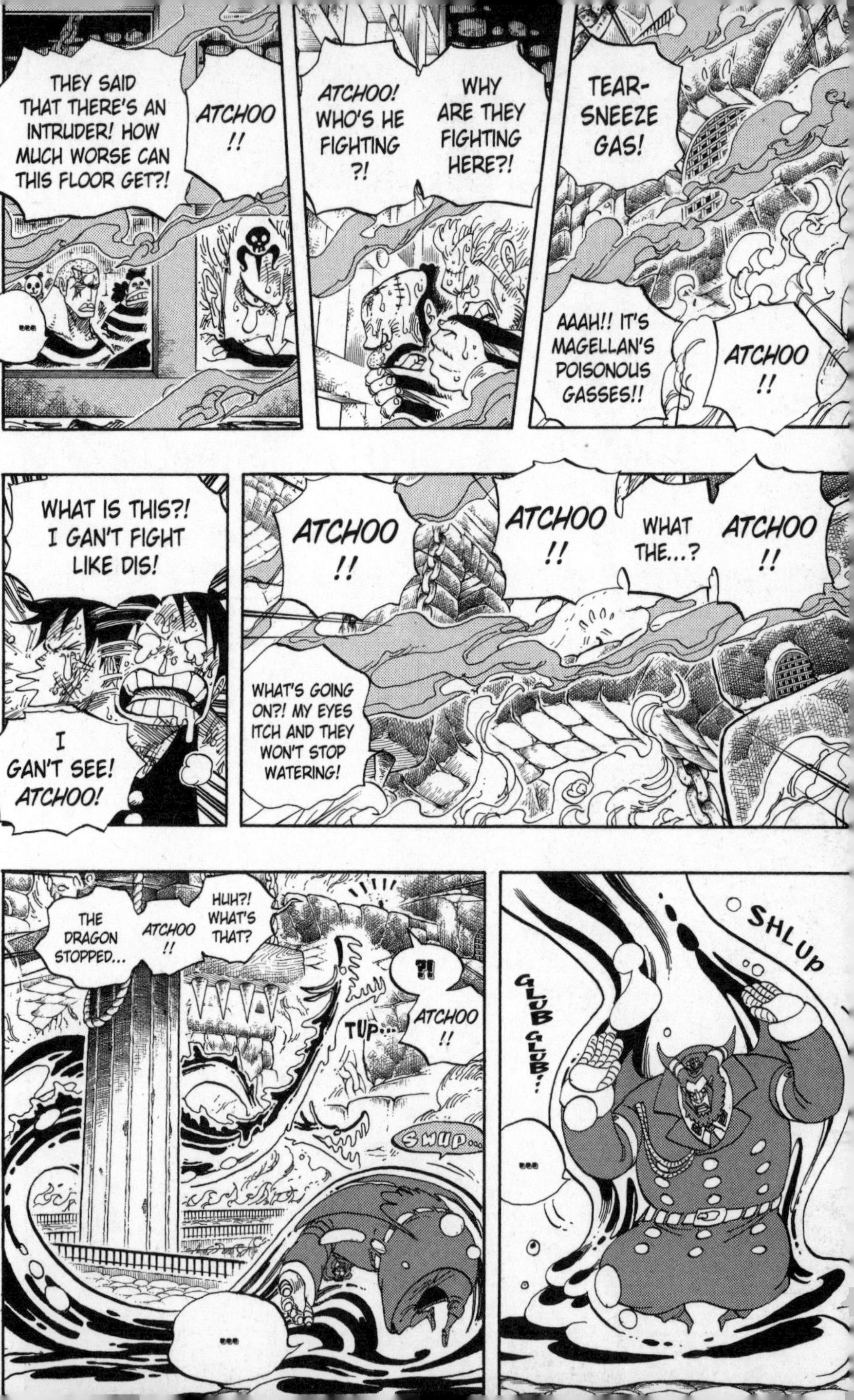
TEAR-SNEEZE GAS!
ATCHOO!!
AAAH!! IT'S MAGELLAN'S POISONOUS GASSES!!
WHY ARE THEY FIGHTING HERE?!
ATCHOO! WHO'S HE FIGHTING?!
ATCHOO!!
THEY SAID THAT THERE'S AN INTRUDER! HOW MUCH WORSE CAN THIS FLOOR GET?!
...
ATCHOO!!
WHAT THE...?
ATCHOO!!
ATCHOO!!
WHAT'S GOING ON?! MY EYES ITCH AND THEY WON'T STOP WATERING!
WHAT IS THIS?! I GAN'T FIGHT LIKE DIS!
I GAN'T SEE! ATCHOO!
SHLUP
GLUB GLUB!!
...
?!
HUH?! WHAT'S THAT?
ATCHOO!!
THE DRAGON STOPPED...
ATCHOO!!
TUP...
SWUP...
...

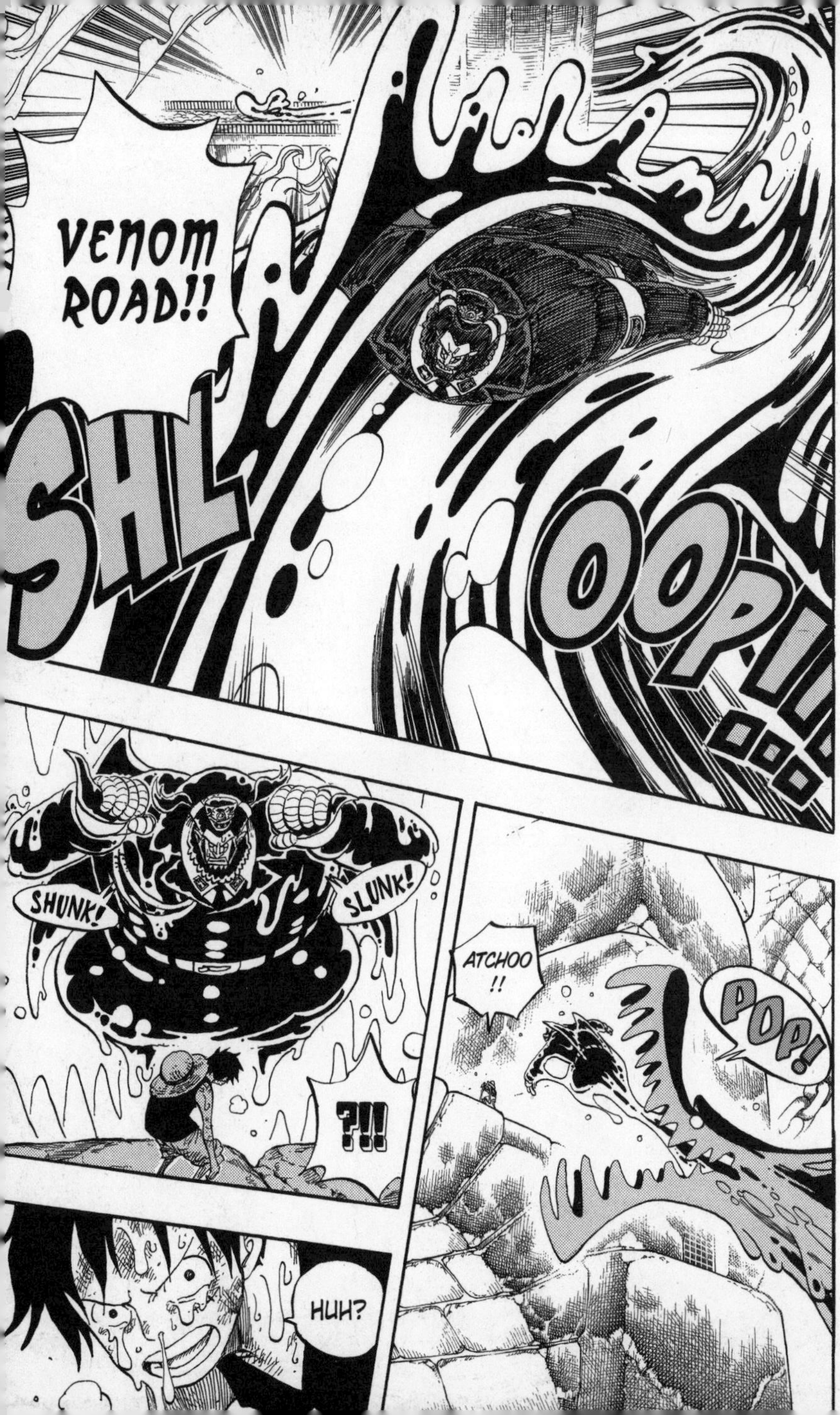
VENOM ROAD!!
SHLOOP!!
ATCHOO!!
POP!
SLUNK!
SHUNK!
?!!
HUH?

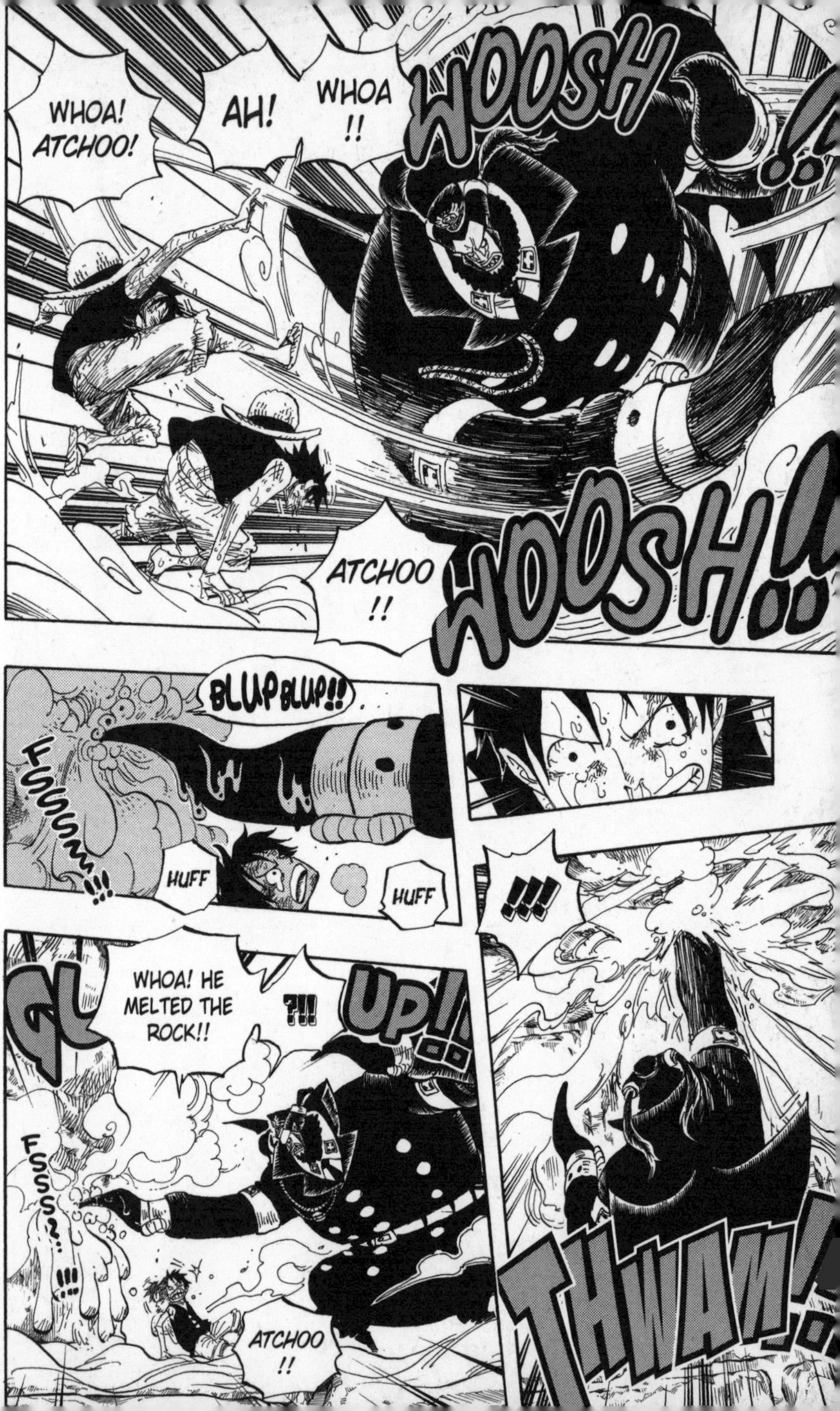
WOOSH!!
WHOA !!
AH!
WHOA! ATCHOO!
WOOSH!!
ATCHOO !!
BLUP BLUP!!
FSSSM!!!
HUFF
HUFF
!!!
THWAM!!
UP!!
?!!
WHOA! HE MELTED THE ROCK!!
GL
FSSS
!!!
ATCHOO !!

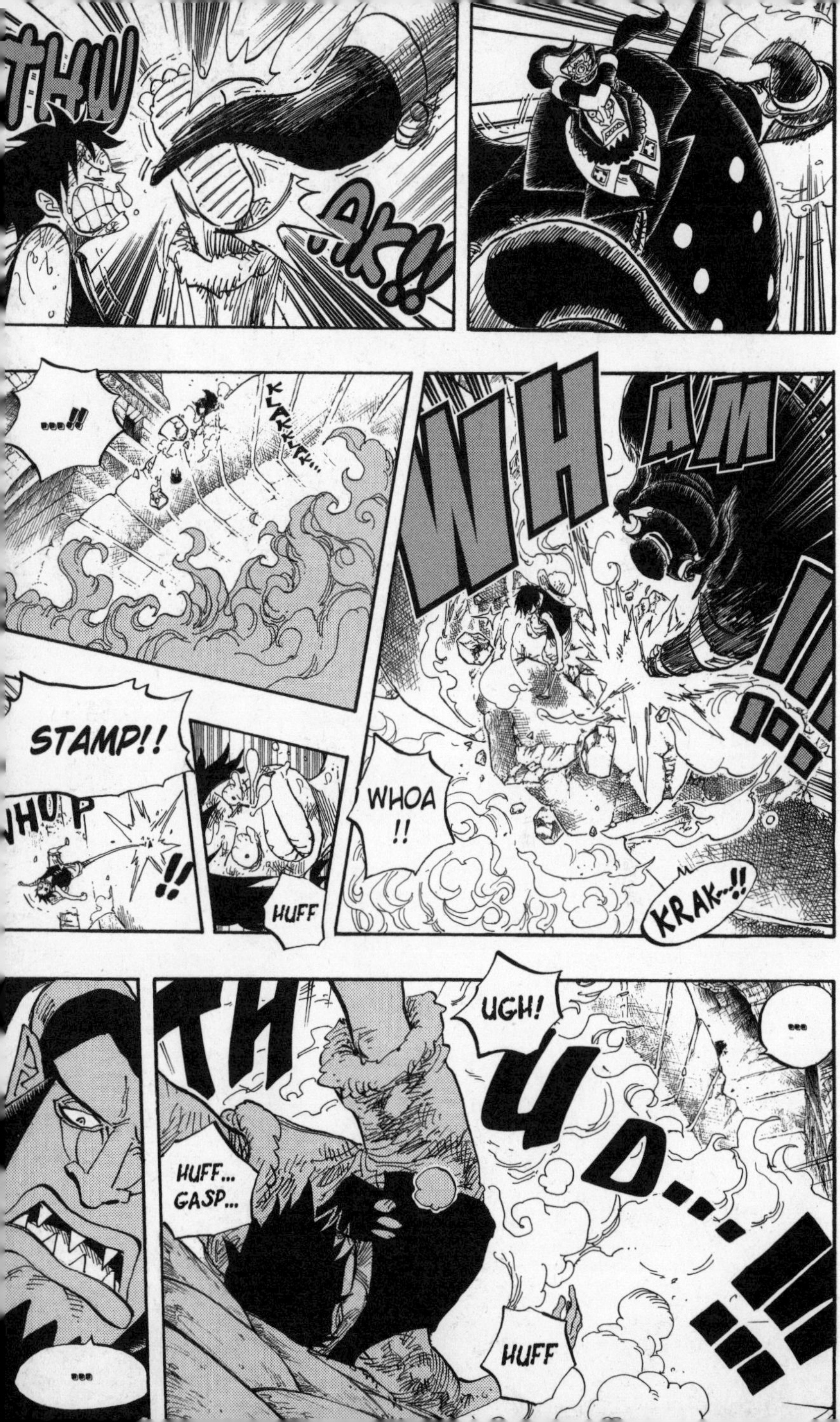
THW
AK!!
WH AM!!
WHOA !!
KRAK..!!
...!!
KLAKKLAK...
HUFF
STAMP!!
WHOP!!
UGH!
...
TH
UD...!!
HUFF... GASP...
HUFF
...

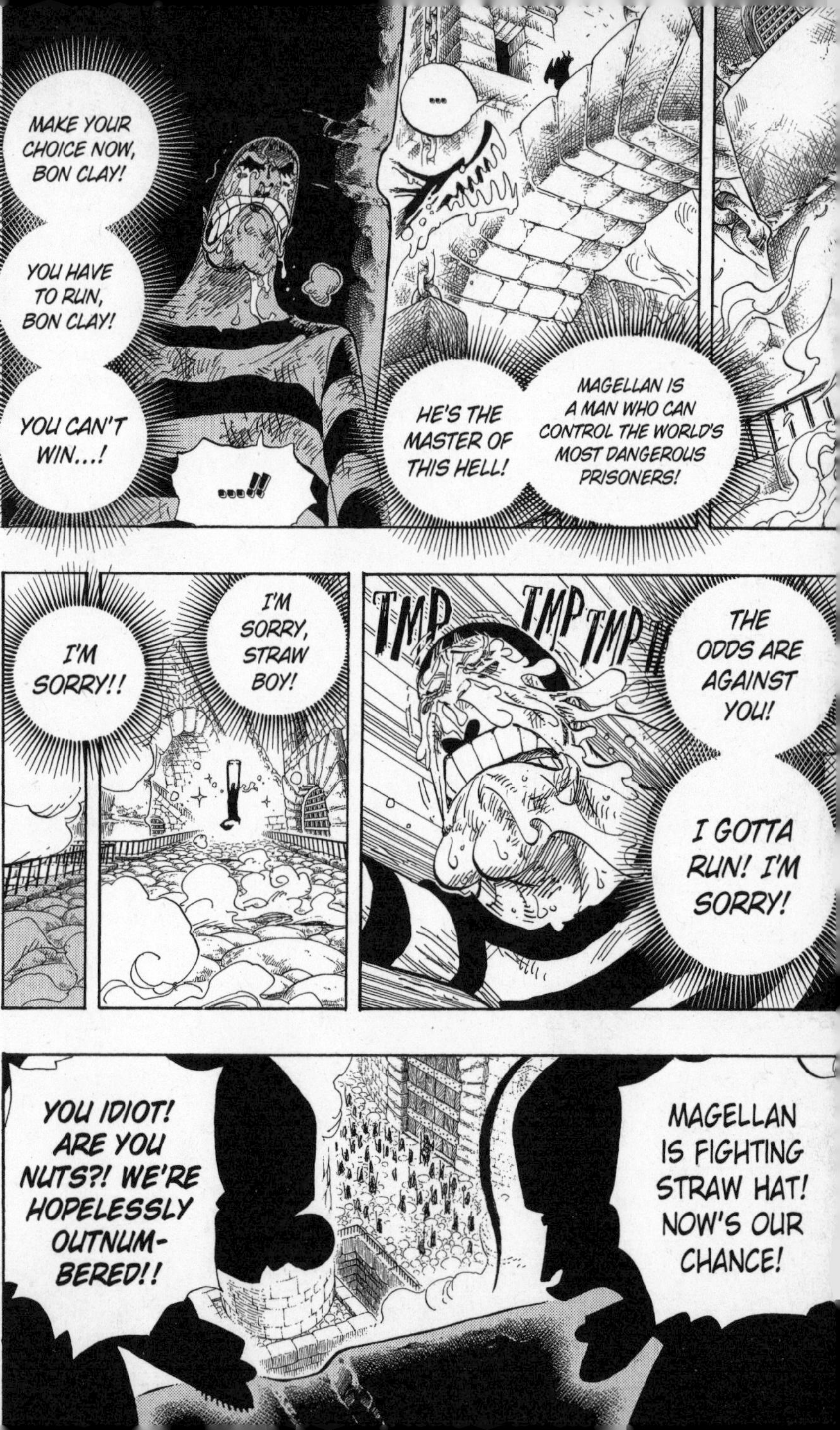
...
MAGELLAN IS A MAN WHO CAN CONTROL THE WORLD'S MOST DANGEROUS PRISONERS!
HE'S THE MASTER OF THIS HELL!
MAKE YOUR CHOICE NOW, BON CLAY!
YOU HAVE TO RUN, BON CLAY!
YOU CAN'T WIN...!
...!!
TMP TMP TMP
THE ODDS ARE AGAINST YOU!
I GOTTA RUN! I'M SORRY!
I'M SORRY, STRAW BOY!
I'M SORRY!!
MAGELLAN IS FIGHTING STRAW HAT! NOW'S OUR CHANCE!
YOU IDIOT! ARE YOU NUTS?! WE'RE HOPELESSLY OUTNUM-BERED!!

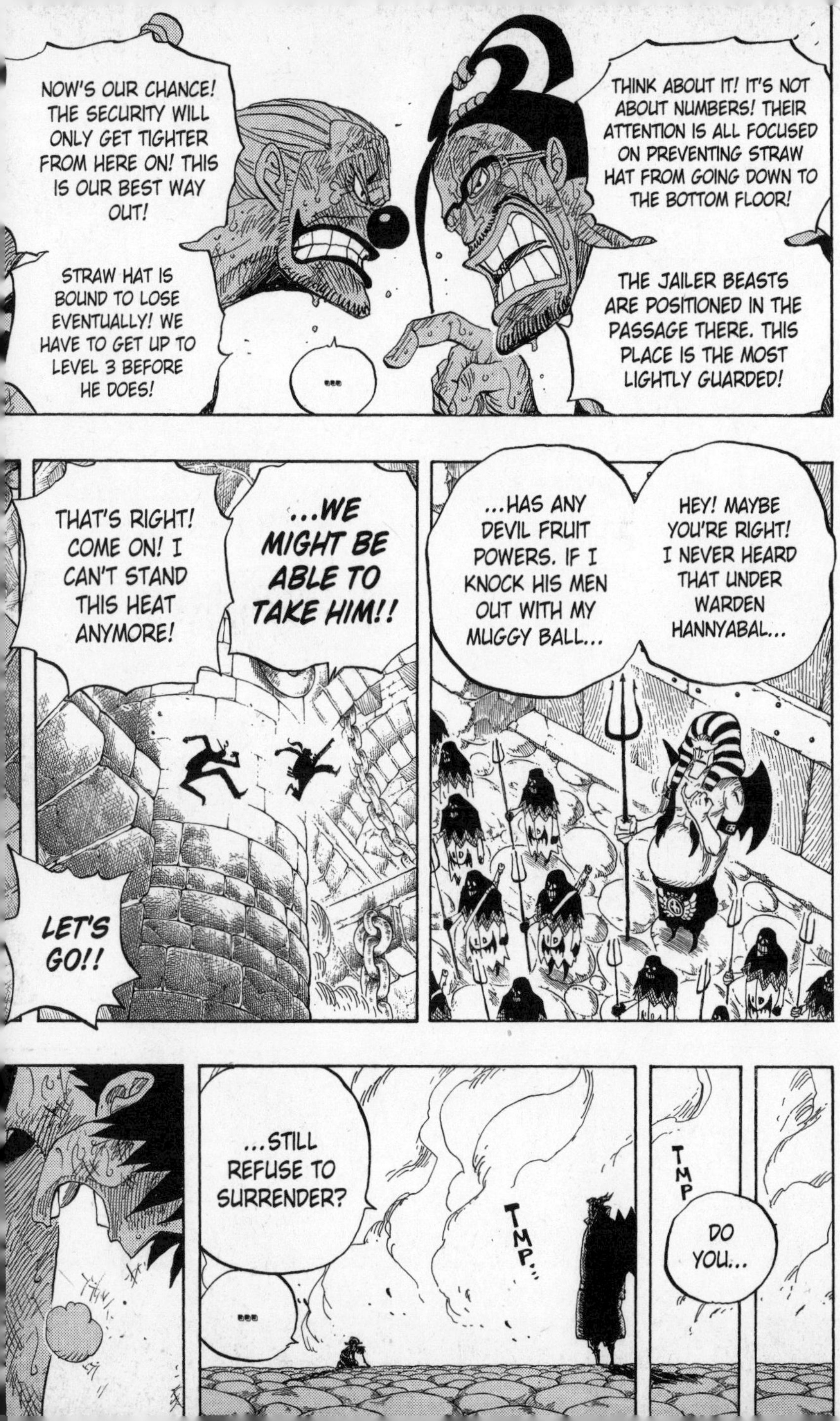
THINK ABOUT IT! IT'S NOT ABOUT NUMBERS! THEIR ATTENTION IS ALL FOCUSED ON PREVENTING STRAW HAT FROM GOING DOWN TO THE BOTTOM FLOOR!
NOW'S OUR CHANCE! THE SECURITY WILL ONLY GET TIGHTER FROM HERE ON! THIS IS OUR BEST WAY OUT!
THE JAILER BEASTS ARE POSITIONED IN THE PASSAGE THERE. THIS PLACE IS THE MOST LIGHTLY GUARDED!
STRAW HAT IS BOUND TO LOSE EVENTUALLY! WE HAVE TO GET UP TO LEVEL 3 BEFORE HE DOES!
...
HEY! MAYBE YOU'RE RIGHT! I NEVER HEARD THAT UNDER WARDEN HANNYABAL...
...HAS ANY DEVIL FRUIT POWERS. IF I KNOCK HIS MEN OUT WITH MY MUGGY BALL...
...WE MIGHT BE ABLE TO TAKE HIM!!
THAT'S RIGHT! COME ON! I CAN'T STAND THIS HEAT ANYMORE!
LET'S GO!!
TMP
DO YOU...
...STILL REFUSE TO SURRENDER?
TMP...
...

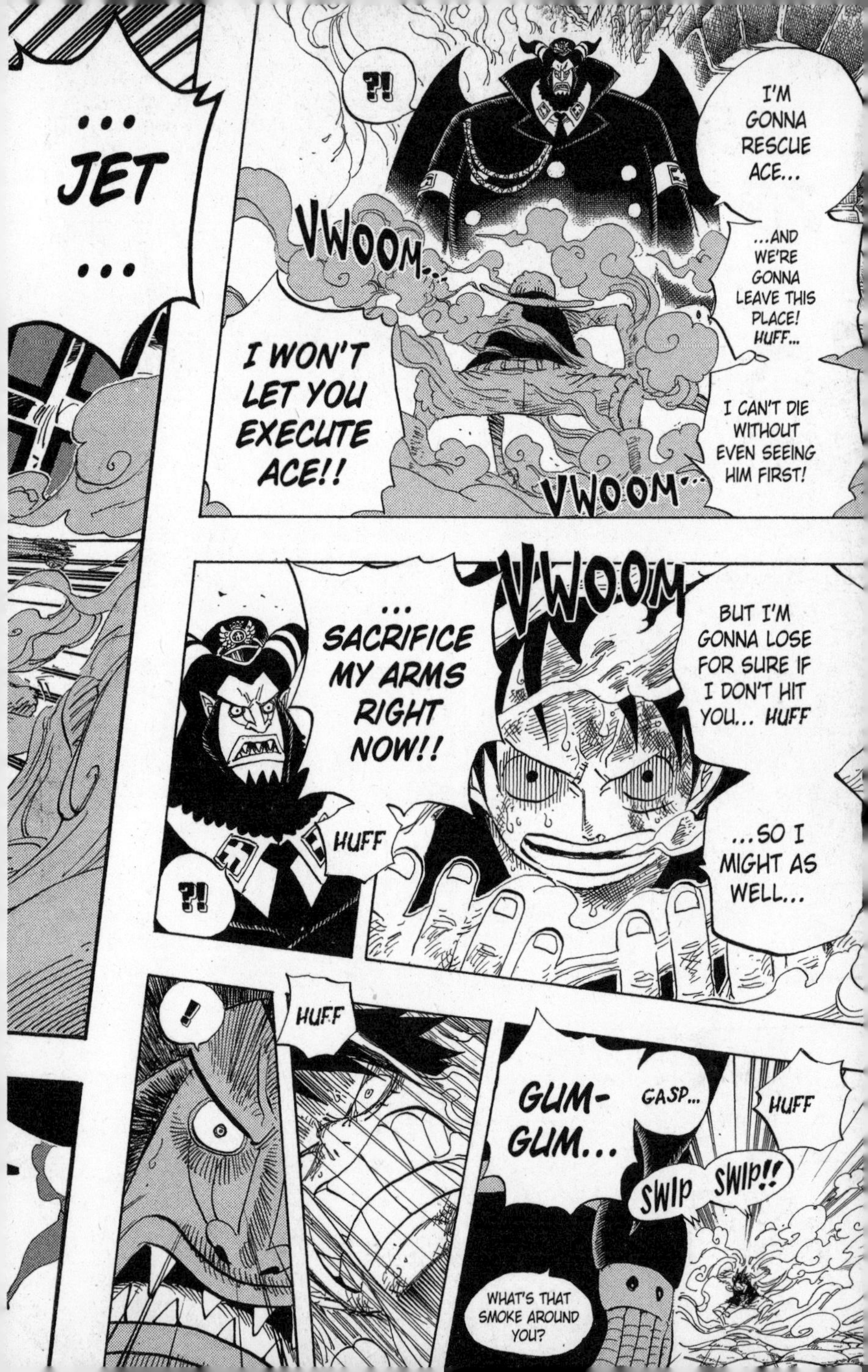

I'M GONNA RESCUE ACE...
...AND WE'RE GONNA LEAVE THIS PLACE! HUFF...
?!
VWOOM...
I CAN'T DIE WITHOUT EVEN SEEING HIM FIRST!
VWOOM...
I WON'T LET YOU EXECUTE ACE!!
VWOOM
BUT I'M GONNA LOSE FOR SURE IF I DON'T HIT YOU... HUFF
...SO I MIGHT AS WELL...
...SACRIFICE MY ARMS RIGHT NOW!!
HUFF
?!
HUFF
GUM-GUM...
GASP...
SWIP SWIP!!
WHAT'S THAT SMOKE AROUND YOU?
HUFF
!
...JET...

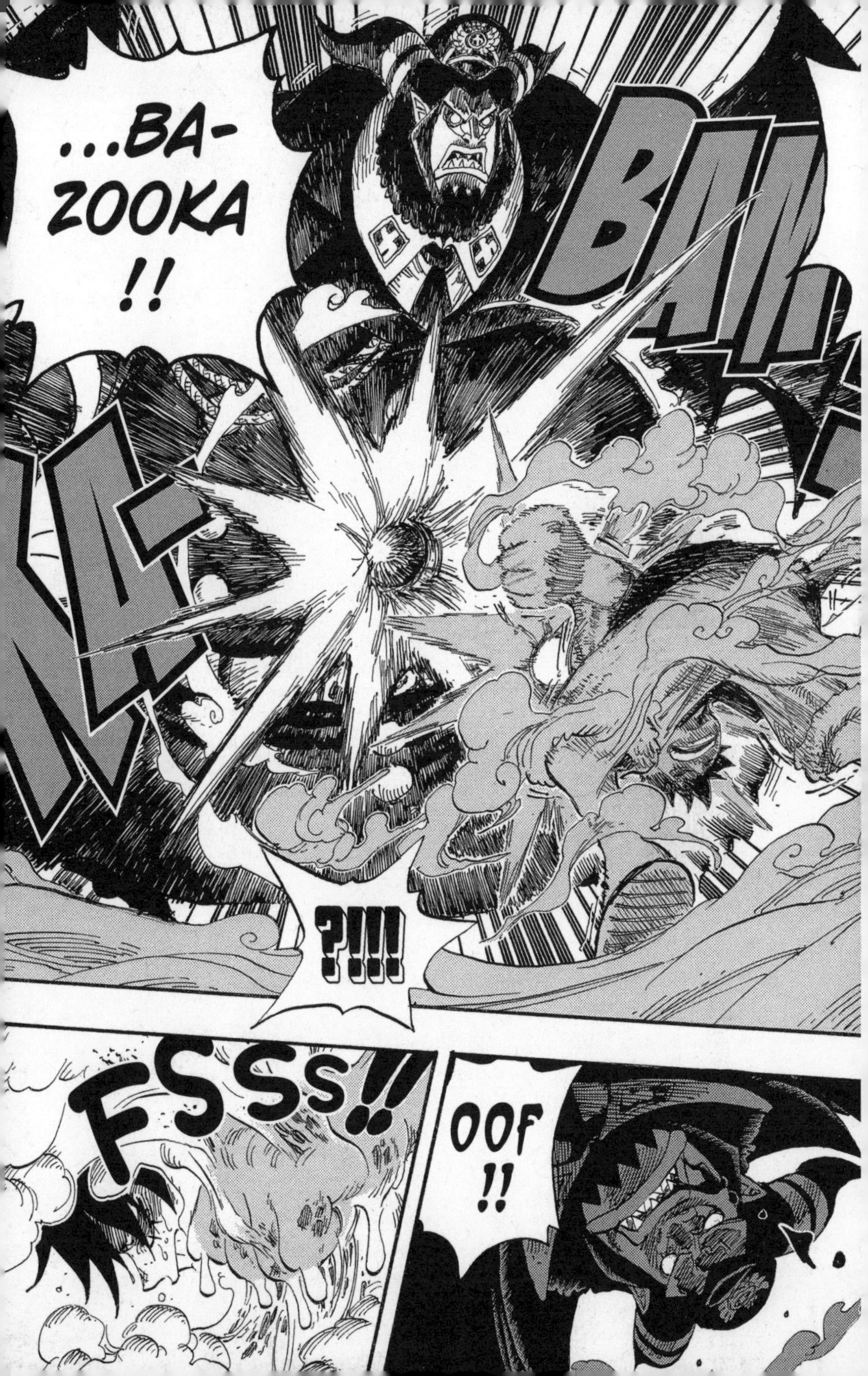
...BA-ZOOKA!!
?!!!
OOF!!
FSSS!!

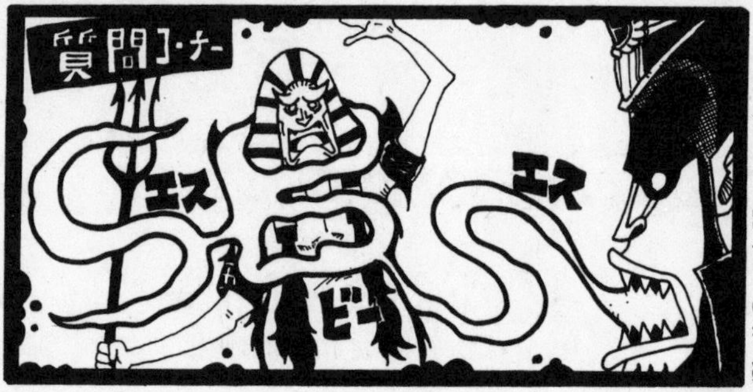
質問コーナー
エス
エス
ビー

(Shoji Omori, Kanagawa)

Q: Mr. Oda! The other day I saw on the news that you can make electricity with a cola drink! It's called a "bio battery"! When I saw this, the first thing I thought of was Franky and Sunny! Now that one of your ideas has become a reality, what do you think will be next?

--Gako Mini-Bear (Age 31)

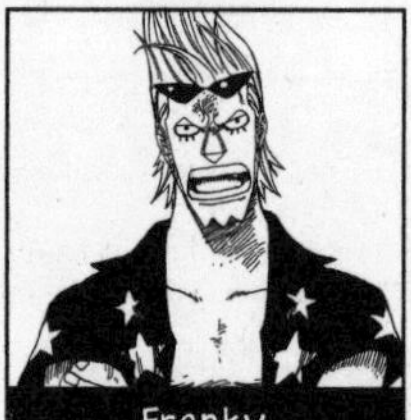

Franky

A: Really? You can make electricity with cola? Hey! W-well... I knew about that! Yeah! Let's see, the next thing to become a reality? How about the sea train? I wish I could ride that.

Q: Have the CP9 ever messed up the Finger Pistol and jammed their fingers? I have.

--Ussa-man

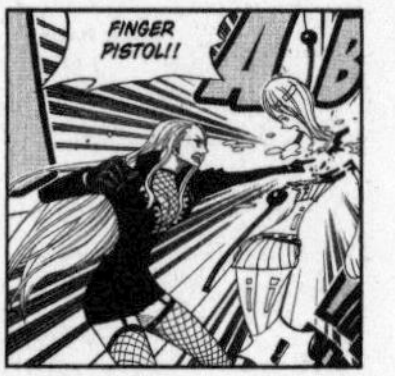
FINGER PISTOL!!

A: What are you doing?! Stop that! I'm sure the CP9 members sometimes jammed their fingers when they were still in training. Don't try it at home, kids! The PTA is on my case all the time as it is!

Q: Hello. I'd just like to say that my whole family is hooked on *One Piece*. And now for the matter at hand... When Luffy got sent to the Island of Women in volume 53, I saw this. (➡) It was in the third panel on page 101, the second panel on page 140, the first panel on page 153, etc. What are these Panda Man-like creatures?

--Yutaka

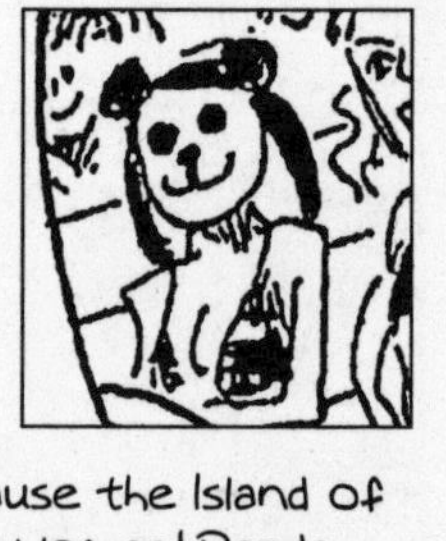

A: So you found them. It's not Panda Man because the Island of Women is forbidden to any man. It's Panda Woman! Panda Man loves her. But I'm not quite sure his love is reciprocated.

Chapter 535: FRIEND

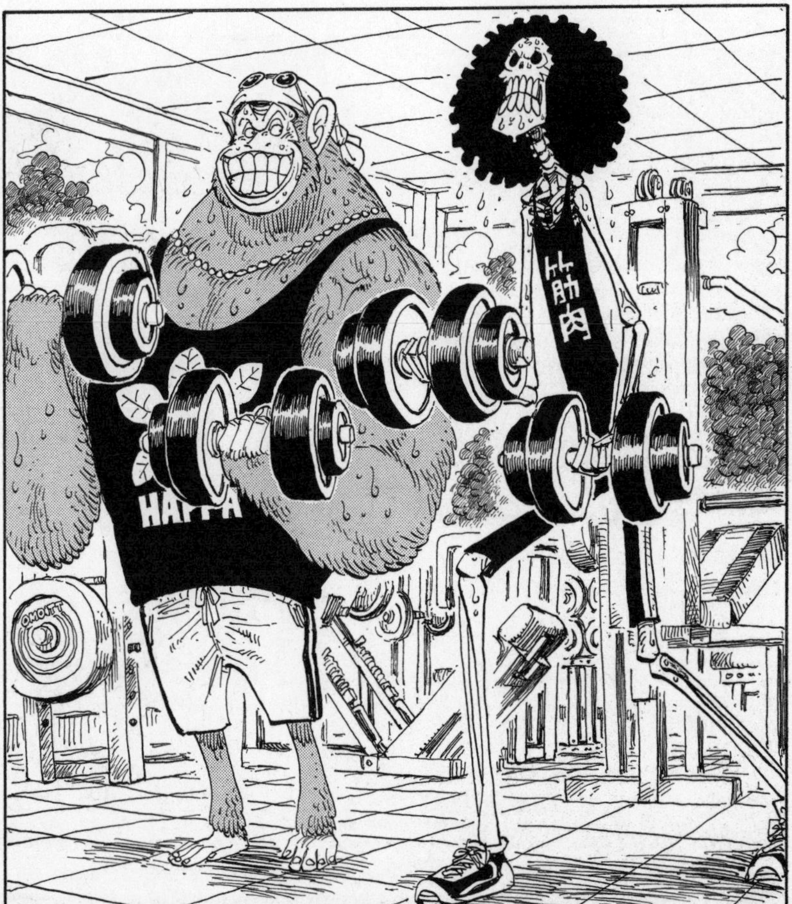
HAPPA
筋肉

BROOK'S SHIRT SAYS "MUSCLE" --ED.

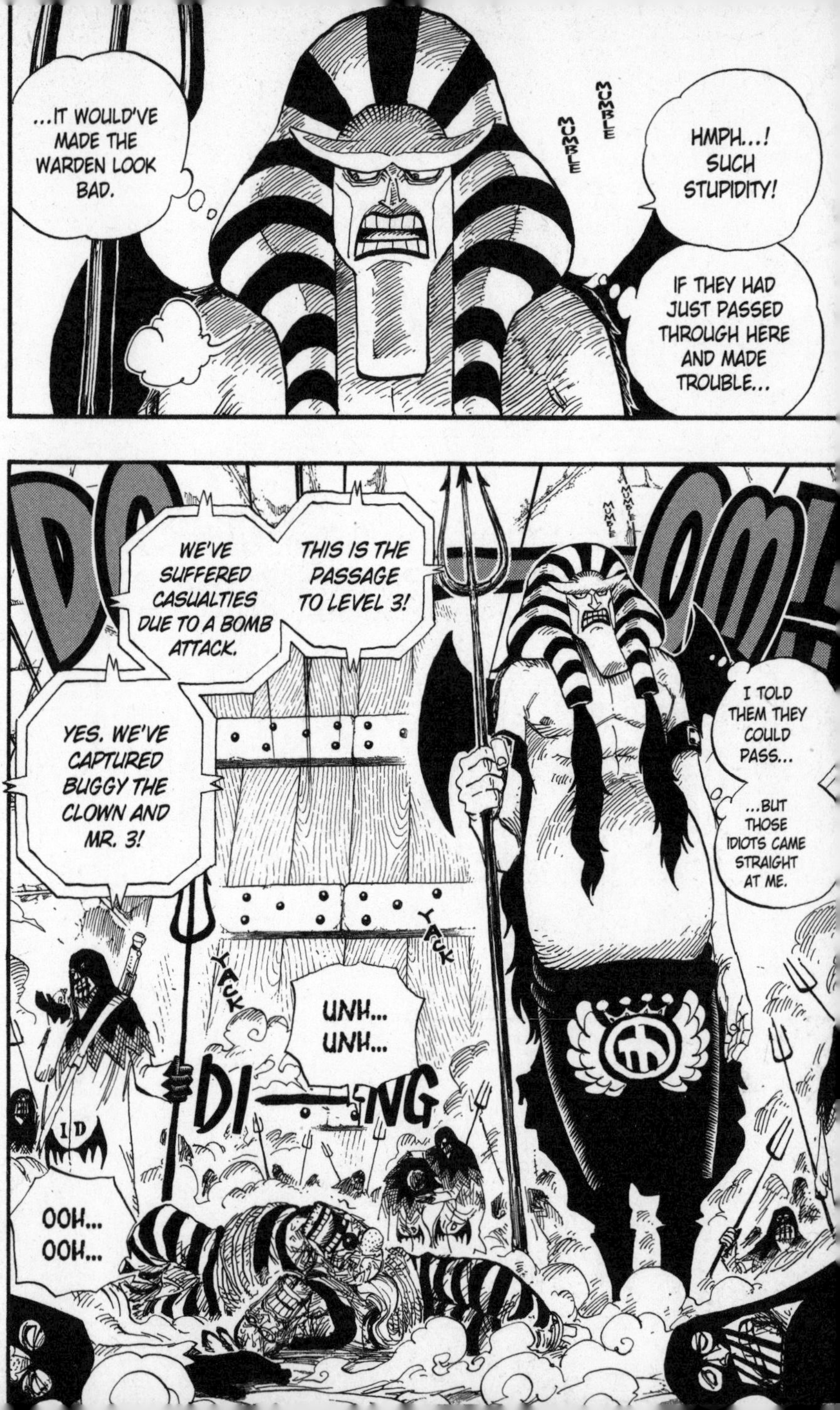
HMPH...! SUCH STUPIDITY!
IF THEY HAD JUST PASSED THROUGH HERE AND MADE TROUBLE...
MUMBLE
MUMBLE
...IT WOULD'VE MADE THE WARDEN LOOK BAD.
DOOM!
MUMBLE
MUMBLE
I TOLD THEM THEY COULD PASS...
...BUT THOSE IDIOTS CAME STRAIGHT AT ME.
THIS IS THE PASSAGE TO LEVEL 3!
WE'VE SUFFERED CASUALTIES DUE TO A BOMB ATTACK.
YES. WE'VE CAPTURED BUGGY THE CLOWN AND MR. 3!
YACK
YACK
UNH... UNH...
DI—NG
OOH... OOH...

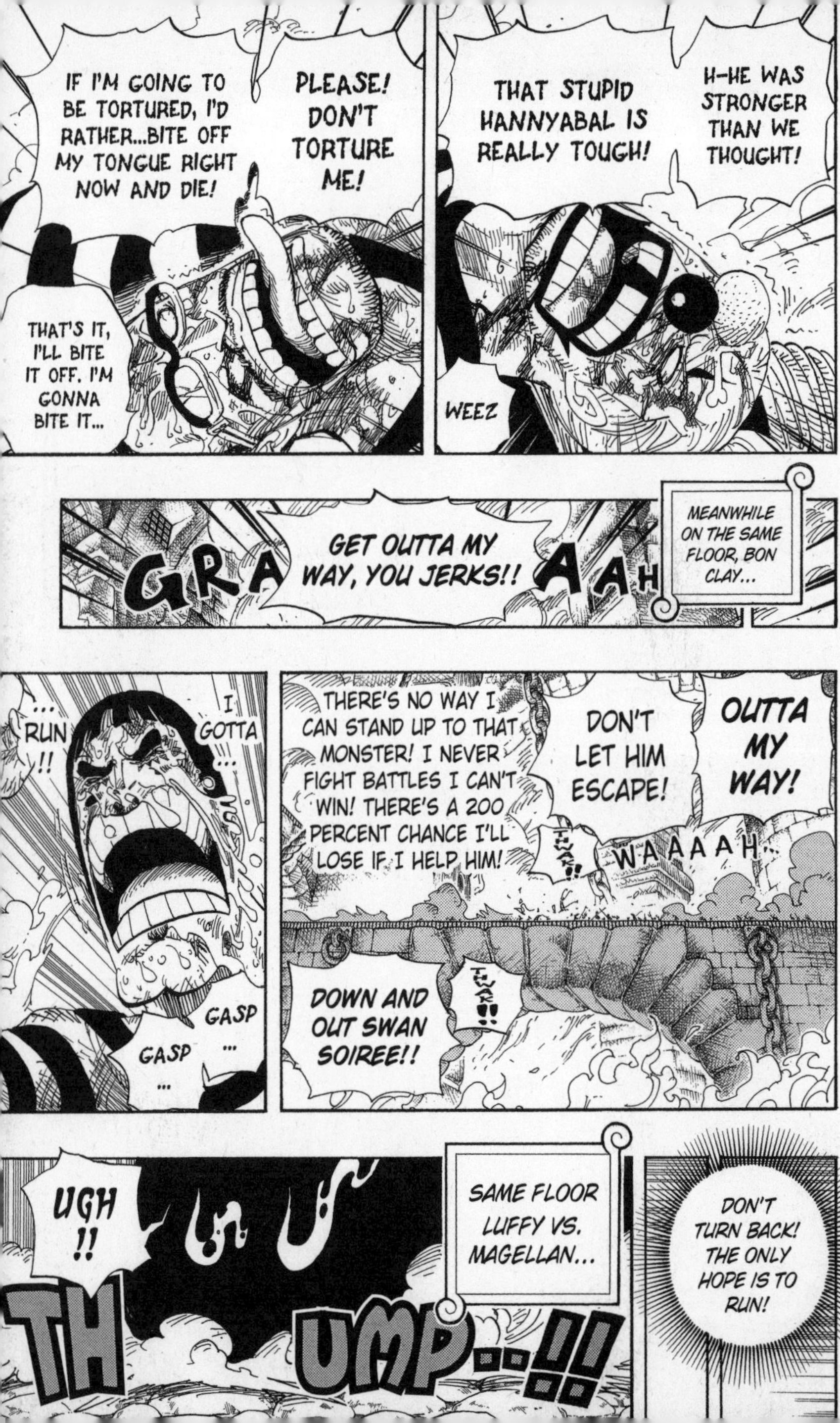
H-HE WAS STRONGER THAN WE THOUGHT!
THAT STUPID HANNYABAL IS REALLY TOUGH!
WEEZ
PLEASE! DON'T TORTURE ME!
IF I'M GOING TO BE TORTURED, I'D RATHER...BITE OFF MY TONGUE RIGHT NOW AND DIE!
THAT'S IT, I'LL BITE IT OFF. I'M GONNA BITE IT...
MEANWHILE ON THE SAME FLOOR, BON CLAY...
GRAAAH
GET OUTTA MY WAY, YOU JERKS!!
OUTTA MY WAY!
DON'T LET HIM ESCAPE!
THERE'S NO WAY I CAN STAND UP TO THAT MONSTER! I NEVER FIGHT BATTLES I CAN'T WIN! THERE'S A 200 PERCENT CHANCE I'LL LOSE IF I HELP HIM!
WAAAAH...
THWAK!!
DOWN AND OUT SWAN SOIREE!!
THWAK!!
I GOTTA ...
... RUN !!
GASP ...
GASP ...
DON'T TURN BACK! THE ONLY HOPE IS TO RUN!
SAME FLOOR LUFFY VS. MAGELLAN...
UGH !!
THUMP...!!

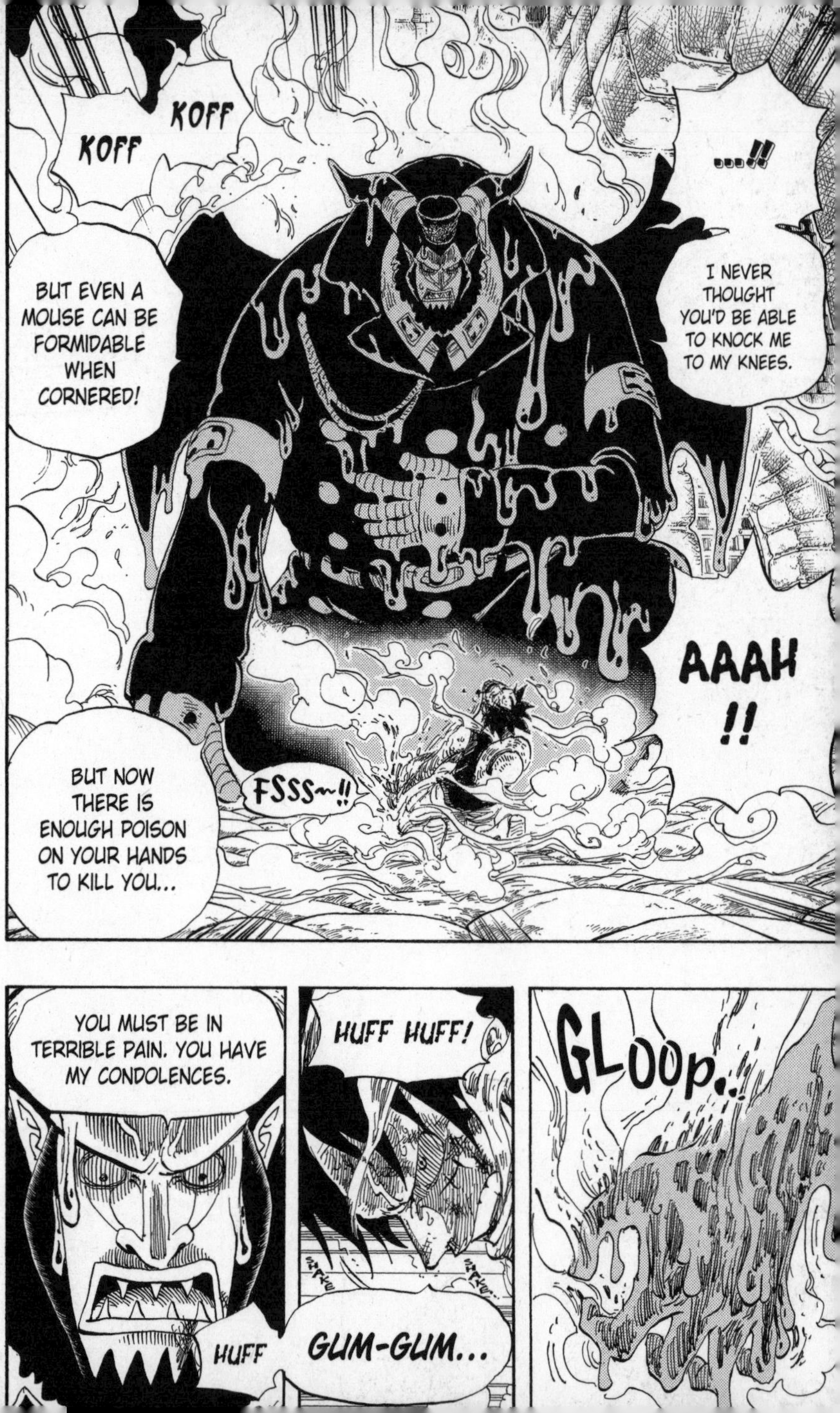
...!!
I NEVER THOUGHT YOU'D BE ABLE TO KNOCK ME TO MY KNEES.
KOFF
KOFF
BUT EVEN A MOUSE CAN BE FORMIDABLE WHEN CORNERED!
AAAH !!
FSSS~!!
BUT NOW THERE IS ENOUGH POISON ON YOUR HANDS TO KILL YOU...
GLOOP..!
HUFF HUFF!
SHAKE
SHAKE...
GUM-GUM...
YOU MUST BE IN TERRIBLE PAIN. YOU HAVE MY CONDOLENCES.
HUFF

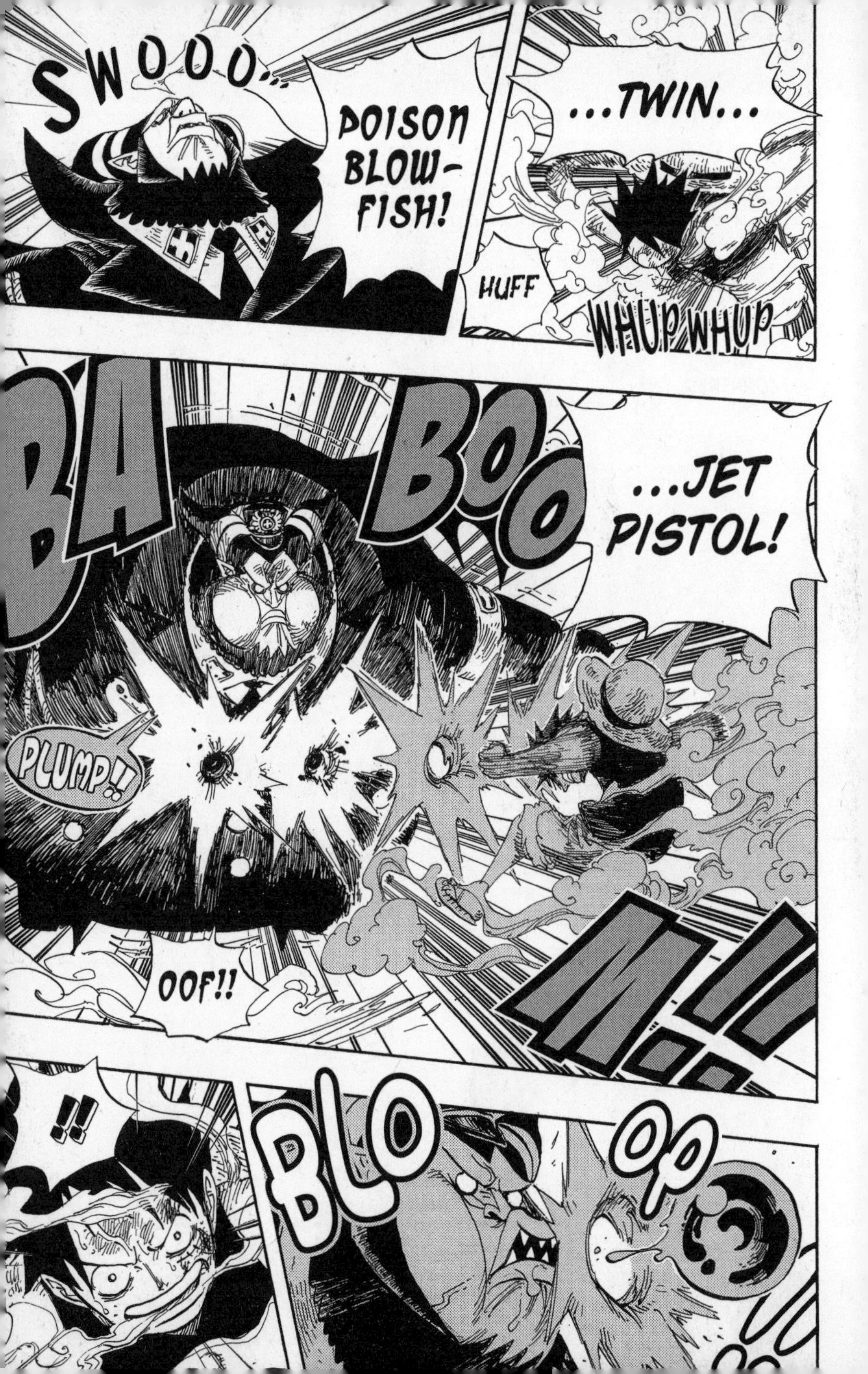
...TWIN...
HUFF
WHUP WHUP
SWOOO...
POISON BLOW-FISH!
...JET PISTOL!
BABOOM!!
PLUMP!!
OOF!!
BLOOP
!!

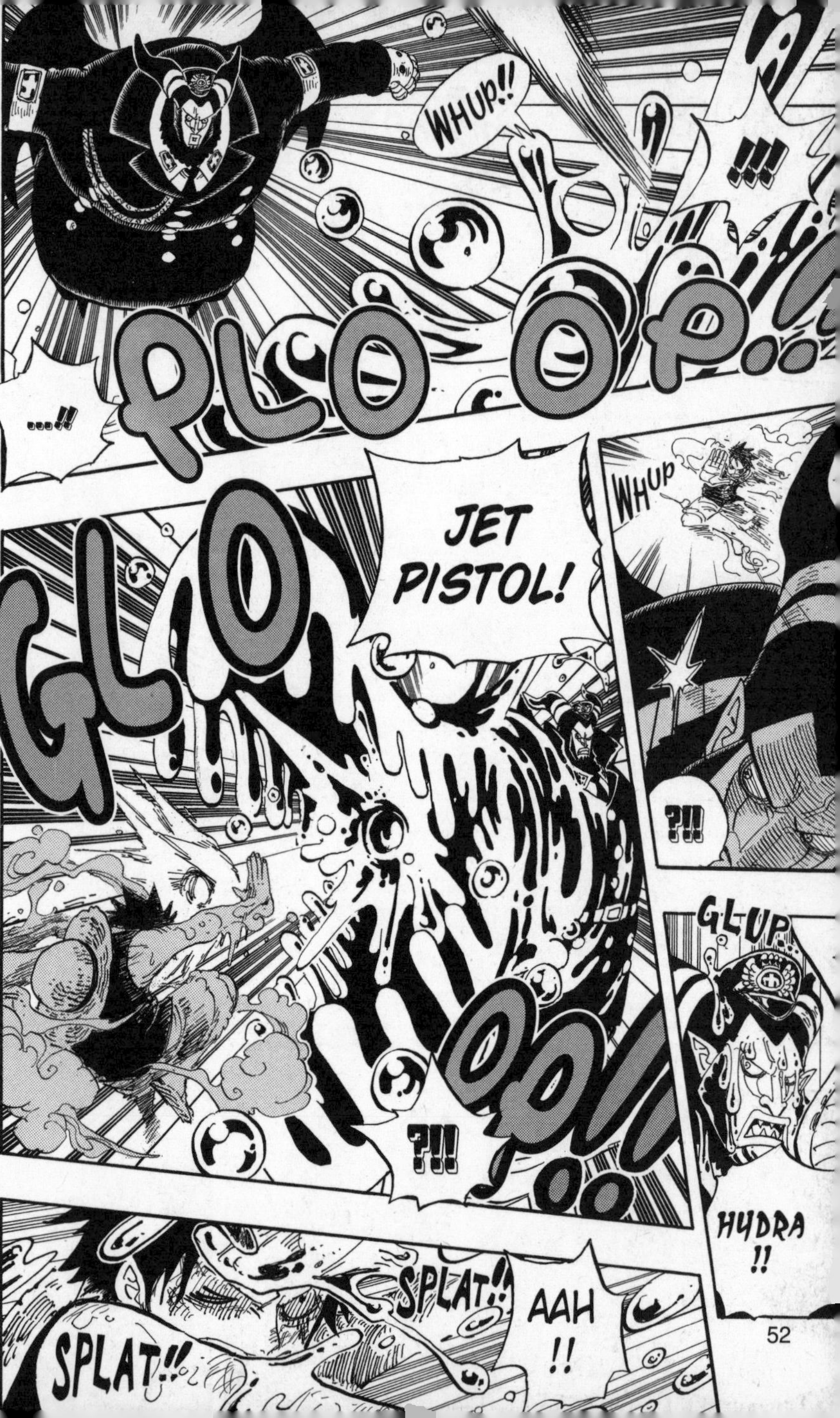
!!!
WHUP!!
PLOO OP...!!
...!!
WHUP
?!!
GLUP...
HYDRA !!
JET PISTOL!
GLOOOP...
?!!
AAH !!
SPLAT!!
SPLAT!!

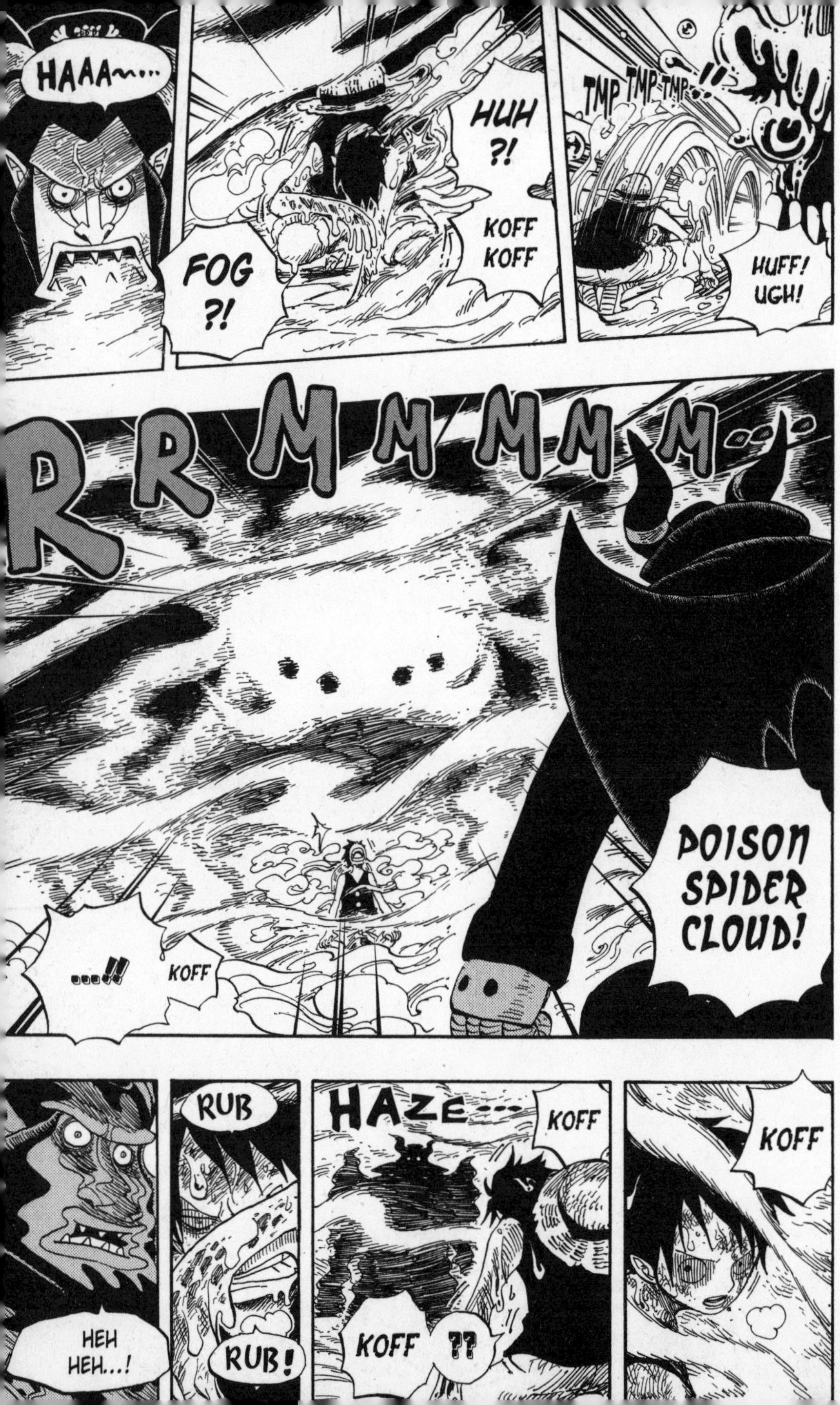

TMP TMP TMP...!!
HUFF! UGH!
HUH ?!
KOFF KOFF
FOG ?!
HAAA~...
RRMMMMMM...
POISON SPIDER CLOUD!
KOFF
...!!
KOFF
HAZE...
KOFF
??
KOFF
RUB
RUB!
HEH HEH...!

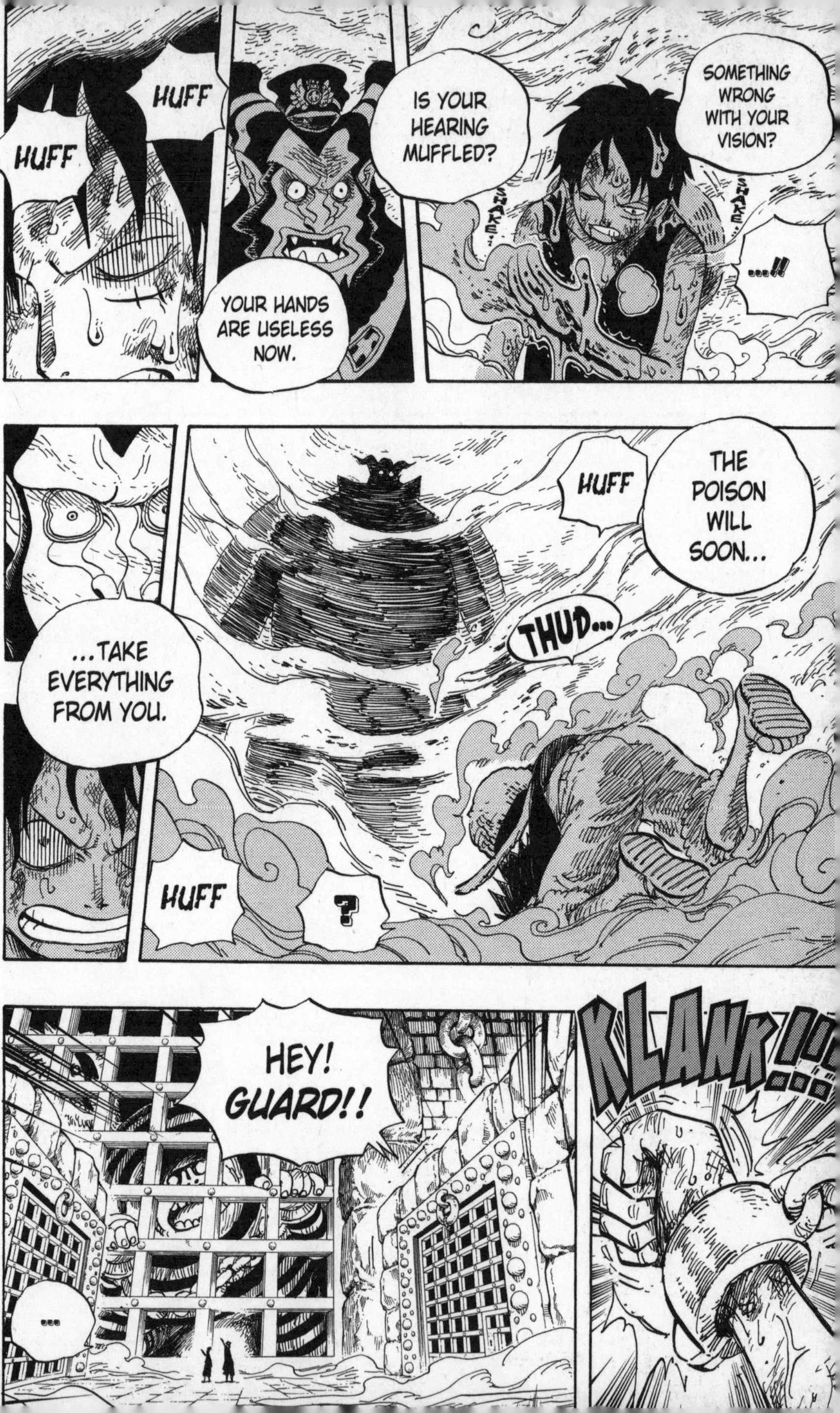
SOMETHING WRONG WITH YOUR VISION?
IS YOUR HEARING MUFFLED?
SHAKE...
SHAKE...
...!!
YOUR HANDS ARE USELESS NOW.
HUFF
HUFF
THE POISON WILL SOON...
HUFF
THUD...
HUFF
?
...TAKE EVERYTHING FROM YOU.
KLANK!!...
HEY! GUARD!!
...

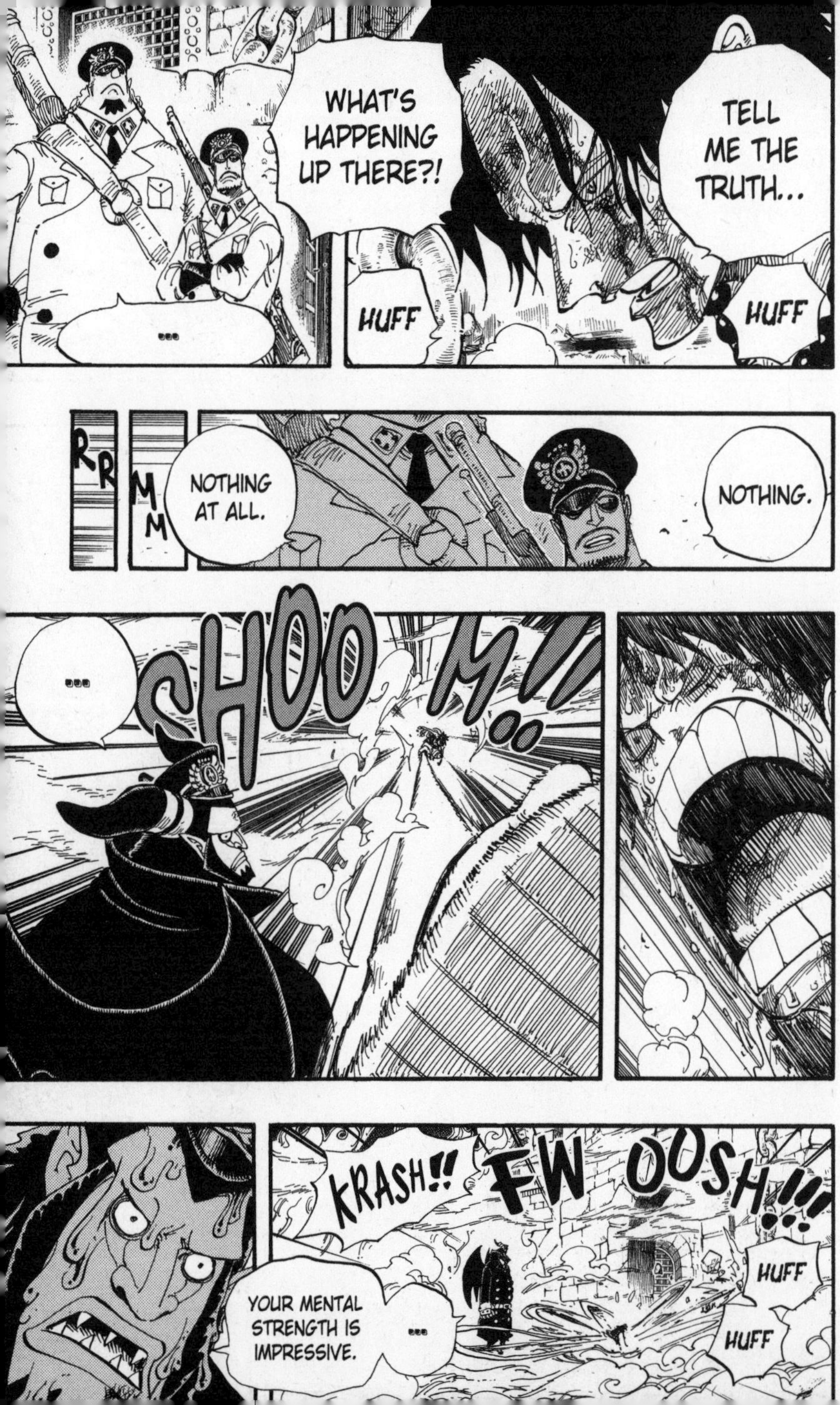
TELL ME THE TRUTH...
HUFF
HUFF
WHAT'S HAPPENING UP THERE?!
...
NOTHING.
NOTHING AT ALL.
RRMM
SHOOM!!
...
FWOOSH!!!
KRASH!!
HUFF
HUFF
...
YOUR MENTAL STRENGTH IS IMPRESSIVE.

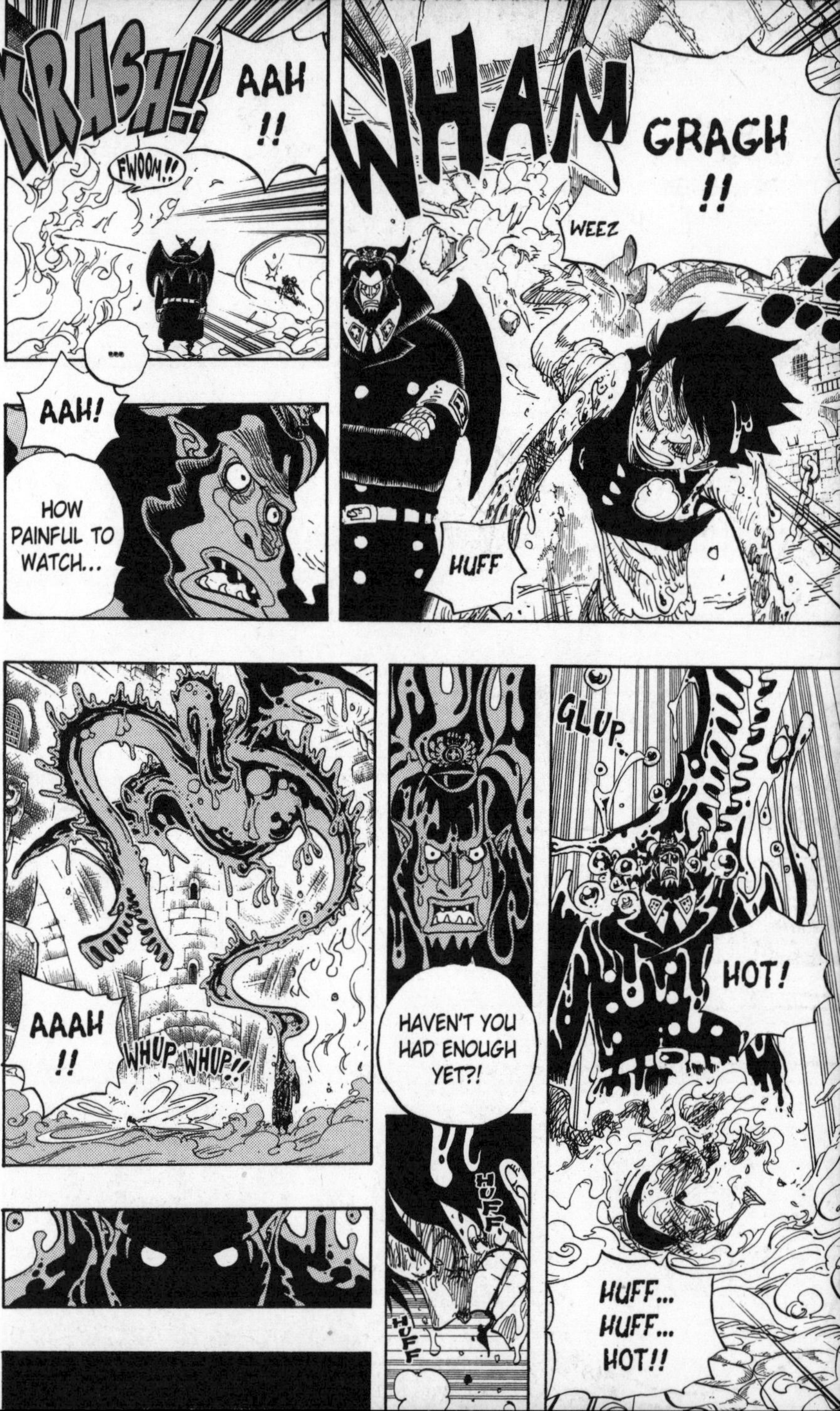
WHAM
GRAGH !!
WEEZ
HUFF
KRASH!!
AAH !!
FWOOM!!
...
AAH!
HOW PAINFUL TO WATCH...
GLUP...
HOT!
HUFF... HUFF... HOT!!
HAVEN'T YOU HAD ENOUGH YET?!
HUFF
HUFF
AAAH !!
WHUP WHUP!!

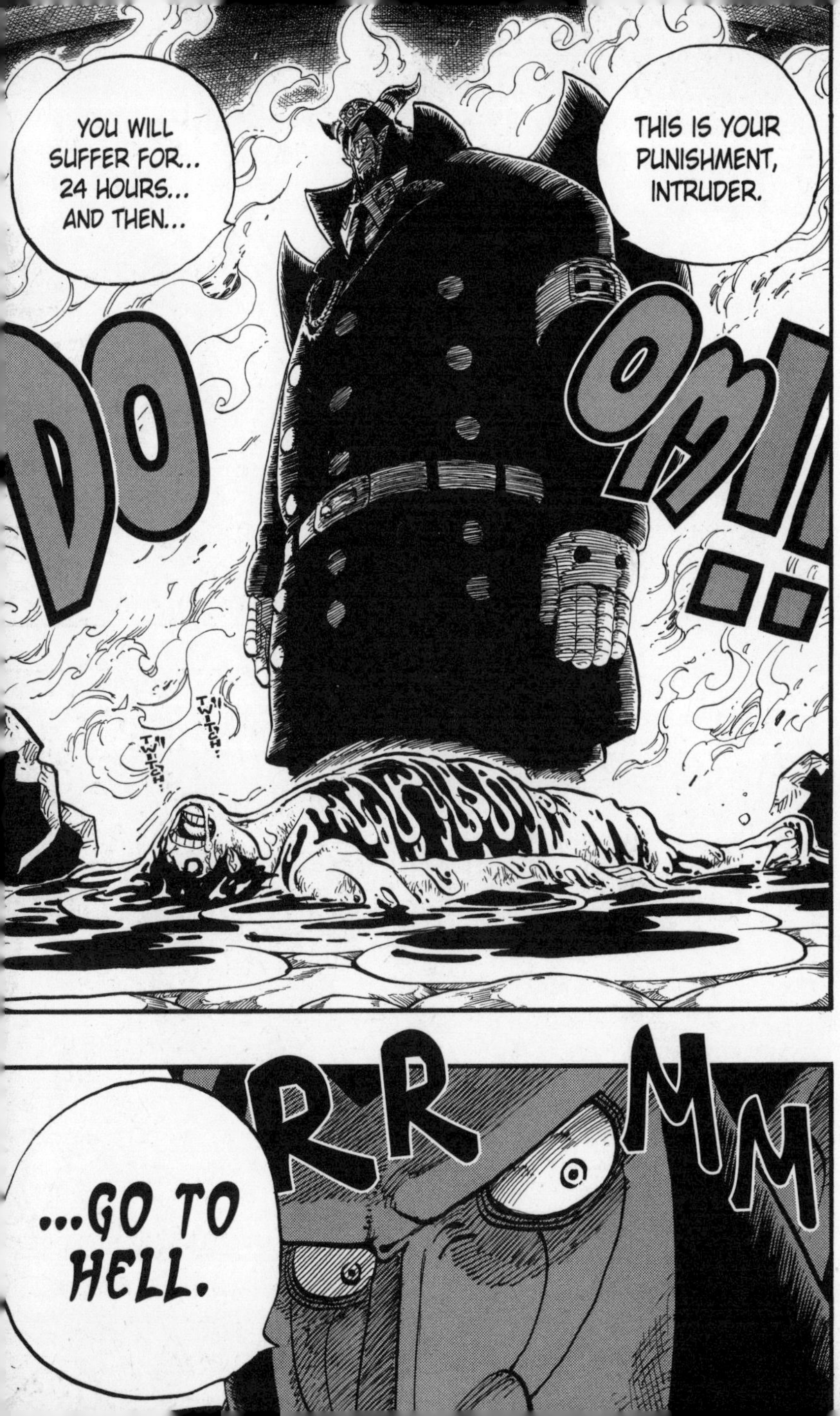
THIS IS YOUR PUNISHMENT, INTRUDER.
YOU WILL SUFFER FOR... 24 HOURS... AND THEN...
DOOM!!
TWITCH
TWITCH
RRMM
...GO TO HELL.

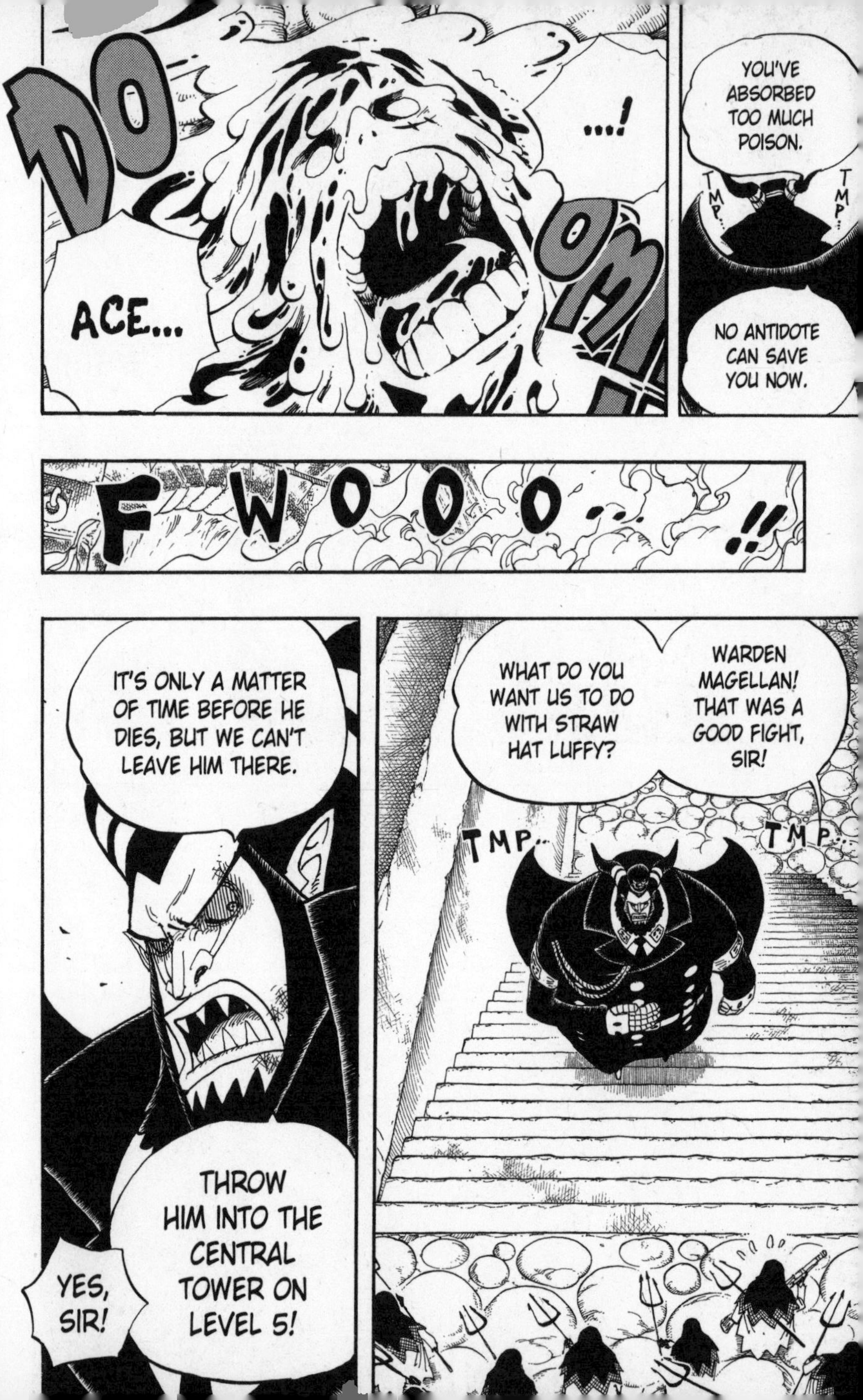
YOU'VE ABSORBED TOO MUCH POISON.
TMP...
TMP...
NO ANTIDOTE CAN SAVE YOU NOW.
DOOM
...!
ACE...
FWOOO...!!
WARDEN MAGELLAN! THAT WAS A GOOD FIGHT, SIR!
WHAT DO YOU WANT US TO DO WITH STRAW HAT LUFFY?
TMP...
TMP...
IT'S ONLY A MATTER OF TIME BEFORE HE DIES, BUT WE CAN'T LEAVE HIM THERE.
THROW HIM INTO THE CENTRAL TOWER ON LEVEL 5!
YES, SIR!

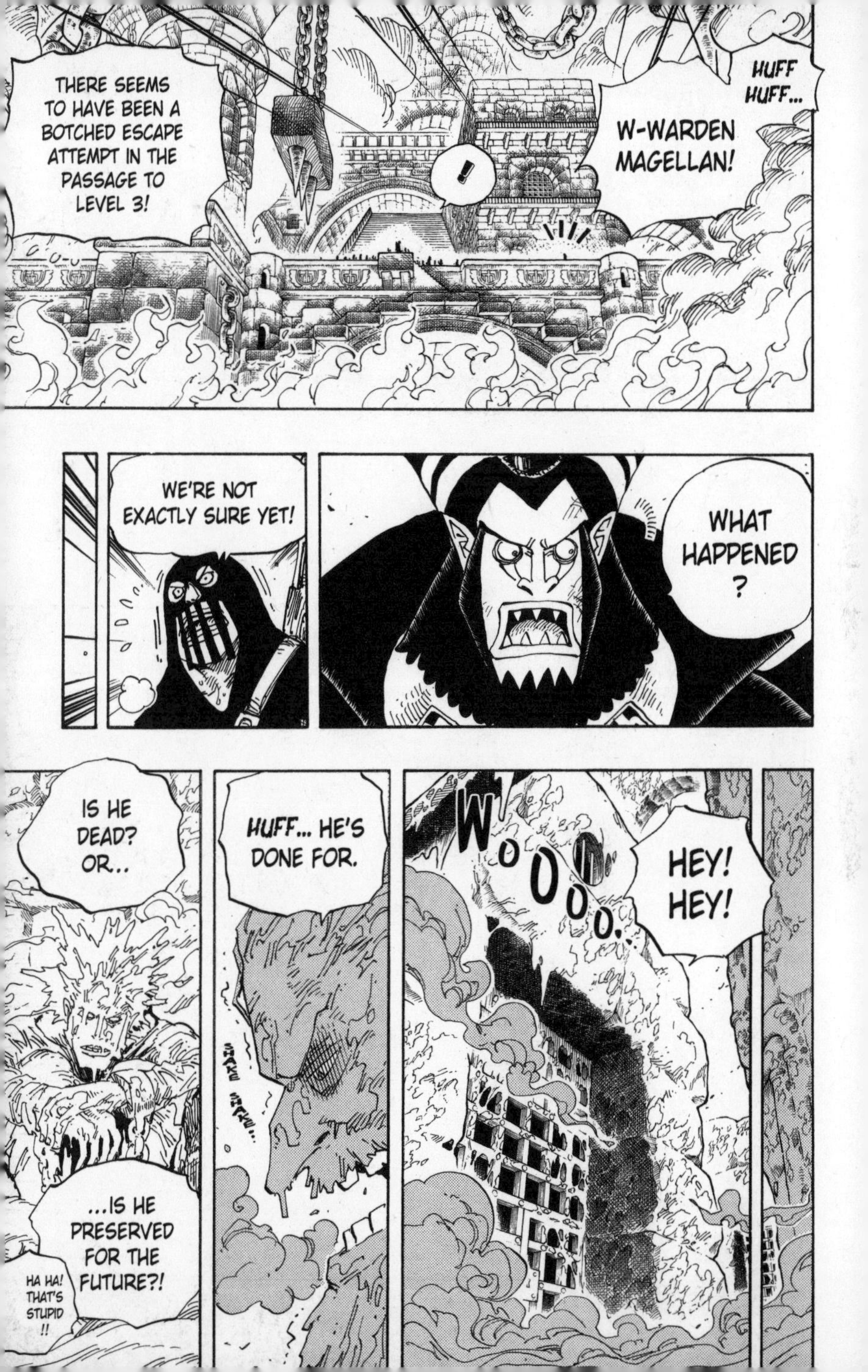
HUFF HUFF...
W-WARDEN MAGELLAN!
!
THERE SEEMS TO HAVE BEEN A BOTCHED ESCAPE ATTEMPT IN THE PASSAGE TO LEVEL 3!
WHAT HAPPENED ?
WE'RE NOT EXACTLY SURE YET!
WOOOO..
HEY! HEY!
HUFF... HE'S DONE FOR.
SHAKE SHAKE...
IS HE DEAD? OR...
...IS HE PRESERVED FOR THE FUTURE?!
HA HA! THAT'S STUPID !!

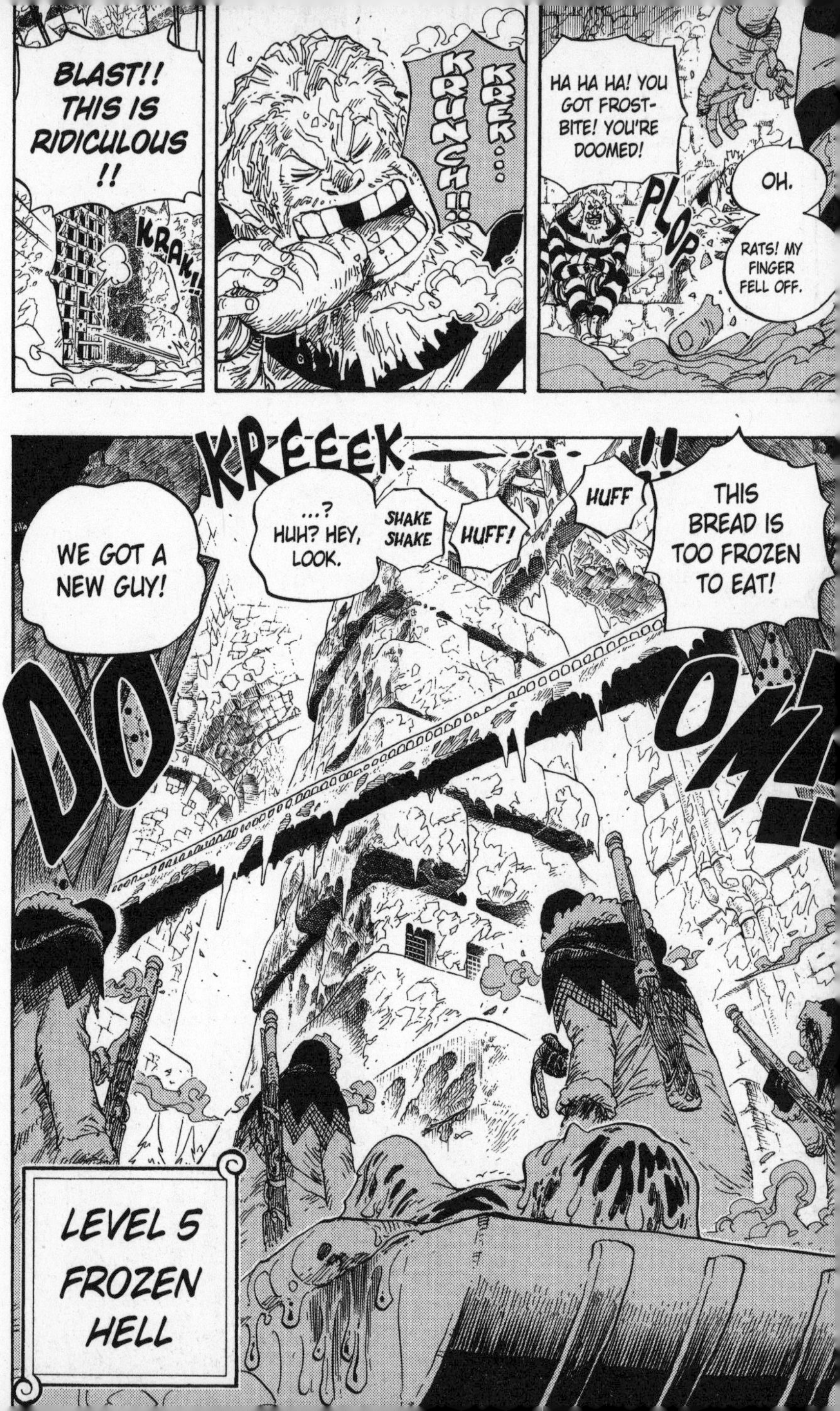
HA HA HA! YOU GOT FROST-BITE! YOU'RE DOOMED!
PLOP
OH.
RATS! MY FINGER FELL OFF.
KREK...
KRUNCH!!
BLAST!! THIS IS RIDICULOUS!!
KRAK!!
THIS BREAD IS TOO FROZEN TO EAT!
HUFF
HUFF!
SHAKE SHAKE
...? HUH? HEY, LOOK.
KREEEK
WE GOT A NEW GUY!
DO
OM!!
LEVEL 5 FROZEN HELL

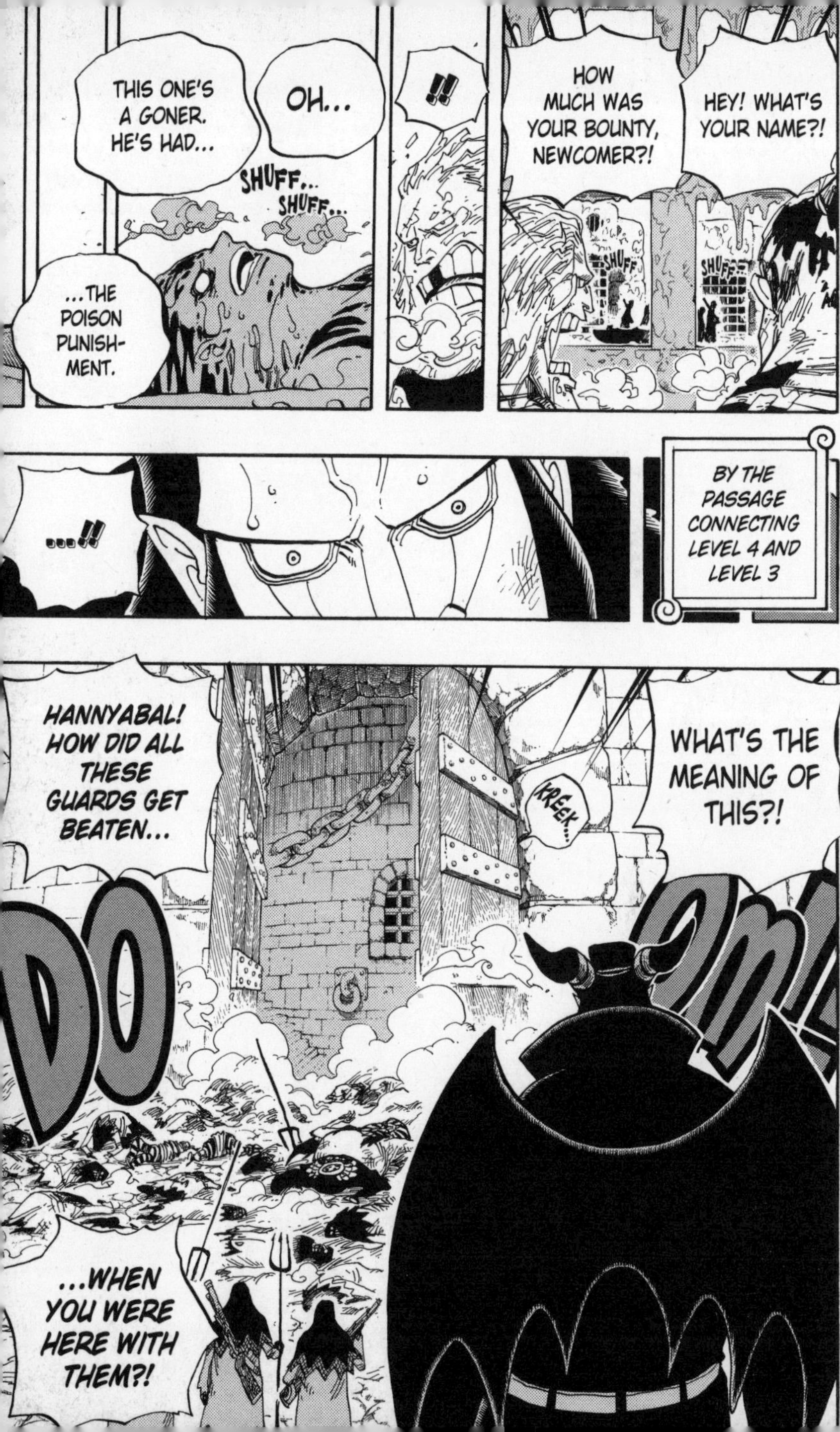
HEY! WHAT'S YOUR NAME?!
HOW MUCH WAS YOUR BOUNTY, NEWCOMER?!
SHUFF
SHUFF...
!!
OH...
THIS ONE'S A GONER. HE'S HAD...
SHUFF... SHUFF...
...THE POISON PUNISH-MENT.
BY THE PASSAGE CONNECTING LEVEL 4 AND LEVEL 3
...!!
WHAT'S THE MEANING OF THIS?!
KREEK...
HANNYABAL! HOW DID ALL THESE GUARDS GET BEATEN...
DO
OM
...WHEN YOU WERE HERE WITH THEM?!

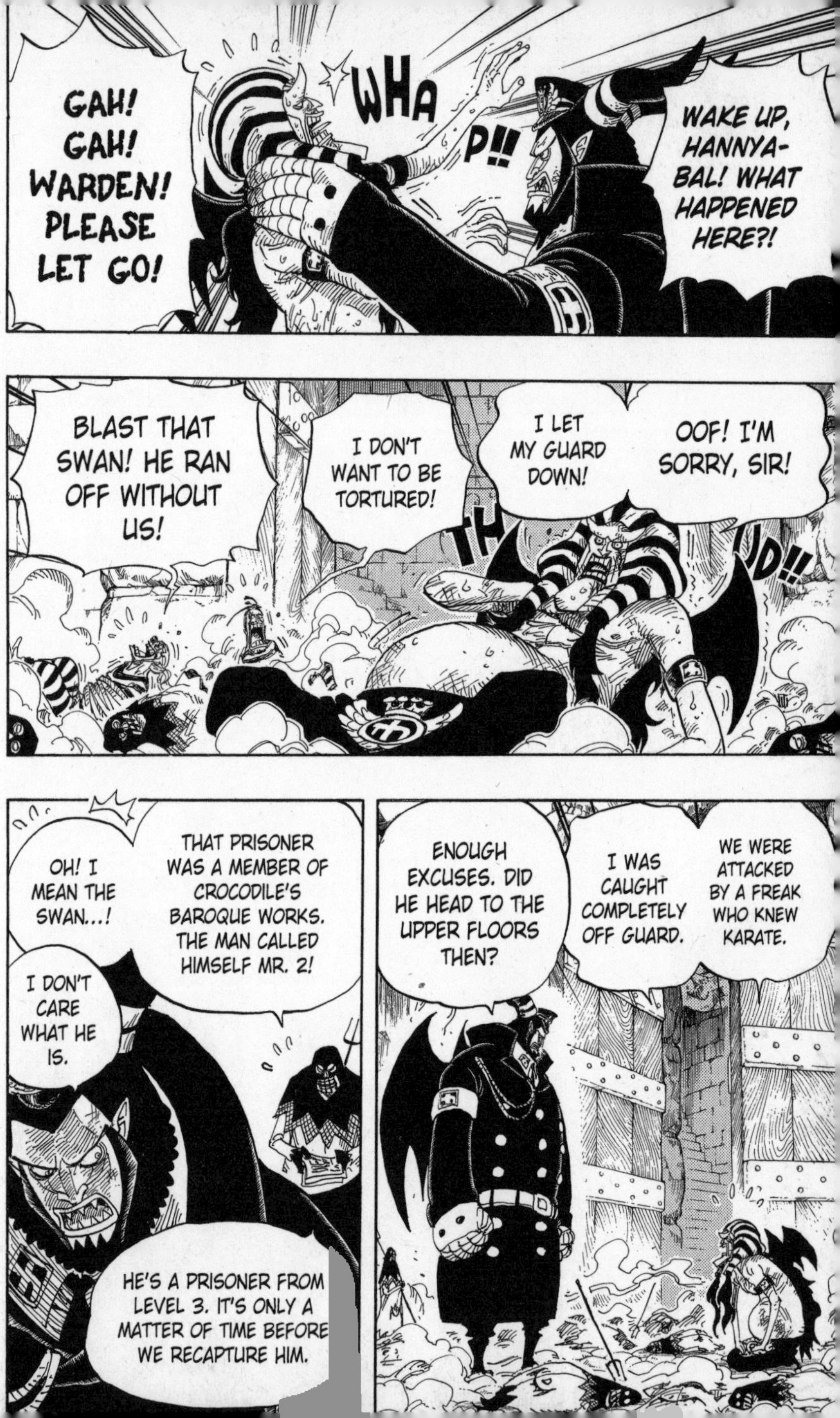
WAKE UP, HANNYA-BAL! WHAT HAPPENED HERE?!
WHA
P!!
GAH! GAH! WARDEN! PLEASE LET GO!
OOF! I'M SORRY, SIR!
I LET MY GUARD DOWN!
UD!!
TH
I DON'T WANT TO BE TORTURED!
BLAST THAT SWAN! HE RAN OFF WITHOUT US!
WE WERE ATTACKED BY A FREAK WHO KNEW KARATE.
I WAS CAUGHT COMPLETELY OFF GUARD.
ENOUGH EXCUSES. DID HE HEAD TO THE UPPER FLOORS THEN?
THAT PRISONER WAS A MEMBER OF CROCODILE'S BAROQUE WORKS. THE MAN CALLED HIMSELF MR. 2!
OH! I MEAN THE SWAN...!
I DON'T CARE WHAT HE IS.
HE'S A PRISONER FROM LEVEL 3. IT'S ONLY A MATTER OF TIME BEFORE WE RECAPTURE HIM.

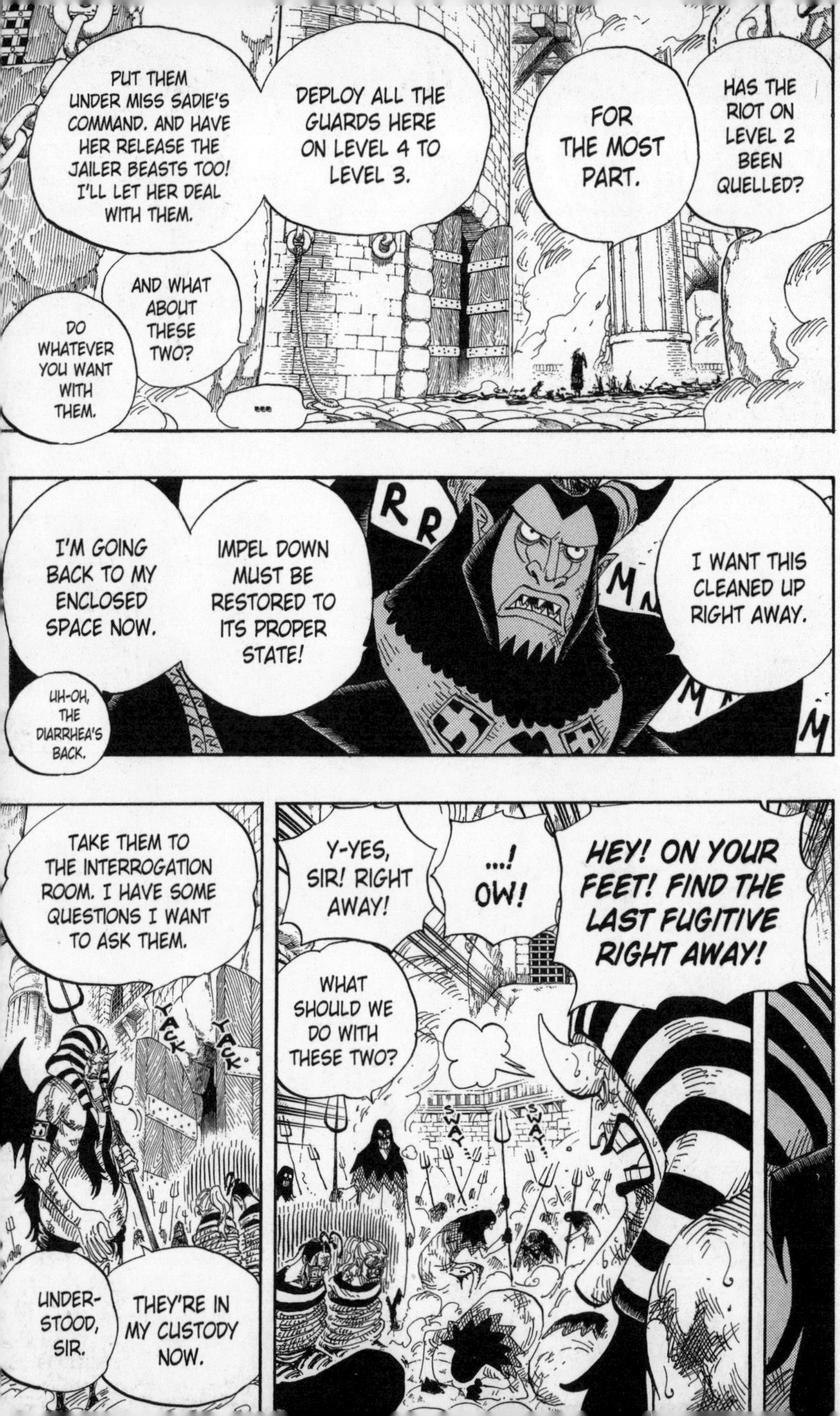
HAS THE RIOT ON LEVEL 2 BEEN QUELLED?
FOR THE MOST PART.
DEPLOY ALL THE GUARDS HERE ON LEVEL 4 TO LEVEL 3.
PUT THEM UNDER MISS SADIE'S COMMAND. AND HAVE HER RELEASE THE JAILER BEASTS TOO! I'LL LET HER DEAL WITH THEM.
AND WHAT ABOUT THESE TWO?
...
DO WHATEVER YOU WANT WITH THEM.
I WANT THIS CLEANED UP RIGHT AWAY.
RRMMMM
IMPEL DOWN MUST BE RESTORED TO ITS PROPER STATE!
I'M GOING BACK TO MY ENCLOSED SPACE NOW.
UH-OH, THE DIARRHEA'S BACK.
HEY! ON YOUR FEET! FIND THE LAST FUGITIVE RIGHT AWAY!
...! OW!
Y-YES, SIR! RIGHT AWAY!
WHAT SHOULD WE DO WITH THESE TWO?
SWAY...
SWAY...
TAKE THEM TO THE INTERROGATION ROOM. I HAVE SOME QUESTIONS I WANT TO ASK THEM.
YACK
YACK
THEY'RE IN MY CUSTODY NOW.
UNDER-STOOD, SIR.

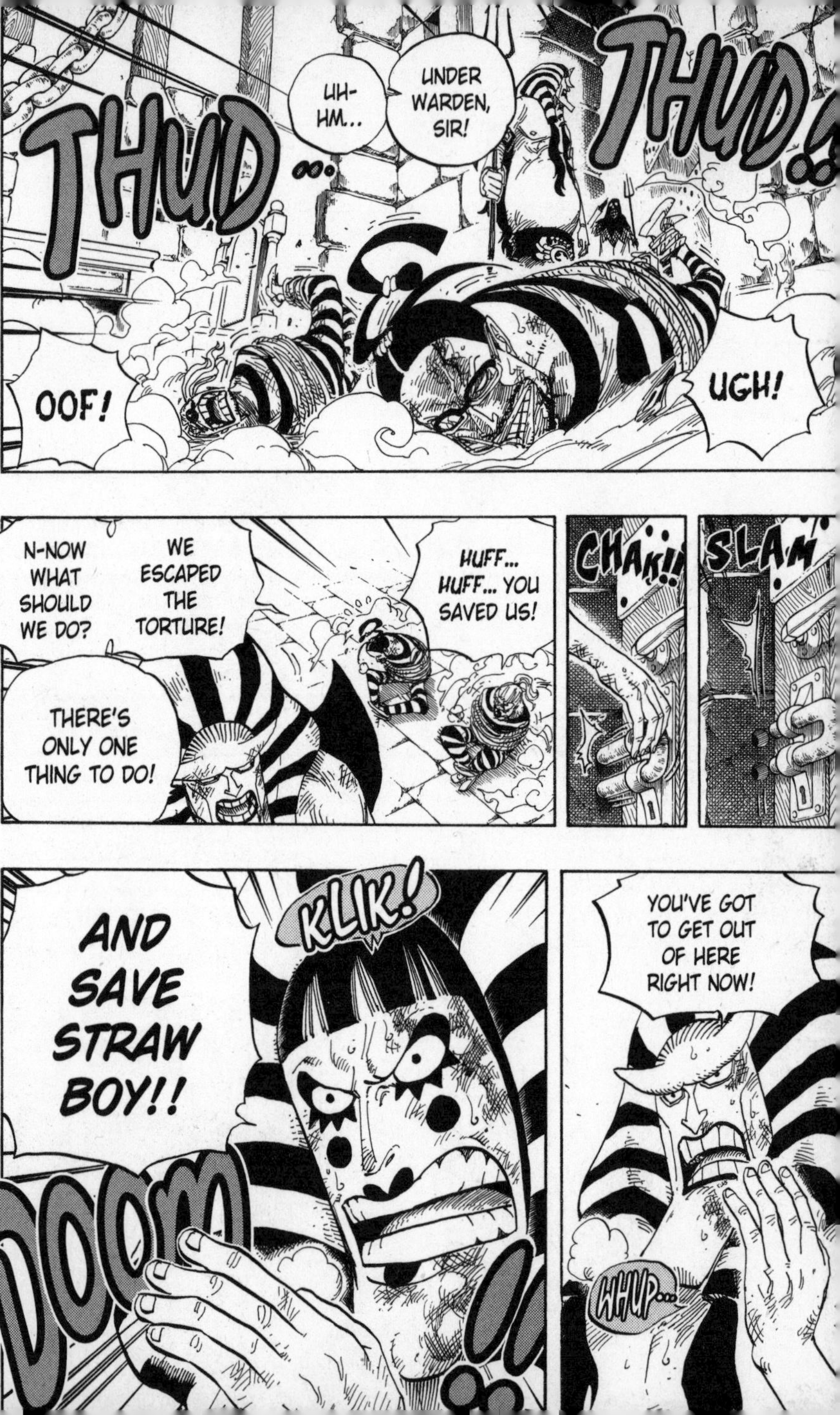
THUD!!
UNDER WARDEN, SIR!
UH-HM...
THUD...
UGH!
OOF!
SLAM
CHAK!!
HUFF... HUFF... YOU SAVED US!
WE ESCAPED THE TORTURE!
N-NOW WHAT SHOULD WE DO?
THERE'S ONLY ONE THING TO DO!
YOU'VE GOT TO GET OUT OF HERE RIGHT NOW!
WHUP...
KLIK!
AND SAVE STRAW BOY!!
DOOM...

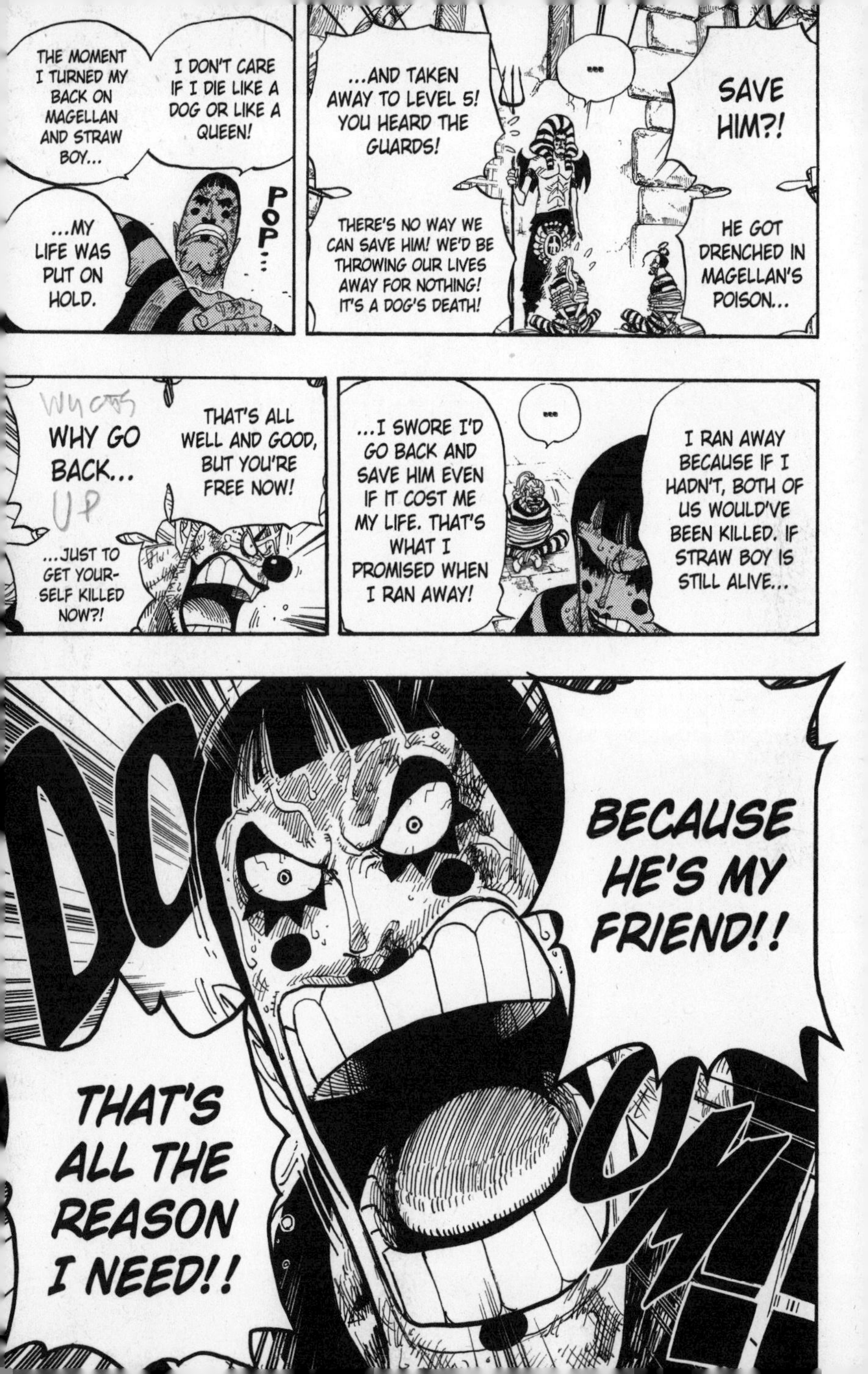
SAVE HIM?!
HE GOT DRENCHED IN MAGELLAN'S POISON...
...
...AND TAKEN AWAY TO LEVEL 5! YOU HEARD THE GUARDS!
THERE'S NO WAY WE CAN SAVE HIM! WE'D BE THROWING OUR LIVES AWAY FOR NOTHING! IT'S A DOG'S DEATH!
I DON'T CARE IF I DIE LIKE A DOG OR LIKE A QUEEN!
THE MOMENT I TURNED MY BACK ON MAGELLAN AND STRAW BOY...
...MY LIFE WAS PUT ON HOLD.
POP...
I RAN AWAY BECAUSE IF I HADN'T, BOTH OF US WOULD'VE BEEN KILLED. IF STRAW BOY IS STILL ALIVE...
...
...I SWORE I'D GO BACK AND SAVE HIM EVEN IF IT COST ME MY LIFE. THAT'S WHAT I PROMISED WHEN I RAN AWAY!
THAT'S ALL WELL AND GOOD, BUT YOU'RE FREE NOW!
WHY GO BACK...
...JUST TO GET YOURSELF KILLED NOW?!
BECAUSE HE'S MY FRIEND!!
THAT'S ALL THE REASON I NEED!!

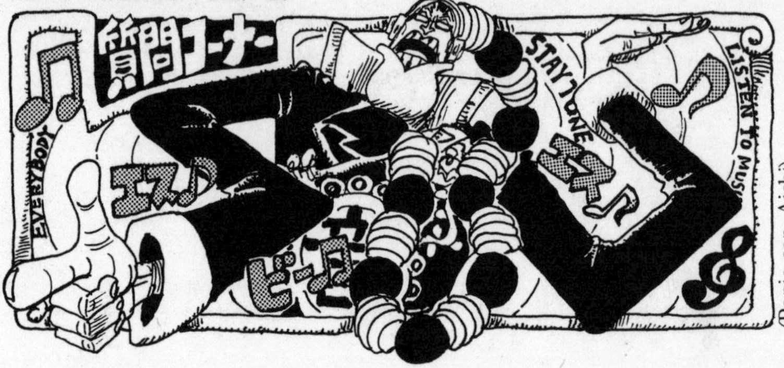
質問コーナー
STAY TUNE
LISTEN TO MUS
EVERYBODY
(Ponio-san, Aichi)

Q: Hello, pleased to meet you! We are the Panda Pirates, the biggest band of pirates in all of China. We've recruited people from all over the world via the Internet. We recently reached 40,000 members! (What?! You're not surprised because China's so big?! Oh, well…) My Question is: The buildings and scenery on the Island of Women look sort of Chinese. Was this intentional?

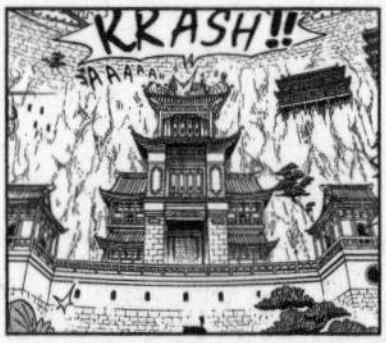
KRASH!!

--Chang Xing Xiang, Panda Pirates

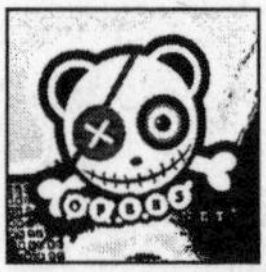

A: Yes, that's true of Amazon Lily. I did model it on China. In movies and stories Amazons often lack elegance, so I wanted this nation of women to inhabit a more cultured setting. And Chinese women are really sexy! I love those dresses! Sanji does too. By the way, this message arrived in a huge envelope labeled the "Panda Pirates." There was a list of members in the envelope. They turned out to be *One Piece* fans from all over the world. This made me really happy. I hope they'll all continue to enjoy *One Piece*.

Q: Mr. Oda, Chopper is so cute! I want him for a pet. What? No? Then make me Nami's pet!

--Shimizu Chamoroe

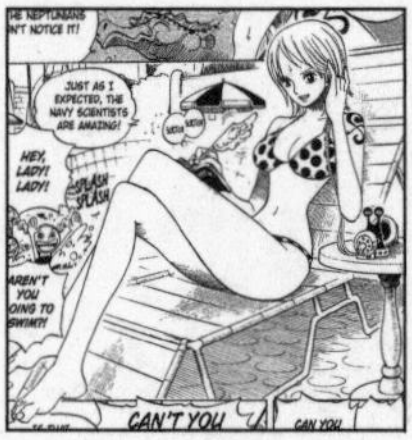
JUST AS I EXPECTED, THE NAVY SCIENTISTS ARE AMAZING!
HEY, LADY! LADY!
CAN'T YOU
CAN YOU

A: What are you talking about?!
Hey! Sheriff! You showed up just in time! We have a weirdo here. Thank you! (siren) Hey! No, not me! Wait!!

Q: Odacchi! ♡ Will you come tomorrow?

--KURI

A: Sure. Where?!

Chapter 536:
LEVEL 5: FROZEN HELL

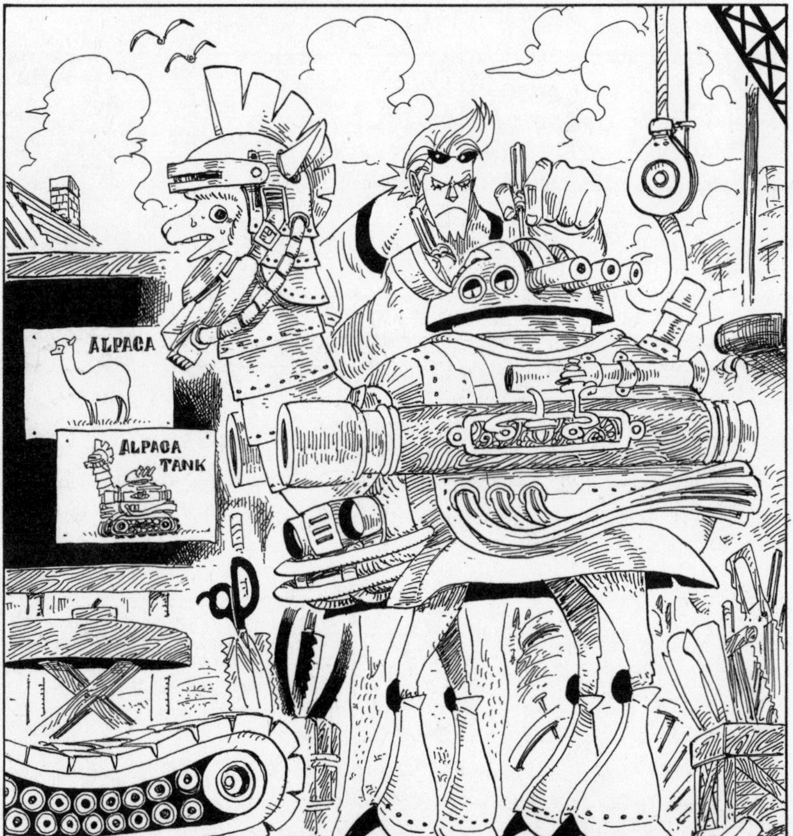
ALPACA
ALPACA TANK

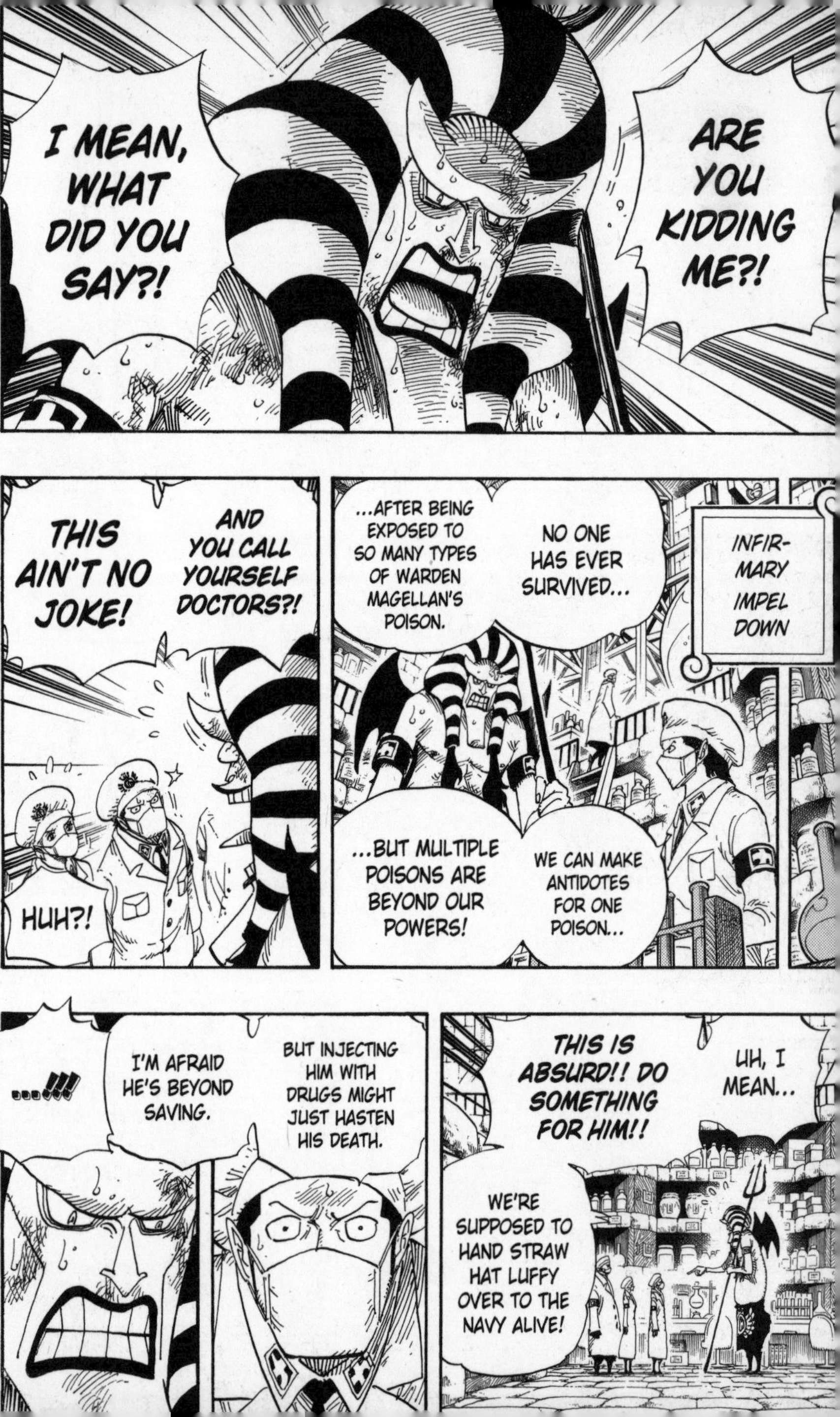
ARE YOU KIDDING ME?!
I MEAN, WHAT DID YOU SAY?!
INFIRMARY IMPEL DOWN
NO ONE HAS EVER SURVIVED...
...AFTER BEING EXPOSED TO SO MANY TYPES OF WARDEN MAGELLAN'S POISON.
WE CAN MAKE ANTIDOTES FOR ONE POISON...
...BUT MULTIPLE POISONS ARE BEYOND OUR POWERS!
AND YOU CALL YOURSELF DOCTORS?!
THIS AIN'T NO JOKE!
HUH?!
UH, I MEAN...
THIS IS ABSURD!! DO SOMETHING FOR HIM!!
WE'RE SUPPOSED TO HAND STRAW HAT LUFFY OVER TO THE NAVY ALIVE!
BUT INJECTING HIM WITH DRUGS MIGHT JUST HASTEN HIS DEATH.
I'M AFRAID HE'S BEYOND SAVING.
...!!!

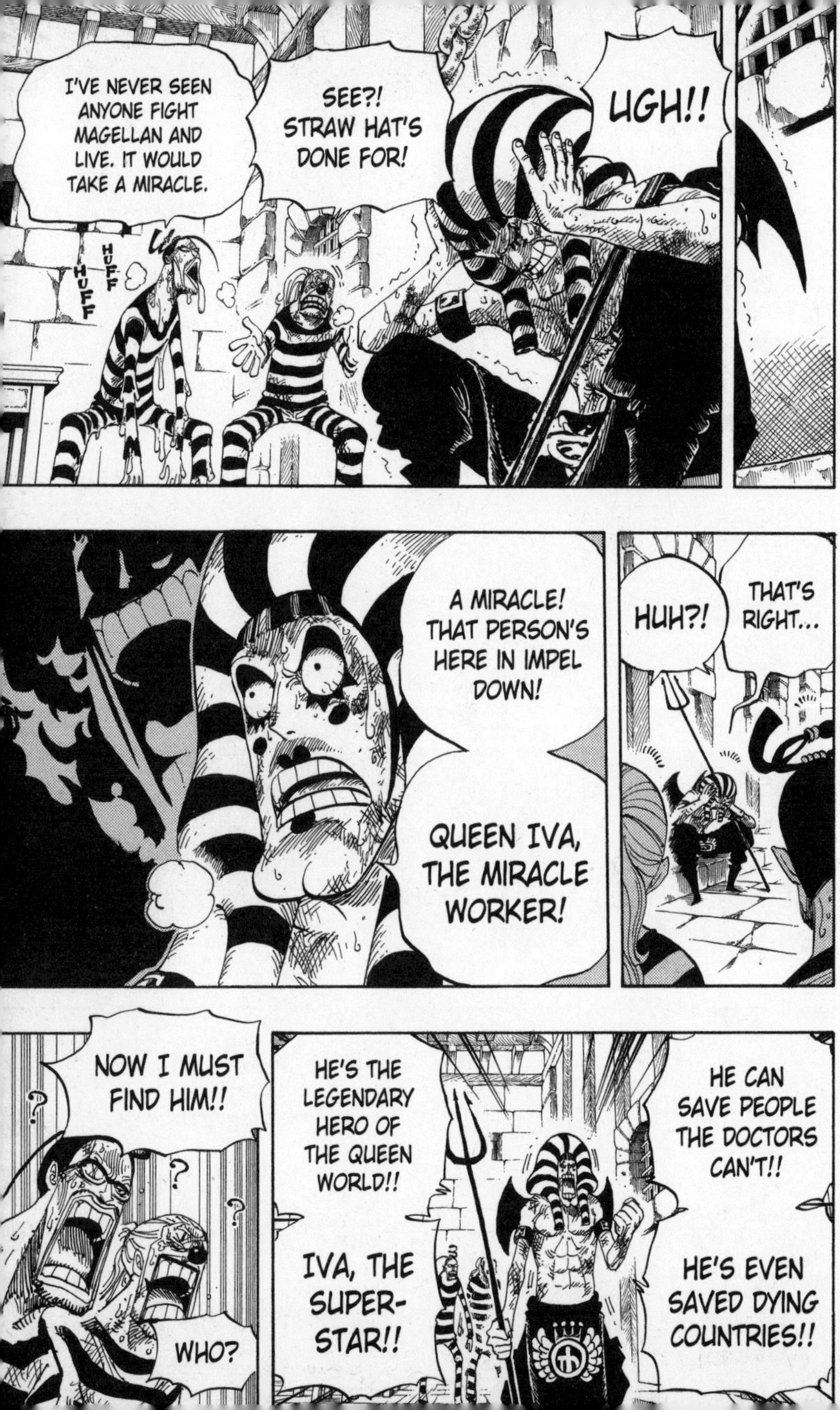
UGH!!
SEE?! STRAW HAT'S DONE FOR!
I'VE NEVER SEEN ANYONE FIGHT MAGELLAN AND LIVE. IT WOULD TAKE A MIRACLE.
HUFF
HUFF
THAT'S RIGHT...
HUH?!
A MIRACLE! THAT PERSON'S HERE IN IMPEL DOWN!
QUEEN IVA, THE MIRACLE WORKER!
HE CAN SAVE PEOPLE THE DOCTORS CAN'T!!
HE'S EVEN SAVED DYING COUNTRIES!!
HE'S THE LEGENDARY HERO OF THE QUEEN WORLD!!
IVA, THE SUPER-STAR!!
NOW I MUST FIND HIM!!
WHO?

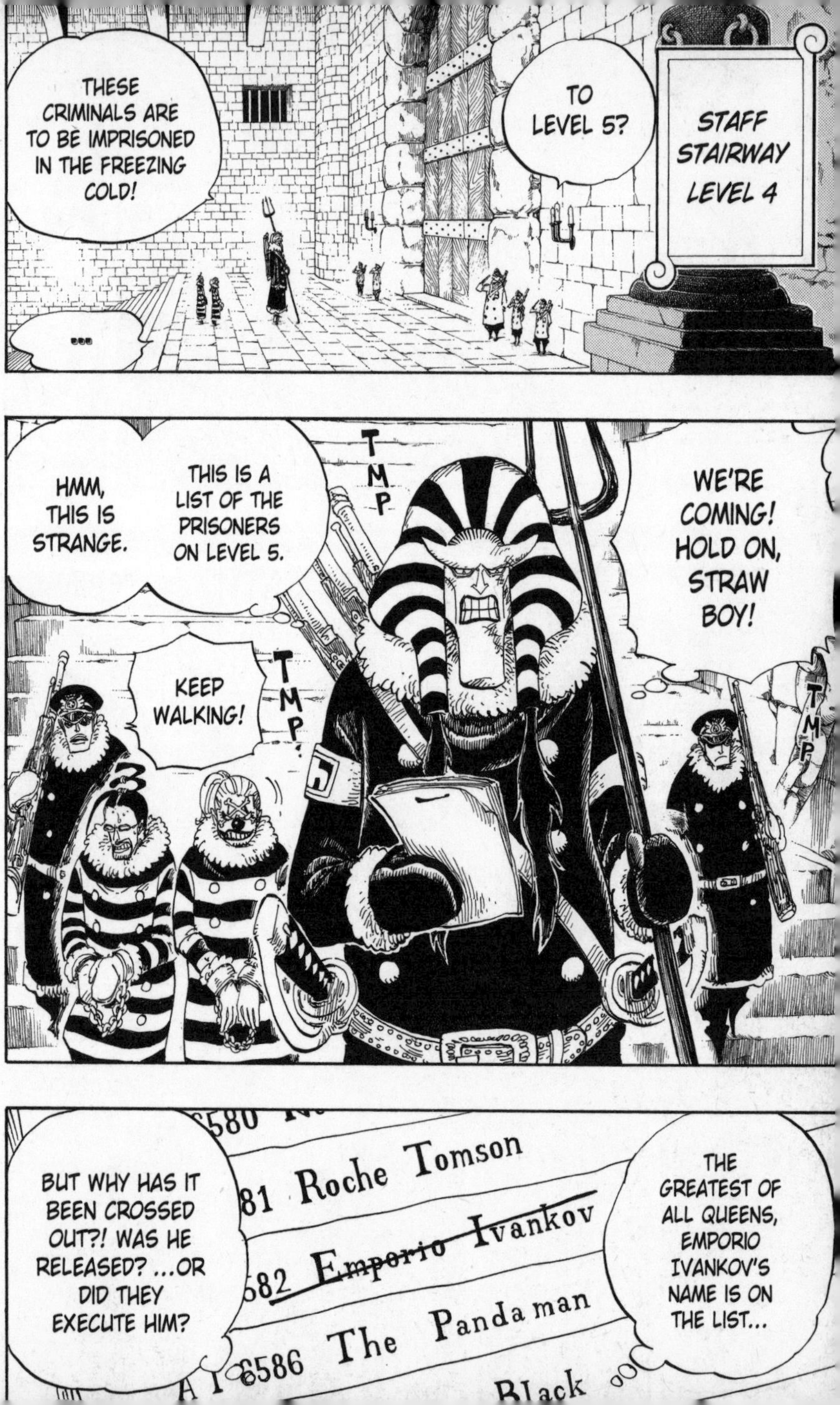
STAFF STAIRWAY LEVEL 4
TO LEVEL 5?
THESE CRIMINALS ARE TO BE IMPRISONED IN THE FREEZING COLD!
...
WE'RE COMING! HOLD ON, STRAW BOY!
TMP
HMM, THIS IS STRANGE.
THIS IS A LIST OF THE PRISONERS ON LEVEL 5.
TMP
TMP
KEEP WALKING!
THE GREATEST OF ALL QUEENS, EMPORIO IVANKOV'S NAME IS ON THE LIST...
6580
81 Roche Tomson
682 Emporio Ivankov
6586 The Pandaman
Black
BUT WHY HAS IT BEEN CROSSED OUT?! WAS HE RELEASED? ...OR DID THEY EXECUTE HIM?

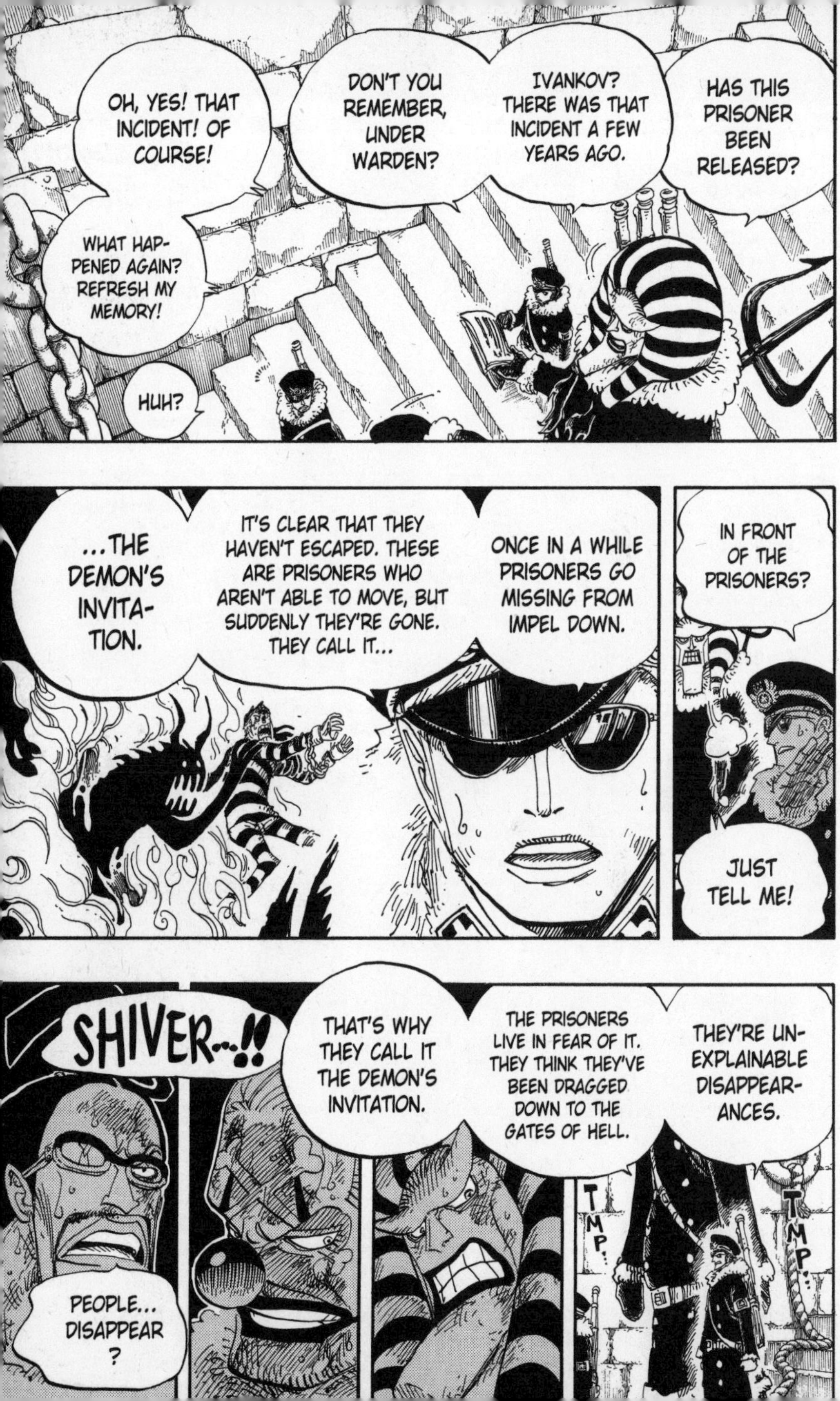
HAS THIS PRISONER BEEN RELEASED?
IVANKOV? THERE WAS THAT INCIDENT A FEW YEARS AGO.
DON'T YOU REMEMBER, UNDER WARDEN?
OH, YES! THAT INCIDENT! OF COURSE!
WHAT HAP-PENED AGAIN? REFRESH MY MEMORY!
HUH?
IN FRONT OF THE PRISONERS?
JUST TELL ME!
ONCE IN A WHILE PRISONERS GO MISSING FROM IMPEL DOWN.
IT'S CLEAR THAT THEY HAVEN'T ESCAPED. THESE ARE PRISONERS WHO AREN'T ABLE TO MOVE, BUT SUDDENLY THEY'RE GONE. THEY CALL IT...
...THE DEMON'S INVITA-TION.
THEY'RE UN-EXPLAINABLE DISAPPEAR-ANCES.
TMP...
TMP...
THE PRISONERS LIVE IN FEAR OF IT. THEY THINK THEY'VE BEEN DRAGGED DOWN TO THE GATES OF HELL.
THAT'S WHY THEY CALL IT THE DEMON'S INVITATION.
SHIVER...!!
PEOPLE... DISAPPEAR?

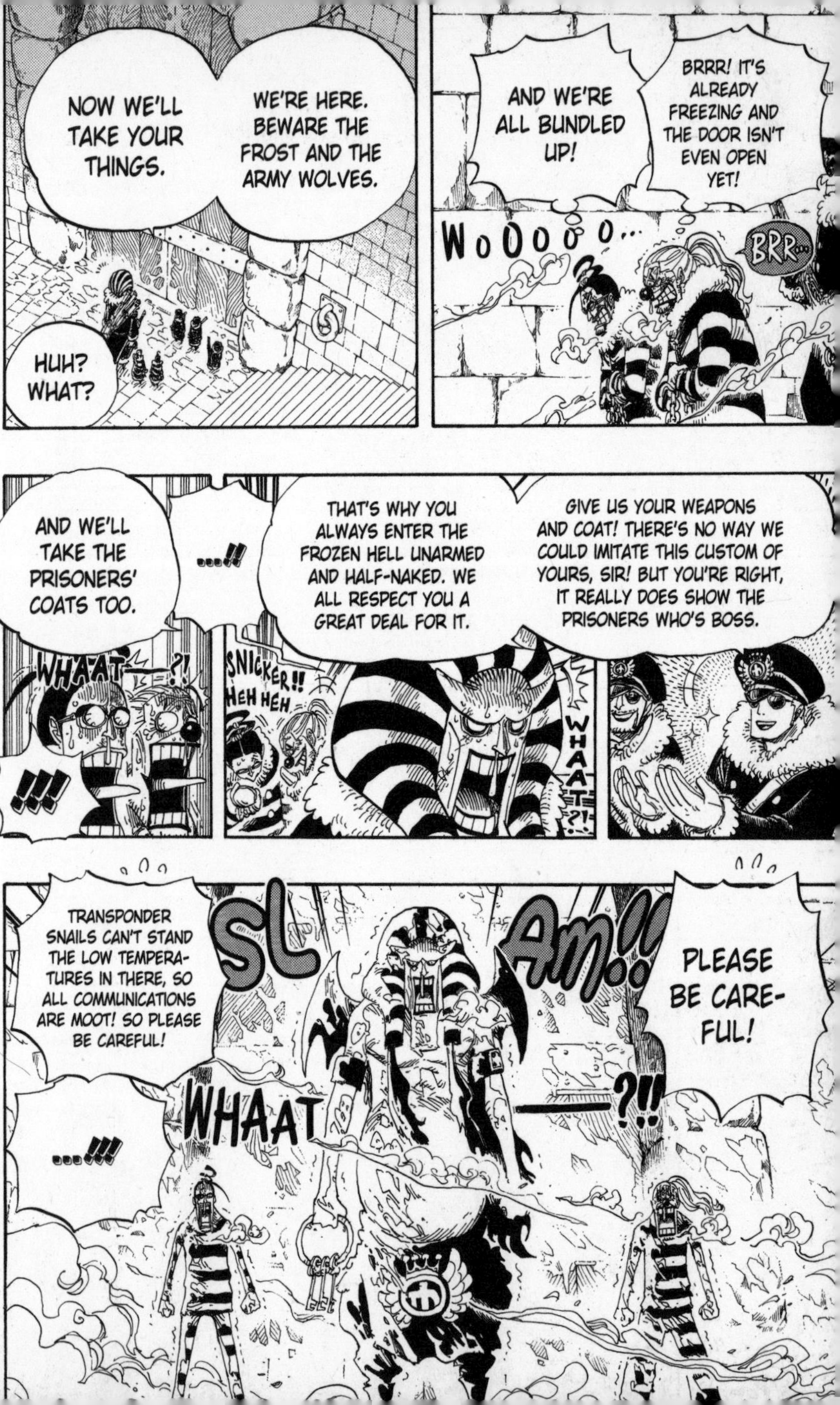
BRRR! IT'S ALREADY FREEZING AND THE DOOR ISN'T EVEN OPEN YET!
AND WE'RE ALL BUNDLED UP!
BRR...
WoOOOO...
WE'RE HERE. BEWARE THE FROST AND THE ARMY WOLVES.
NOW WE'LL TAKE YOUR THINGS.
HUH? WHAT?
GIVE US YOUR WEAPONS AND COAT! THERE'S NO WAY WE COULD IMITATE THIS CUSTOM OF YOURS, SIR! BUT YOU'RE RIGHT, IT REALLY DOES SHOW THE PRISONERS WHO'S BOSS.
THAT'S WHY YOU ALWAYS ENTER THE FROZEN HELL UNARMED AND HALF-NAKED. WE ALL RESPECT YOU A GREAT DEAL FOR IT.
WHAAAT?!
SNICKER!! HEH HEH
...!!
AND WE'LL TAKE THE PRISONERS' COATS TOO.
WHAAT—?!
!!!
PLEASE BE CARE-FUL!
TRANSPONDER SNAILS CAN'T STAND THE LOW TEMPERA-TURES IN THERE, SO ALL COMMUNICATIONS ARE MOOT! SO PLEASE BE CAREFUL!
SLAM!!
WHAAT—?!!
...!!!

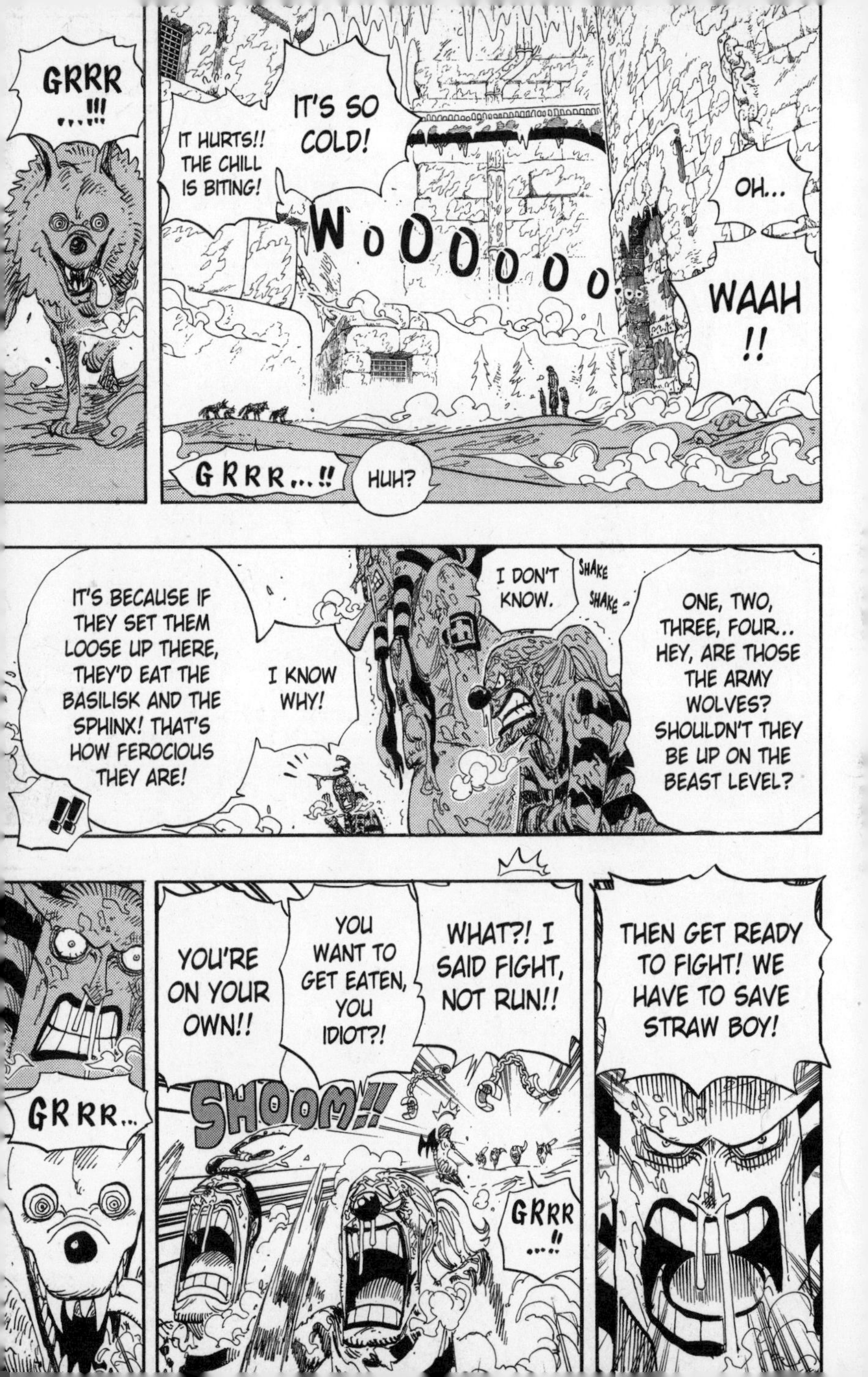
OH...
WAAH!!
IT'S SO COLD!
IT HURTS!! THE CHILL IS BITING!
WOOOOOOO
HUH?
GRRR...!!
GRRR...!!!
ONE, TWO, THREE, FOUR... HEY, ARE THOSE THE ARMY WOLVES? SHOULDN'T THEY BE UP ON THE BEAST LEVEL?
SHAKE SHAKE
I DON'T KNOW.
I KNOW WHY!
IT'S BECAUSE IF THEY SET THEM LOOSE UP THERE, THEY'D EAT THE BASILISK AND THE SPHINX! THAT'S HOW FEROCIOUS THEY ARE!
!!
THEN GET READY TO FIGHT! WE HAVE TO SAVE STRAW BOY!
WHAT?! I SAID FIGHT, NOT RUN!!
YOU WANT TO GET EATEN, YOU IDIOT?!
YOU'RE ON YOUR OWN!!
SHOOM!!
GRRR...!!
GRRR...

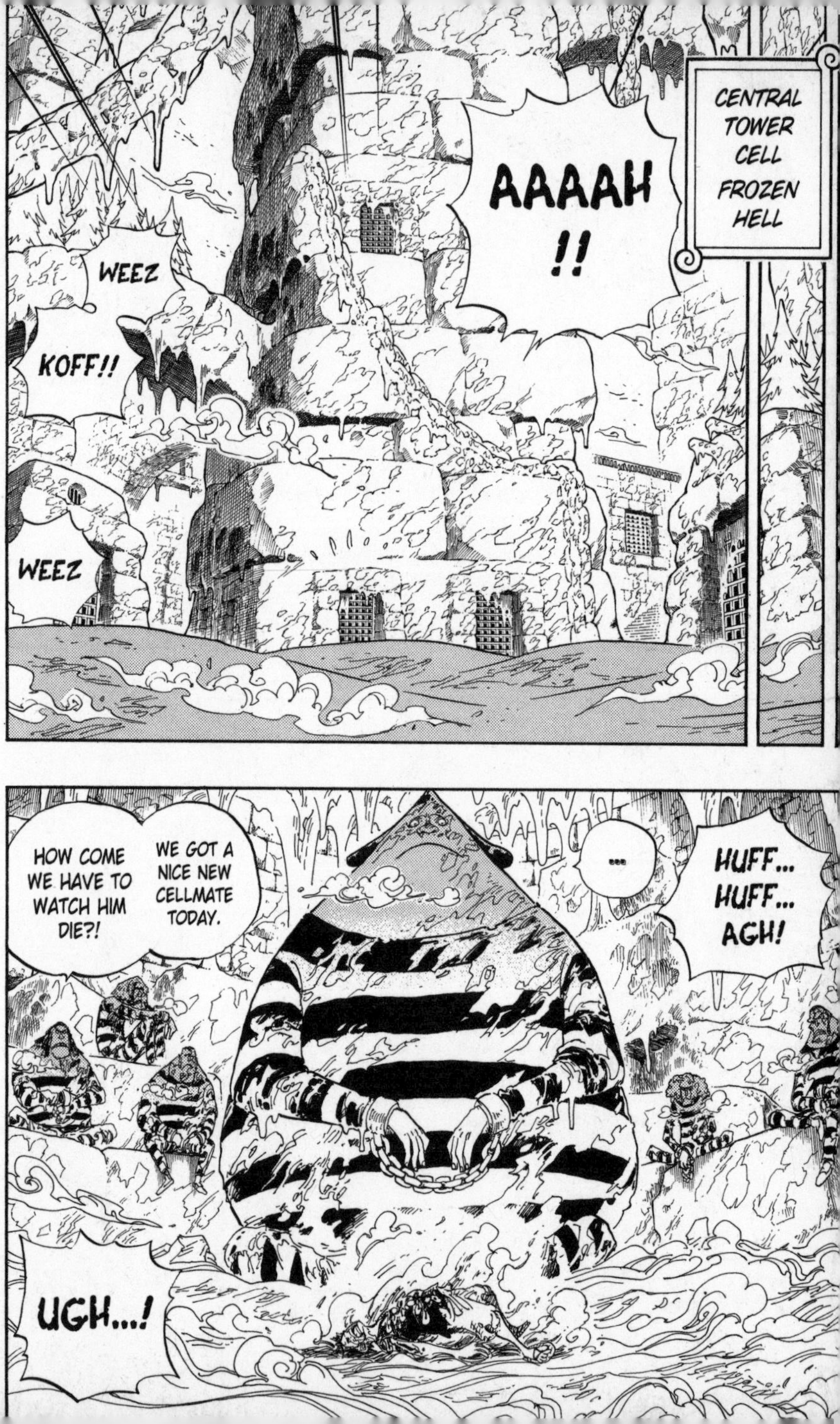

CENTRAL TOWER CELL FROZEN HELL
AAAAH !!
WEEZ
KOFF!!
WEEZ
HUFF... HUFF... AGH!
...
WE GOT A NICE NEW CELLMATE TODAY.
HOW COME WE HAVE TO WATCH HIM DIE?!
UGH...!

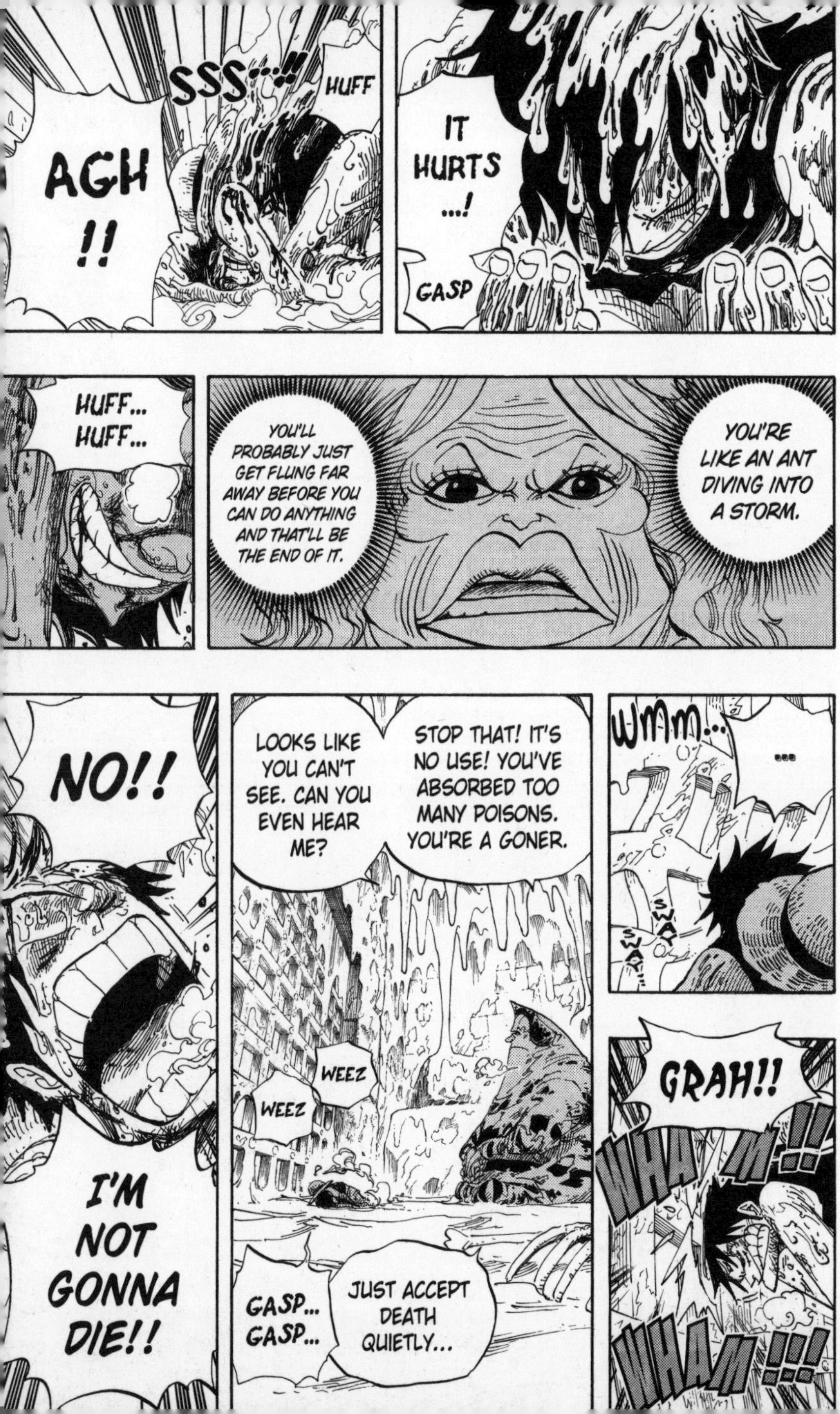
IT HURTS ...!
GASP
SSS...!!
HUFF
AGH!!
YOU'RE LIKE AN ANT DIVING INTO A STORM.
YOU'LL PROBABLY JUST GET FLUNG FAR AWAY BEFORE YOU CAN DO ANYTHING AND THAT'LL BE THE END OF IT.
HUFF... HUFF...
WMM...
...
SWAY
SWAY
GRAH!!
WHAM!!
WHAM!!!
STOP THAT! IT'S NO USE! YOU'VE ABSORBED TOO MANY POISONS. YOU'RE A GONER.
LOOKS LIKE YOU CAN'T SEE. CAN YOU EVEN HEAR ME?
WEEZ
WEEZ
JUST ACCEPT DEATH QUIETLY...
GASP... GASP...
NO!!
I'M NOT GONNA DIE!!

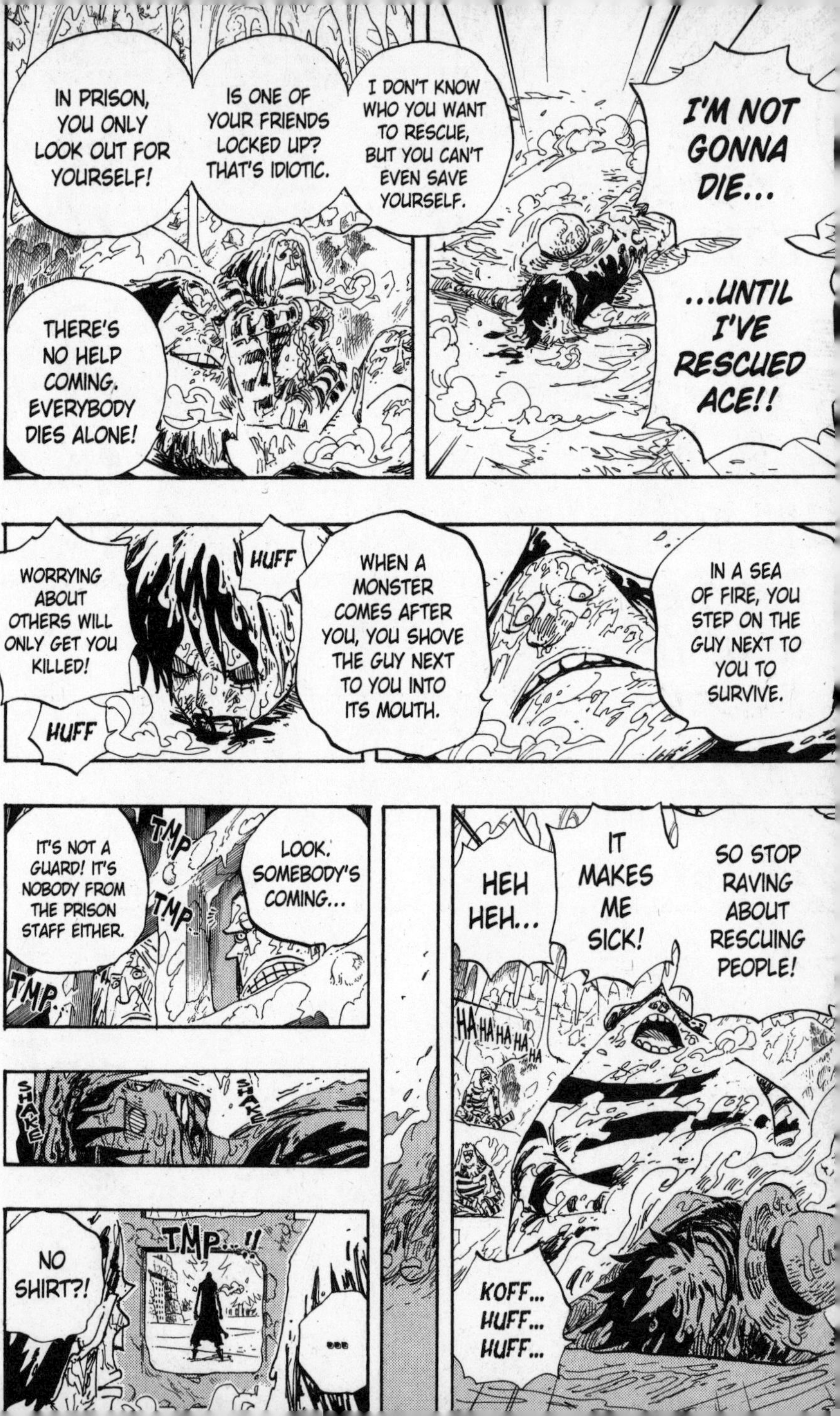
I'M NOT GONNA DIE...
...UNTIL I'VE RESCUED ACE!!
I DON'T KNOW WHO YOU WANT TO RESCUE, BUT YOU CAN'T EVEN SAVE YOURSELF.
IS ONE OF YOUR FRIENDS LOCKED UP? THAT'S IDIOTIC.
IN PRISON, YOU ONLY LOOK OUT FOR YOURSELF!
THERE'S NO HELP COMING. EVERYBODY DIES ALONE!
IN A SEA OF FIRE, YOU STEP ON THE GUY NEXT TO YOU TO SURVIVE.
WHEN A MONSTER COMES AFTER YOU, YOU SHOVE THE GUY NEXT TO YOU INTO ITS MOUTH.
HUFF
WORRYING ABOUT OTHERS WILL ONLY GET YOU KILLED!
HUFF
SO STOP RAVING ABOUT RESCUING PEOPLE!
IT MAKES ME SICK!
HEH HEH...
HA HA HA HA HA HA
KOFF... HUFF... HUFF...
LOOK. SOMEBODY'S COMING...
TMP
TMP
IT'S NOT A GUARD! IT'S NOBODY FROM THE PRISON STAFF EITHER.
TMP..
SHAKE
SHAKE
TMP...!!
...
NO SHIRT?!

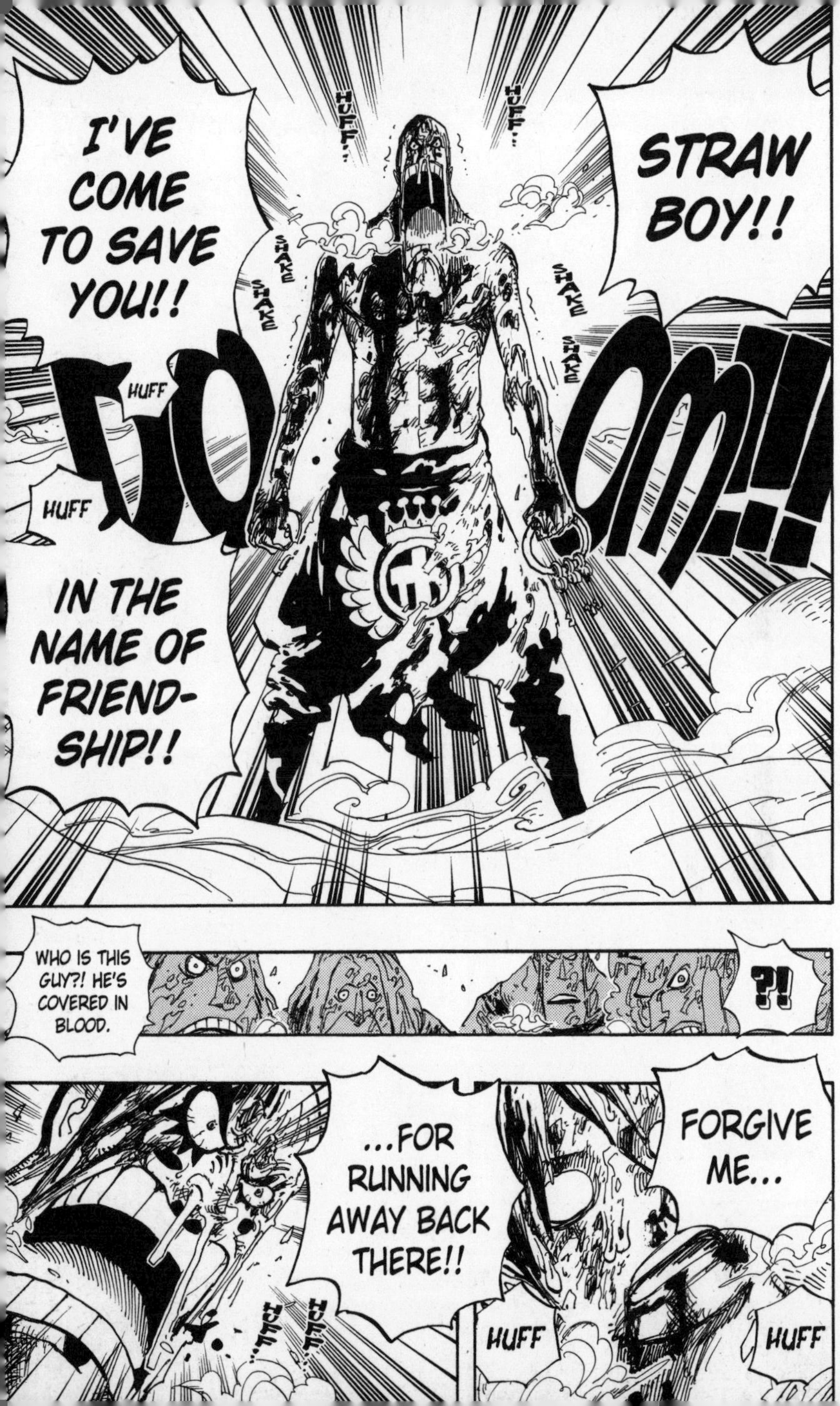
STRAW BOY!!
HUFF HUFF...
HUFF HUFF...
I'VE COME TO SAVE YOU!!
SHAKE SHAKE
SHAKE SHAKE
DOOM!!!
HUFF
HUFF
IN THE NAME OF FRIEND-SHIP!!
?!
WHO IS THIS GUY?! HE'S COVERED IN BLOOD.
FORGIVE ME...
HUFF
HUFF
...FOR RUNNING AWAY BACK THERE!!
HUFF HUFF...

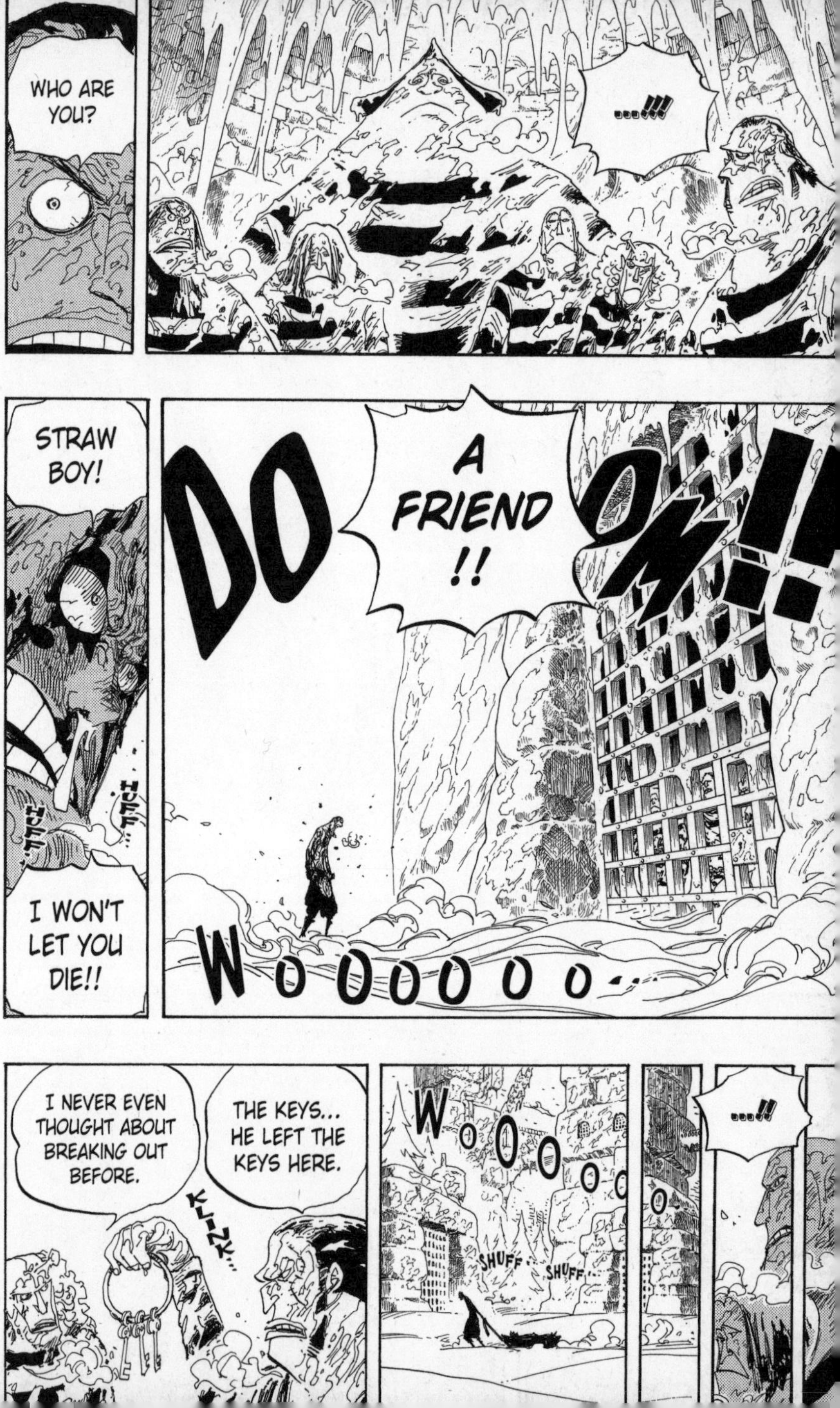

...!!!
WHO ARE YOU?
DO
A FRIEND !!
OM!!
WOOOOOOO...
STRAW BOY!
HUFF HUFF...
I WON'T LET YOU DIE!!
...!!
WOOOOO
SHUFF... SHUFF...
THE KEYS... HE LEFT THE KEYS HERE.
I NEVER EVEN THOUGHT ABOUT BREAKING OUT BEFORE.
KLINK...

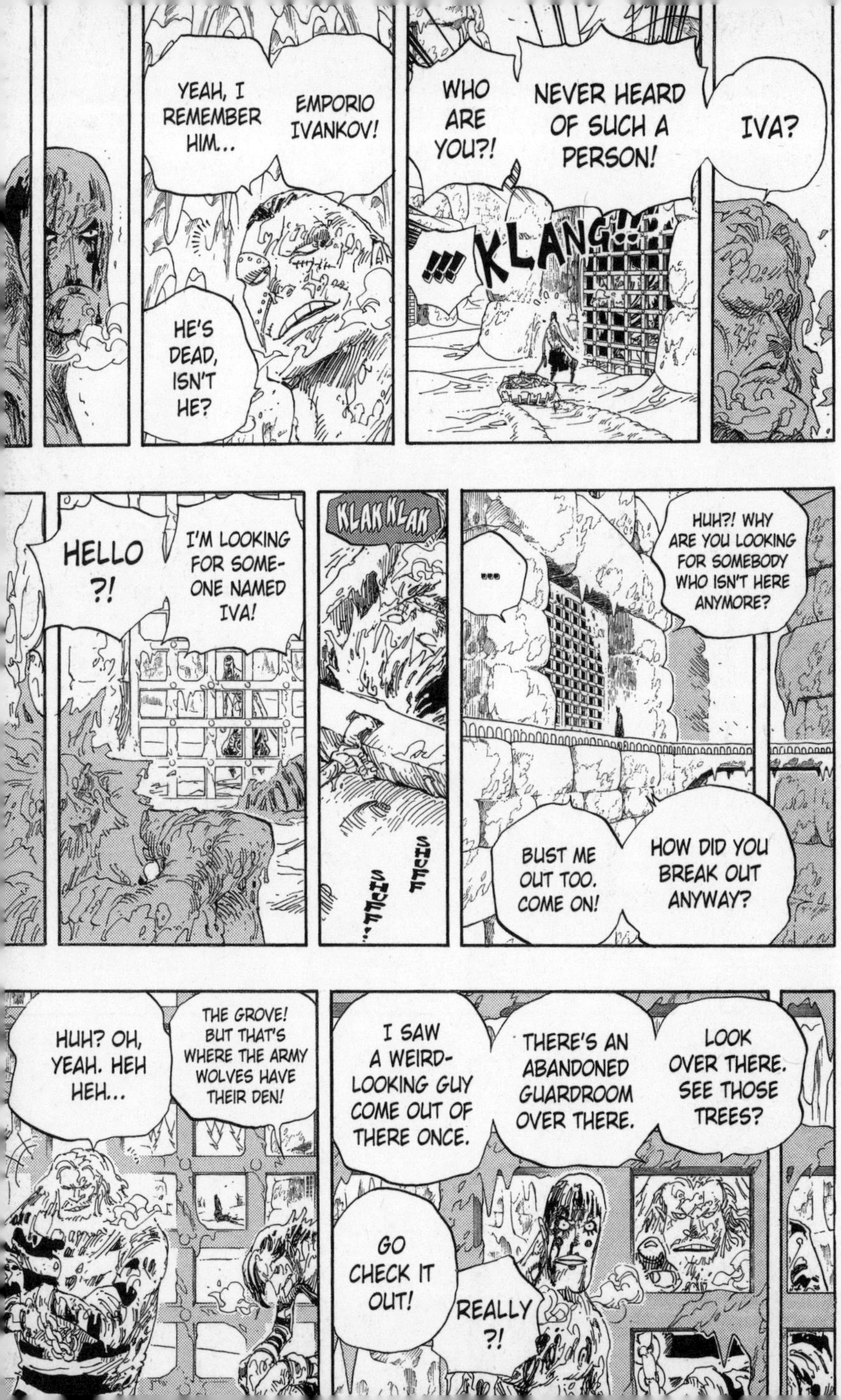
IVA?
NEVER HEARD OF SUCH A PERSON!
WHO ARE YOU?!
KLANG!!!
!!!
EMPORIO IVANKOV!
YEAH, I REMEMBER HIM...
HE'S DEAD, ISN'T HE?
HUH?! WHY ARE YOU LOOKING FOR SOMEBODY WHO ISN'T HERE ANYMORE?
...
HOW DID YOU BREAK OUT ANYWAY?
BUST ME OUT TOO. COME ON!
KLAK KLAK
SHUFF
SHUFF
I'M LOOKING FOR SOME-ONE NAMED IVA!
HELLO ?!
LOOK OVER THERE. SEE THOSE TREES?
THERE'S AN ABANDONED GUARDROOM OVER THERE.
I SAW A WEIRD-LOOKING GUY COME OUT OF THERE ONCE.
REALLY ?!
GO CHECK IT OUT!
THE GROVE! BUT THAT'S WHERE THE ARMY WOLVES HAVE THEIR DEN!
HUH? OH, YEAH. HEH HEH...

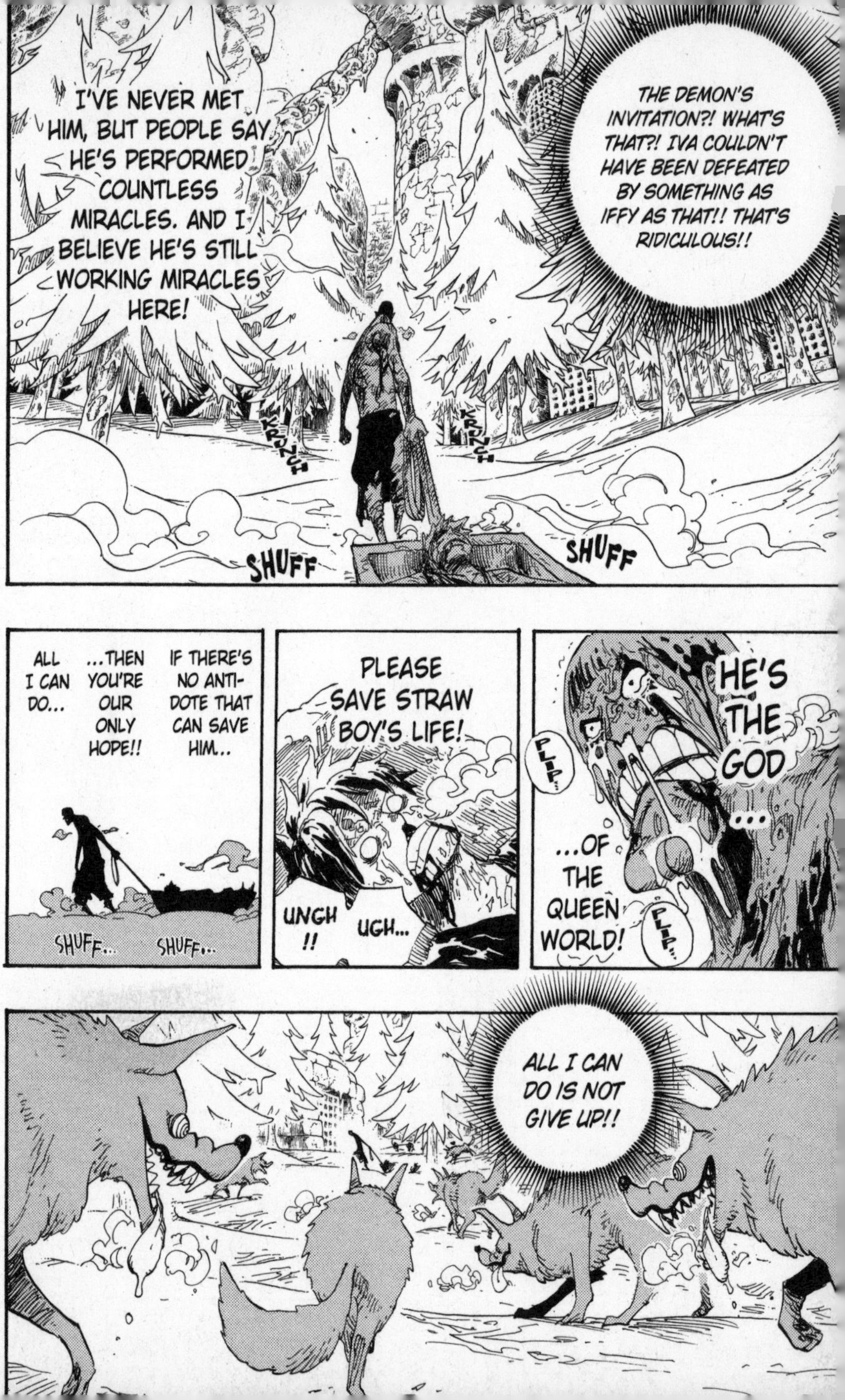
THE DEMON'S INVITATION?! WHAT'S THAT?! IVA COULDN'T HAVE BEEN DEFEATED BY SOMETHING AS IFFY AS THAT!! THAT'S RIDICULOUS!!
I'VE NEVER MET HIM, BUT PEOPLE SAY HE'S PERFORMED COUNTLESS MIRACLES. AND I BELIEVE HE'S STILL WORKING MIRACLES HERE!
KRUNCH
KRUNCH
SHUFF
SHUFF
HE'S THE GOD...
...OF THE QUEEN WORLD!
FLIP...
FLIP...
PLEASE SAVE STRAW BOY'S LIFE!
UNGH!!
UGH...
IF THERE'S NO ANTI-DOTE THAT CAN SAVE HIM...
...THEN YOU'RE OUR ONLY HOPE!!
ALL I CAN DO...
SHUFF...
SHUFF...
ALL I CAN DO IS NOT GIVE UP!!

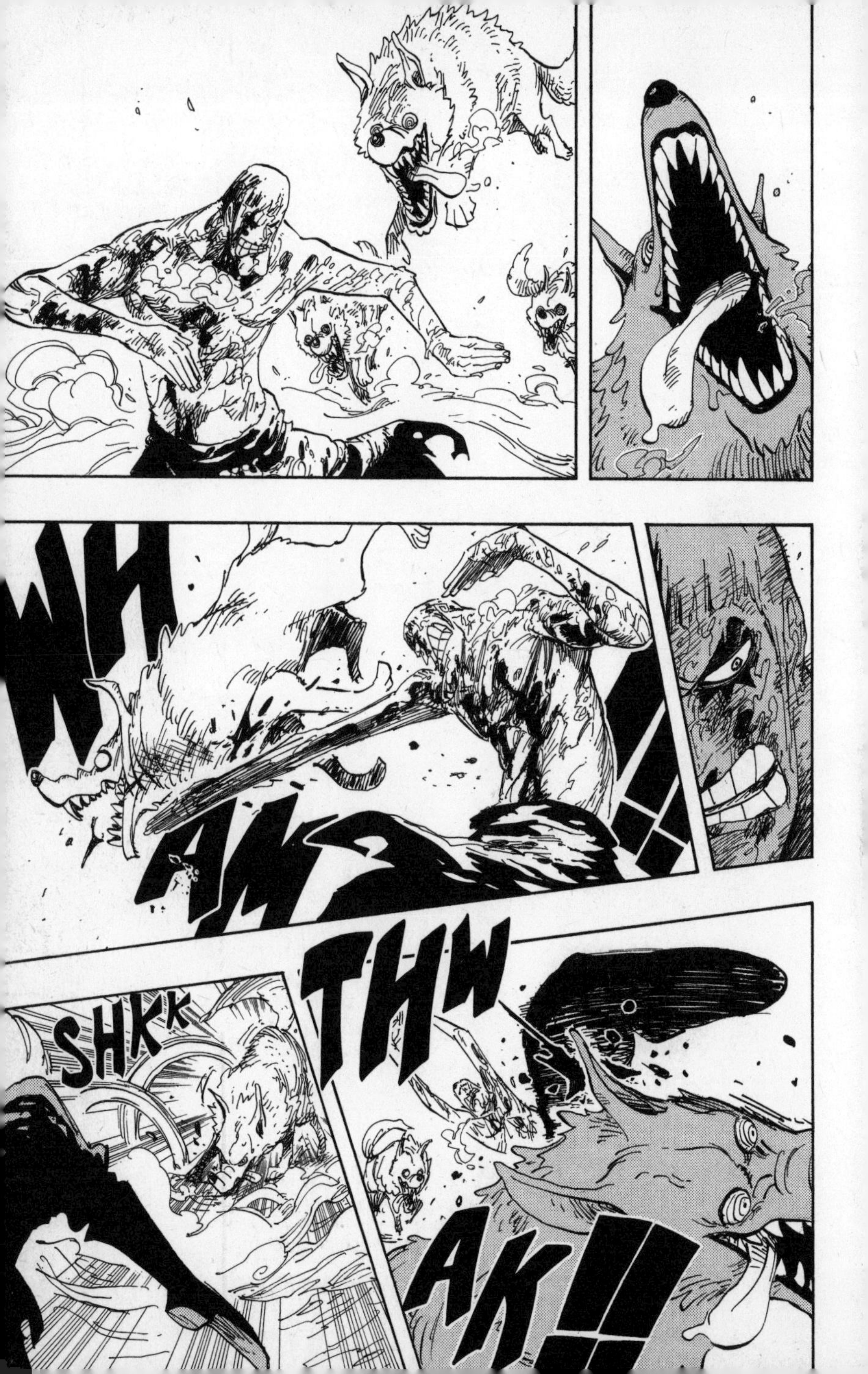
WHAM!!
THWAK!!
SHKK

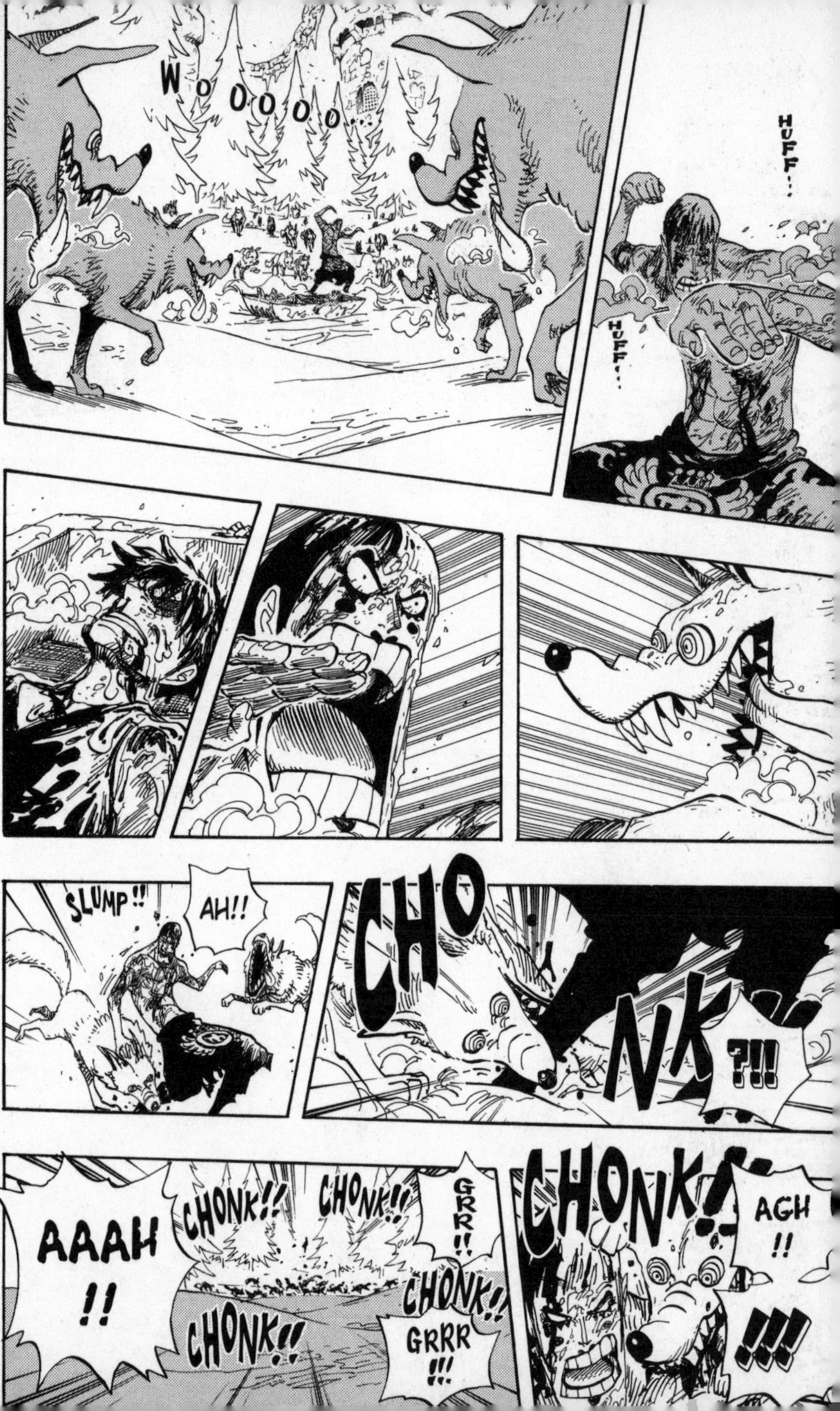
HUFF...
HUFF...
WOOOOOO
AH!!
SLUMP!!
CHONK
?!!
AGH!!
CHONK!
!!!
GRR!!
CHONK!!
CHONK!!
CHONK!!
GRRR!!!
CHONK!!
AAAH!!

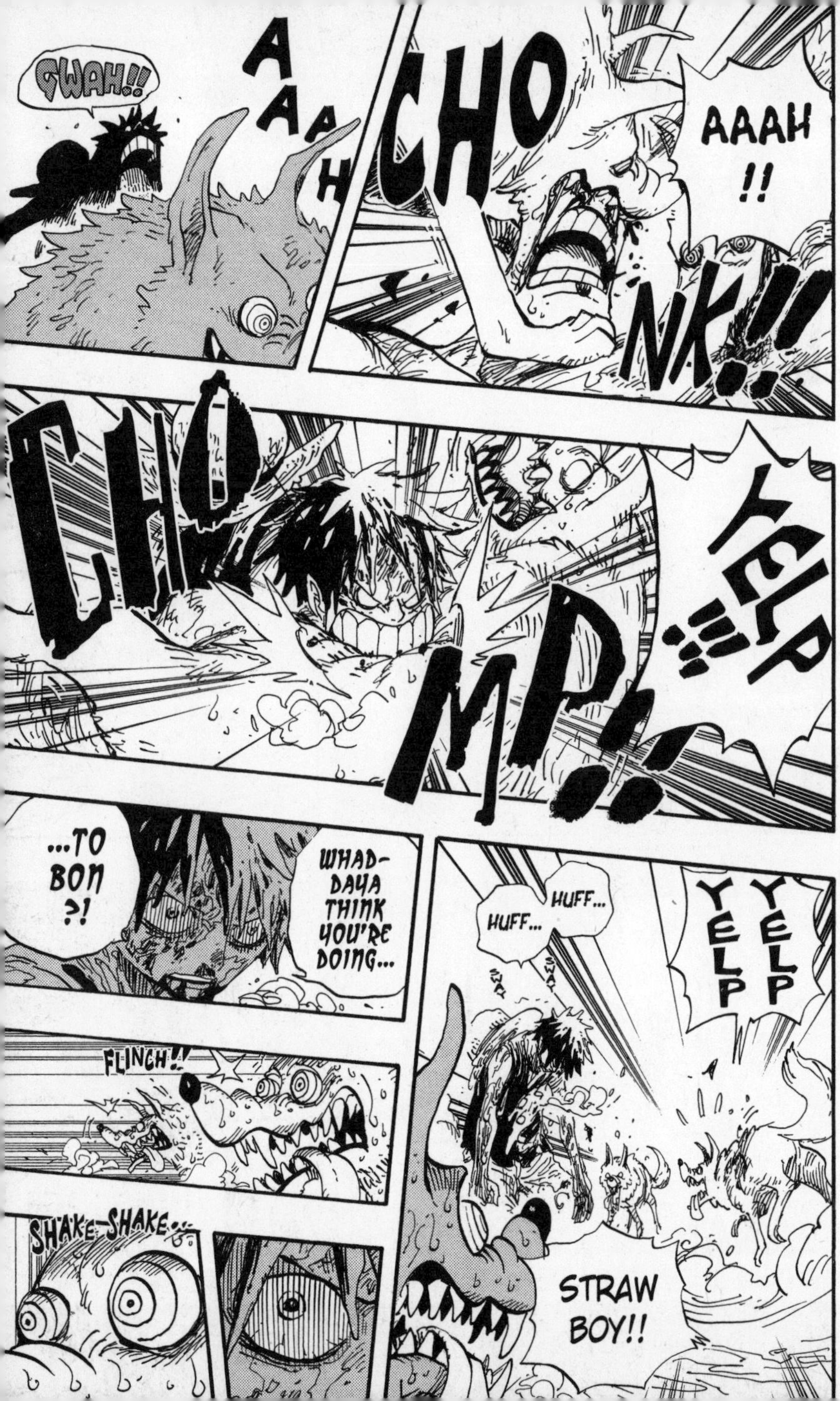
AAAH!!
CHONK!!
GWAH!!
AAPH
YELP!!
CHOMP!!
YELP YELP
HUFF...
HUFF...
SWAY
SWAY
STRAW BOY!!
WHADDAYA THINK YOU'RE DOING...
...TO BON?!
FLINCH!!
SHAKE-SHAKE...

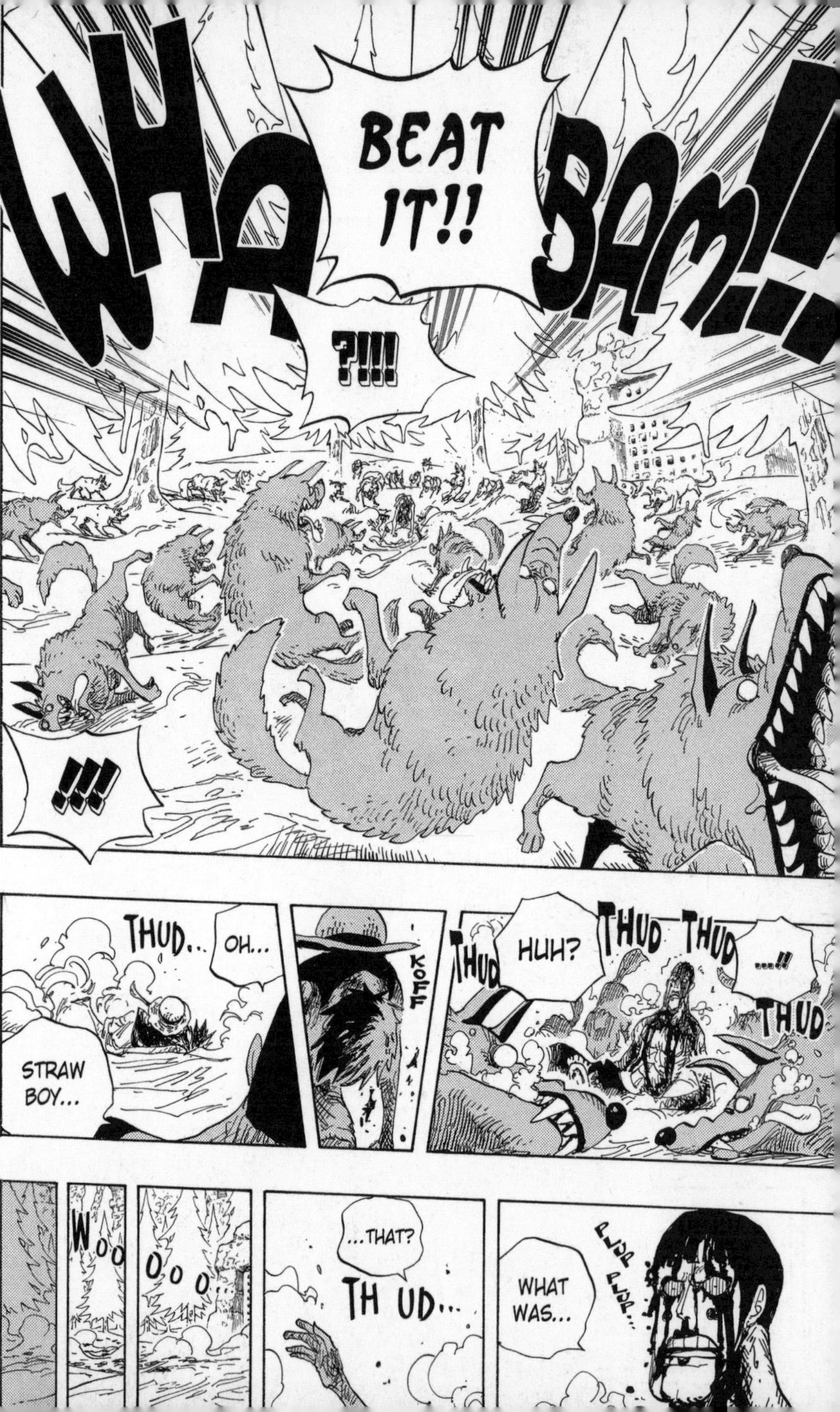
BAM!!
BEAT IT!!
WHA
?!!!
!!!
THUD
...!!
THUD THUD
HUH?
THUD
KOFF
OH...
THUD...
STRAW BOY...
PLOP PLOP...
WHAT WAS...
...THAT?
TH UD...
WOOOOO...

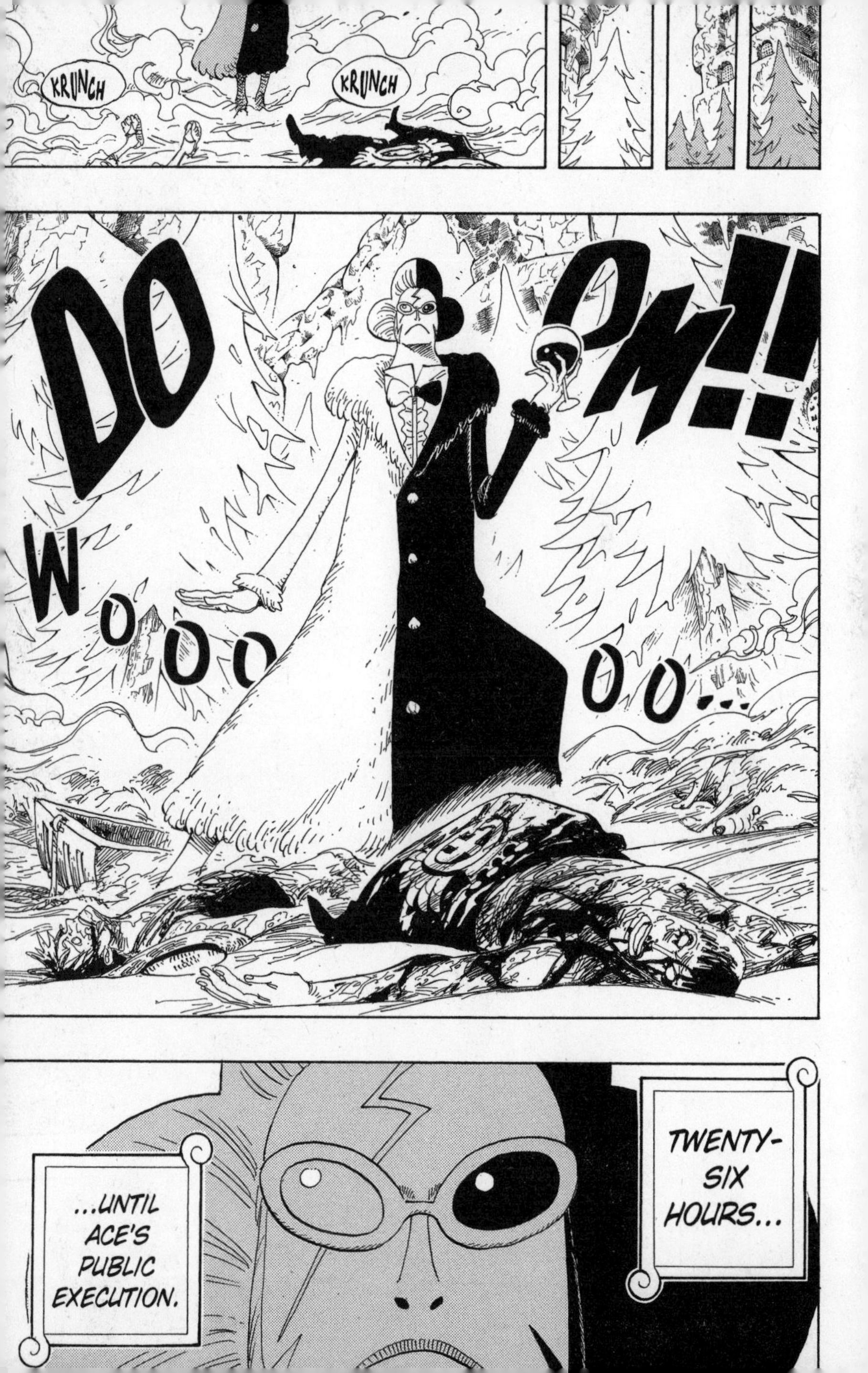
KRUNCH
KRUNCH
DOOM!!
WOOOOOO...
TWENTY-SIX HOURS...
...UNTIL ACE'S PUBLIC EXECUTION.

A RAY OF HOPE

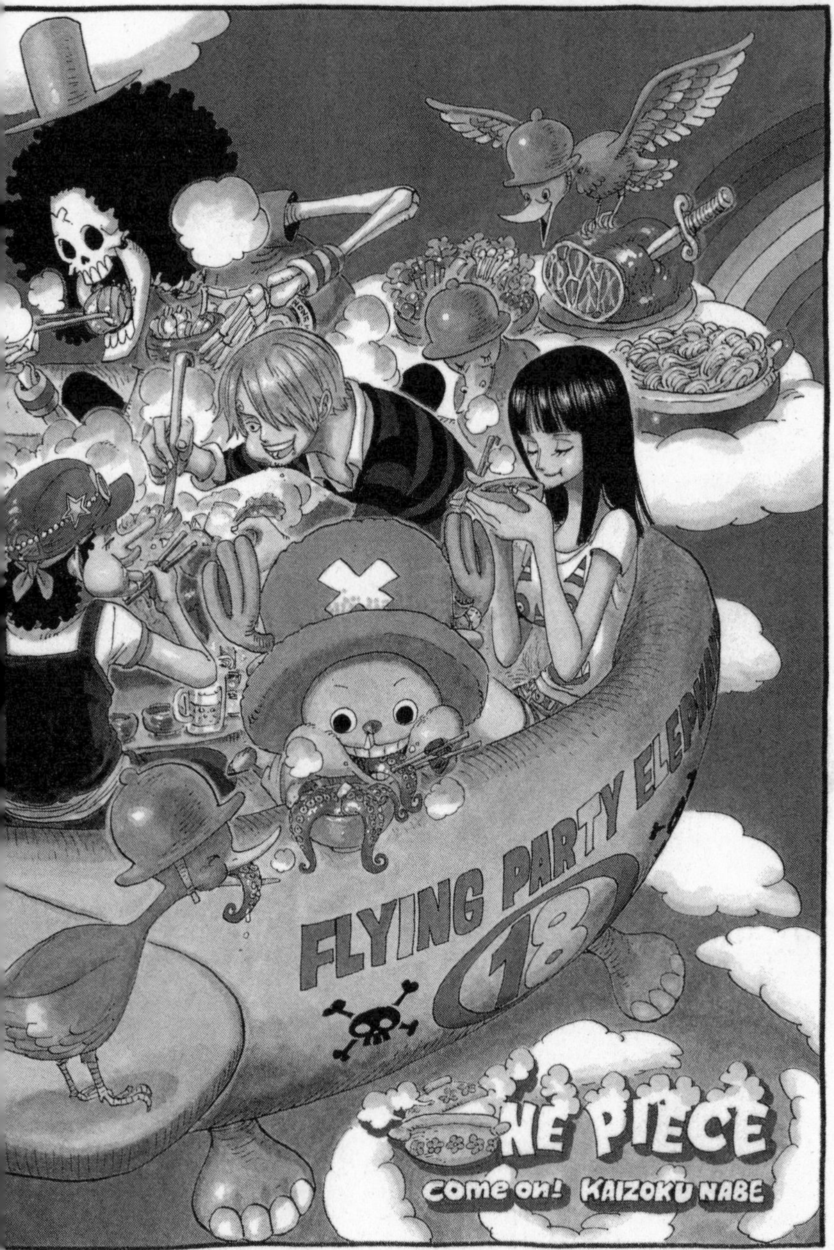
FLYING PARTY ELEPHANT
18
ONE PIECE
come on! KAIZOKU NABE

Chapter 537:

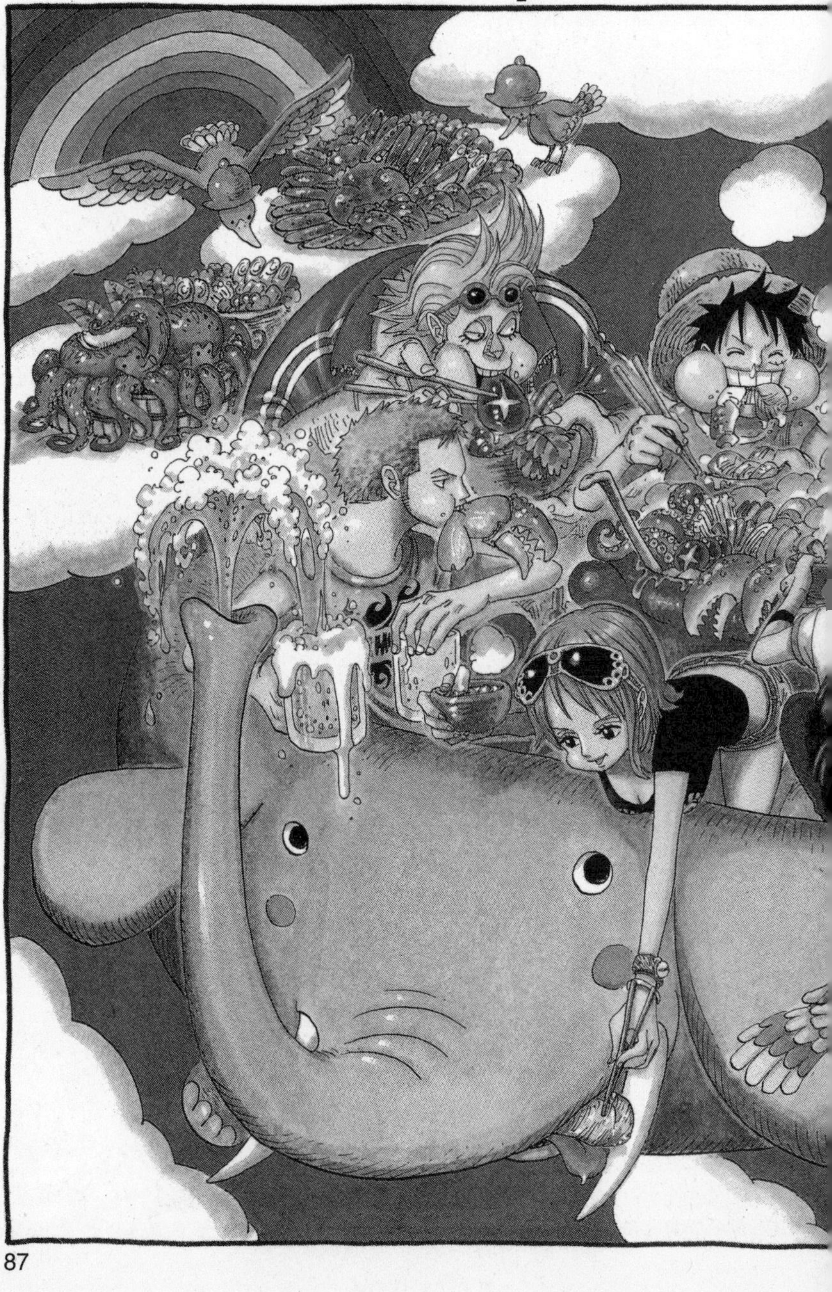

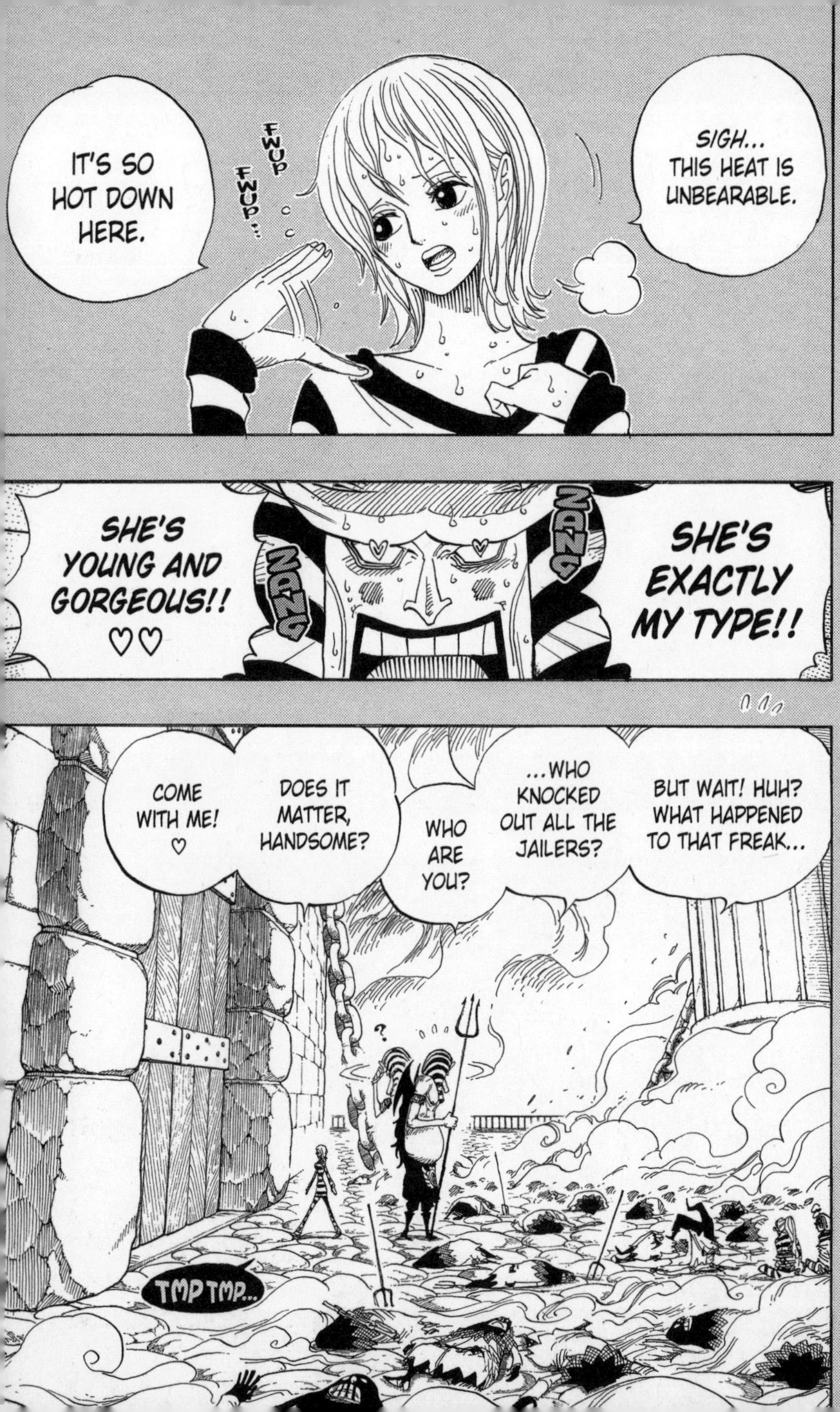
SIGH... THIS HEAT IS UNBEARABLE.
FWUP FWUP...
IT'S SO HOT DOWN HERE.
SHE'S EXACTLY MY TYPE!!
ZANG
ZANG
SHE'S YOUNG AND GORGEOUS!! ♡♡
BUT WAIT! HUH? WHAT HAPPENED TO THAT FREAK...
...WHO KNOCKED OUT ALL THE JAILERS?
WHO ARE YOU?
DOES IT MATTER, HANDSOME?
COME WITH ME! ♡
TMP TMP...

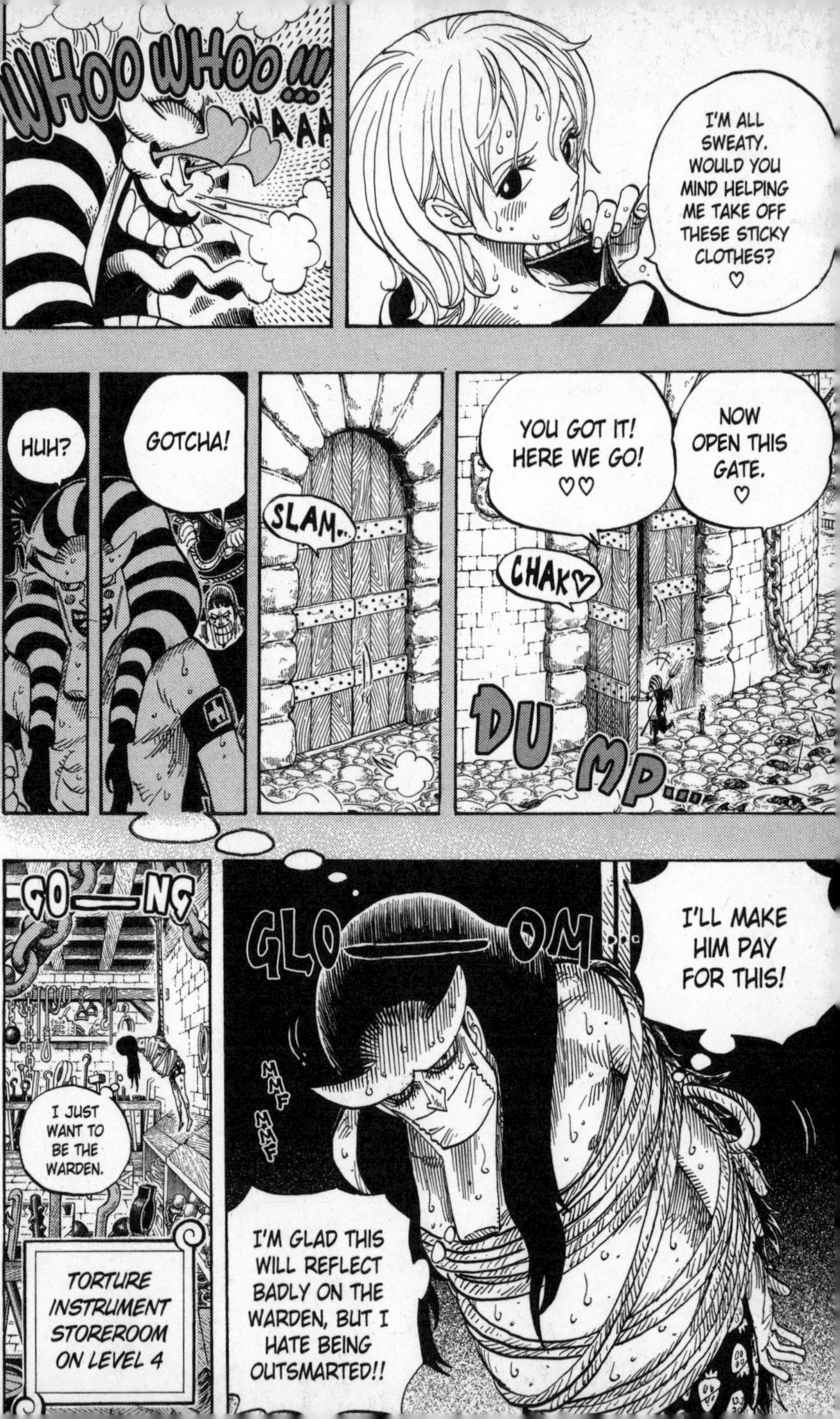
I'M ALL SWEATY. WOULD YOU MIND HELPING ME TAKE OFF THESE STICKY CLOTHES? ♡
WHOO WHOO!!!
WAAA
NOW OPEN THIS GATE. ♡
YOU GOT IT! HERE WE GO! ♡♡
CHAK♡
DUMP...
SLAM..
GOTCHA!
HUH?
I'LL MAKE HIM PAY FOR THIS!
GLO—OM..
MMF
MMF
I'M GLAD THIS WILL REFLECT BADLY ON THE WARDEN, BUT I HATE BEING OUTSMARTED!!
GO—NG
I JUST WANT TO BE THE WARDEN.
TORTURE INSTRUMENT STOREROOM ON LEVEL 4

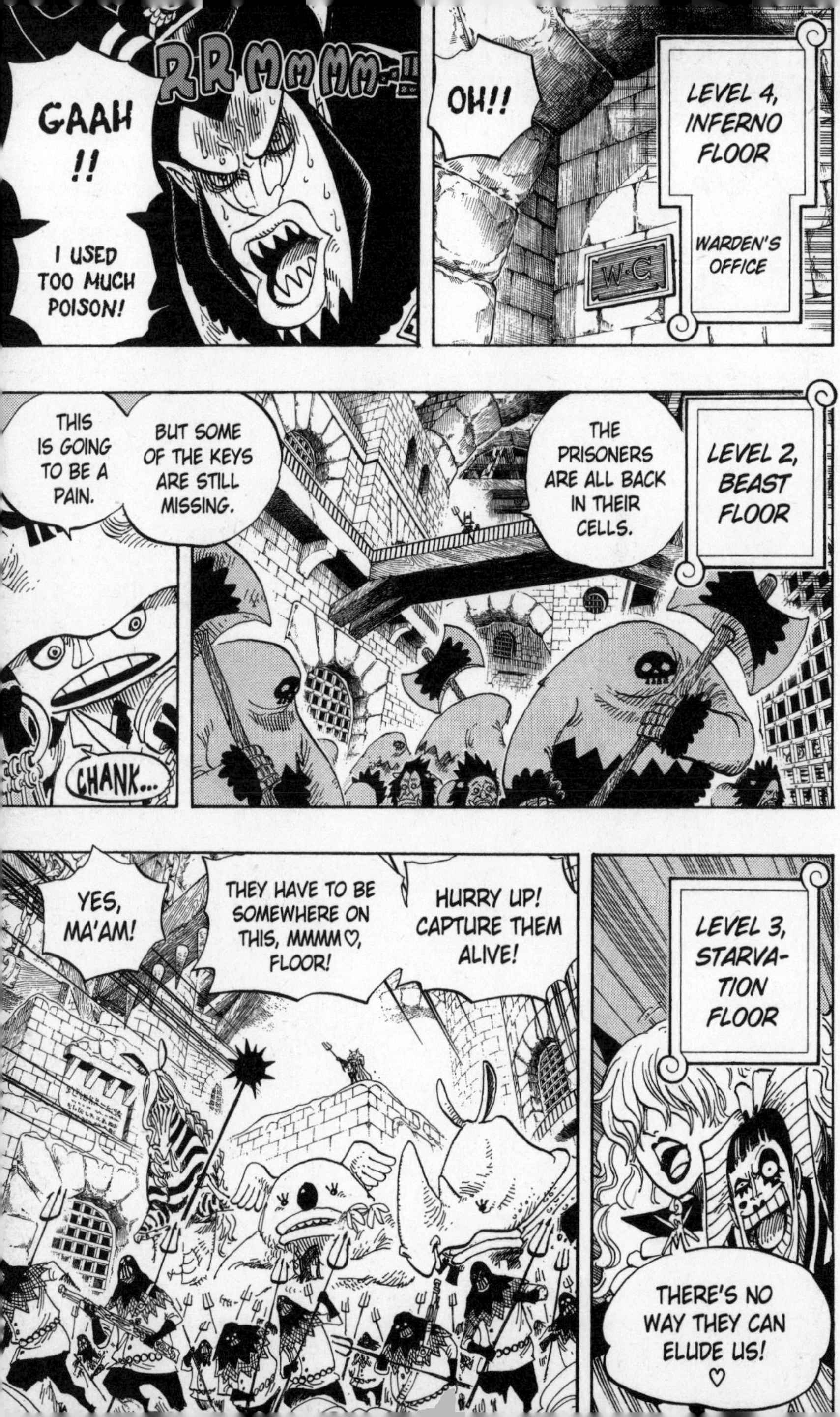
LEVEL 4, INFERNO FLOOR
WARDEN'S OFFICE
W·C
OH!!
RRMMMMM-!!
GAAH !!
I USED TOO MUCH POISON!
LEVEL 2, BEAST FLOOR
THE PRISONERS ARE ALL BACK IN THEIR CELLS.
BUT SOME OF THE KEYS ARE STILL MISSING.
THIS IS GOING TO BE A PAIN.
CHANK...
LEVEL 3, STARVATION FLOOR
THERE'S NO WAY THEY CAN ELUDE US! ♡
HURRY UP! CAPTURE THEM ALIVE!
THEY HAVE TO BE SOMEWHERE ON THIS, MMMM♡, FLOOR!
YES, MA'AM!

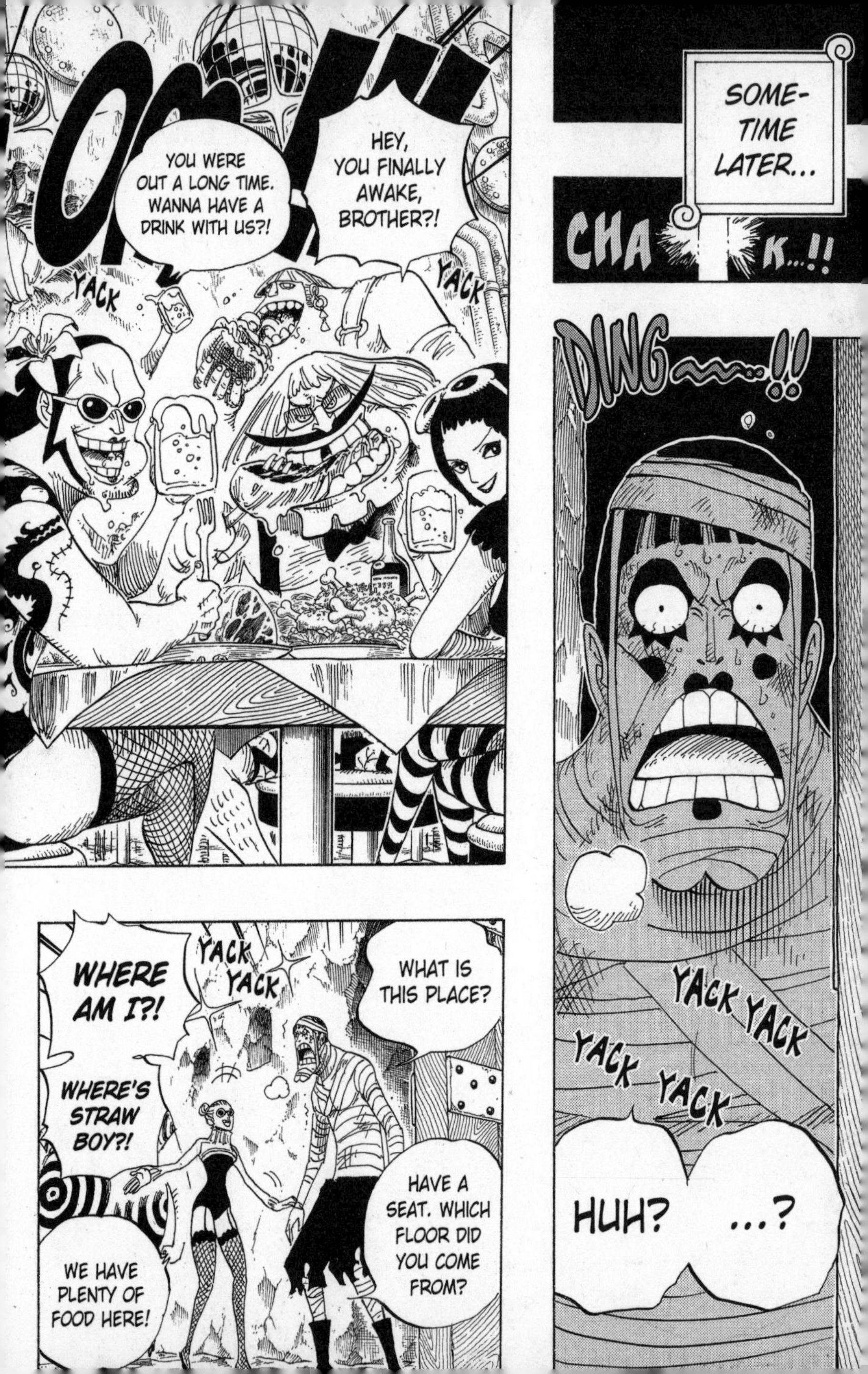
SOME-TIME LATER...
CHA K...!!
DING~~!!
YACK YACK
YACK YACK
...?
HUH?
YACK
HEY, YOU FINALLY AWAKE, BROTHER?!
YOU WERE OUT A LONG TIME. WANNA HAVE A DRINK WITH US?!
YACK
WHAT IS THIS PLACE?
YACK YACK
WHERE AM I?!
WHERE'S STRAW BOY?!
HAVE A SEAT. WHICH FLOOR DID YOU COME FROM?
WE HAVE PLENTY OF FOOD HERE!

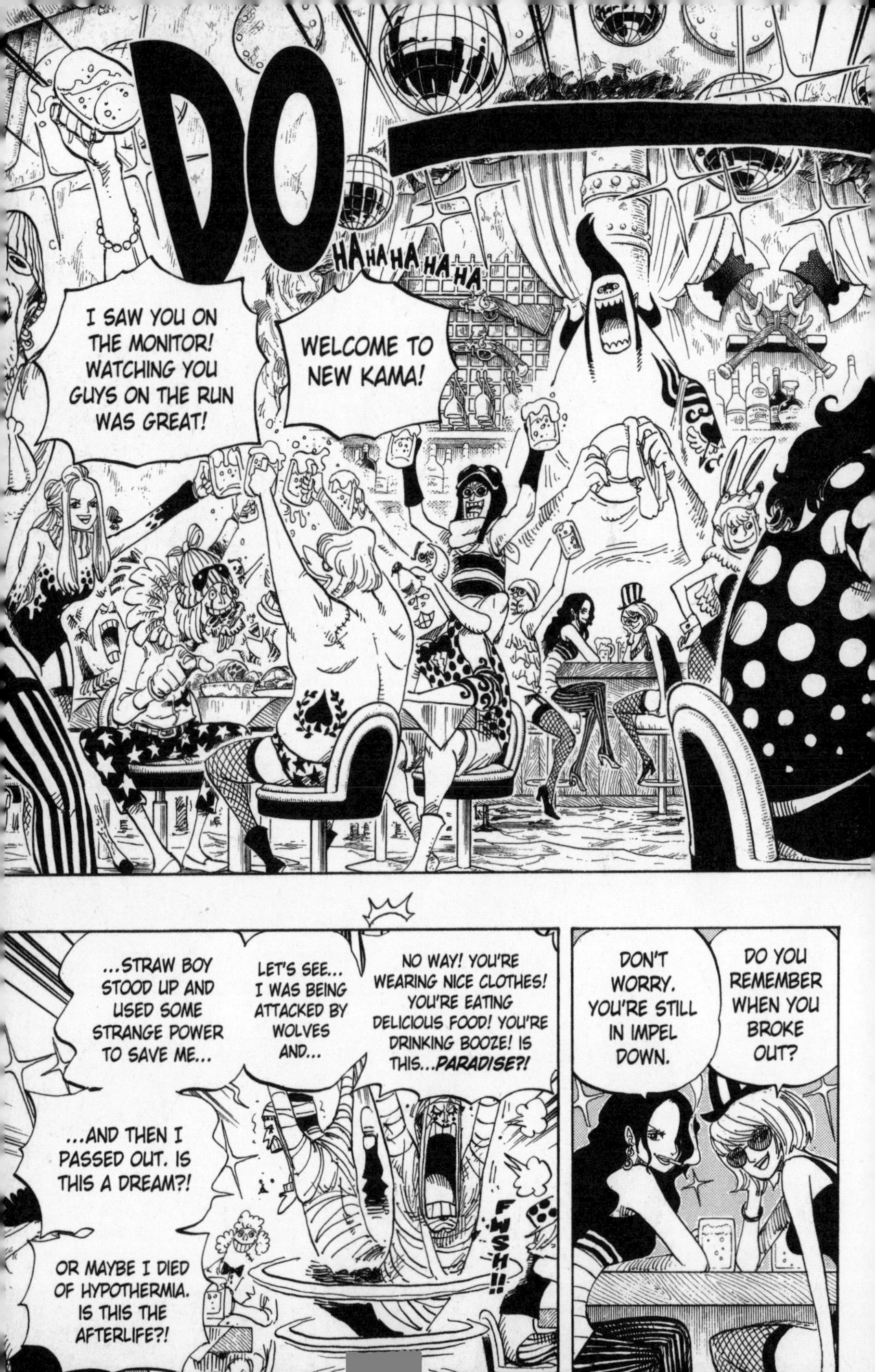
DO—
HAHAHAHAHAHA
WELCOME TO NEW KAMA!
I SAW YOU ON THE MONITOR! WATCHING YOU GUYS ON THE RUN WAS GREAT!
DO YOU REMEMBER WHEN YOU BROKE OUT?
DON'T WORRY. YOU'RE STILL IN IMPEL DOWN.
NO WAY! YOU'RE WEARING NICE CLOTHES! YOU'RE EATING DELICIOUS FOOD! YOU'RE DRINKING BOOZE! IS THIS...*PARADISE?!*
LET'S SEE... I WAS BEING ATTACKED BY WOLVES AND...
...STRAW BOY STOOD UP AND USED SOME STRANGE POWER TO SAVE ME...
...AND THEN I PASSED OUT. IS THIS A DREAM?!
OR MAYBE I DIED OF HYPOTHERMIA. IS THIS THE AFTERLIFE?!
FWSH!!

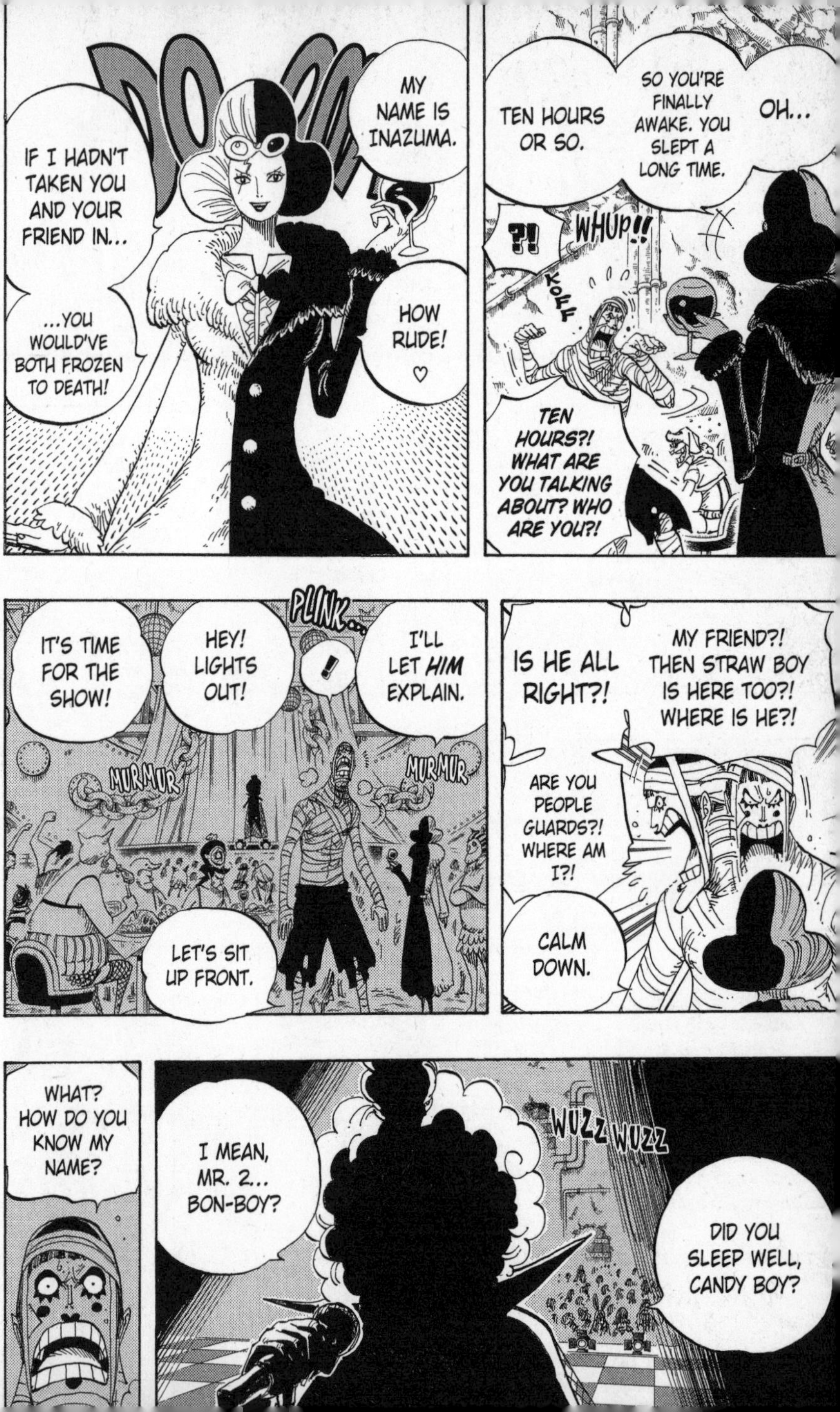
OH...
SO YOU'RE FINALLY AWAKE. YOU SLEPT A LONG TIME.
TEN HOURS OR SO.
?!
WHUP!!
KOFF
TEN HOURS?! WHAT ARE YOU TALKING ABOUT? WHO ARE YOU?!
MY NAME IS INAZUMA.
HOW RUDE! ♡
IF I HADN'T TAKEN YOU AND YOUR FRIEND IN...
...YOU WOULD'VE BOTH FROZEN TO DEATH!
MY FRIEND?! THEN STRAW BOY IS HERE TOO?! WHERE IS HE?!
IS HE ALL RIGHT?!
ARE YOU PEOPLE GUARDS?! WHERE AM I?!
CALM DOWN.
I'LL LET *HIM* EXPLAIN.
PLINK...
!
HEY! LIGHTS OUT!
IT'S TIME FOR THE SHOW!
MURMUR
MURMUR
LET'S SIT UP FRONT.
DID YOU SLEEP WELL, CANDY BOY?
WUZZ WUZZ
I MEAN, MR. 2... BON-BOY?
WHAT? HOW DO YOU KNOW MY NAME?

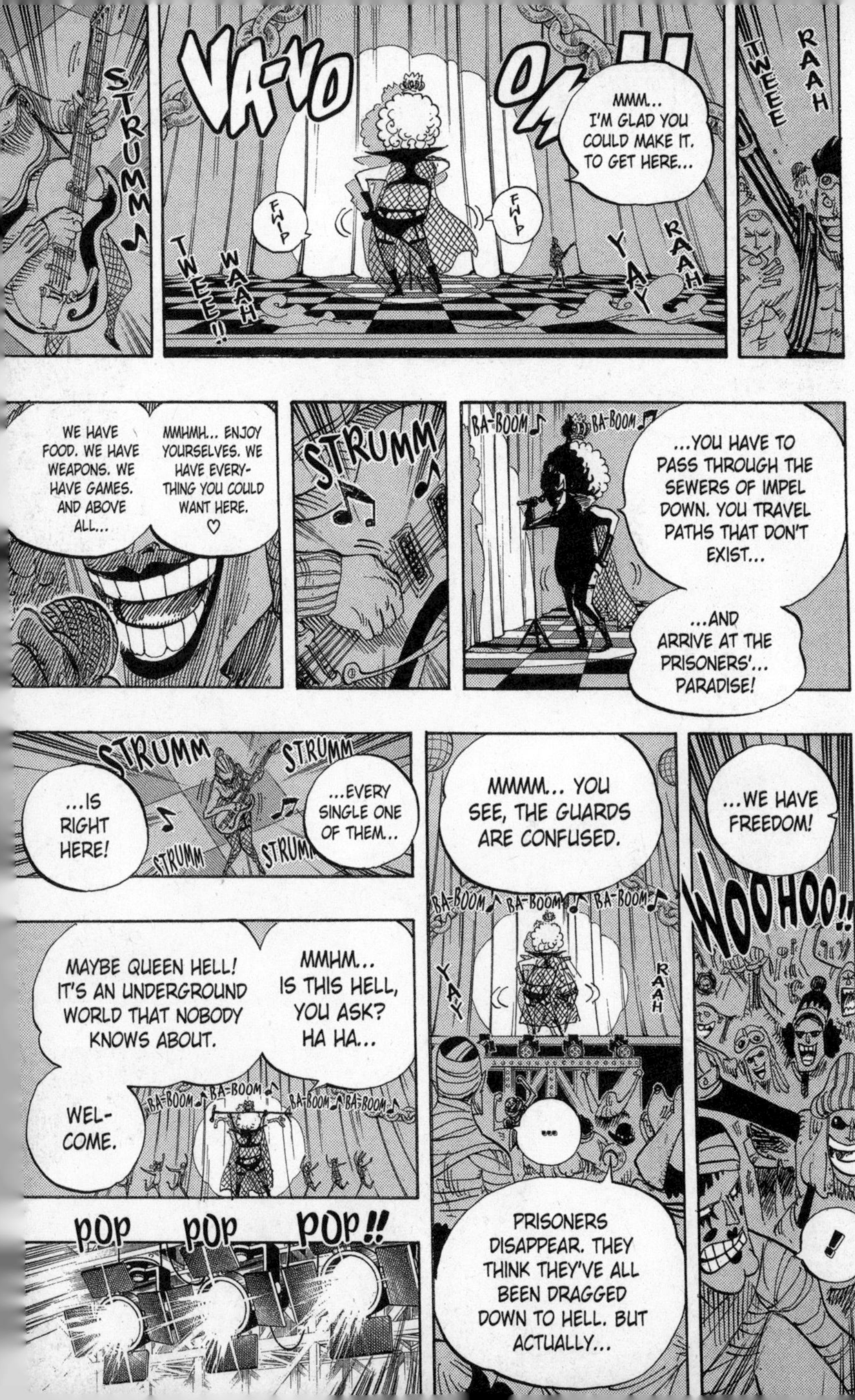
TWEEE
RAAH
VA-VO
OM
MMM... I'M GLAD YOU COULD MAKE IT. TO GET HERE...
FWIP
FWIP
RAAH
YAY
WAAH
TWEEE!!
STRUMM
BA-BOOM
BA-BOOM
...YOU HAVE TO PASS THROUGH THE SEWERS OF IMPEL DOWN. YOU TRAVEL PATHS THAT DON'T EXIST...
...AND ARRIVE AT THE PRISONERS'... PARADISE!
STRUMM
MMHMH... ENJOY YOURSELVES. WE HAVE EVERY-THING YOU COULD WANT HERE. ♡
WE HAVE FOOD. WE HAVE WEAPONS. WE HAVE GAMES. AND ABOVE ALL...
...WE HAVE FREEDOM!
WOOHOO!!
!
MMMM... YOU SEE, THE GUARDS ARE CONFUSED.
BA-BOOM
BA-BOOM
BA-BOOM
RAAH
YAY
...
PRISONERS DISAPPEAR. THEY THINK THEY'VE ALL BEEN DRAGGED DOWN TO HELL. BUT ACTUALLY...
STRUMM
STRUMM
...EVERY SINGLE ONE OF THEM...
...IS RIGHT HERE!
STRUMM
STRUMM
MMHM... IS THIS HELL, YOU ASK? HA HA...
MAYBE QUEEN HELL! IT'S AN UNDERGROUND WORLD THAT NOBODY KNOWS ABOUT.
BA-BOOM
BA-BOOM
BA-BOOM
BA-BOOM
WEL-COME.
POP!!
POP
POP

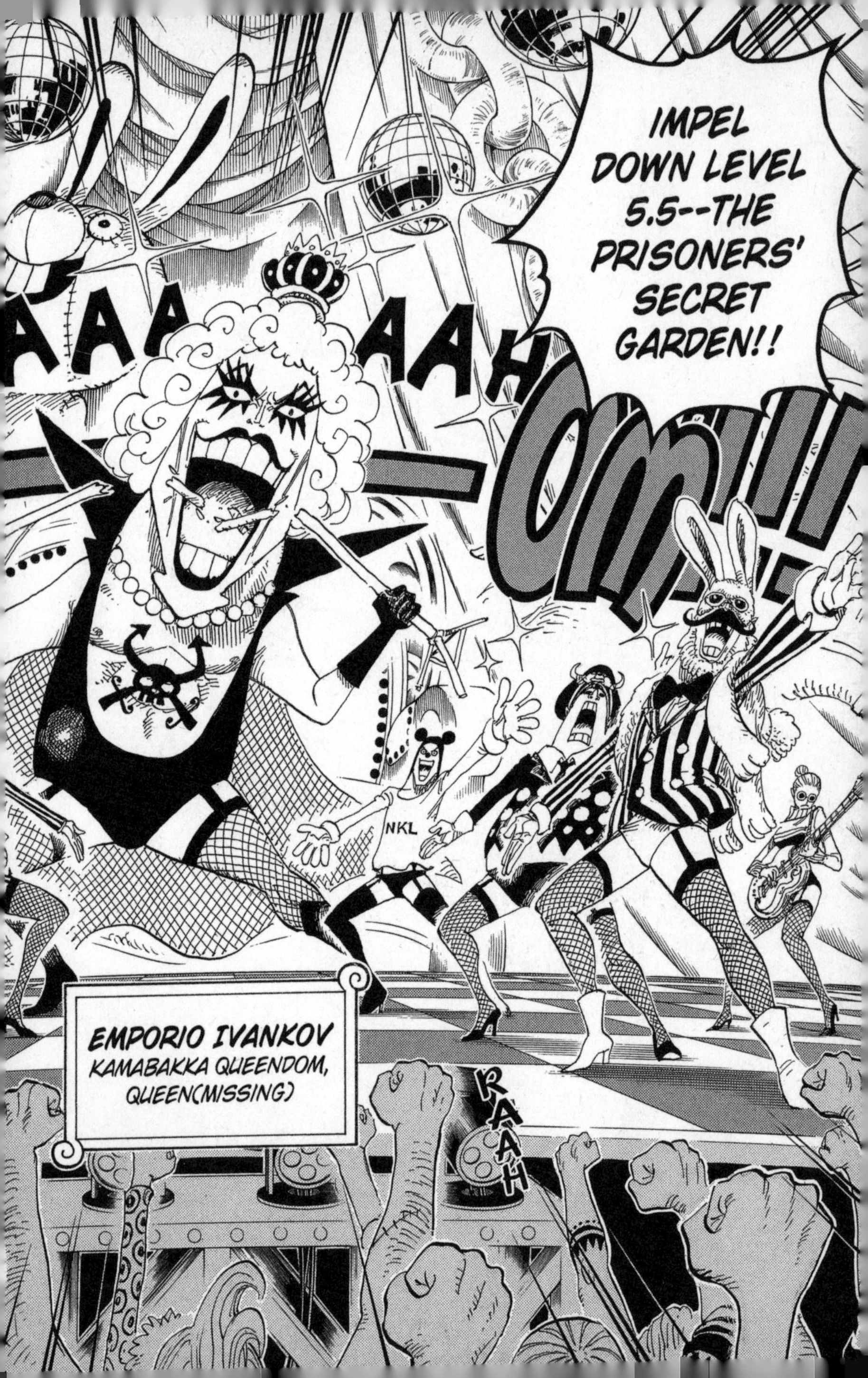
IMPEL DOWN LEVEL 5.5--THE PRISONERS' SECRET GARDEN!!
AAAAAAH
OMW
NKL
EMPORIO IVANKOV
KAMABAKKA QUEENDOM, QUEEN(MISSING)
RAAAH

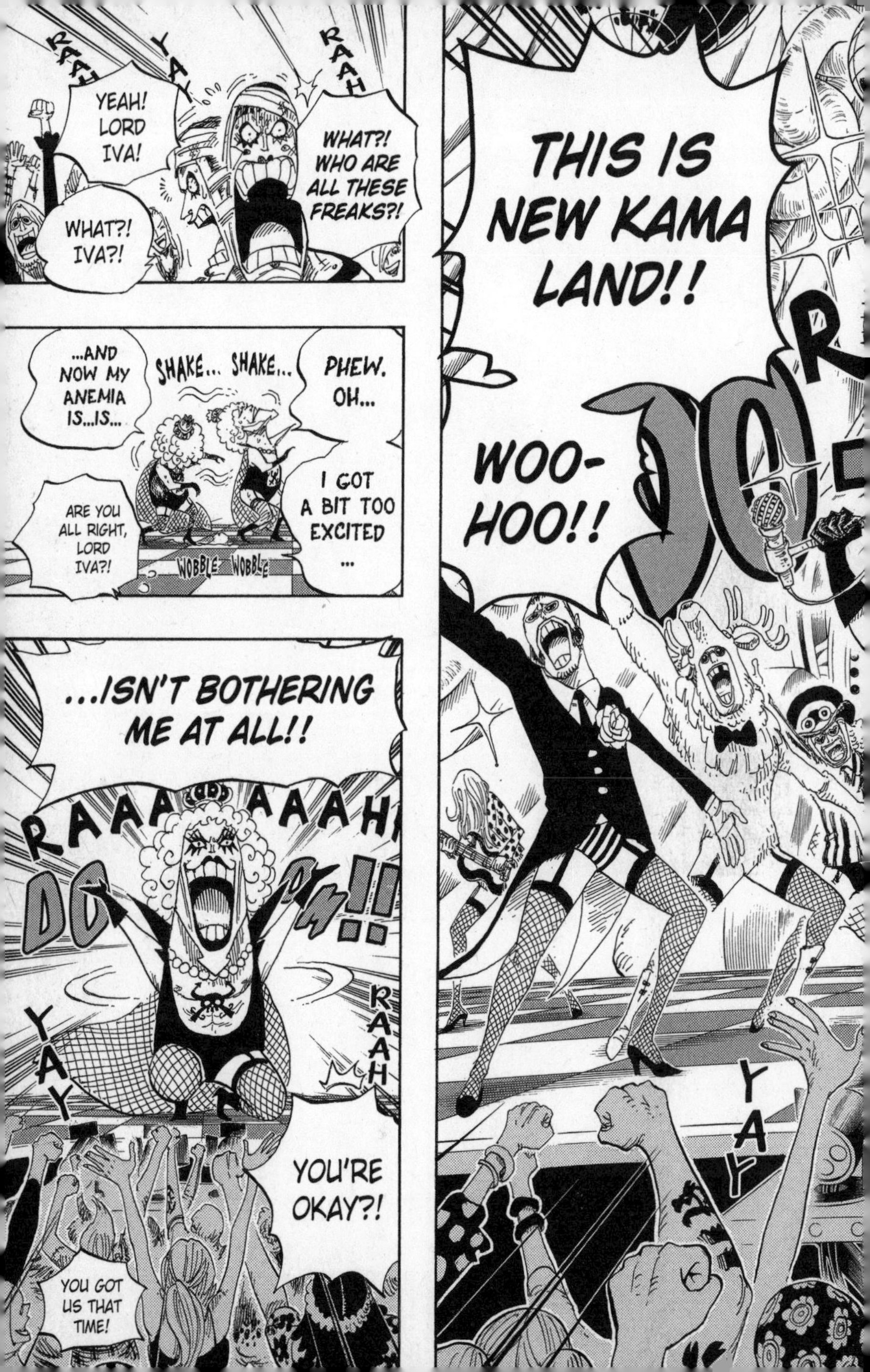
THIS IS NEW KAMA LAND!!
WOO-HOO!!
YAY
RAAH
WHAT?! WHO ARE ALL THESE FREAKS?!
YAY
RAAH
YEAH! LORD IVA!
WHAT?! IVA?!
PHEW. OH...
I GOT A BIT TOO EXCITED ...
SHAKE... SHAKE...
...AND NOW MY ANEMIA IS...IS...
WOBBLE WOBBLE
ARE YOU ALL RIGHT, LORD IVA?!
...ISN'T BOTHERING ME AT ALL!!
RAAAAAAAH!
RAAH
YAY
YOU'RE OKAY?!
YOU GOT US THAT TIME!

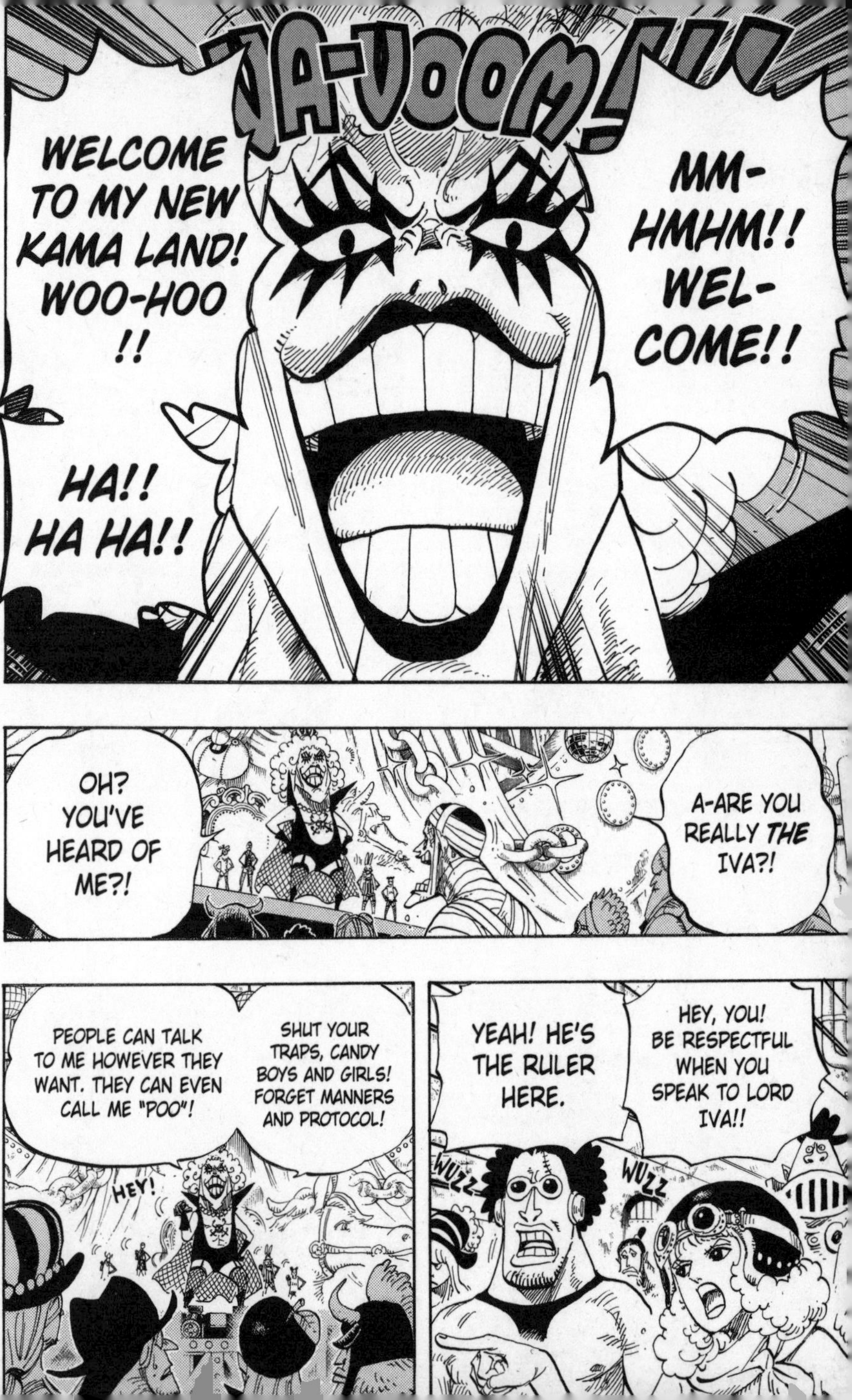
JA-VOOM!!!
MM-HMHM!! WEL-COME!!
WELCOME TO MY NEW KAMA LAND! WOO-HOO!!
HA!! HA HA!!
A-ARE YOU REALLY *THE* IVA?!
OH? YOU'VE HEARD OF ME?!
HEY, YOU! BE RESPECTFUL WHEN YOU SPEAK TO LORD IVA!!
YEAH! HE'S THE RULER HERE.
WUZZ
WUZZ
SHUT YOUR TRAPS, CANDY BOYS AND GIRLS! FORGET MANNERS AND PROTOCOL!
PEOPLE CAN TALK TO ME HOWEVER THEY WANT. THEY CAN EVEN CALL ME "POO"!
HEY!

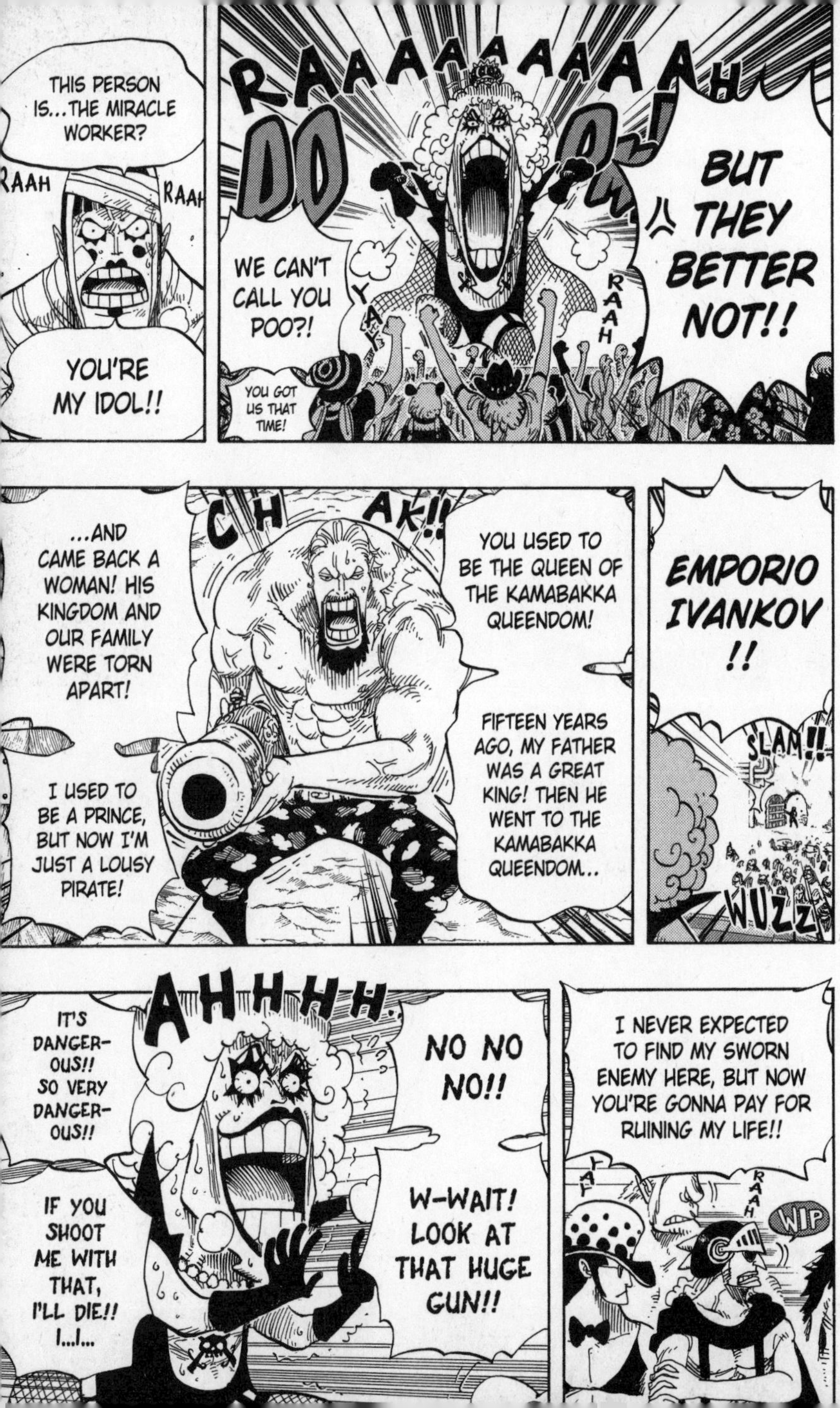
RAAAAAAAAAH!
DO
BUT THEY BETTER NOT!!
RAAH
WE CAN'T CALL YOU POO?!
YAY
YOU GOT US THAT TIME!
THIS PERSON IS...THE MIRACLE WORKER?
RAAH
RAAH
YOU'RE MY IDOL!!
EMPORIO IVANKOV!!
SLAM!!
WUZZ
CH AK!!
YOU USED TO BE THE QUEEN OF THE KAMABAKKA QUEENDOM!
FIFTEEN YEARS AGO, MY FATHER WAS A GREAT KING! THEN HE WENT TO THE KAMABAKKA QUEENDOM...
...AND CAME BACK A WOMAN! HIS KINGDOM AND OUR FAMILY WERE TORN APART!
I USED TO BE A PRINCE, BUT NOW I'M JUST A LOUSY PIRATE!
I NEVER EXPECTED TO FIND MY SWORN ENEMY HERE, BUT NOW YOU'RE GONNA PAY FOR RUINING MY LIFE!!
RAAH
YAY
WIP
AHHHH
NO NO NO!!
W-WAIT! LOOK AT THAT HUGE GUN!!
IT'S DANGER-OUS!! SO VERY DANGER-OUS!!
IF YOU SHOOT ME WITH THAT, I'LL DIE!! I...I...

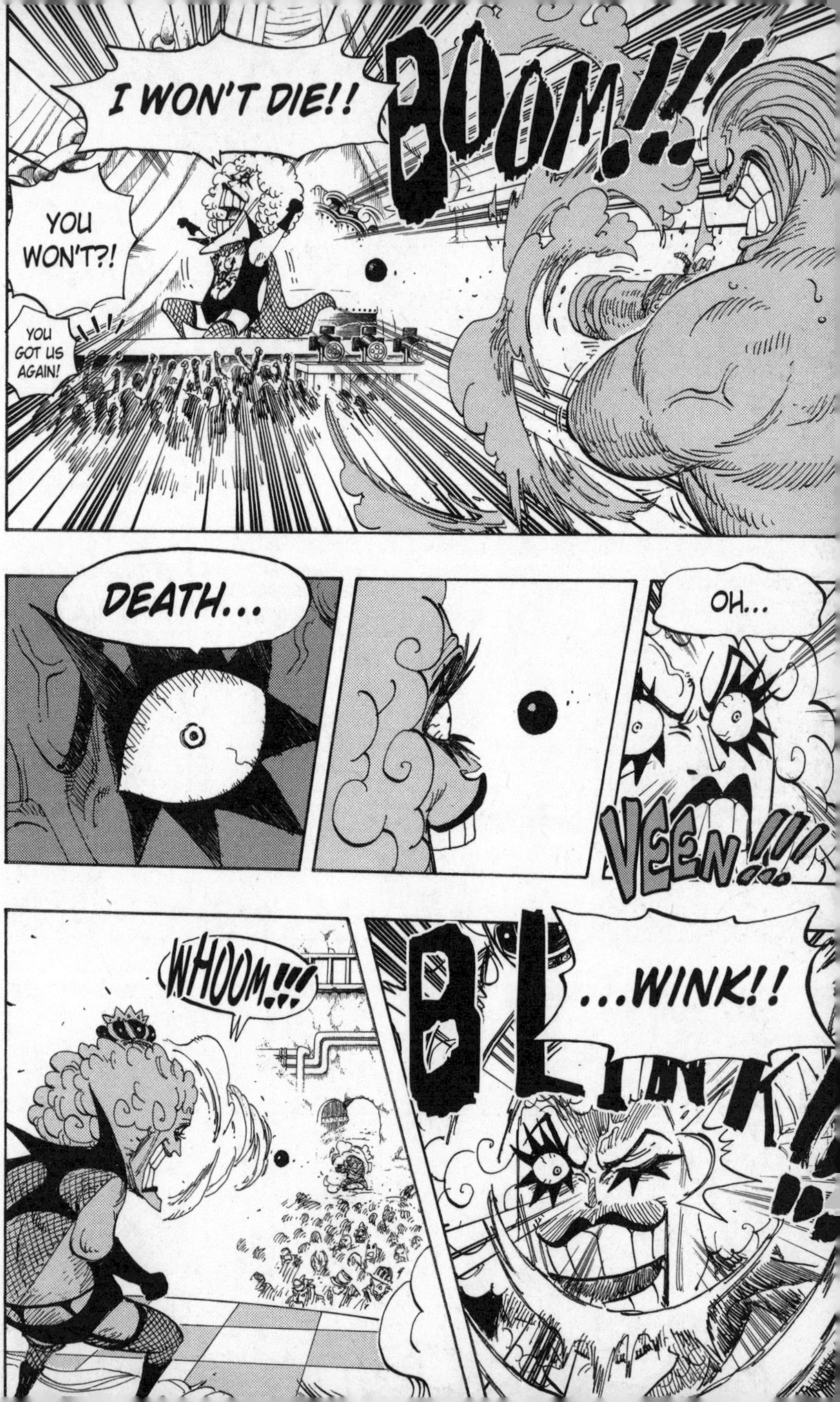
BOOM!!!
I WON'T DIE!!
YOU WON'T?!
YOU GOT US AGAIN!
OH...
VEEN!!!
DEATH...
BLINK!!
...WINK!!
WHOOM!!!

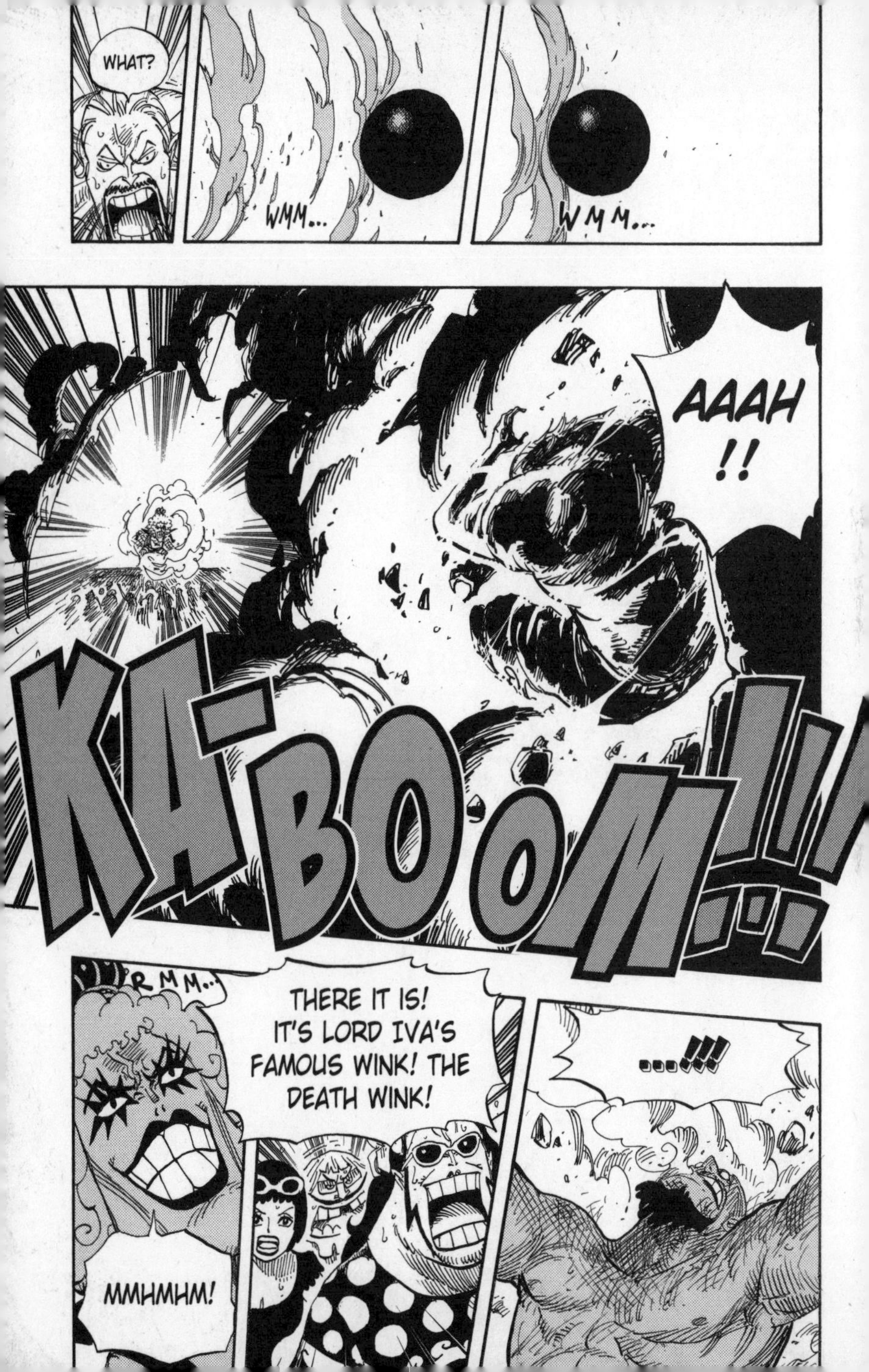
WMM...
WMM...
WHAT?
AAAH!!
KA-BOOM!!!...
...!!!
THERE IT IS! IT'S LORD IVA'S FAMOUS WINK! THE DEATH WINK!
RMM...
MMHMHM!

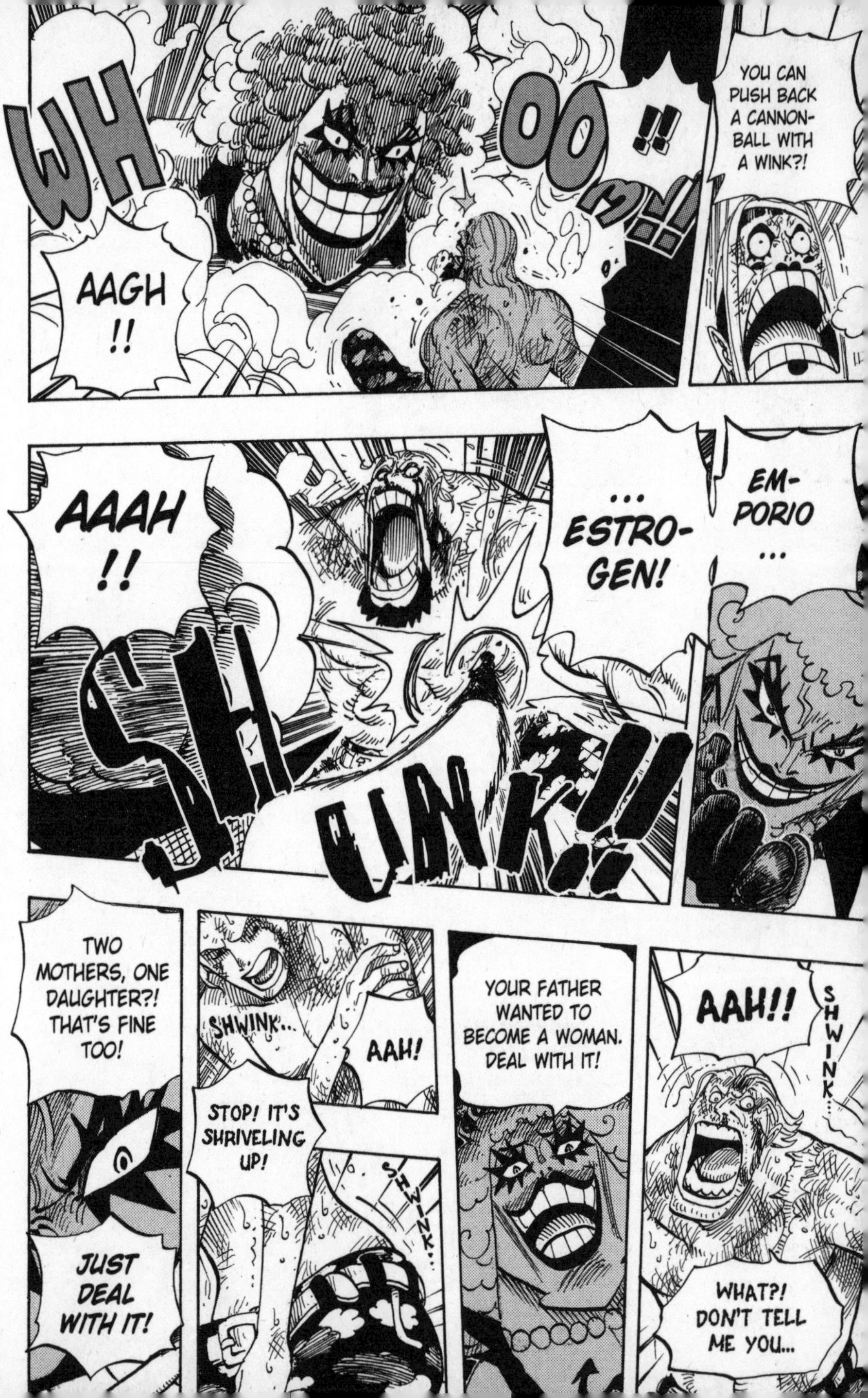
YOU CAN PUSH BACK A CANNON-BALL WITH A WINK?!
WH
OO!!
AAGH!!
EM-PORIO...
...ESTRO-GEN!
AAAH!!
SH
UNK!!
AAH!!
SHWINK...
WHAT?! DON'T TELL ME YOU...
YOUR FATHER WANTED TO BECOME A WOMAN. DEAL WITH IT!
SHWINK...
AAH!
STOP! IT'S SHRIVELING UP!
SHWINK...
TWO MOTHERS, ONE DAUGHTER?! THAT'S FINE TOO!
JUST DEAL WITH IT!

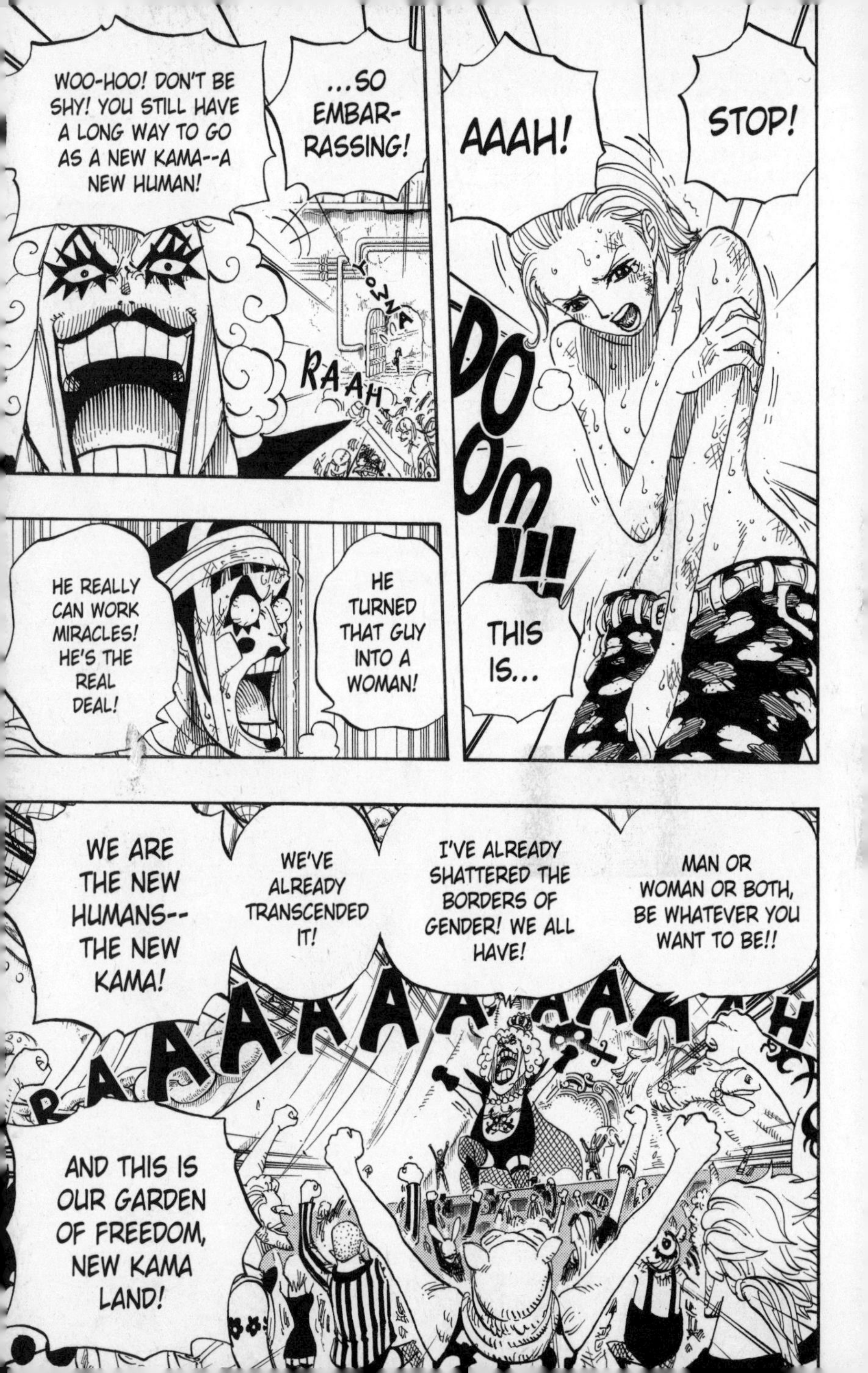
STOP!
AAAH!
DOOOM!!
THIS IS...
...SO EMBARRASSING!
YOWZA
RAAAH
WOO-HOO! DON'T BE SHY! YOU STILL HAVE A LONG WAY TO GO AS A NEW KAMA--A NEW HUMAN!
HE TURNED THAT GUY INTO A WOMAN!
HE REALLY CAN WORK MIRACLES! HE'S THE REAL DEAL!
MAN OR WOMAN OR BOTH, BE WHATEVER YOU WANT TO BE!!
I'VE ALREADY SHATTERED THE BORDERS OF GENDER! WE ALL HAVE!
WE'VE ALREADY TRANSCENDED IT!
WE ARE THE NEW HUMANS-- THE NEW KAMA!
RAAAAAAAAAAAH
AND THIS IS OUR GARDEN OF FREEDOM, NEW KAMA LAND!

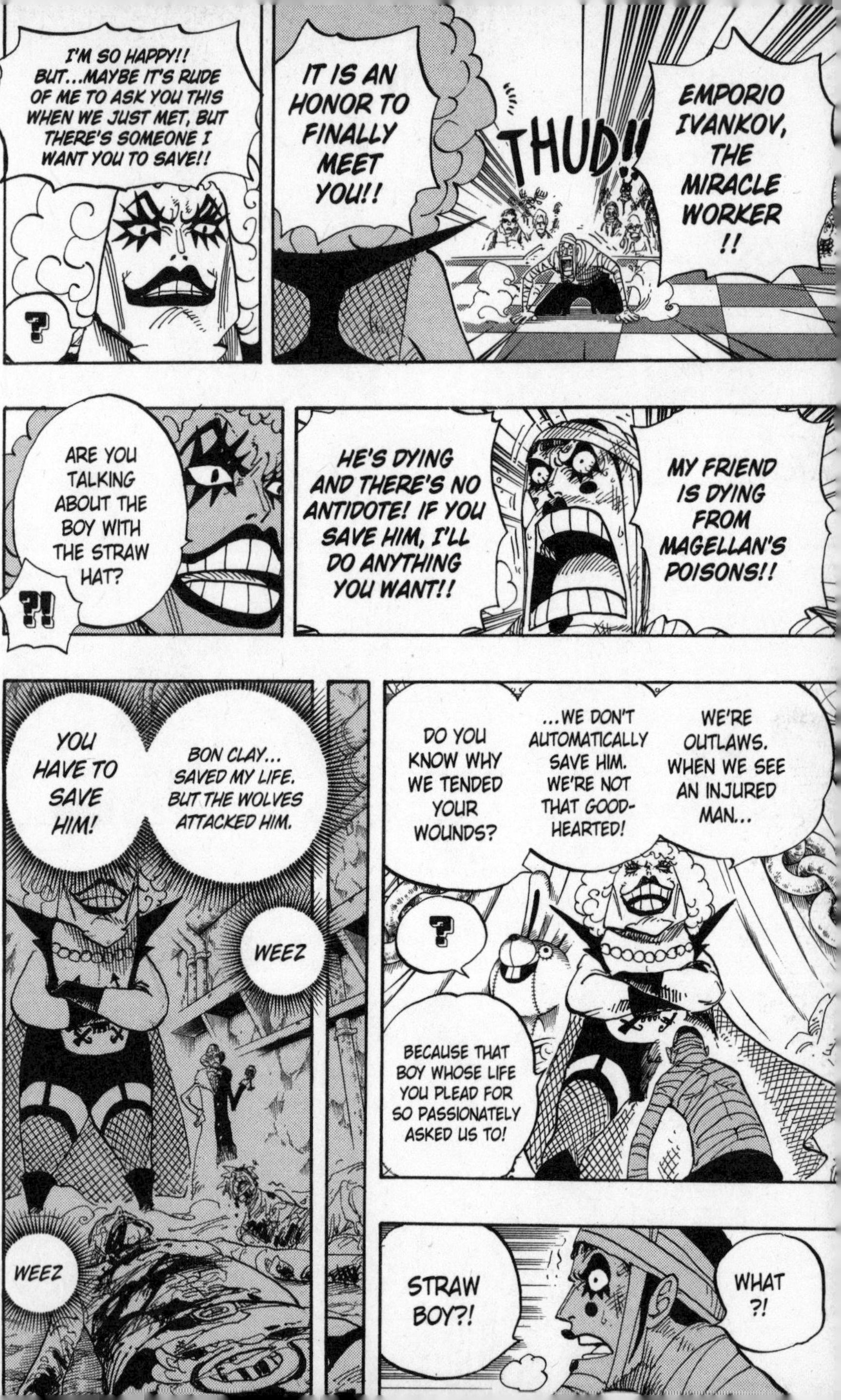
EMPORIO IVANKOV, THE MIRACLE WORKER!!
THUD!!
IT IS AN HONOR TO FINALLY MEET YOU!!
I'M SO HAPPY!! BUT...MAYBE IT'S RUDE OF ME TO ASK YOU THIS WHEN WE JUST MET, BUT THERE'S SOMEONE I WANT YOU TO SAVE!!
?
MY FRIEND IS DYING FROM MAGELLAN'S POISONS!!
HE'S DYING AND THERE'S NO ANTIDOTE! IF YOU SAVE HIM, I'LL DO ANYTHING YOU WANT!!
ARE YOU TALKING ABOUT THE BOY WITH THE STRAW HAT?
?!
WE'RE OUTLAWS. WHEN WE SEE AN INJURED MAN...
...WE DON'T AUTOMATICALLY SAVE HIM. WE'RE NOT THAT GOOD-HEARTED!
DO YOU KNOW WHY WE TENDED YOUR WOUNDS?
?
BECAUSE THAT BOY WHOSE LIFE YOU PLEAD FOR SO PASSIONATELY ASKED US TO!
WHAT ?!
STRAW BOY?!
BON CLAY... SAVED MY LIFE. BUT THE WOLVES ATTACKED HIM.
YOU HAVE TO SAVE HIM!
WEEZ
WEEZ

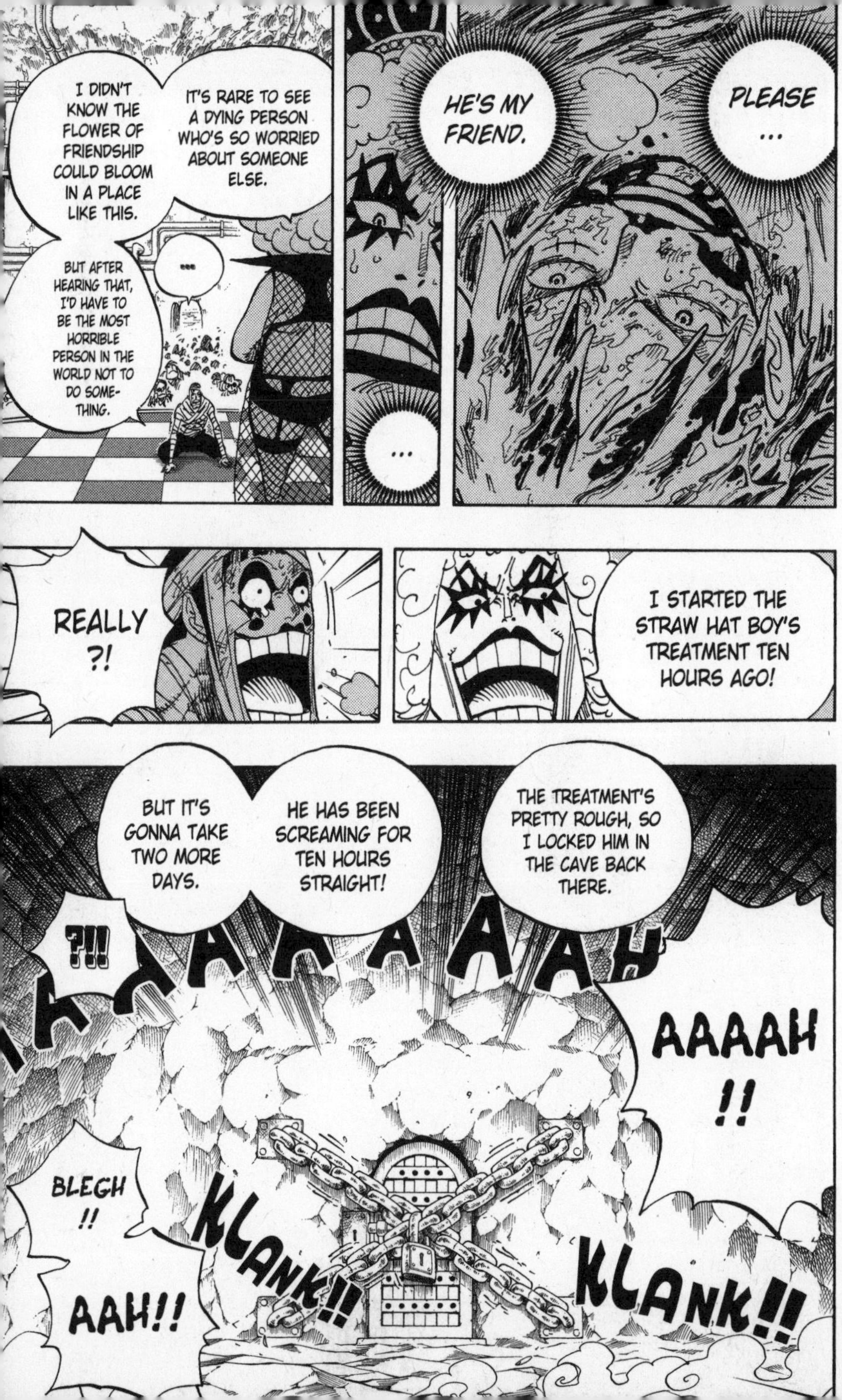
PLEASE ...
HE'S MY FRIEND.
...
IT'S RARE TO SEE A DYING PERSON WHO'S SO WORRIED ABOUT SOMEONE ELSE.
I DIDN'T KNOW THE FLOWER OF FRIENDSHIP COULD BLOOM IN A PLACE LIKE THIS.
...
BUT AFTER HEARING THAT, I'D HAVE TO BE THE MOST HORRIBLE PERSON IN THE WORLD NOT TO DO SOME-THING.
I STARTED THE STRAW HAT BOY'S TREATMENT TEN HOURS AGO!
REALLY ?!
THE TREATMENT'S PRETTY ROUGH, SO I LOCKED HIM IN THE CAVE BACK THERE.
HE HAS BEEN SCREAMING FOR TEN HOURS STRAIGHT!
BUT IT'S GONNA TAKE TWO MORE DAYS.
?!!
AAAAH !!
KLANK!!
KLANK!!
BLEGH !!
AAH!!

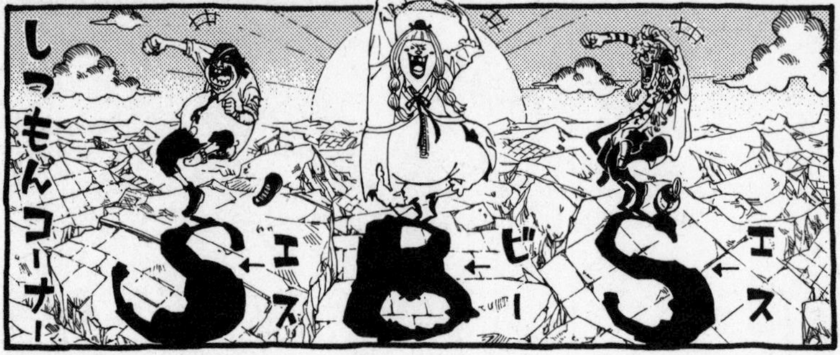
しつもんコーナー
エス
ビー
エス

(Ham Ster, Tokyo)

Q: Odacchi! It'll be okay!

--Shuyu

A: Thanks. I may suck, but I'll keep trying.

Q: What's that mark that's on people like Magellan in Impel Down?

--Jonjororin

A: Toei Animation asked me about that too, but the symbols on the neck and the ones on the arm are slightly different. There are actually two variations, but they're based on the same thing. It's the initials of Impel Down, "I" and "D." If you combine them...

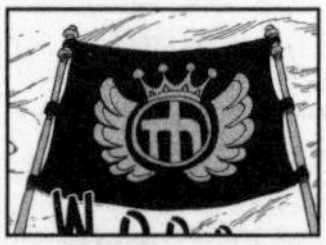

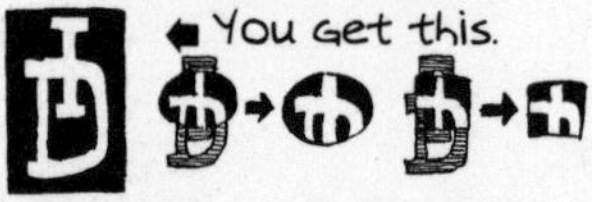
You get this.

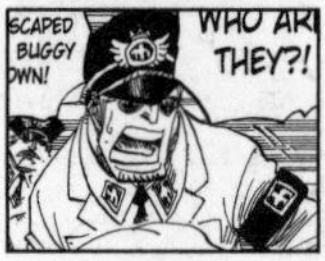
SCAPED BUGGY DWN!
WHO AR THEY?!

You get a different symbol depending on which part you cut out. Both of these symbols represent Impel Down. But they're not really very important.

Q: Hello, Mr. Oda! I stayed up three days and three nights to come up with this. Since your name is Eiichiro (ichi = 1, ro = sounds like 6 in Japanese), can we make your birthday January 6?

--Barcode

A: Sure.

Q: This chapter is called "I Have a Question for Odacchi!" There's a huge bookshelf inside the *Thousand Sunny!* But it says that everybody's books are there except Luffy's! Now on to the main point! I have no idea what kind of books a certain person reads, and that's…Zolo. What does he read? Call this chapter "Tell me!"

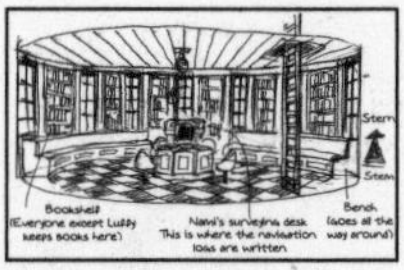
Stern
Stem
Bookshelf
(Everyone except Luffy keeps books here)
Nami's surveying desk
This is where the navigation logs are written
Bench
(goes all the way around)

--Twisted Love ♡

A: You're right that Zolo doesn't seem to be the book-reading type. He doesn't really read books, he just looks at them--martial arts manuals, weapons listings, bounty lists, as well as other things. That's what he reads.

Chapter 538:
LEVEL 5.5: NEW KAMA LAND

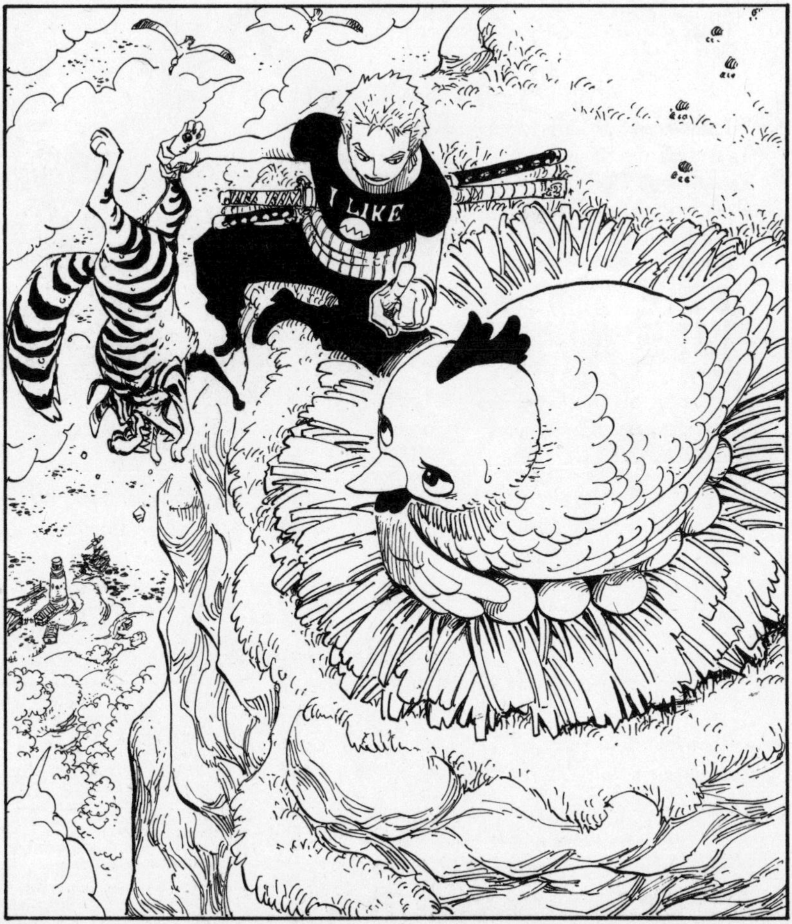
I LIKE

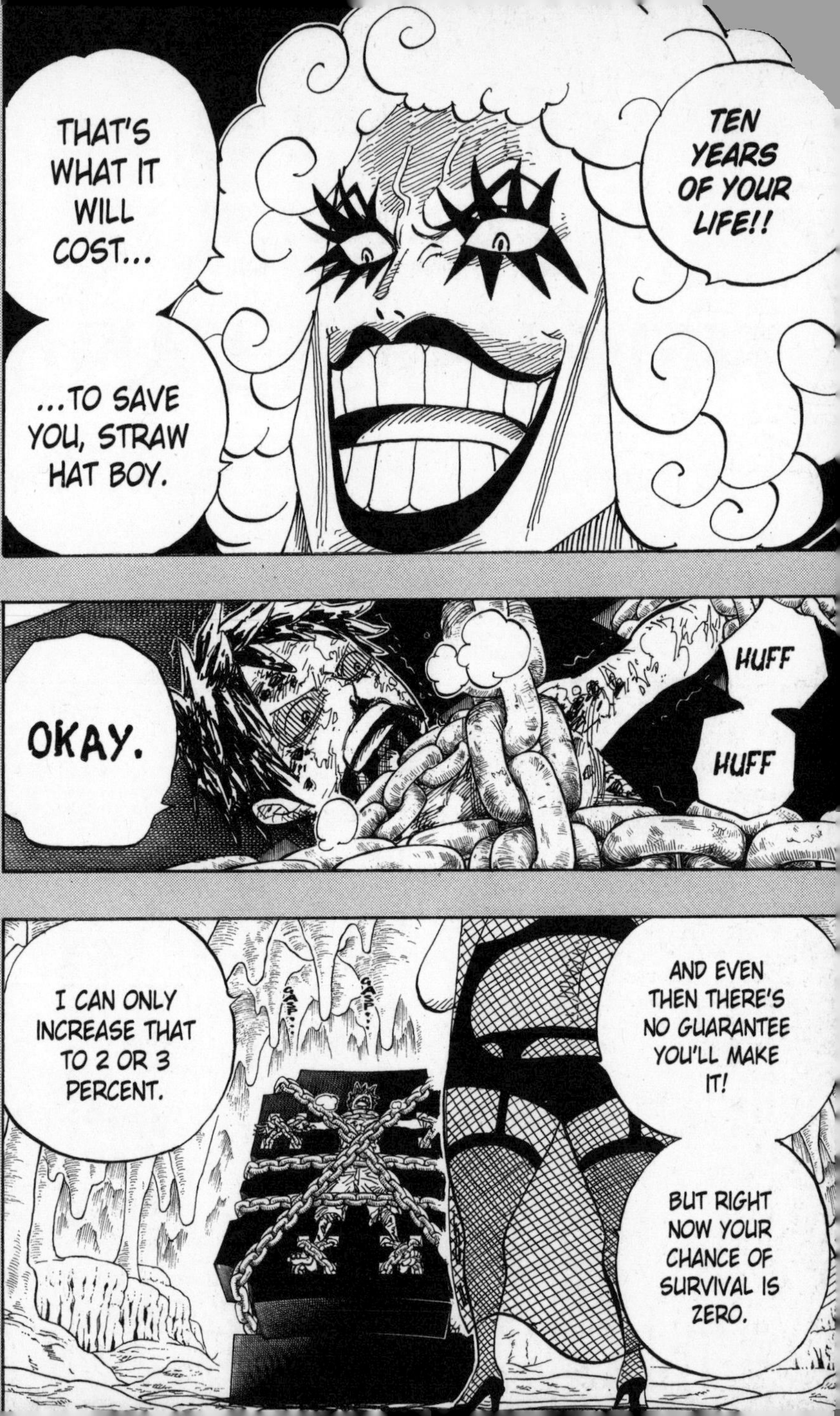
TEN YEARS OF YOUR LIFE!!
THAT'S WHAT IT WILL COST...
...TO SAVE YOU, STRAW HAT BOY.
HUFF
HUFF
OKAY.
AND EVEN THEN THERE'S NO GUARANTEE YOU'LL MAKE IT!
BUT RIGHT NOW YOUR CHANCE OF SURVIVAL IS ZERO.
GASP...
GASP...
I CAN ONLY INCREASE THAT TO 2 OR 3 PERCENT.

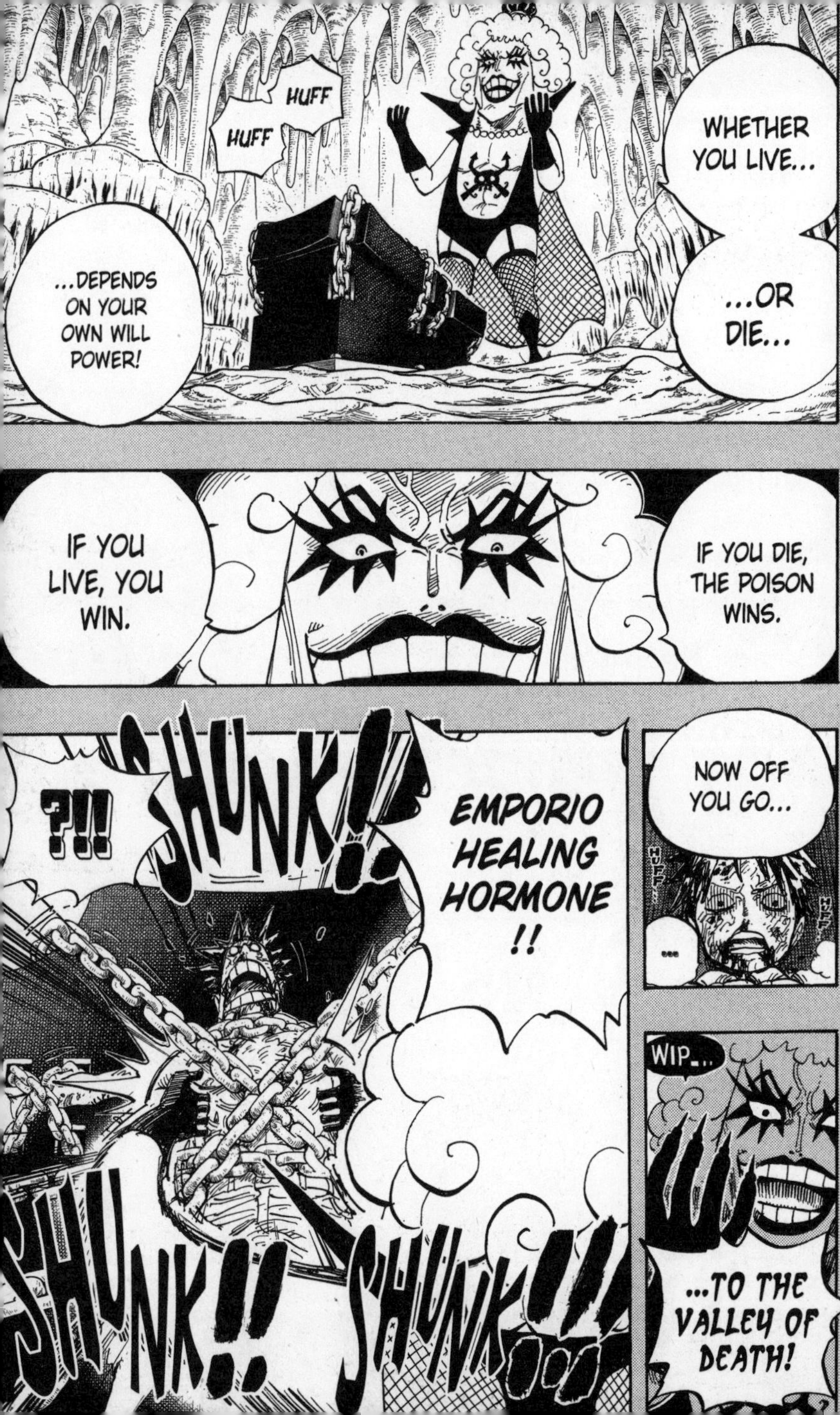
WHETHER YOU LIVE...
...OR DIE...
HUFF
HUFF
...DEPENDS ON YOUR OWN WILL POWER!
IF YOU DIE, THE POISON WINS.
IF YOU LIVE, YOU WIN.
NOW OFF YOU GO...
HUFF
HUFF
...
WIP...
...TO THE VALLEY OF DEATH!
EMPORIO HEALING HORMONE !!
SHUNK!!
?!!
SHUNK!!
SHUNK!!

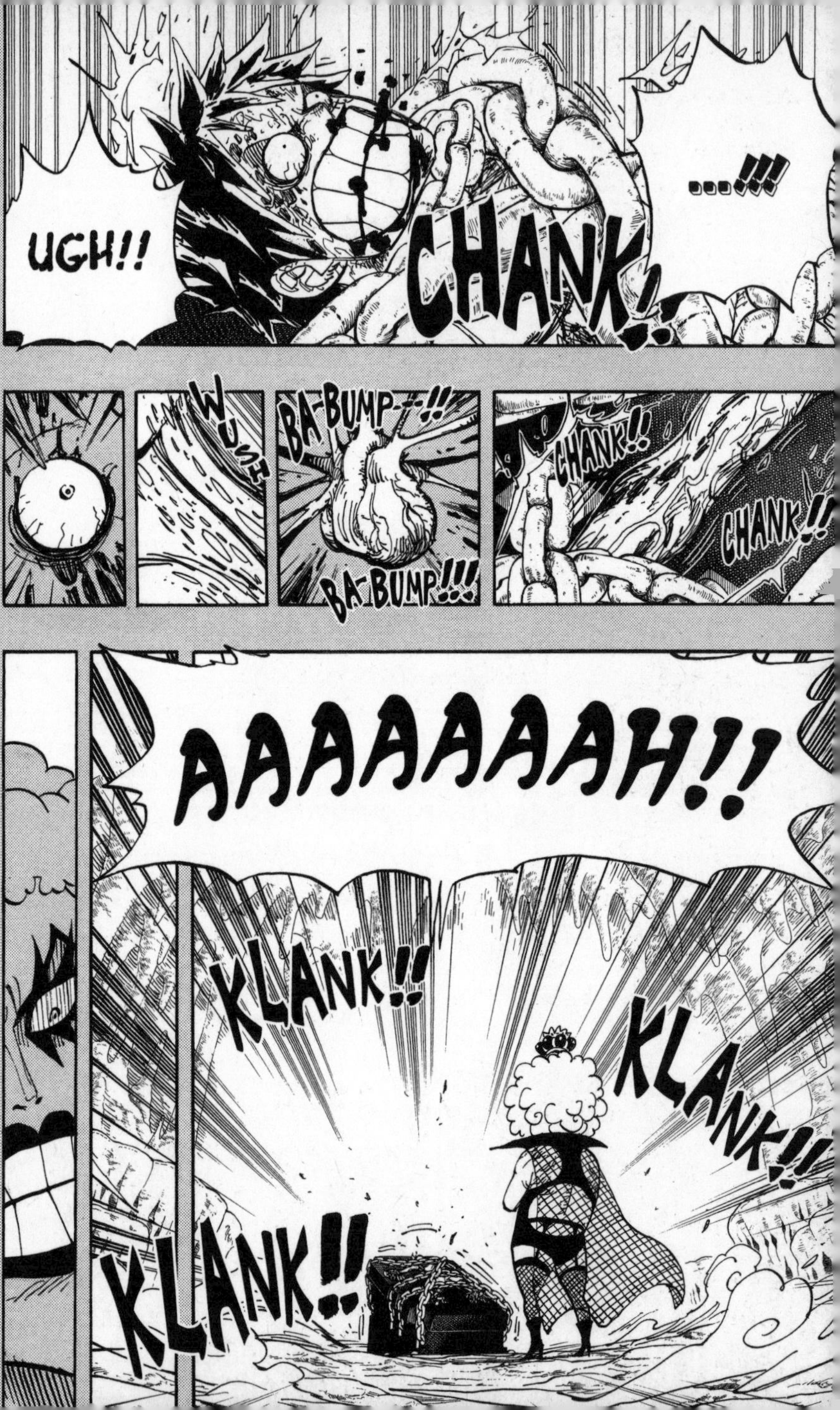
...!!!
CHANK
UGH!!
CHANK!!
CHANK!!
BA-BUMP--!!
BA-BUMP!!!
WUSH
AAAAAAAH!!
KLANK!!
KLANK!!
KLANK!!

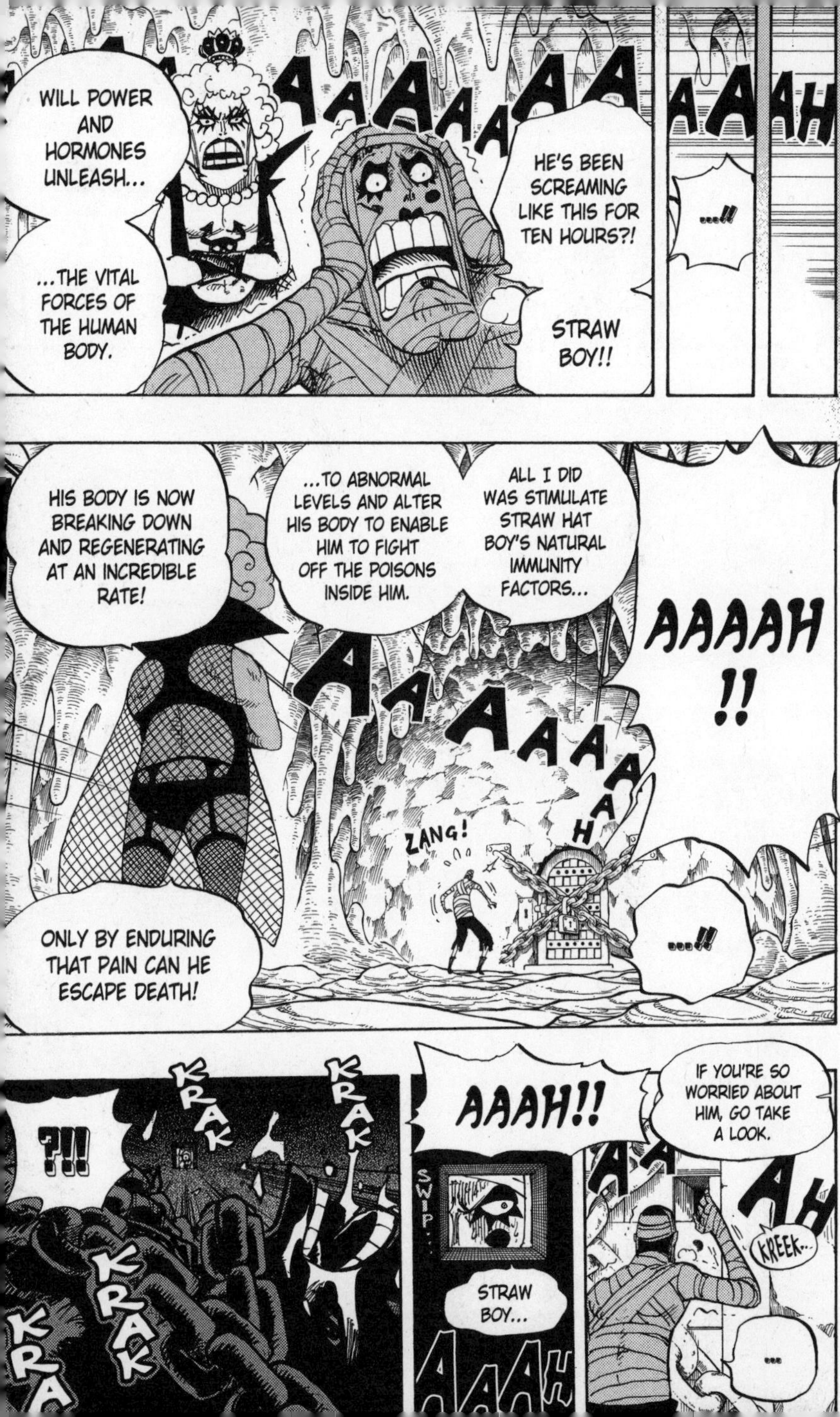
AH
A
...!!
AAAAAAAAA
HE'S BEEN SCREAMING LIKE THIS FOR TEN HOURS?!
STRAW BOY!!
WILL POWER AND HORMONES UNLEASH...
...THE VITAL FORCES OF THE HUMAN BODY.
AAAAH!!
...!!
ALL I DID WAS STIMULATE STRAW HAT BOY'S NATURAL IMMUNITY FACTORS...
...TO ABNORMAL LEVELS AND ALTER HIS BODY TO ENABLE HIM TO FIGHT OFF THE POISONS INSIDE HIM.
HIS BODY IS NOW BREAKING DOWN AND REGENERATING AT AN INCREDIBLE RATE!
AAAAAAAH
ZANG!
ONLY BY ENDURING THAT PAIN CAN HE ESCAPE DEATH!
IF YOU'RE SO WORRIED ABOUT HIM, GO TAKE A LOOK.
AAAH!!
AAAH
KREEK..
...
SWIP...
STRAW BOY...
AAAH
KRAK
KRAK
?!!
KRAK
KRAK
KRA

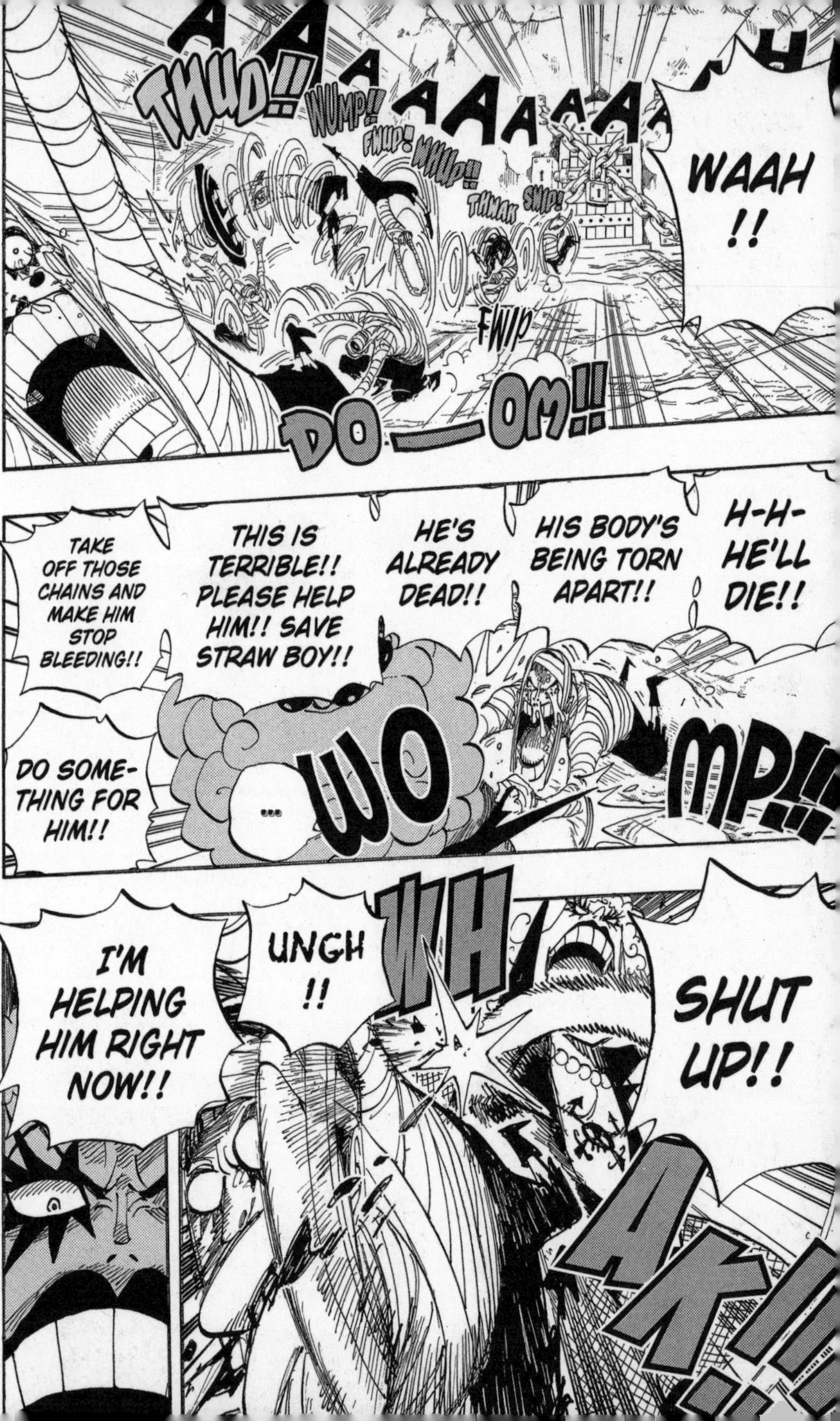
WAAH!!
AAAAAAAAA
SHIP!
THWAK
WHUP!!
FWUP!
WUMP!!
THUD!!
FWIP
DO—OM!!
H-H-HE'LL DIE!!
HIS BODY'S BEING TORN APART!!
HE'S ALREADY DEAD!!
THIS IS TERRIBLE!! PLEASE HELP HIM!! SAVE STRAW BOY!!
TAKE OFF THOSE CHAINS AND MAKE HIM STOP BLEEDING!!
WOMP!!!
...
DO SOME-THING FOR HIM!!
SHUT UP!!
WHAK!!
UNGH!!
I'M HELPING HIM RIGHT NOW!!

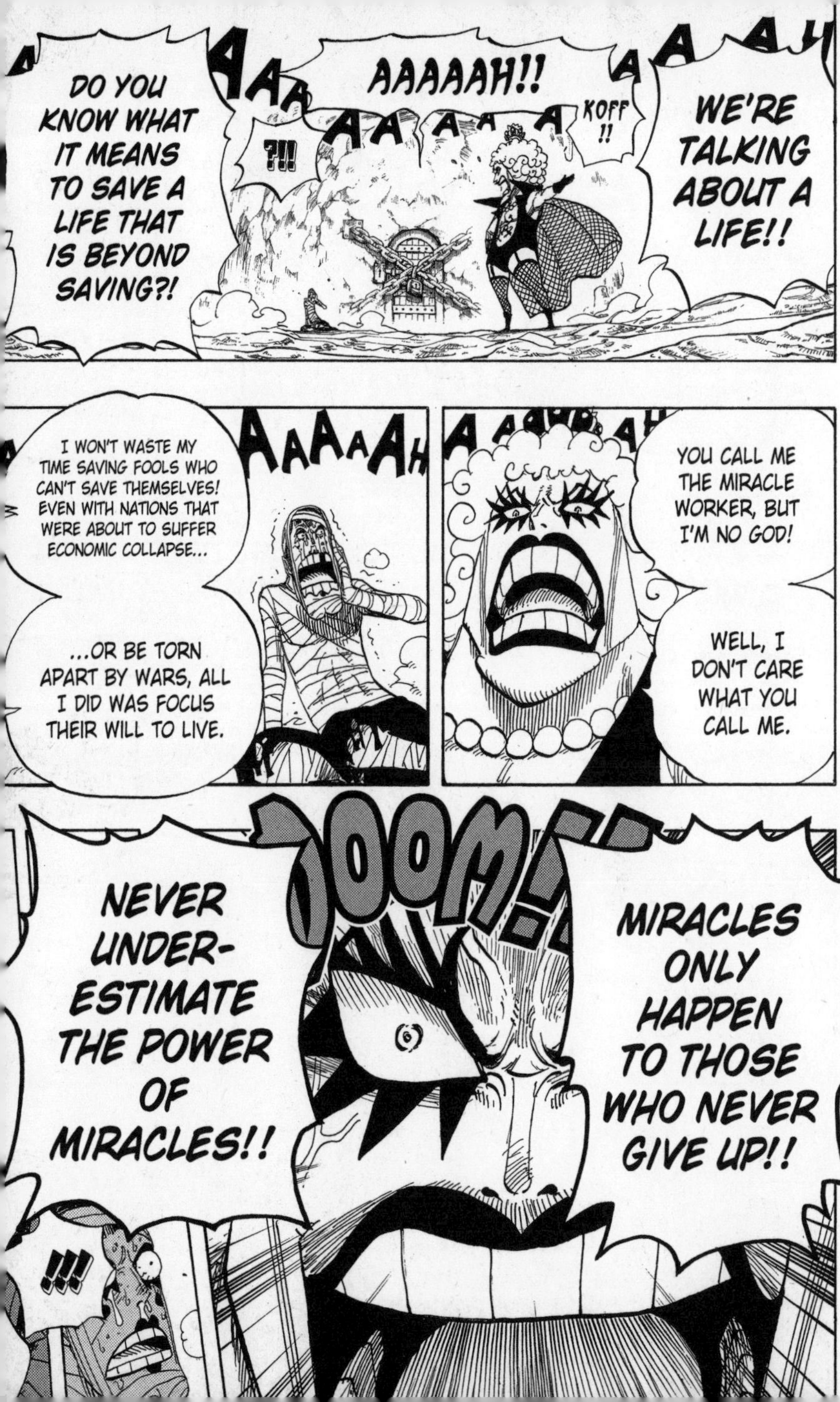
AAAAAH!!
WE'RE TALKING ABOUT A LIFE!!
KOFF !!
?!!
DO YOU KNOW WHAT IT MEANS TO SAVE A LIFE THAT IS BEYOND SAVING?!
YOU CALL ME THE MIRACLE WORKER, BUT I'M NO GOD!
WELL, I DON'T CARE WHAT YOU CALL ME.
I WON'T WASTE MY TIME SAVING FOOLS WHO CAN'T SAVE THEMSELVES! EVEN WITH NATIONS THAT WERE ABOUT TO SUFFER ECONOMIC COLLAPSE...
...OR BE TORN APART BY WARS, ALL I DID WAS FOCUS THEIR WILL TO LIVE.
MIRACLES ONLY HAPPEN TO THOSE WHO NEVER GIVE UP!!
NEVER UNDER-ESTIMATE THE POWER OF MIRACLES!!
!!!

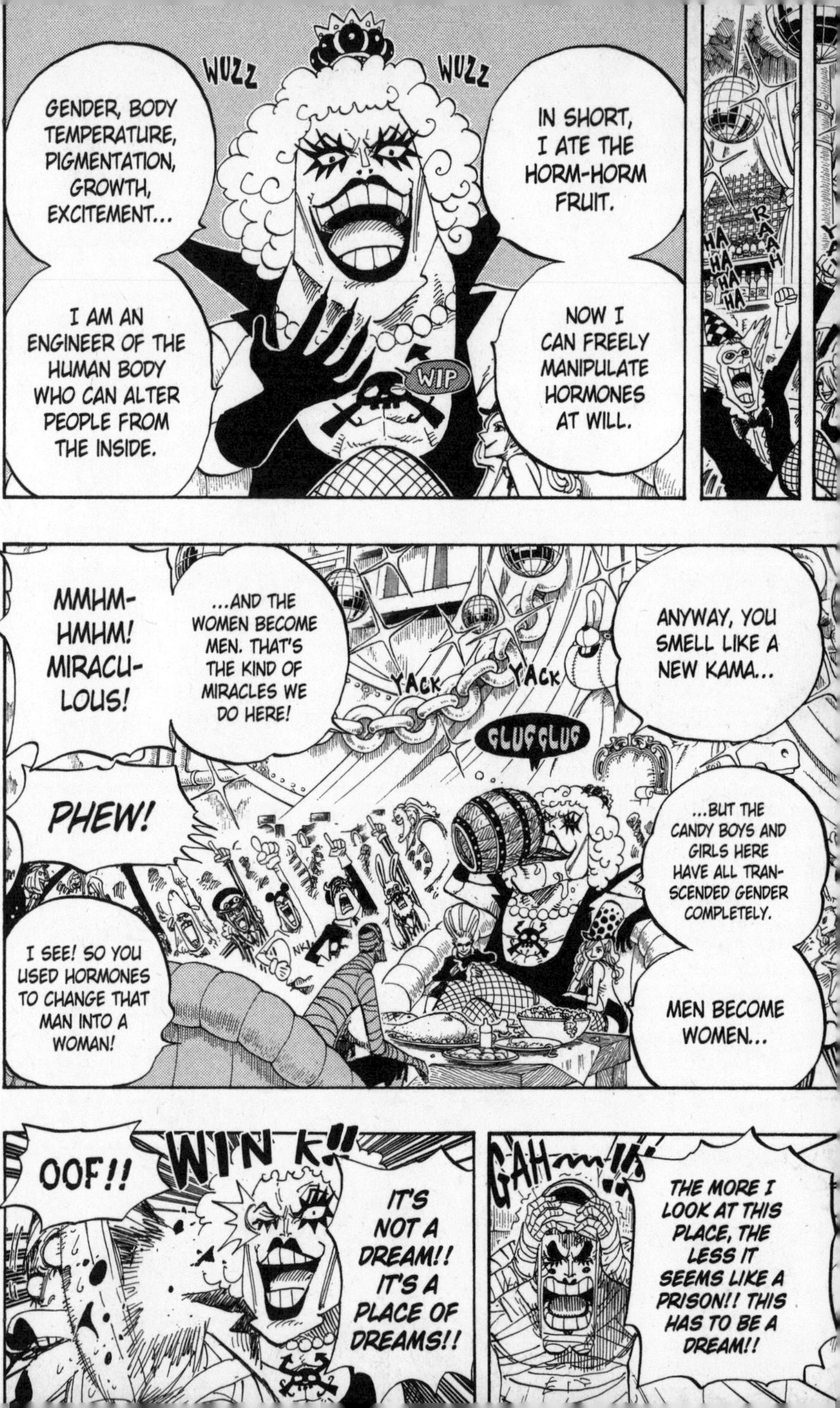
RAAH
HA HA HA HA HA
IN SHORT, I ATE THE HORM-HORM FRUIT.
NOW I CAN FREELY MANIPULATE HORMONES AT WILL.
WUZZ
WUZZ
GENDER, BODY TEMPERATURE, PIGMENTATION, GROWTH, EXCITEMENT...
I AM AN ENGINEER OF THE HUMAN BODY WHO CAN ALTER PEOPLE FROM THE INSIDE.
WIP
ANYWAY, YOU SMELL LIKE A NEW KAMA...
...BUT THE CANDY BOYS AND GIRLS HERE HAVE ALL TRANSCENDED GENDER COMPLETELY.
MEN BECOME WOMEN...
YACK
YACK
GLUGGLUG
...AND THE WOMEN BECOME MEN. THAT'S THE KIND OF MIRACLES WE DO HERE!
MMHM-HMHM! MIRACULOUS!
PHEW!
I SEE! SO YOU USED HORMONES TO CHANGE THAT MAN INTO A WOMAN!
GAH!!
THE MORE I LOOK AT THIS PLACE, THE LESS IT SEEMS LIKE A PRISON!! THIS HAS TO BE A DREAM!!
WINK!!
IT'S NOT A DREAM!! IT'S A PLACE OF DREAMS!!
OOF!!

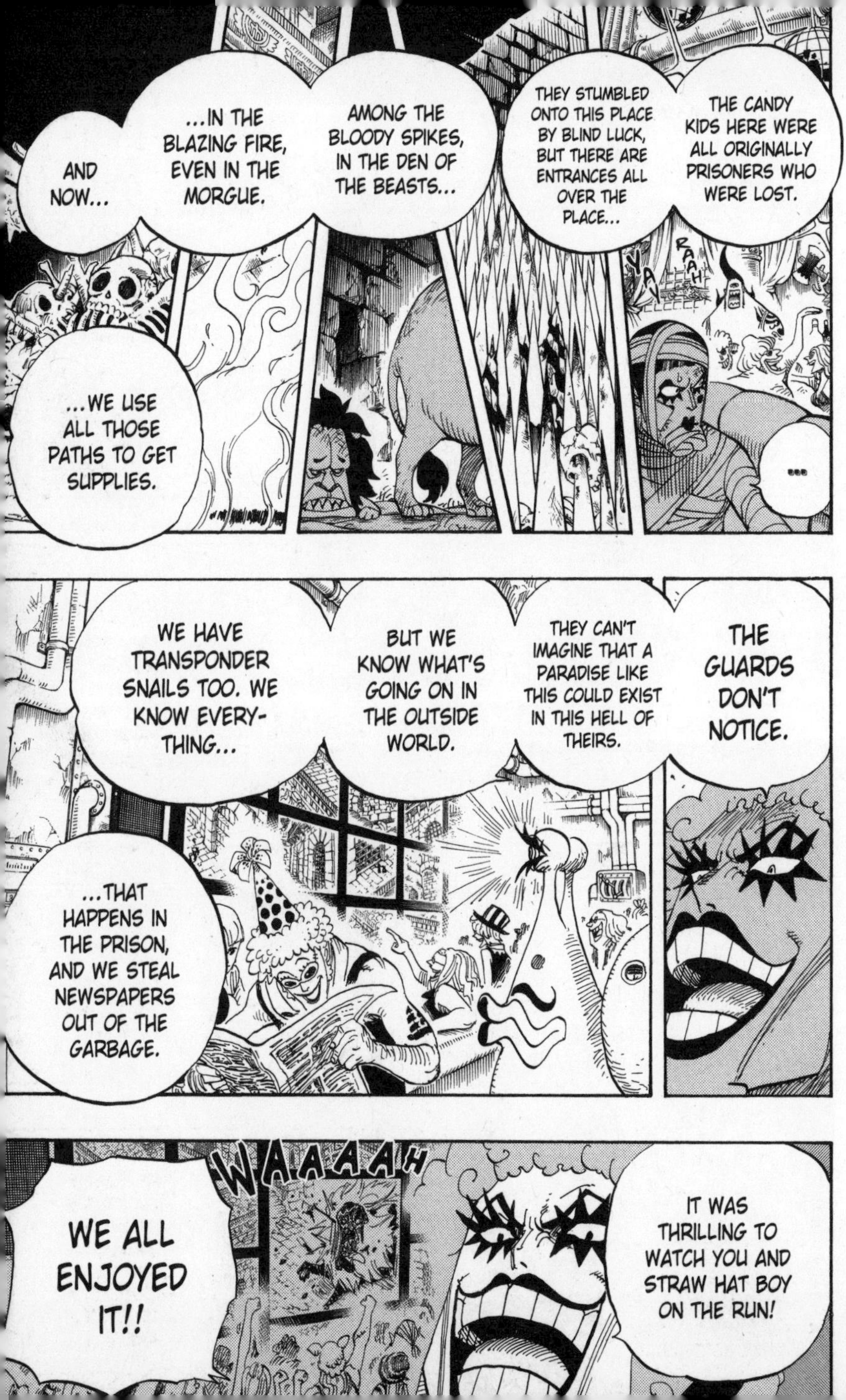
THE CANDY KIDS HERE WERE ALL ORIGINALLY PRISONERS WHO WERE LOST.
...
THEY STUMBLED ONTO THIS PLACE BY BLIND LUCK, BUT THERE ARE ENTRANCES ALL OVER THE PLACE...
AMONG THE BLOODY SPIKES, IN THE DEN OF THE BEASTS...
...IN THE BLAZING FIRE, EVEN IN THE MORGUE.
AND NOW...
...WE USE ALL THOSE PATHS TO GET SUPPLIES.
THE GUARDS DON'T NOTICE.
THEY CAN'T IMAGINE THAT A PARADISE LIKE THIS COULD EXIST IN THIS HELL OF THEIRS.
BUT WE KNOW WHAT'S GOING ON IN THE OUTSIDE WORLD.
WE HAVE TRANSPONDER SNAILS TOO. WE KNOW EVERY-THING...
...THAT HAPPENS IN THE PRISON, AND WE STEAL NEWSPAPERS OUT OF THE GARBAGE.
IT WAS THRILLING TO WATCH YOU AND STRAW HAT BOY ON THE RUN!
WAAAAAH
WE ALL ENJOYED IT!!

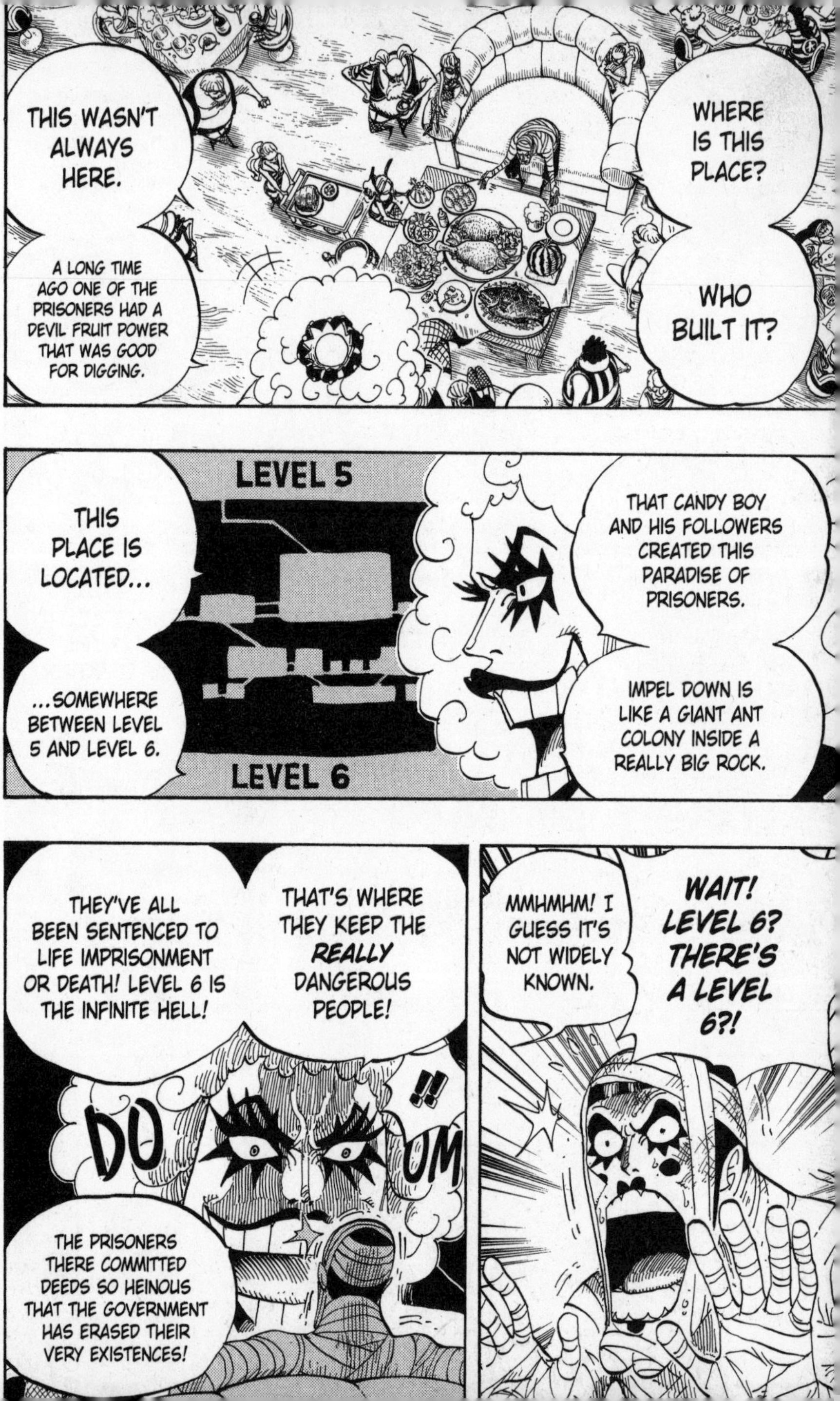
WHERE IS THIS PLACE?
WHO BUILT IT?
THIS WASN'T ALWAYS HERE.
A LONG TIME AGO ONE OF THE PRISONERS HAD A DEVIL FRUIT POWER THAT WAS GOOD FOR DIGGING.
THAT CANDY BOY AND HIS FOLLOWERS CREATED THIS PARADISE OF PRISONERS.
IMPEL DOWN IS LIKE A GIANT ANT COLONY INSIDE A REALLY BIG ROCK.
THIS PLACE IS LOCATED...
LEVEL 5
...SOMEWHERE BETWEEN LEVEL 5 AND LEVEL 6.
LEVEL 6
WAIT! LEVEL 6? THERE'S A LEVEL 6?!
MMHMHM! I GUESS IT'S NOT WIDELY KNOWN.
THAT'S WHERE THEY KEEP THE *REALLY* DANGEROUS PEOPLE!
THEY'VE ALL BEEN SENTENCED TO LIFE IMPRISONMENT OR DEATH! LEVEL 6 IS THE INFINITE HELL!
DO
!!
UM
THE PRISONERS THERE COMMITTED DEEDS SO HEINOUS THAT THE GOVERNMENT HAS ERASED THEIR VERY EXISTENCES!

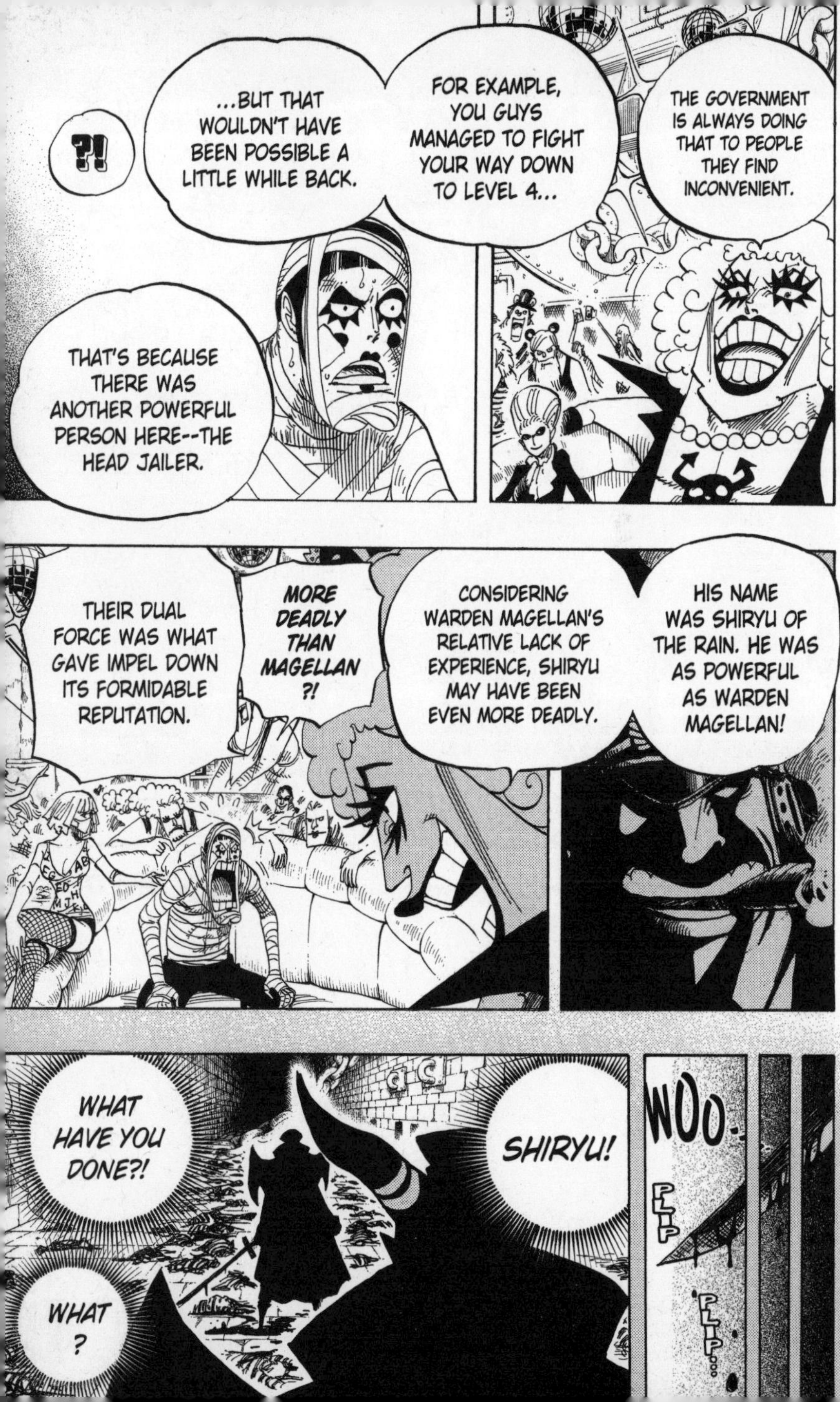
THE GOVERNMENT IS ALWAYS DOING THAT TO PEOPLE THEY FIND INCONVENIENT.
FOR EXAMPLE, YOU GUYS MANAGED TO FIGHT YOUR WAY DOWN TO LEVEL 4...
...BUT THAT WOULDN'T HAVE BEEN POSSIBLE A LITTLE WHILE BACK.
?!
THAT'S BECAUSE THERE WAS ANOTHER POWERFUL PERSON HERE--THE HEAD JAILER.
HIS NAME WAS SHIRYU OF THE RAIN. HE WAS AS POWERFUL AS WARDEN MAGELLAN!
CONSIDERING WARDEN MAGELLAN'S RELATIVE LACK OF EXPERIENCE, SHIRYU MAY HAVE BEEN EVEN MORE DEADLY.
MORE DEADLY THAN MAGELLAN ?!
THEIR DUAL FORCE WAS WHAT GAVE IMPEL DOWN ITS FORMIDABLE REPUTATION.
WOO..
FLIP
FLIP...
SHIRYU!
WHAT HAVE YOU DONE?!
WHAT ?

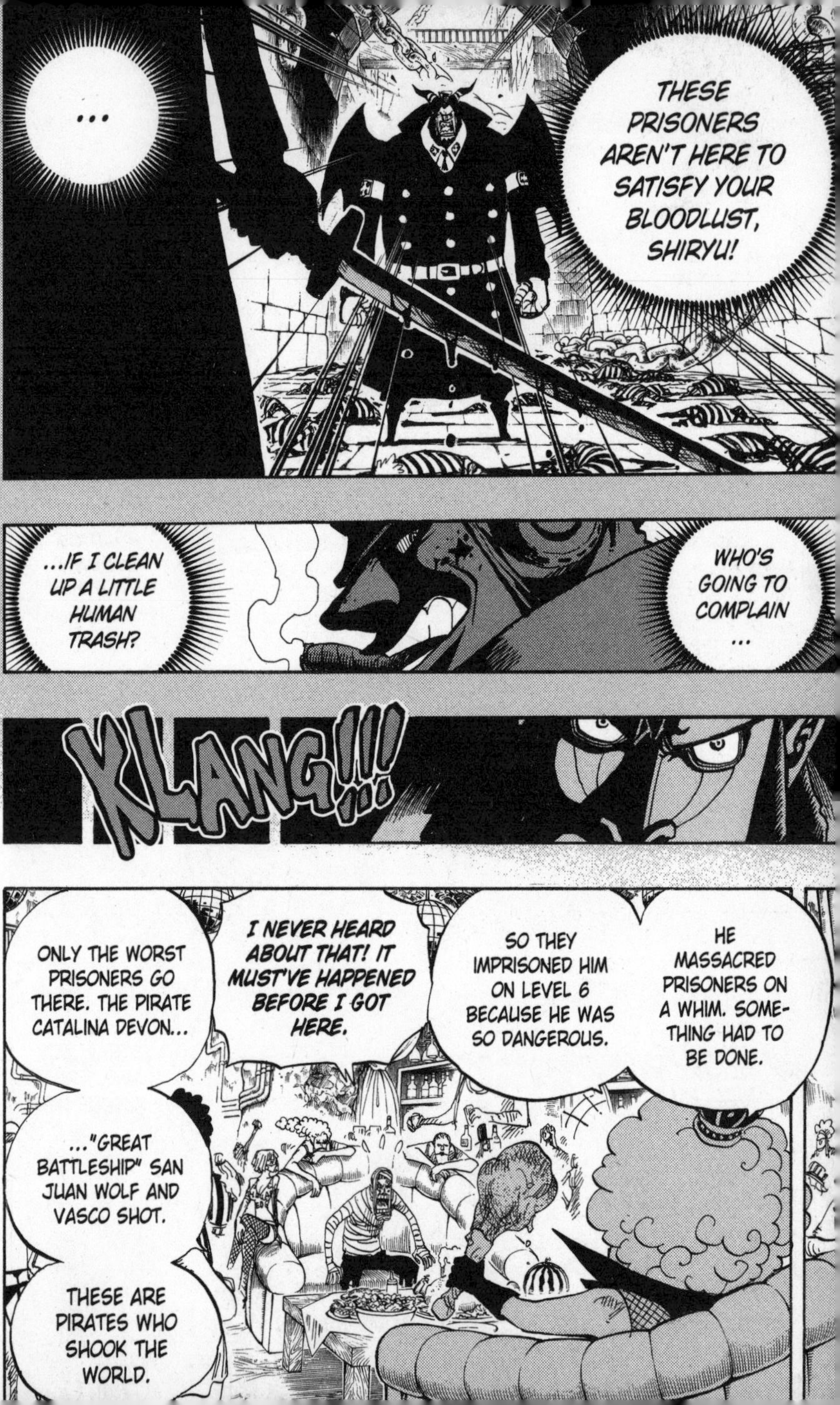
THESE PRISONERS AREN'T HERE TO SATISFY YOUR BLOODLUST, SHIRYU!
...
WHO'S GOING TO COMPLAIN ...
...IF I CLEAN UP A LITTLE HUMAN TRASH?
KLANG!!!
HE MASSACRED PRISONERS ON A WHIM. SOME-THING HAD TO BE DONE.
SO THEY IMPRISONED HIM ON LEVEL 6 BECAUSE HE WAS SO DANGEROUS.
I NEVER HEARD ABOUT THAT! IT MUST'VE HAPPENED BEFORE I GOT HERE.
ONLY THE WORST PRISONERS GO THERE. THE PIRATE CATALINA DEVON...
..."GREAT BATTLESHIP" SAN JUAN WOLF AND VASCO SHOT.
THESE ARE PIRATES WHO SHOOK THE WORLD.

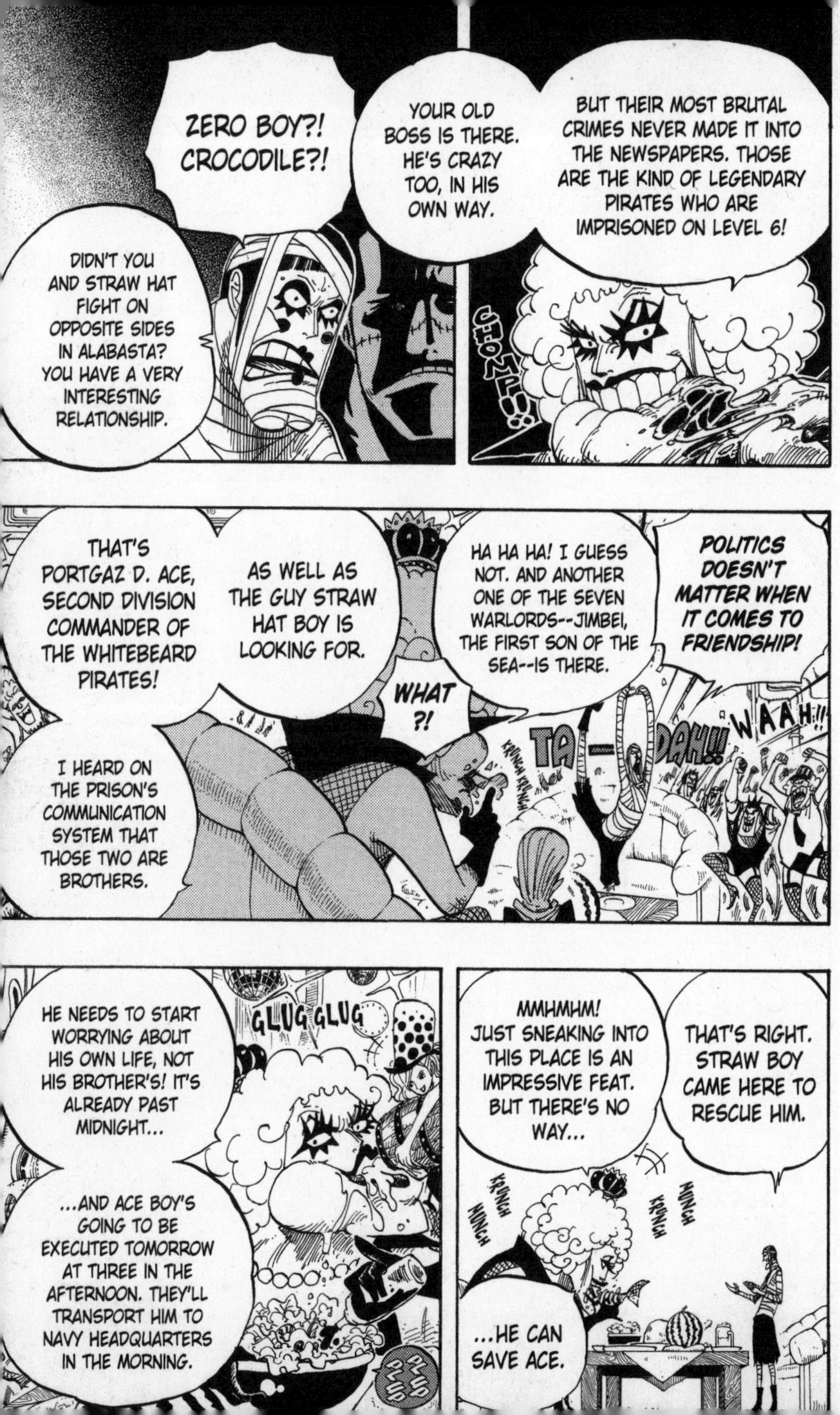
BUT THEIR MOST BRUTAL CRIMES NEVER MADE IT INTO THE NEWSPAPERS. THOSE ARE THE KIND OF LEGENDARY PIRATES WHO ARE IMPRISONED ON LEVEL 6!
CHOMP!!
YOUR OLD BOSS IS THERE. HE'S CRAZY TOO, IN HIS OWN WAY.
ZERO BOY?! CROCODILE?!
DIDN'T YOU AND STRAW HAT FIGHT ON OPPOSITE SIDES IN ALABASTA? YOU HAVE A VERY INTERESTING RELATIONSHIP.
POLITICS DOESN'T MATTER WHEN IT COMES TO FRIENDSHIP!
WAAH!!
HA HA HA! I GUESS NOT. AND ANOTHER ONE OF THE SEVEN WARLORDS--JIMBEI, THE FIRST SON OF THE SEA--IS THERE.
TA-DAH!!
KRUNCH KRUNCH
WHAT?!
AS WELL AS THE GUY STRAW HAT BOY IS LOOKING FOR.
THAT'S PORTGAZ D. ACE, SECOND DIVISION COMMANDER OF THE WHITEBEARD PIRATES!
I HEARD ON THE PRISON'S COMMUNICATION SYSTEM THAT THOSE TWO ARE BROTHERS.
THAT'S RIGHT. STRAW BOY CAME HERE TO RESCUE HIM.
MMHMHM! JUST SNEAKING INTO THIS PLACE IS AN IMPRESSIVE FEAT. BUT THERE'S NO WAY...
MUNCH
KRUNCH
KRUNCH
MUNCH
...HE CAN SAVE ACE.
GLUG GLUG
HE NEEDS TO START WORRYING ABOUT HIS OWN LIFE, NOT HIS BROTHER'S! IT'S ALREADY PAST MIDNIGHT...
...AND ACE BOY'S GOING TO BE EXECUTED TOMORROW AT THREE IN THE AFTERNOON. THEY'LL TRANSPORT HIM TO NAVY HEADQUARTERS IN THE MORNING.

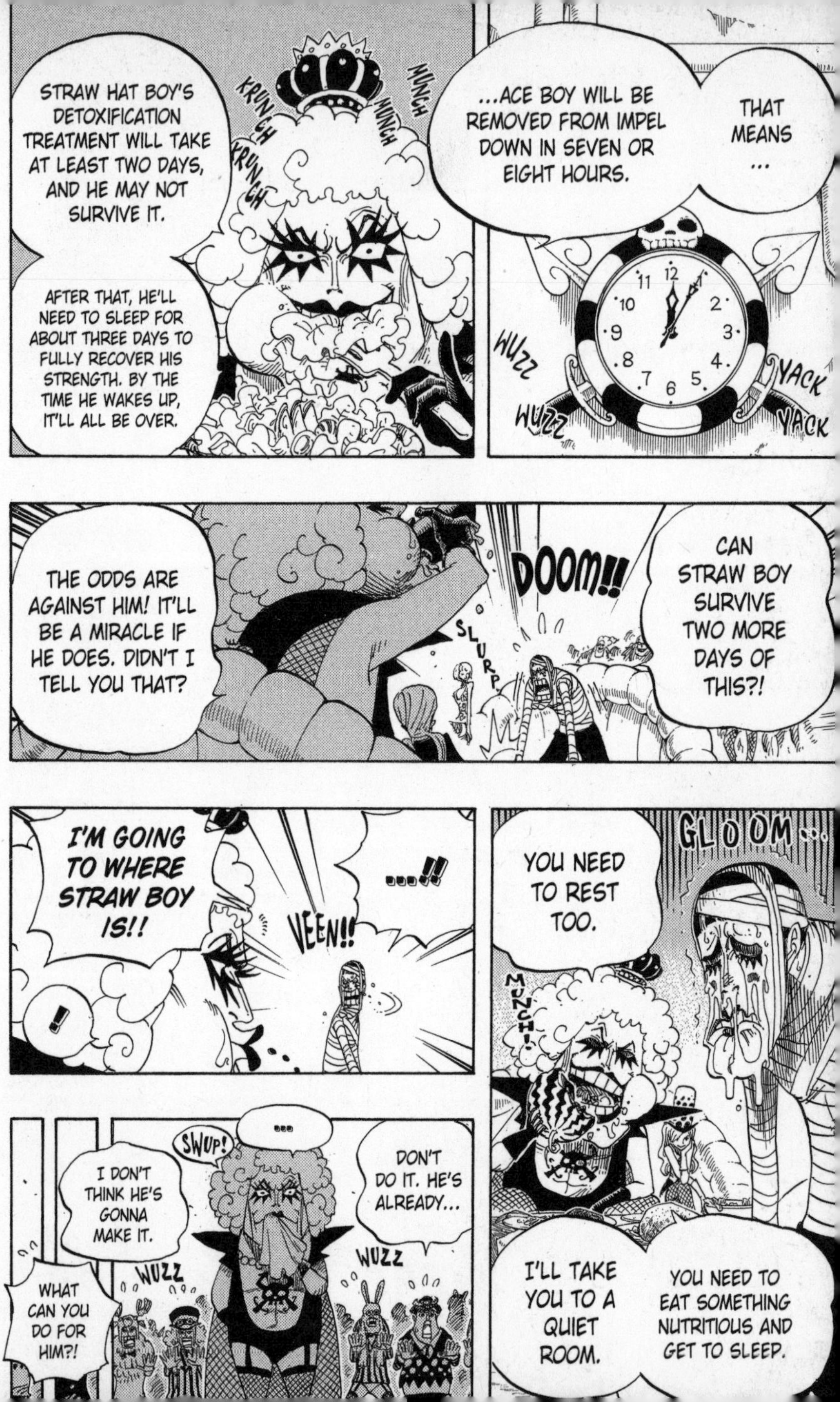
THAT MEANS ...
...ACE BOY WILL BE REMOVED FROM IMPEL DOWN IN SEVEN OR EIGHT HOURS.
WUZZ
WUZZ
YACK
YACK
MUNCH
MUNCH
KRUNCH
KRUNCH
STRAW HAT BOY'S DETOXIFICATION TREATMENT WILL TAKE AT LEAST TWO DAYS, AND HE MAY NOT SURVIVE IT.
AFTER THAT, HE'LL NEED TO SLEEP FOR ABOUT THREE DAYS TO FULLY RECOVER HIS STRENGTH. BY THE TIME HE WAKES UP, IT'LL ALL BE OVER.
CAN STRAW BOY SURVIVE TWO MORE DAYS OF THIS?!
DOOM!!
SLURP
THE ODDS ARE AGAINST HIM! IT'LL BE A MIRACLE IF HE DOES. DIDN'T I TELL YOU THAT?
GLOOM...
YOU NEED TO REST TOO.
MUNCH!
YOU NEED TO EAT SOMETHING NUTRITIOUS AND GET TO SLEEP.
I'LL TAKE YOU TO A QUIET ROOM.
...!!
I'M GOING TO WHERE STRAW BOY IS!!
VEEN!!
!
...
DON'T DO IT. HE'S ALREADY...
SWUP!
I DON'T THINK HE'S GONNA MAKE IT.
WUZZ
WUZZ
WHAT CAN YOU DO FOR HIM?!

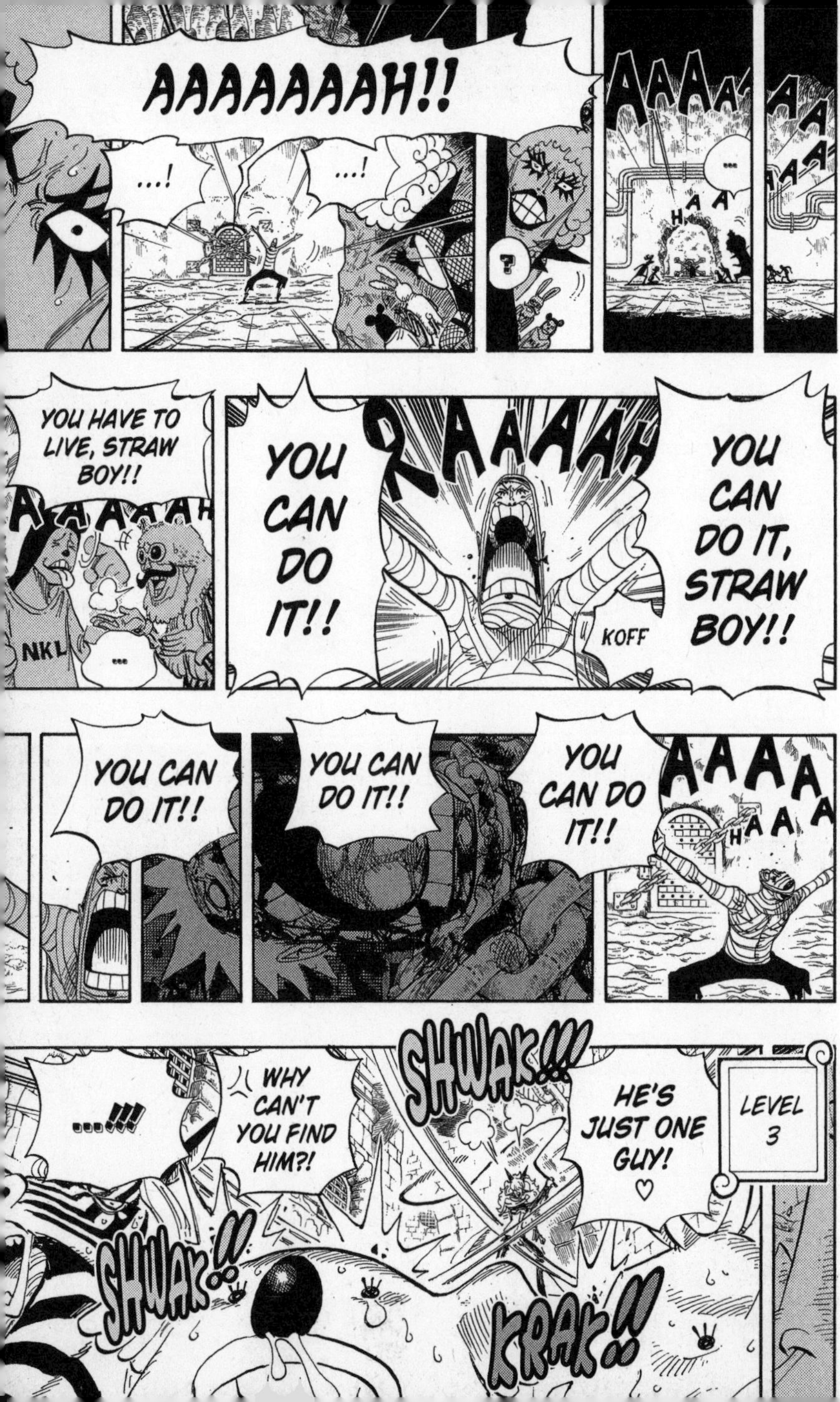

AAAA
HAA
...
?
...!
...!
AAAAAAAH!!
YOU CAN DO IT, STRAW BOY!!
RAAAAAH
KOFF
YOU CAN DO IT!!
YOU HAVE TO LIVE, STRAW BOY!!
AAAAAAH
NKL
...
AAAAA
HAAA
YOU CAN DO IT!!
YOU CAN DO IT!!
YOU CAN DO IT!!
LEVEL 3
HE'S JUST ONE GUY! ♡
SHWAK!!!
WHY CAN'T YOU FIND HIM?!
...!!!
SHWAK!!
KRAK!!

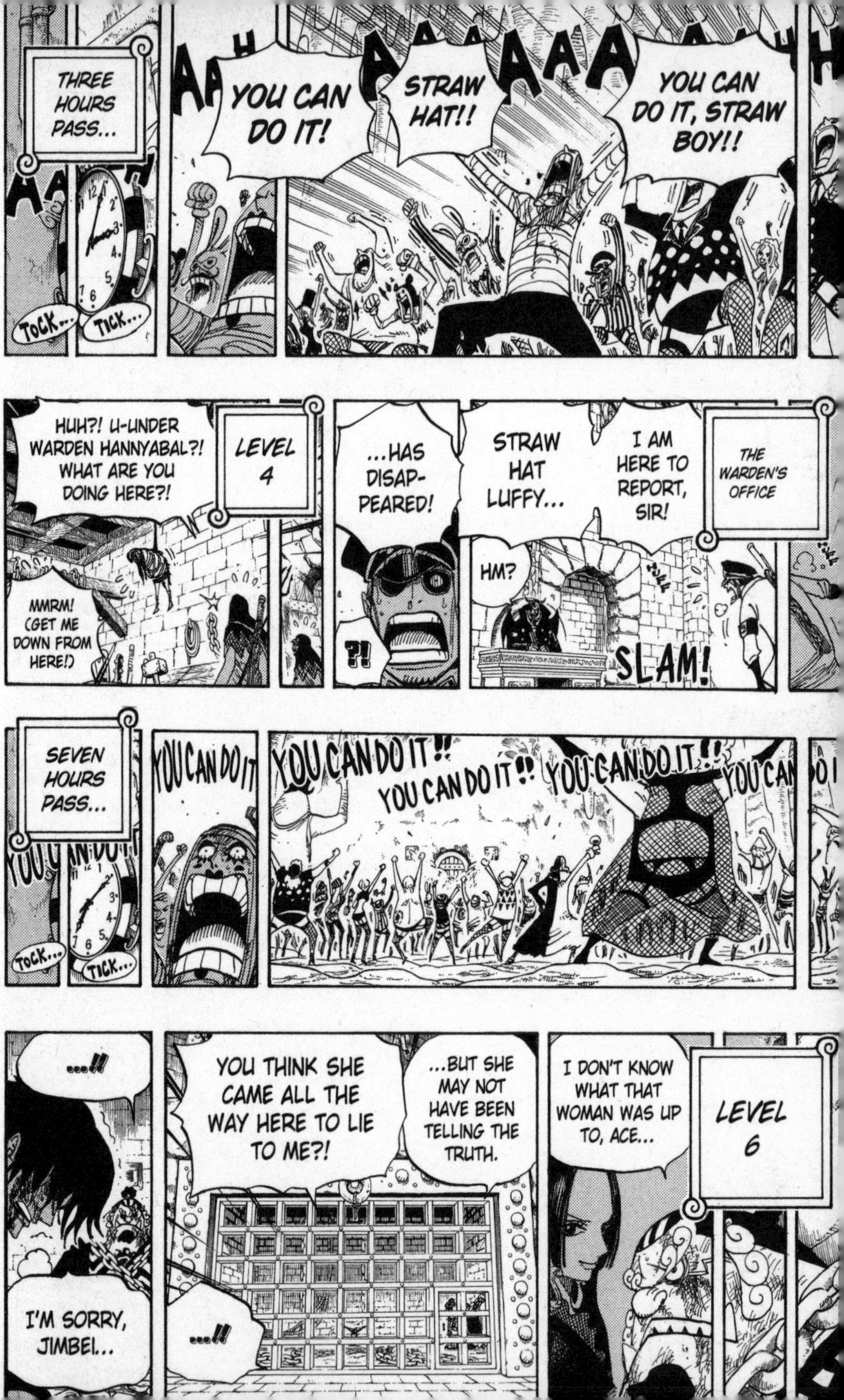

YOU CAN DO IT, STRAW BOY!!
STRAW HAT!!
YOU CAN DO IT!
THREE HOURS PASS...
TICK...
TOCK...
THE WARDEN'S OFFICE
I AM HERE TO REPORT, SIR!
STRAW HAT LUFFY...
SLAM!
HM?
...HAS DISAPPEARED!
?!
LEVEL 4
HUH?! U-UNDER WARDEN HANNYABAL?! WHAT ARE YOU DOING HERE?!
MMRM! (GET ME DOWN FROM HERE!)
YOU CAN DO IT!!
YOU CAN DO IT!!
YOU CAN DO IT!!
YOU CAN DO IT
SEVEN HOURS PASS...
TICK...
TOCK...
LEVEL 6
I DON'T KNOW WHAT THAT WOMAN WAS UP TO, ACE...
...BUT SHE MAY NOT HAVE BEEN TELLING THE TRUTH.
YOU THINK SHE CAME ALL THE WAY HERE TO LIE TO ME?!
...!!
...!!
I'M SORRY, JIMBEI...

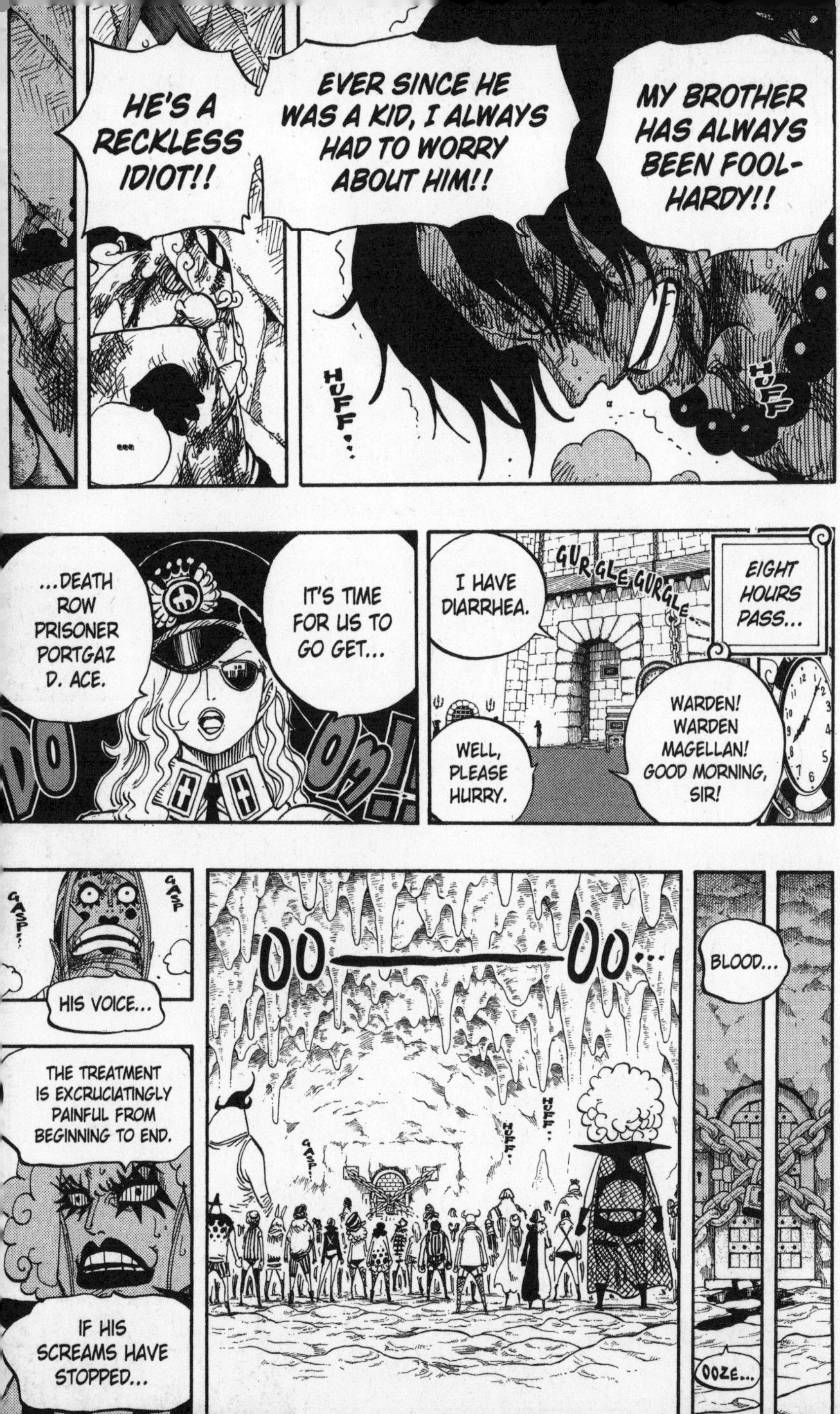
MY BROTHER HAS ALWAYS BEEN FOOL-HARDY!!
HUFF
HUFF...
EVER SINCE HE WAS A KID, I ALWAYS HAD TO WORRY ABOUT HIM!!
HE'S A RECKLESS IDIOT!!
...
EIGHT HOURS PASS...
GURGLE GURGLE...
I HAVE DIARRHEA.
WARDEN! WARDEN MAGELLAN! GOOD MORNING, SIR!
WELL, PLEASE HURRY.
IT'S TIME FOR US TO GO GET...
...DEATH ROW PRISONER PORTGAZ D. ACE.
DOOM!
BLOOD...
OOZE...
OO————OO...
HUFF...
GASP...
GASP
GASP...
HIS VOICE...
THE TREATMENT IS EXCRUCIATINGLY PAINFUL FROM BEGINNING TO END.
IF HIS SCREAMS HAVE STOPPED...

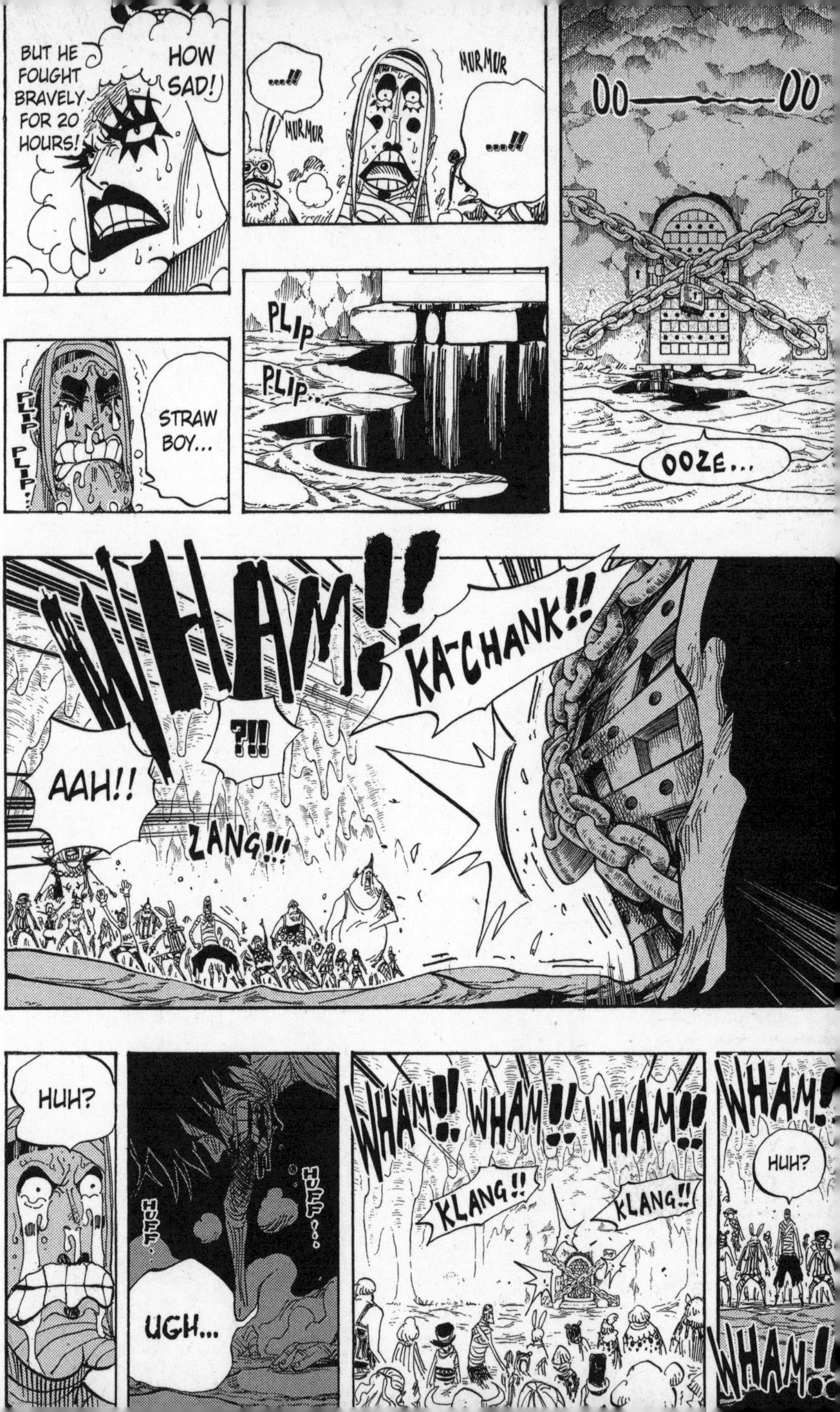
OO——OO
OOZE...
MURMUR
...!!
...!!
MURMUR
HOW SAD!
BUT HE FOUGHT BRAVELY FOR 20 HOURS!
PLIP
PLIP...
STRAW BOY...
PLIP PLIP...
KA-CHANK!!
WHAM!!
?!!
ZANG!!!
AAH!!
WHAM!!
HUH?
WHAM!!
WHAM!!
WHAM!!
WHAM!!
KLANG!!
KLANG!!
HUFF...
HUFF...
UGH...
HUH?

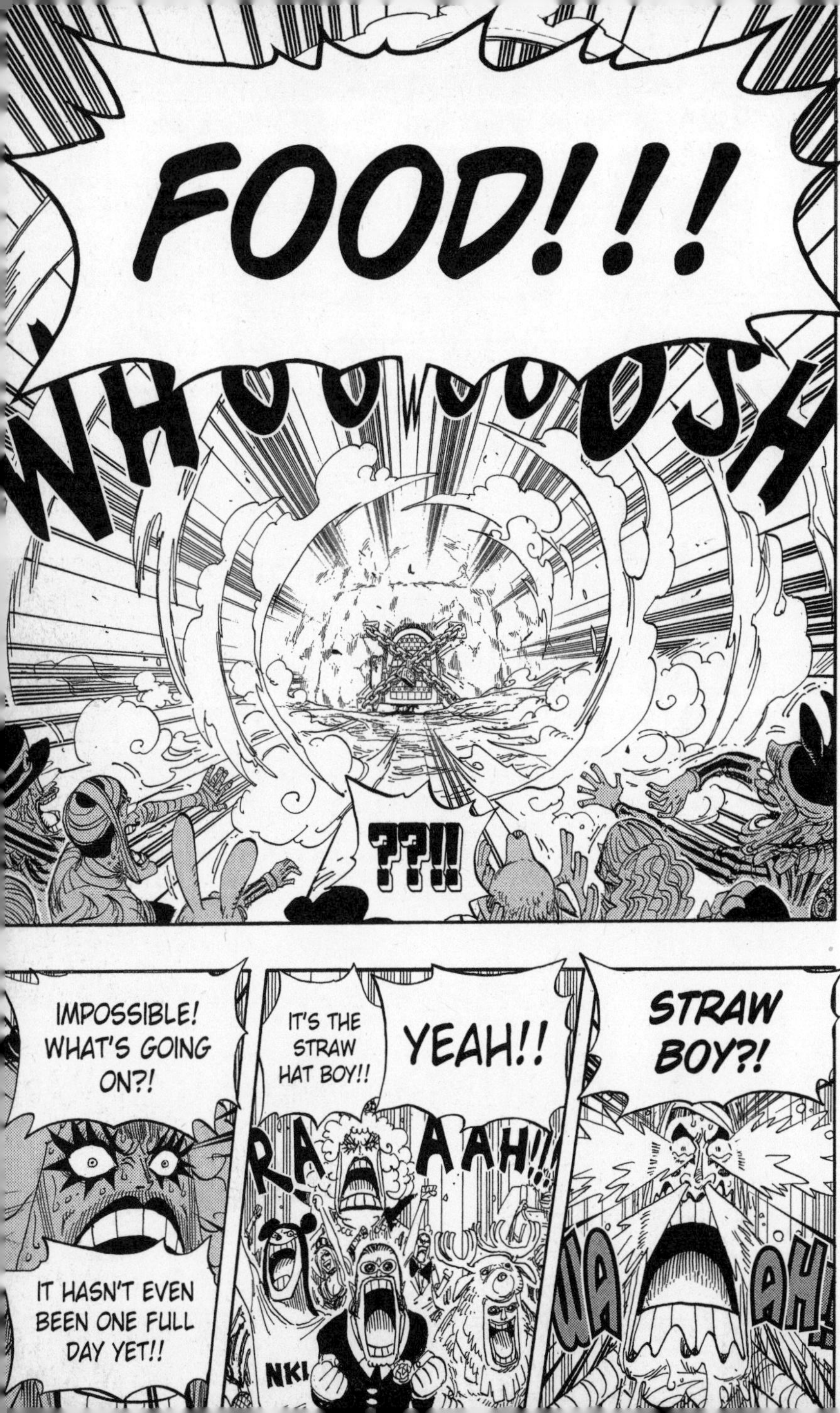
FOOD!!!
WHOOOOOOSH
??!!
STRAW BOY?!
WA
AH!
YEAH!!
IT'S THE STRAW HAT BOY!!
RA
AAH!!
NKI
IMPOSSIBLE! WHAT'S GOING ON?!
IT HASN'T EVEN BEEN ONE FULL DAY YET!!

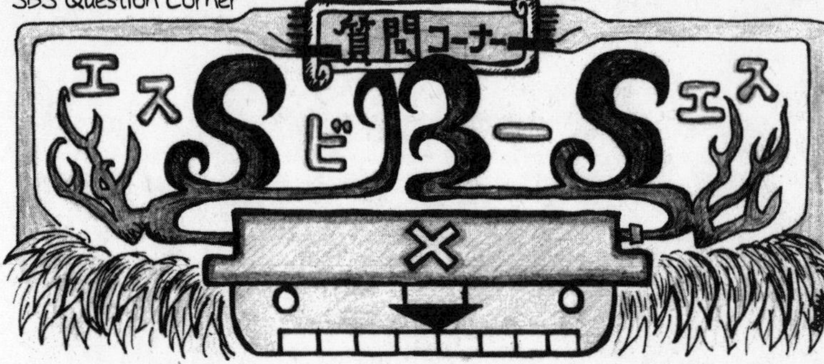
質問コーナー
エスビーエス
SBS

(Mimi 12☆29, Tokyo)

Q: Mr. Oda! Congratulations! There's going to be another *One Piece* movie, and you're writing this one, right? I can't wait! But when I saw the previews on my computer, the words "Golden Lion" jumped out at me. Is this the flying pirate Sengoku spoke of in chapter 530? The one who escaped Impel Down 20 years ago?! Is that who it is?

--12th Rookie Girl

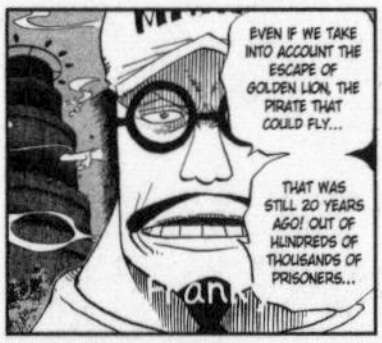
EVEN IF WE TAKE INTO ACCOUNT THE ESCAPE OF GOLDEN LION, THE PIRATE THAT COULD FLY...
THAT WAS STILL 20 YEARS AGO! OUT OF HUNDREDS OF THOUSANDS OF PRISONERS...

A: Yes, it's the very same Golden Lion. I'd planned to insert the name into the conversation between Whitebeard and Shanks in volume 45, but when I was doing the rough draft I thought it might confuse the readers if I put in too much information, so I left it out. He is one of the great pirates who wreaked havoc in the time of Roger. I didn't think I'd ever make a movie about him though. Anyway, the movie's about Golden Lion finally making his move 20 years after he escaped. There will be a preview on page 192.

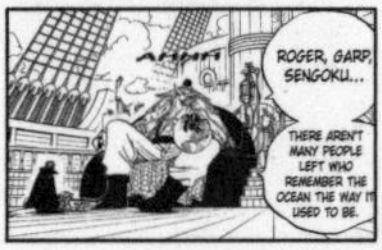
ROGER, GARP, SENGOKU...
THERE AREN'T MANY PEOPLE LEFT WHO REMEMBER THE OCEAN THE WAY IT USED TO BE.

Q: Can I get Sadie to whip me too?

--Shimizu Chamoroe

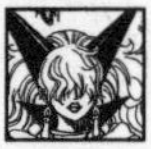

A: What are you talking about?! Is that you again, the 21-year-old guy from Aichi?! Sheriff! We have a weirdo here! No, not me! What?! I'm not allowed to wear underwear on my head?!

Q: When Oars fell and crushed the bridge in volume 48, Franky built a new one to replace it. But where does Franky keep his hammer (and other tools)? Please ask him for me!

--Roll

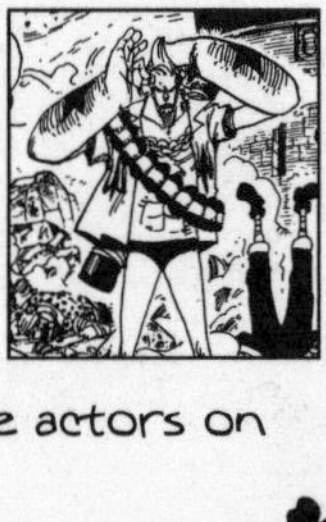

A: In your underwear, right?

Franky: **Yeah.**

A: Okay! This is the last Question Corner for this volume! But we'll be talking to some voice actors on page 166!

Chapter 539:
EMPORIO ENERGY HORMONE

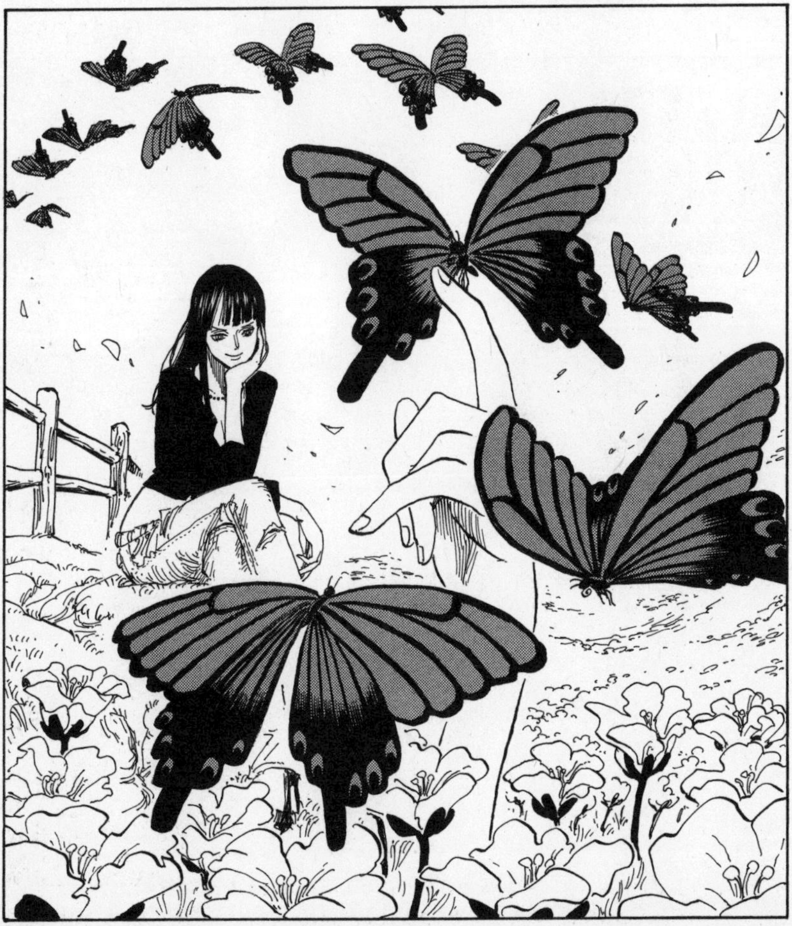

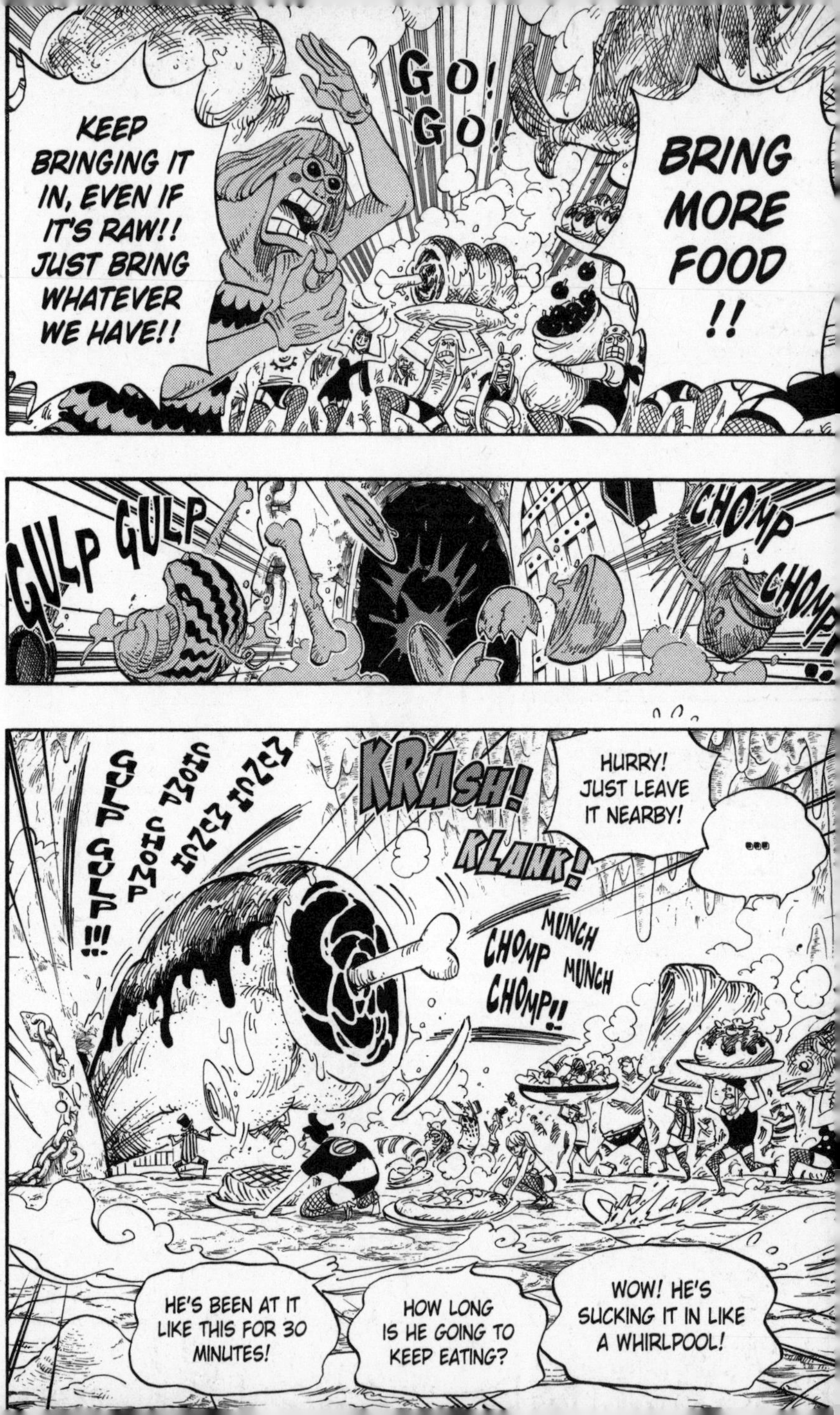
BRING MORE FOOD!!
GO! GO!
KEEP BRINGING IT IN, EVEN IF IT'S RAW!! JUST BRING WHATEVER WE HAVE!!
CHOMP CHOMP!!
GULP GULP
...
HURRY! JUST LEAVE IT NEARBY!
KRASH!
KLANK!
MUNCH MUNCH
CHOMP CHOMP!!
CHOMP CHOMP
GULP GULP!!!
WOW! HE'S SUCKING IT IN LIKE A WHIRLPOOL!
HOW LONG IS HE GOING TO KEEP EATING?
HE'S BEEN AT IT LIKE THIS FOR 30 MINUTES!

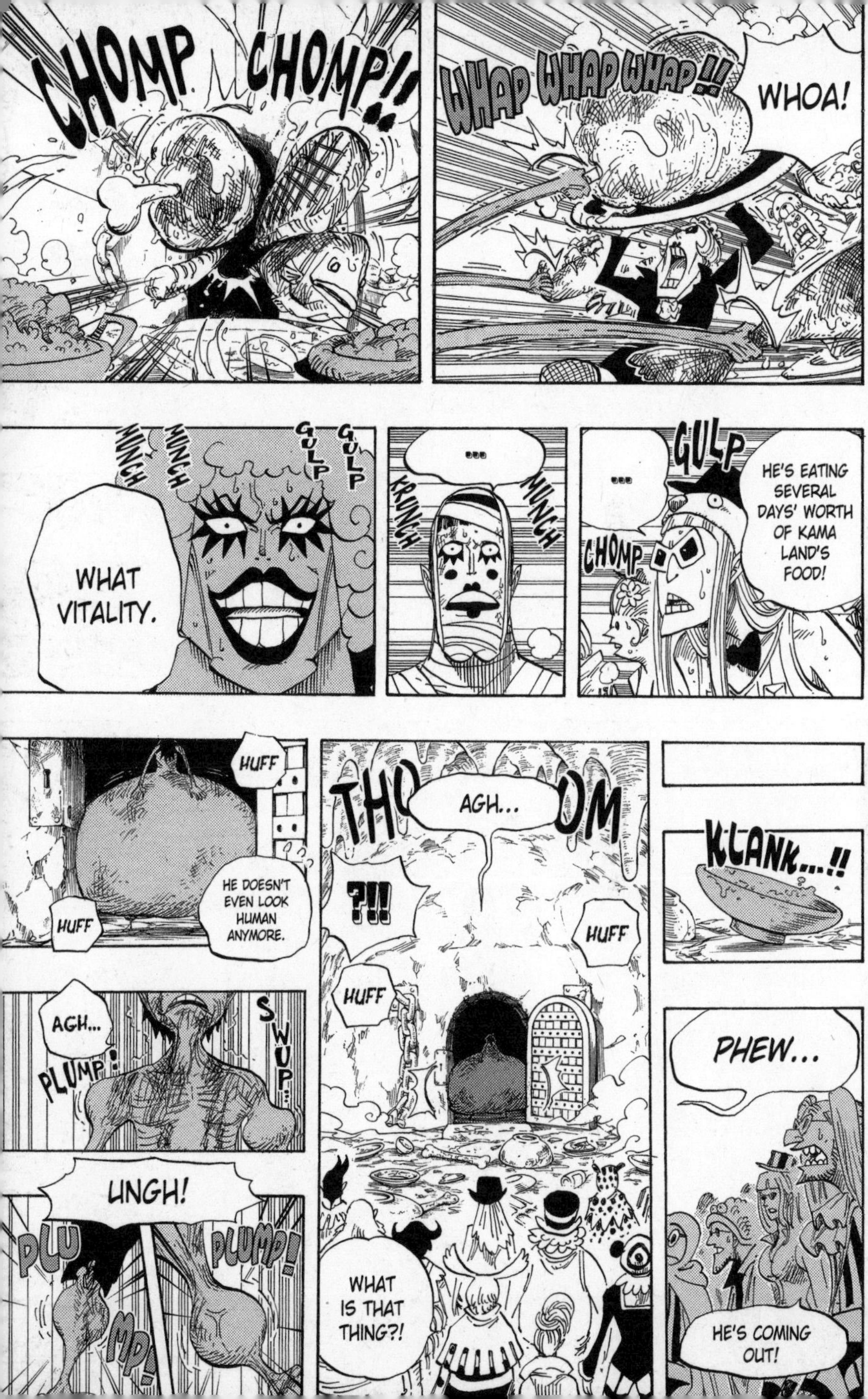

WHAP WHAP WHAP!!
WHOA!
CHOMP
CHOMP!!
GULP
HE'S EATING SEVERAL DAYS' WORTH OF KAMA LAND'S FOOD!
...
CHOMP
...
MUNCH
KRUNCH
GULP
GULP
MUNCH
MUNCH
WHAT VITALITY.
KLANK...!!
PHEW...
HE'S COMING OUT!
THO
OM
AGH...
?!!
HUFF
HUFF
WHAT IS THAT THING?!
HUFF
HE DOESN'T EVEN LOOK HUMAN ANYMORE.
HUFF
AGH...
SWUP...
PLUMP!
UNGH!
PLUMP!
PLU
MP!

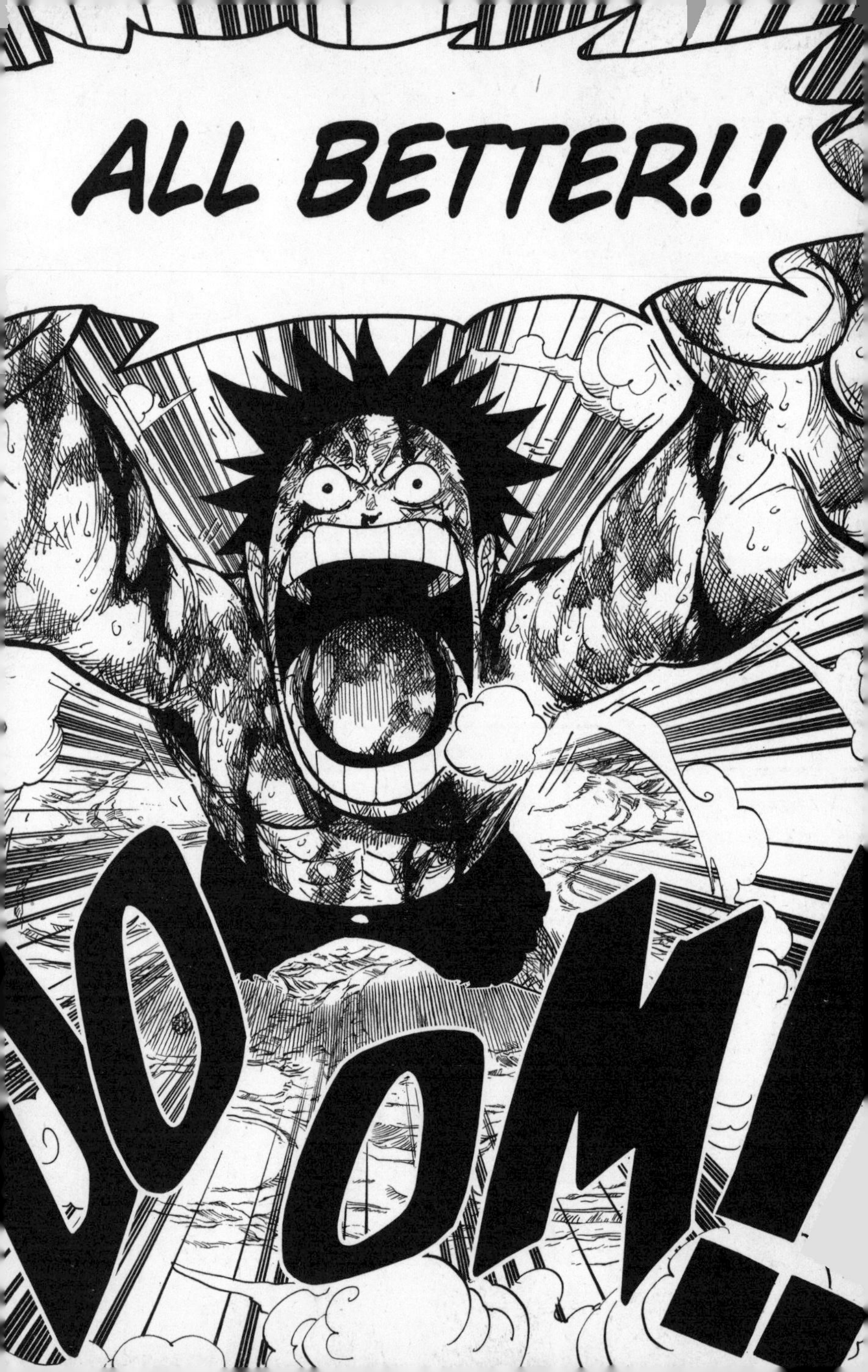
ALL BETTER!!
DOOM!!

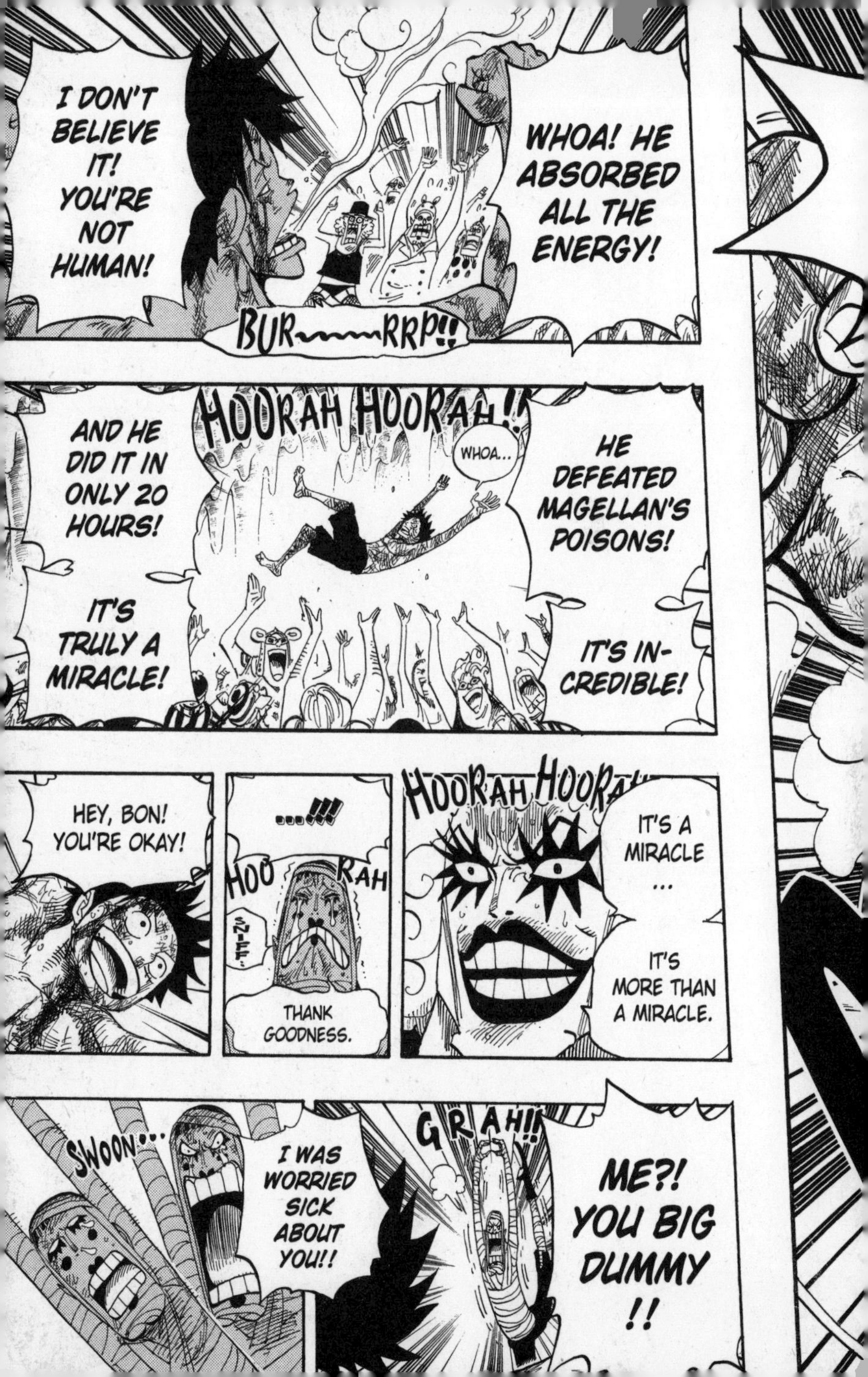
WHOA! HE ABSORBED ALL THE ENERGY!
I DON'T BELIEVE IT! YOU'RE NOT HUMAN!
BUR~~~~RRP!!
HOORAH HOORAH!!
HE DEFEATED MAGELLAN'S POISONS!
WHOA...
AND HE DID IT IN ONLY 20 HOURS!
IT'S IN-CREDIBLE!
IT'S TRULY A MIRACLE!
HOORAH HOORA
IT'S A MIRACLE ...
IT'S MORE THAN A MIRACLE.
...!!!
HOO RAH
SNIFF..
THANK GOODNESS.
HEY, BON! YOU'RE OKAY!
ME?! YOU BIG DUMMY!!
GRAH!!
I WAS WORRIED SICK ABOUT YOU!!
SWOON...

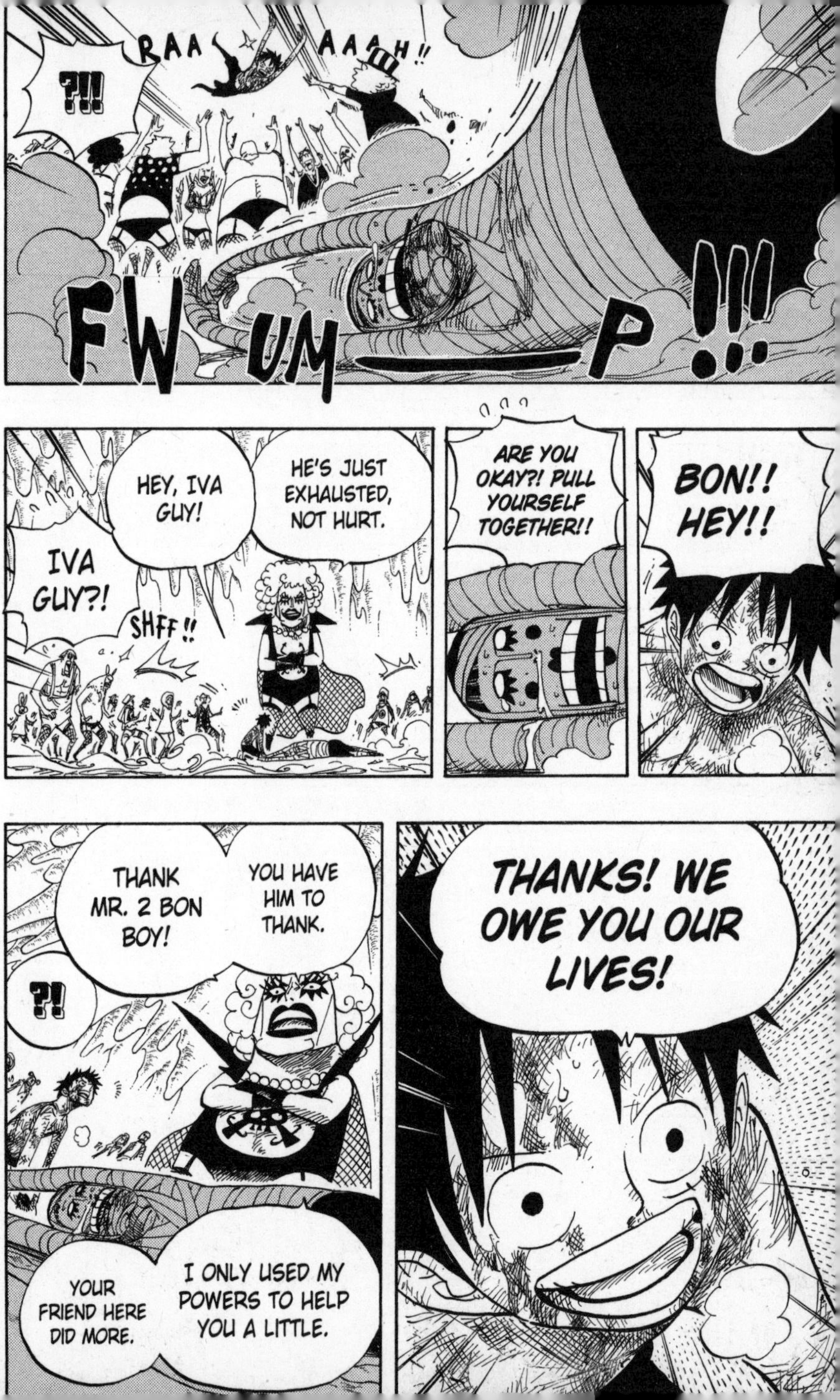
?!!
RAAA
AAAAH!!
FWUM—P!!!
BON!! HEY!!
ARE YOU OKAY?! PULL YOURSELF TOGETHER!!
HE'S JUST EXHAUSTED, NOT HURT.
HEY, IVA GUY!
IVA GUY?!
SHFF!!
THANKS! WE OWE YOU OUR LIVES!
YOU HAVE HIM TO THANK.
THANK MR. 2 BON BOY!
?!
I ONLY USED MY POWERS TO HELP YOU A LITTLE.
YOUR FRIEND HERE DID MORE.

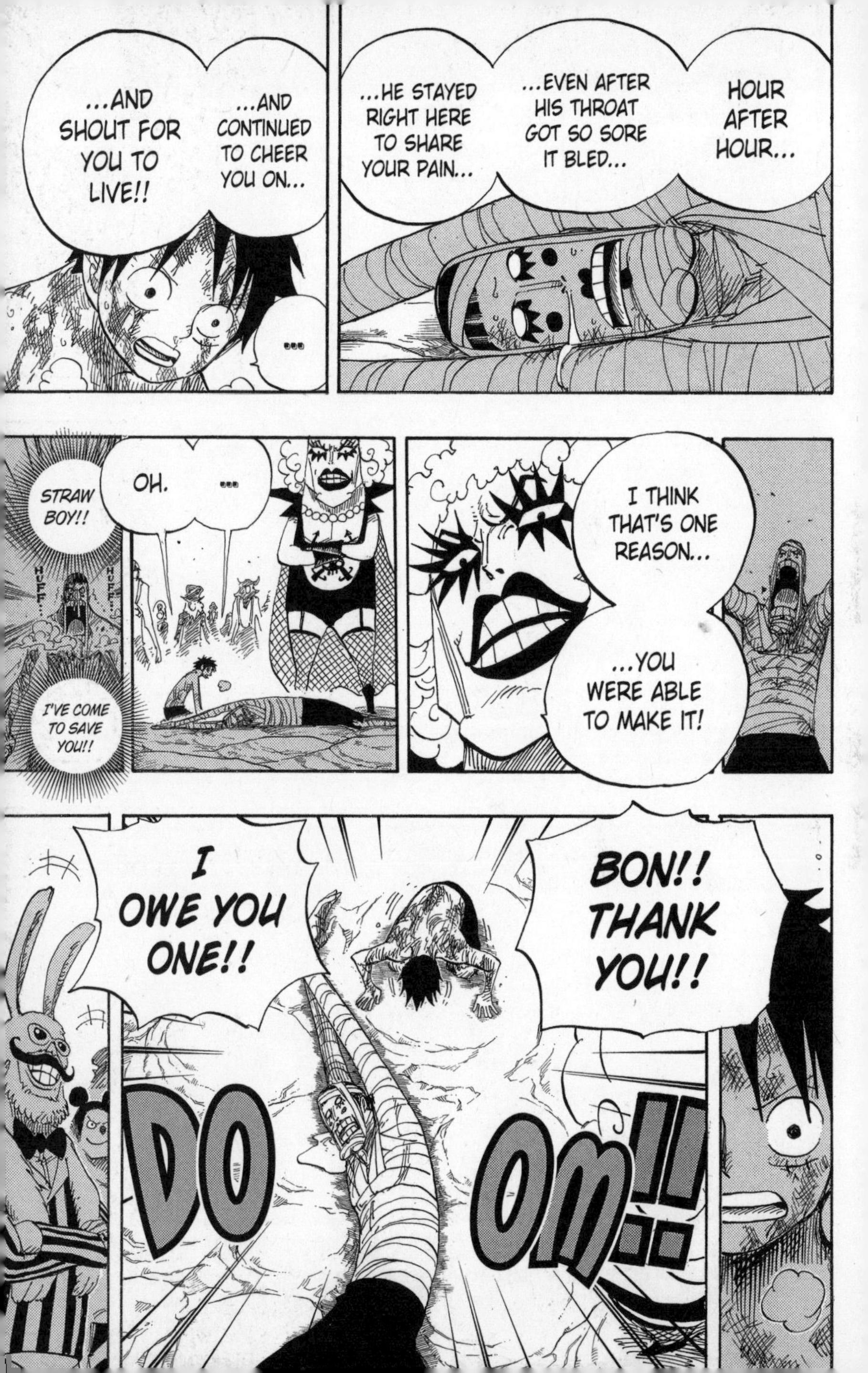
HOUR AFTER HOUR...
...EVEN AFTER HIS THROAT GOT SO SORE IT BLED...
...HE STAYED RIGHT HERE TO SHARE YOUR PAIN...
...AND CONTINUED TO CHEER YOU ON...
...AND SHOUT FOR YOU TO LIVE!!
...
I THINK THAT'S ONE REASON...
...YOU WERE ABLE TO MAKE IT!
OH. ...
STRAW BOY!!
HUFF...
HUFF...
I'VE COME TO SAVE YOU!!
BON!! THANK YOU!!
I OWE YOU ONE!!
DOOM!!

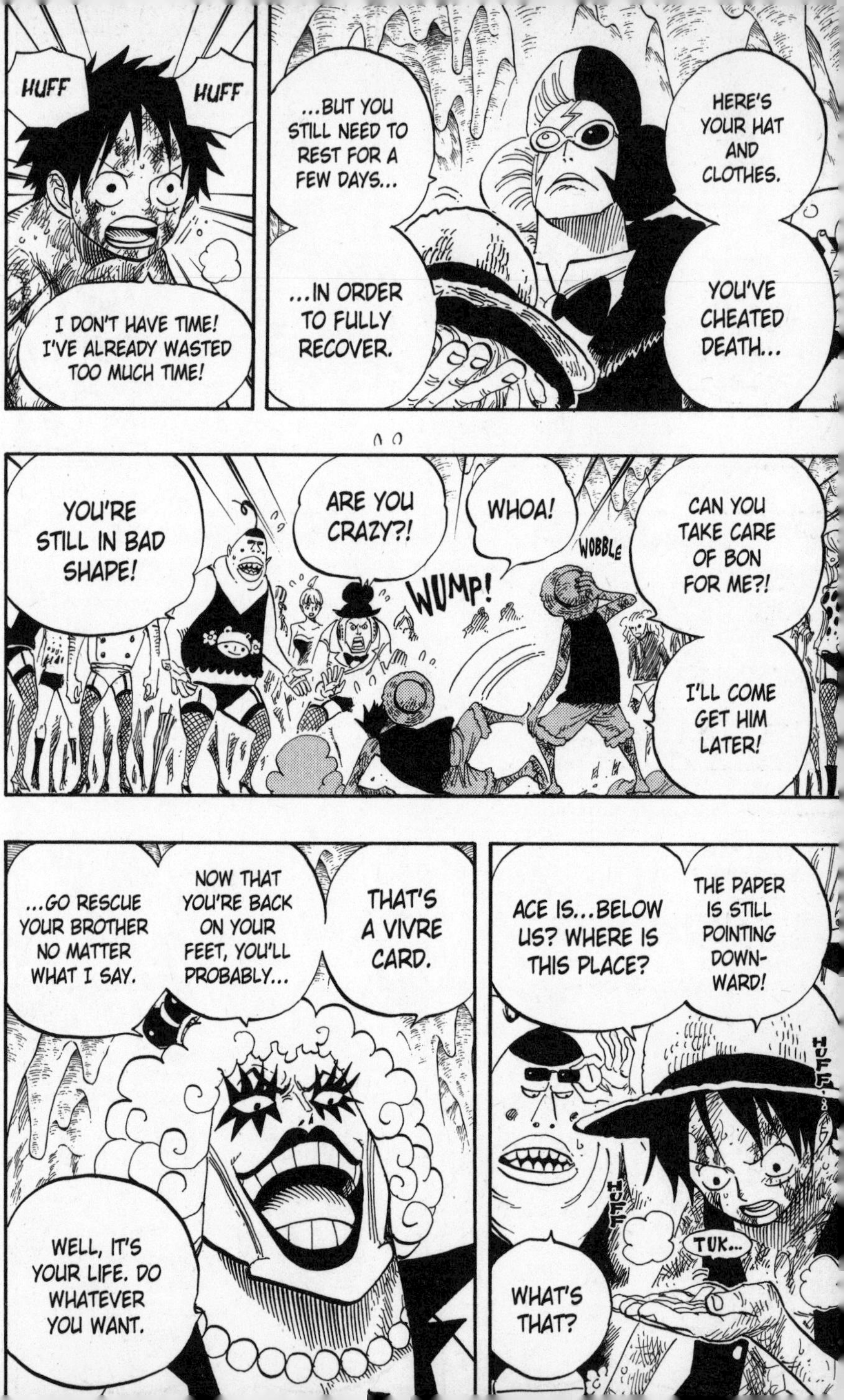
HERE'S YOUR HAT AND CLOTHES.
YOU'VE CHEATED DEATH...
...BUT YOU STILL NEED TO REST FOR A FEW DAYS...
...IN ORDER TO FULLY RECOVER.
HUFF
HUFF
I DON'T HAVE TIME! I'VE ALREADY WASTED TOO MUCH TIME!
CAN YOU TAKE CARE OF BON FOR ME?!
I'LL COME GET HIM LATER!
WOBBLE
WHOA!
WUMP!
ARE YOU CRAZY?!
YOU'RE STILL IN BAD SHAPE!
THE PAPER IS STILL POINTING DOWNWARD!
HUFF
ACE IS...BELOW US? WHERE IS THIS PLACE?
HUFF
TUK...
WHAT'S THAT?
THAT'S A VIVRE CARD.
NOW THAT YOU'RE BACK ON YOUR FEET, YOU'LL PROBABLY...
...GO RESCUE YOUR BROTHER NO MATTER WHAT I SAY.
WELL, IT'S YOUR LIFE. DO WHATEVER YOU WANT.

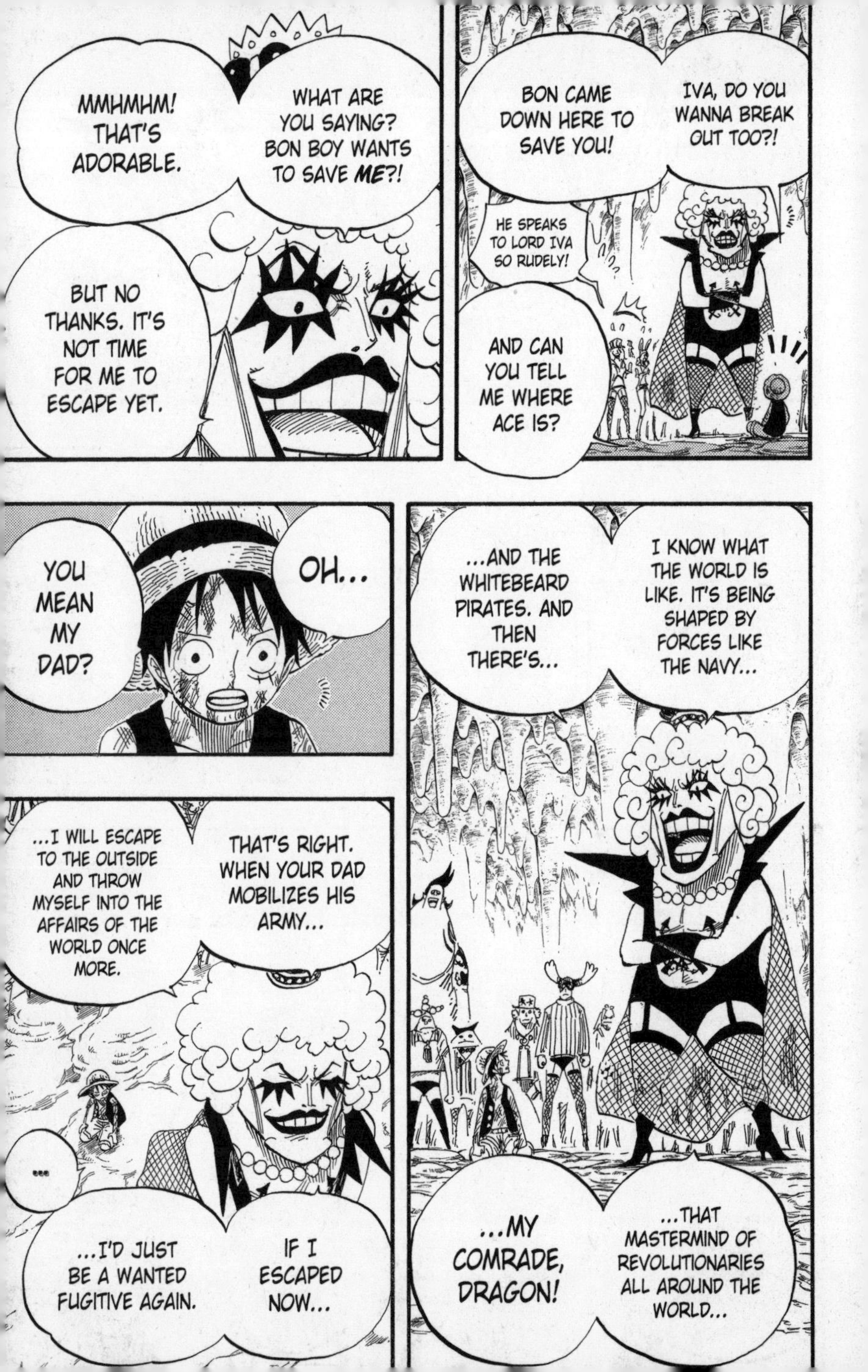
IVA, DO YOU WANNA BREAK OUT TOO?!
BON CAME DOWN HERE TO SAVE YOU!
HE SPEAKS TO LORD IVA SO RUDELY!
AND CAN YOU TELL ME WHERE ACE IS?
WHAT ARE YOU SAYING? BON BOY WANTS TO SAVE ME?!
MMHMHM! THAT'S ADORABLE.
BUT NO THANKS. IT'S NOT TIME FOR ME TO ESCAPE YET.
I KNOW WHAT THE WORLD IS LIKE. IT'S BEING SHAPED BY FORCES LIKE THE NAVY...
...AND THE WHITEBEARD PIRATES. AND THEN THERE'S...
...THAT MASTERMIND OF REVOLUTIONARIES ALL AROUND THE WORLD...
...MY COMRADE, DRAGON!
OH...
YOU MEAN MY DAD?
THAT'S RIGHT. WHEN YOUR DAD MOBILIZES HIS ARMY...
...I WILL ESCAPE TO THE OUTSIDE AND THROW MYSELF INTO THE AFFAIRS OF THE WORLD ONCE MORE.
...
IF I ESCAPED NOW...
...I'D JUST BE A WANTED FUGITIVE AGAIN.

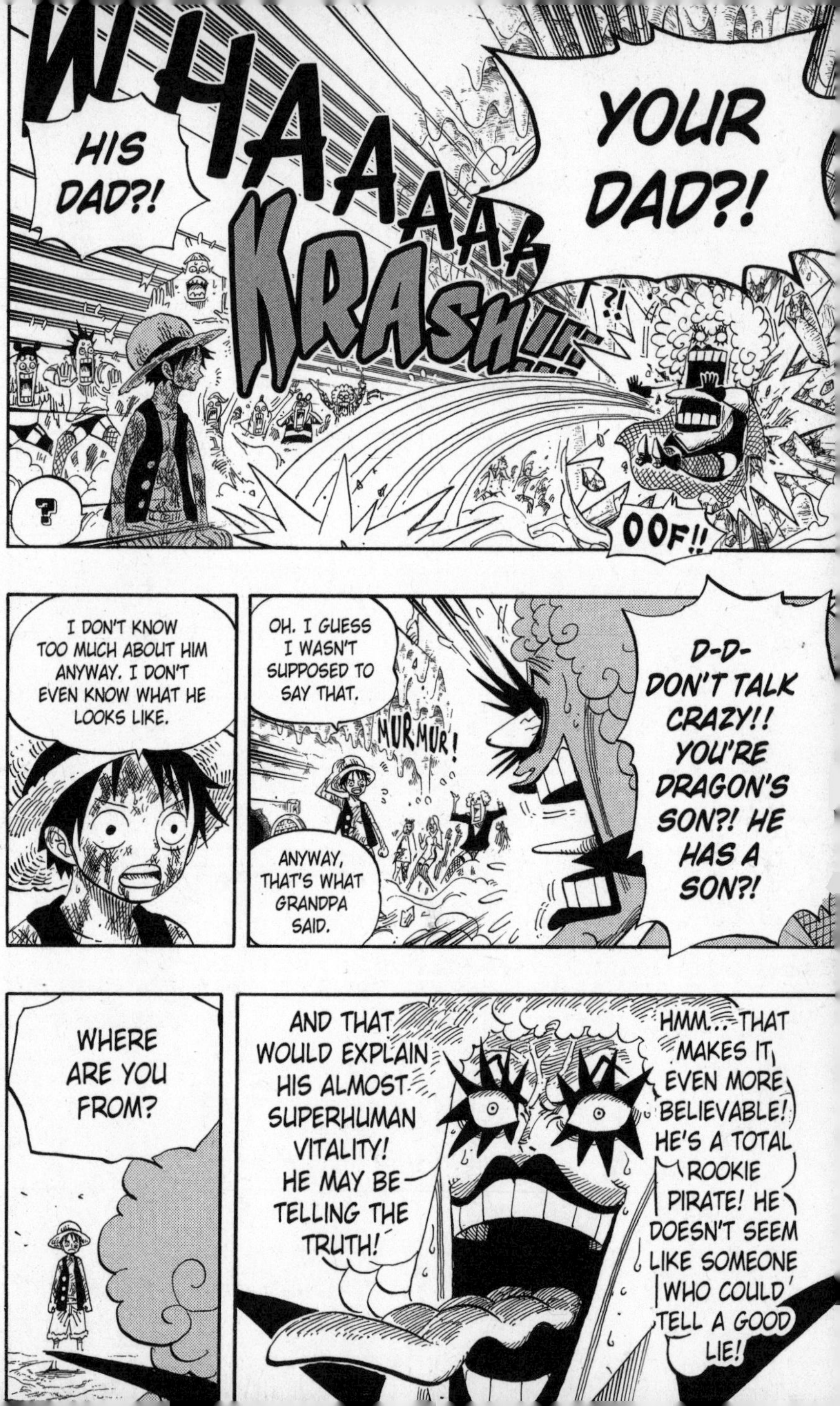
YOUR DAD?!
WHAAAAAK
KRASH!!!
HIS DAD?!
?!
OOF!!
?
D-D-DON'T TALK CRAZY!! YOU'RE DRAGON'S SON?! HE HAS A SON?!
OH. I GUESS I WASN'T SUPPOSED TO SAY THAT.
MURMUR!
ANYWAY, THAT'S WHAT GRANDPA SAID.
I DON'T KNOW TOO MUCH ABOUT HIM ANYWAY. I DON'T EVEN KNOW WHAT HE LOOKS LIKE.
HMM... THAT MAKES IT EVEN MORE BELIEVABLE! HE'S A TOTAL ROOKIE PIRATE! HE DOESN'T SEEM LIKE SOMEONE WHO COULD TELL A GOOD LIE!
AND THAT WOULD EXPLAIN HIS ALMOST SUPERHUMAN VITALITY! HE MAY BE TELLING THE TRUTH!
WHERE ARE YOU FROM?

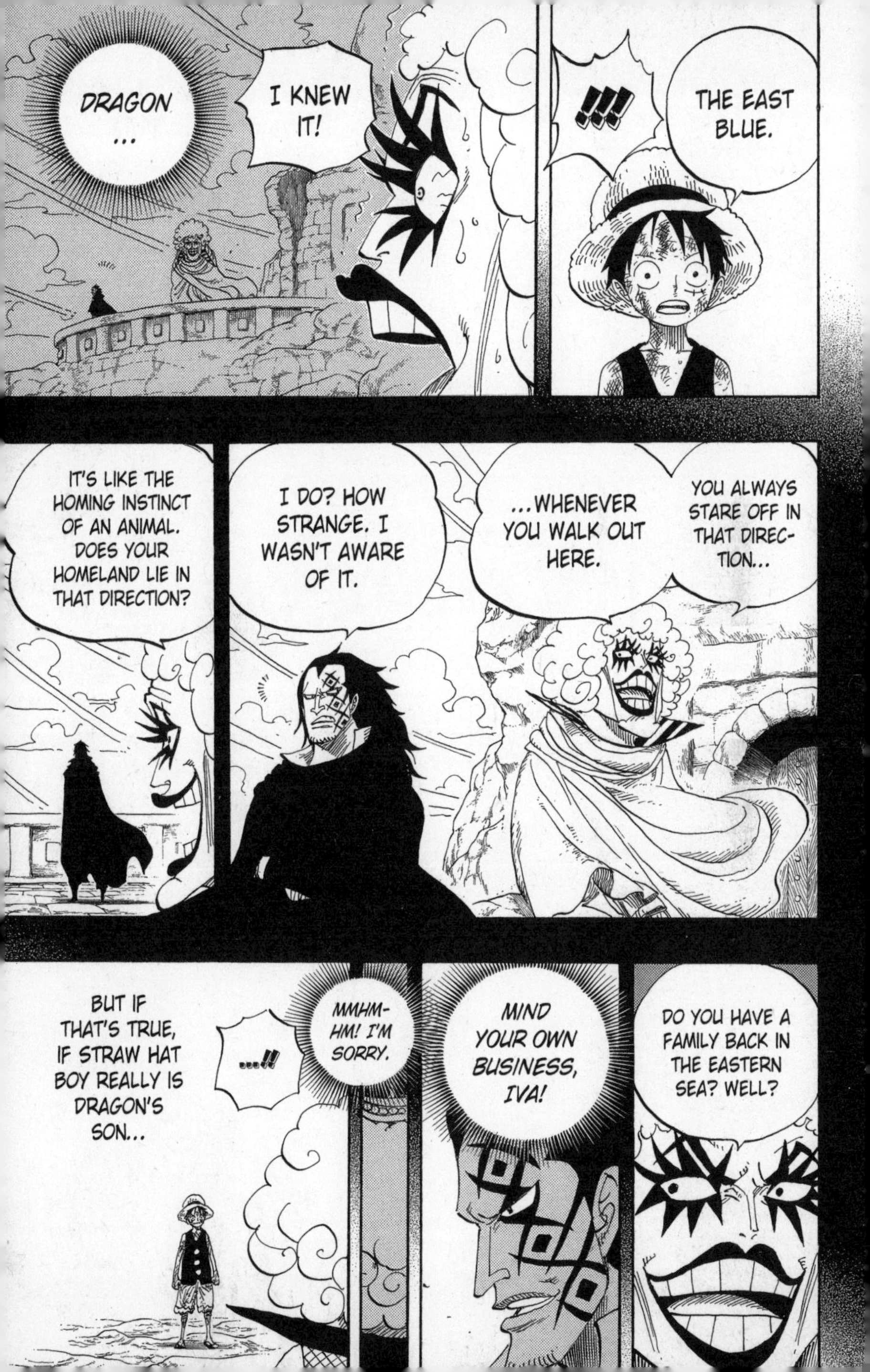
THE EAST BLUE.
!!!
I KNEW IT!
DRAGON ...
YOU ALWAYS STARE OFF IN THAT DIREC-TION...
...WHENEVER YOU WALK OUT HERE.
I DO? HOW STRANGE. I WASN'T AWARE OF IT.
IT'S LIKE THE HOMING INSTINCT OF AN ANIMAL. DOES YOUR HOMELAND LIE IN THAT DIRECTION?
DO YOU HAVE A FAMILY BACK IN THE EASTERN SEA? WELL?
MIND YOUR OWN BUSINESS, IVA!
MMHM-HM! I'M SORRY.
...!!
BUT IF THAT'S TRUE, IF STRAW HAT BOY REALLY IS DRAGON'S SON...

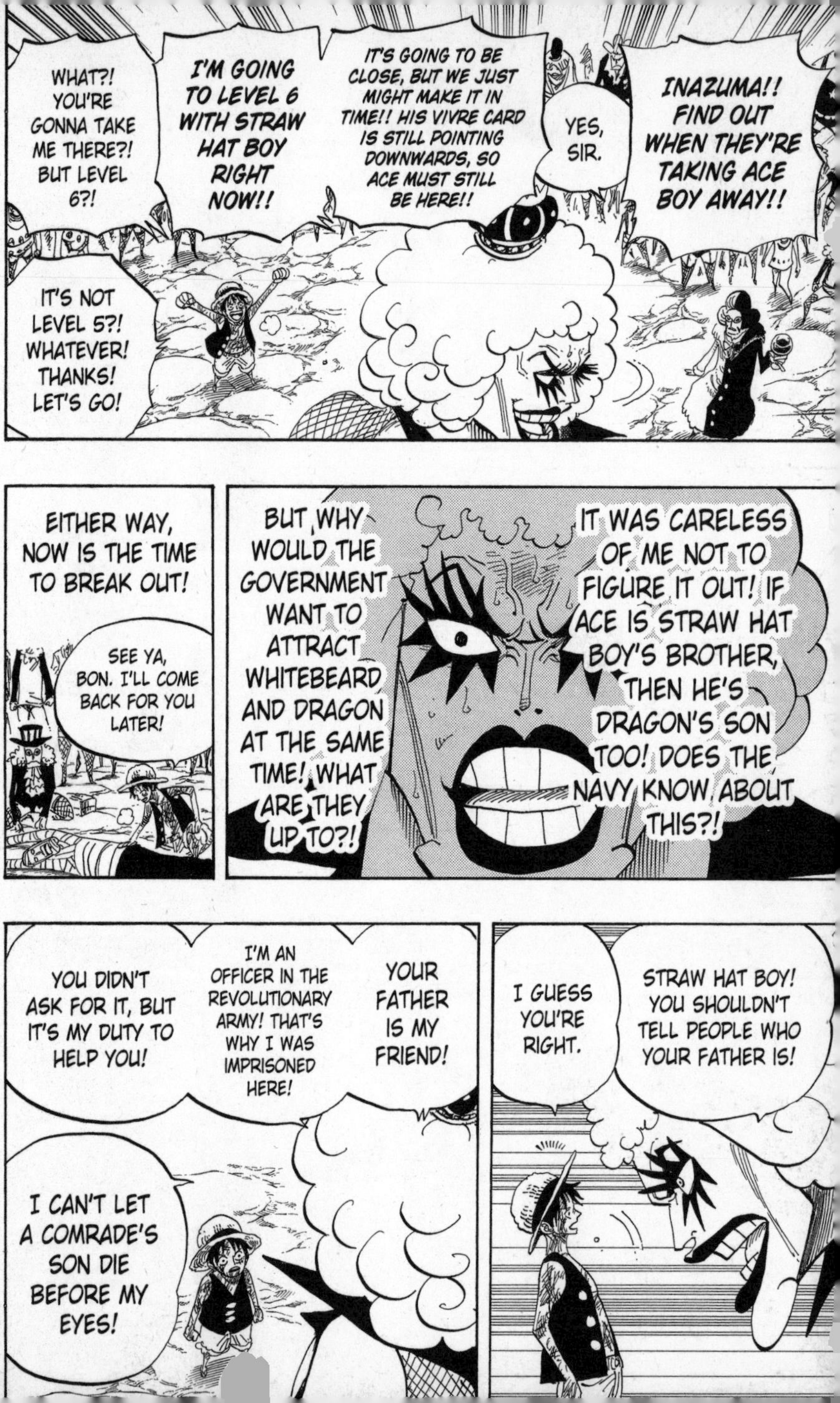
INAZUMA!! FIND OUT WHEN THEY'RE TAKING ACE BOY AWAY!!
YES, SIR.
IT'S GOING TO BE CLOSE, BUT WE JUST MIGHT MAKE IT IN TIME!! HIS VIVRE CARD IS STILL POINTING DOWNWARDS, SO ACE MUST STILL BE HERE!!
I'M GOING TO LEVEL 6 WITH STRAW HAT BOY RIGHT NOW!!
WHAT?! YOU'RE GONNA TAKE ME THERE?! BUT LEVEL 6?!
IT'S NOT LEVEL 5?! WHATEVER! THANKS! LET'S GO!
IT WAS CARELESS OF ME NOT TO FIGURE IT OUT! IF ACE IS STRAW HAT BOY'S BROTHER, THEN HE'S DRAGON'S SON TOO! DOES THE NAVY KNOW ABOUT THIS?!
BUT WHY WOULD THE GOVERNMENT WANT TO ATTRACT WHITEBEARD AND DRAGON AT THE SAME TIME! WHAT ARE THEY UP TO?!
EITHER WAY, NOW IS THE TIME TO BREAK OUT!
SEE YA, BON. I'LL COME BACK FOR YOU LATER!
STRAW HAT BOY! YOU SHOULDN'T TELL PEOPLE WHO YOUR FATHER IS!
I GUESS YOU'RE RIGHT.
YOUR FATHER IS MY FRIEND!
I'M AN OFFICER IN THE REVOLUTIONARY ARMY! THAT'S WHY I WAS IMPRISONED HERE!
YOU DIDN'T ASK FOR IT, BUT IT'S MY DUTY TO HELP YOU!
I CAN'T LET A COMRADE'S SON DIE BEFORE MY EYES!

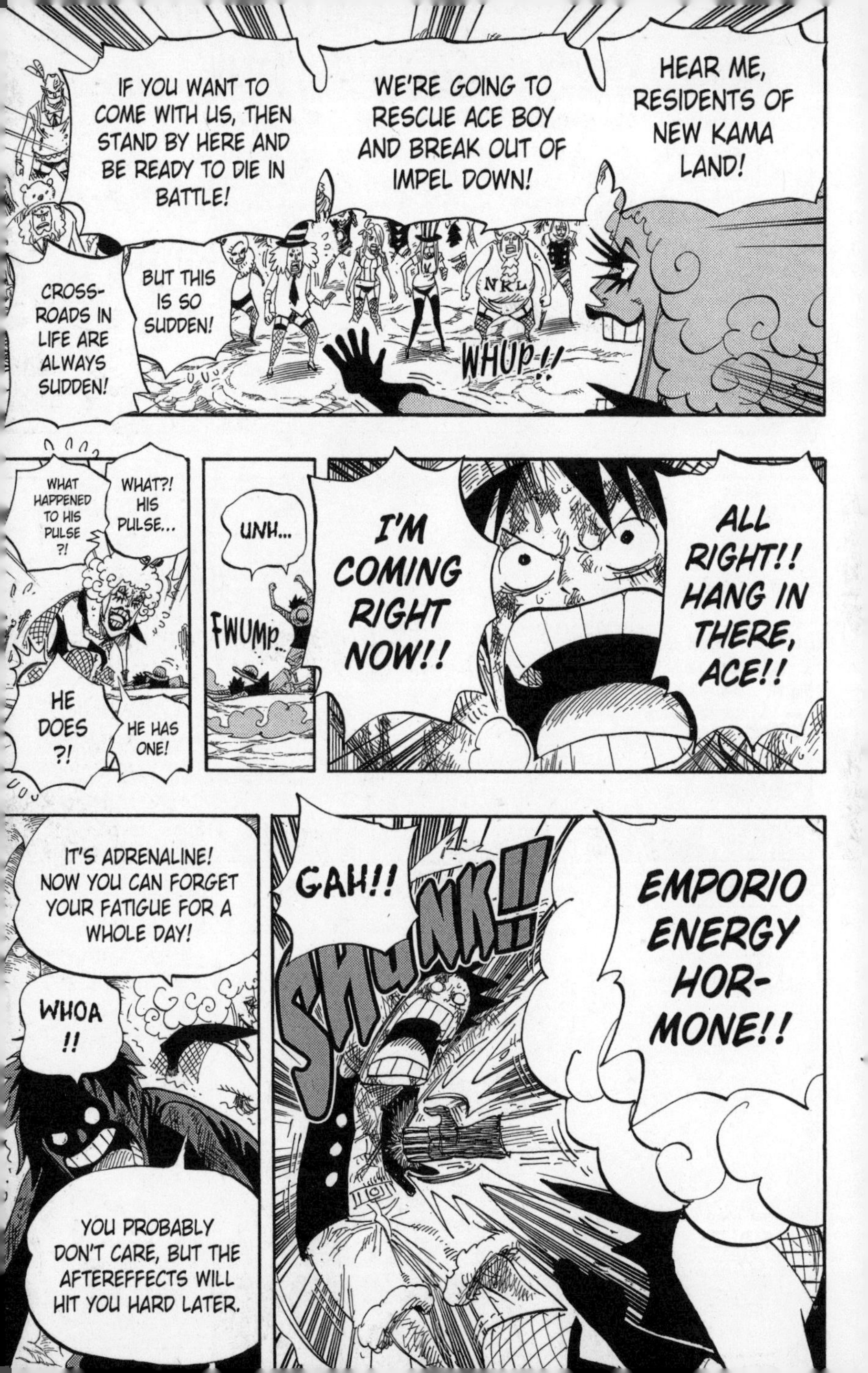
HEAR ME, RESIDENTS OF NEW KAMA LAND!
WE'RE GOING TO RESCUE ACE BOY AND BREAK OUT OF IMPEL DOWN!
IF YOU WANT TO COME WITH US, THEN STAND BY HERE AND BE READY TO DIE IN BATTLE!
WHUP!!
NKL
BUT THIS IS SO SUDDEN!
CROSS-ROADS IN LIFE ARE ALWAYS SUDDEN!
ALL RIGHT!! HANG IN THERE, ACE!!
I'M COMING RIGHT NOW!!
UNH...
FWUMP..
WHAT?! HIS PULSE...
WHAT HAPPENED TO HIS PULSE ?!
HE HAS ONE!
HE DOES ?!
EMPORIO ENERGY HOR-MONE!!
SHUNK!!
GAH!!
IT'S ADRENALINE! NOW YOU CAN FORGET YOUR FATIGUE FOR A WHOLE DAY!
WHOA !!
YOU PROBABLY DON'T CARE, BUT THE AFTEREFFECTS WILL HIT YOU HARD LATER.

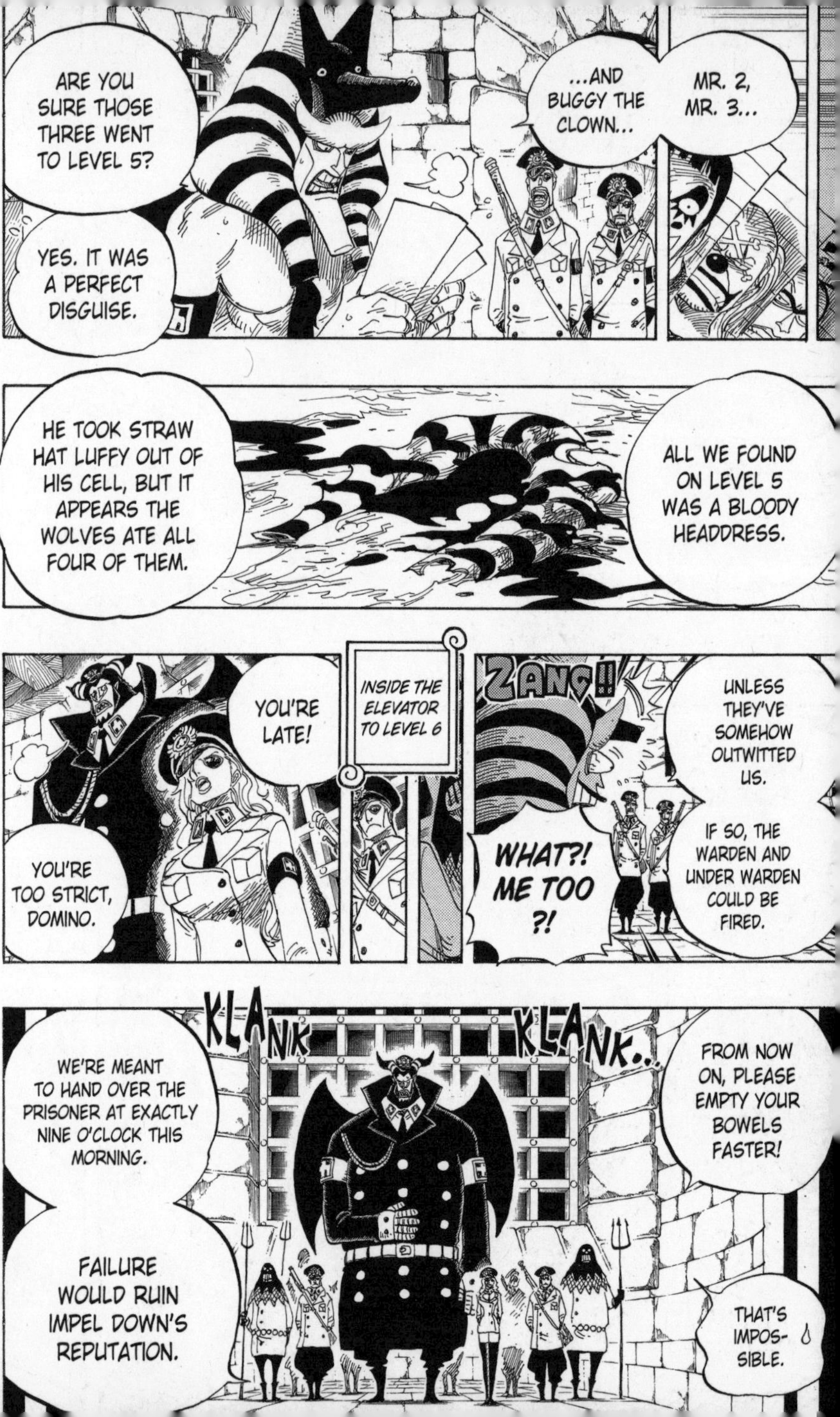
MR. 2, MR. 3...
...AND BUGGY THE CLOWN...
ARE YOU SURE THOSE THREE WENT TO LEVEL 5?
YES. IT WAS A PERFECT DISGUISE.
ALL WE FOUND ON LEVEL 5 WAS A BLOODY HEADDRESS.
HE TOOK STRAW HAT LUFFY OUT OF HIS CELL, BUT IT APPEARS THE WOLVES ATE ALL FOUR OF THEM.
ZANG!!
UNLESS THEY'VE SOMEHOW OUTWITTED US.
IF SO, THE WARDEN AND UNDER WARDEN COULD BE FIRED.
WHAT?! ME TOO ?!
INSIDE THE ELEVATOR TO LEVEL 6
YOU'RE LATE!
YOU'RE TOO STRICT, DOMINO.
KLANK
KLANK...
FROM NOW ON, PLEASE EMPTY YOUR BOWELS FASTER!
WE'RE MEANT TO HAND OVER THE PRISONER AT EXACTLY NINE O'CLOCK THIS MORNING.
FAILURE WOULD RUIN IMPEL DOWN'S REPUTATION.
THAT'S IMPOS-SIBLE.

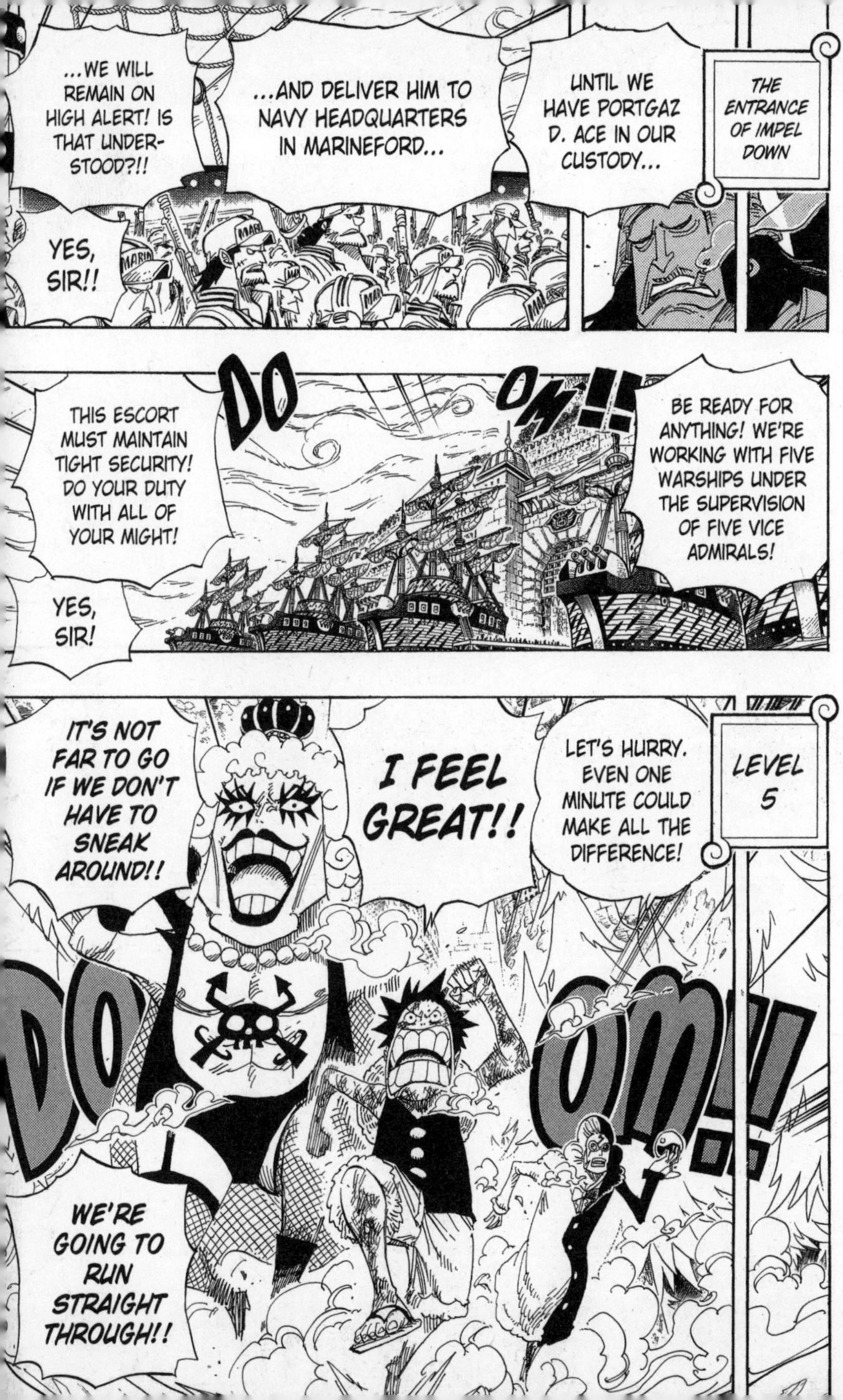
THE ENTRANCE OF IMPEL DOWN
UNTIL WE HAVE PORTGAZ D. ACE IN OUR CUSTODY...
...AND DELIVER HIM TO NAVY HEADQUARTERS IN MARINEFORD...
...WE WILL REMAIN ON HIGH ALERT! IS THAT UNDER-STOOD?!!
YES, SIR!!
DO OM!!
BE READY FOR ANYTHING! WE'RE WORKING WITH FIVE WARSHIPS UNDER THE SUPERVISION OF FIVE VICE ADMIRALS!
THIS ESCORT MUST MAINTAIN TIGHT SECURITY! DO YOUR DUTY WITH ALL OF YOUR MIGHT!
YES, SIR!
LEVEL 5
LET'S HURRY. EVEN ONE MINUTE COULD MAKE ALL THE DIFFERENCE!
I FEEL GREAT!!
IT'S NOT FAR TO GO IF WE DON'T HAVE TO SNEAK AROUND!!
DO OM!!
WE'RE GOING TO RUN STRAIGHT THROUGH!!

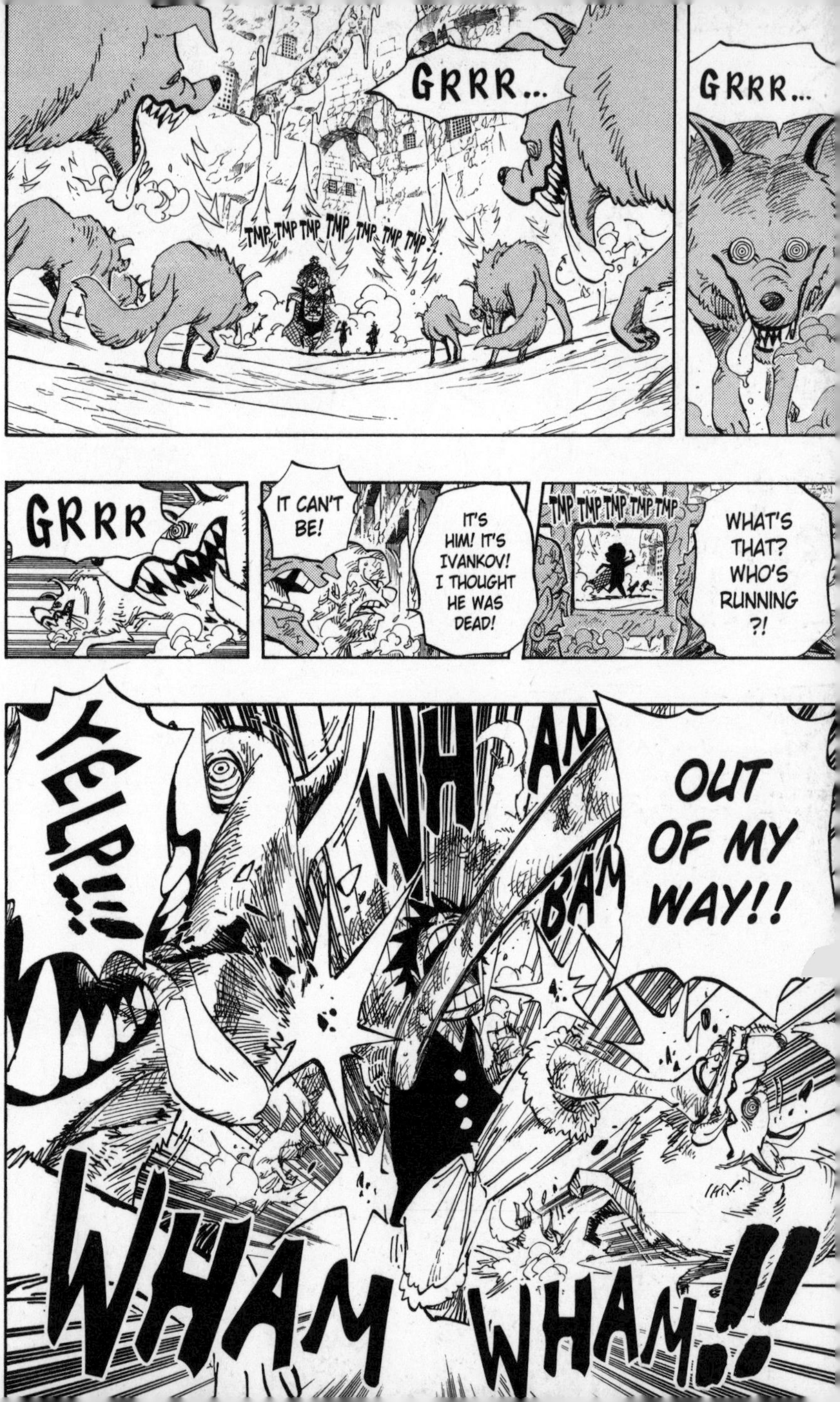
GRRR...
GRRR...
TMP TMP TMP TMP TMP TMP TMP
TMP TMP TMP TMP TMP
WHAT'S THAT? WHO'S RUNNING ?!
IT'S HIM! IT'S IVANKOV! I THOUGHT HE WAS DEAD!
IT CAN'T BE!
GRRR
OUT OF MY WAY!!
WHAM
BAM
YELP!!!
WHAM WHAM!!

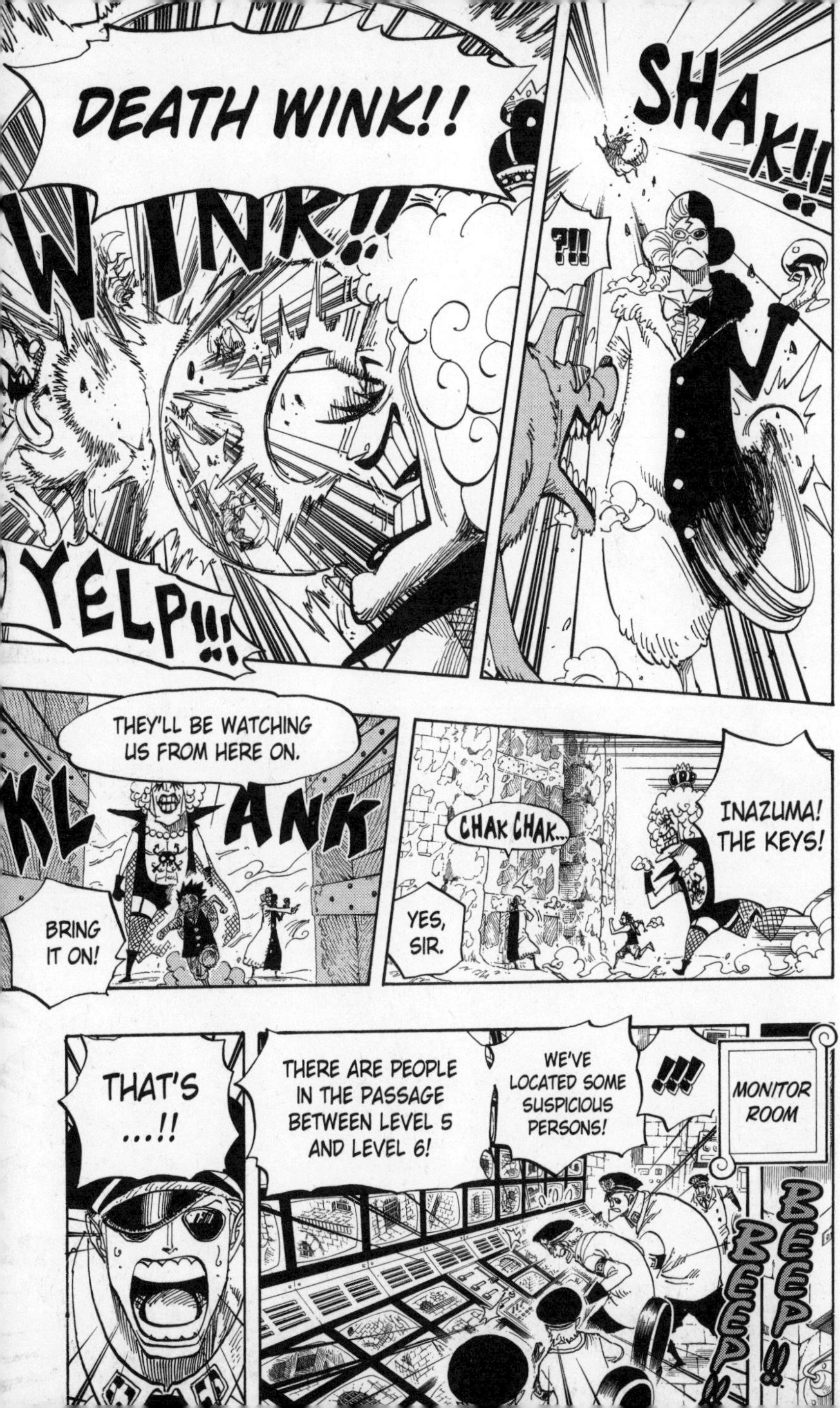
SHAKI!!
?!!
DEATH WINK!!
WINK!!
YELP!!!
INAZUMA! THE KEYS!
CHAK CHAK...
YES, SIR.
THEY'LL BE WATCHING US FROM HERE ON.
KLANK
BRING IT ON!
MONITOR ROOM
!!!
WE'VE LOCATED SOME SUSPICIOUS PERSONS!
THERE ARE PEOPLE IN THE PASSAGE BETWEEN LEVEL 5 AND LEVEL 6!
BEEP
BEEP!!
THAT'S ...!!

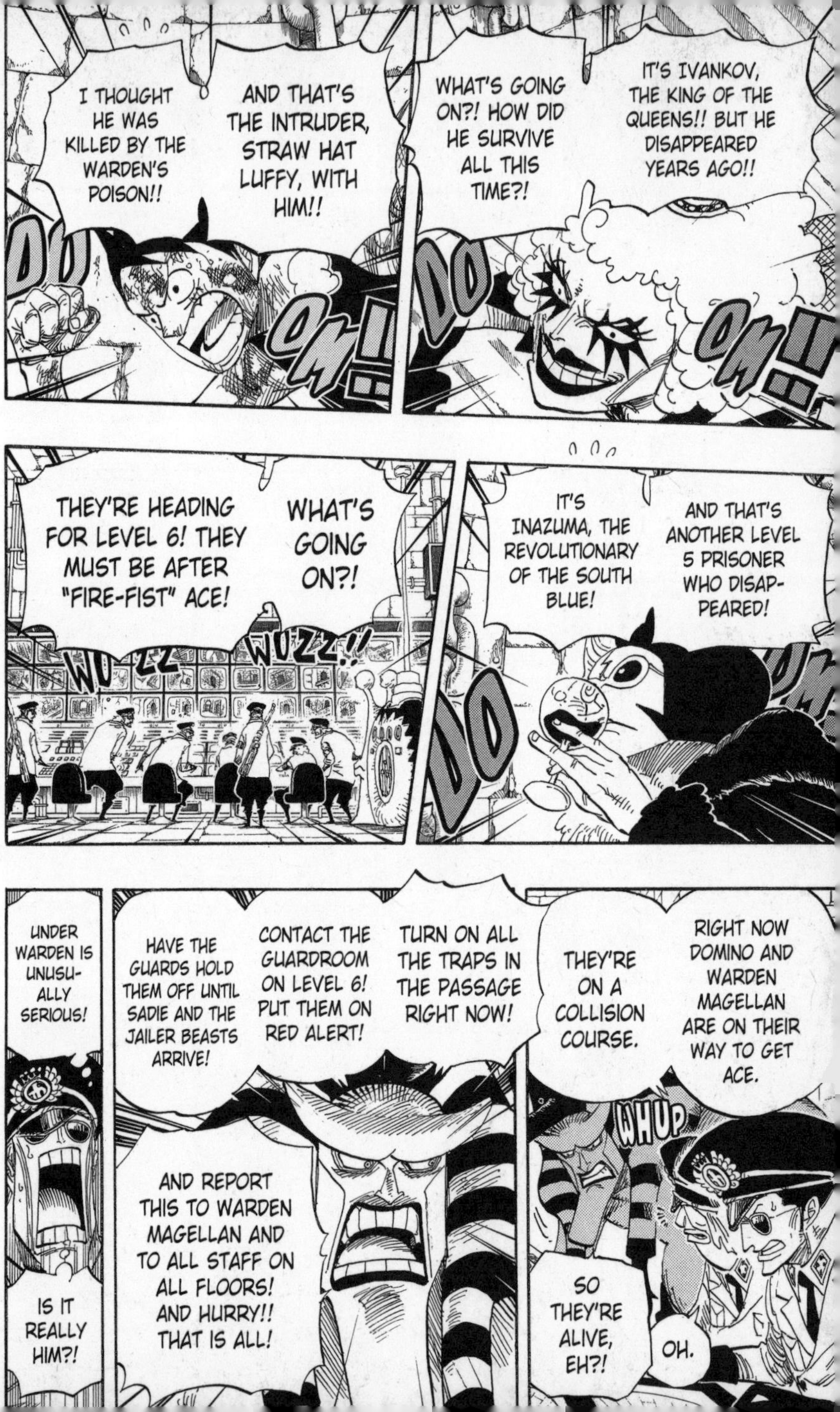
IT'S IVANKOV, THE KING OF THE QUEENS!! BUT HE DISAPPEARED YEARS AGO!!
WHAT'S GOING ON?! HOW DID HE SURVIVE ALL THIS TIME?!
DOOON!!
AND THAT'S THE INTRUDER, STRAW HAT LUFFY, WITH HIM!!
I THOUGHT HE WAS KILLED BY THE WARDEN'S POISON!!
DOOON!!
AND THAT'S ANOTHER LEVEL 5 PRISONER WHO DISAPPEARED!
IT'S INAZUMA, THE REVOLUTIONARY OF THE SOUTH BLUE!
DOO
WHAT'S GOING ON?!
THEY'RE HEADING FOR LEVEL 6! THEY MUST BE AFTER "FIRE-FIST" ACE!
WUZZ!!
WUZZ
RIGHT NOW DOMINO AND WARDEN MAGELLAN ARE ON THEIR WAY TO GET ACE.
THEY'RE ON A COLLISION COURSE.
WHUP
OH.
SO THEY'RE ALIVE, EH?!
TURN ON ALL THE TRAPS IN THE PASSAGE RIGHT NOW!
CONTACT THE GUARDROOM ON LEVEL 6! PUT THEM ON RED ALERT!
HAVE THE GUARDS HOLD THEM OFF UNTIL SADIE AND THE JAILER BEASTS ARRIVE!
AND REPORT THIS TO WARDEN MAGELLAN AND TO ALL STAFF ON ALL FLOORS! AND HURRY!! THAT IS ALL!
UNDER WARDEN IS UNUSUALLY SERIOUS!
IS IT REALLY HIM?!

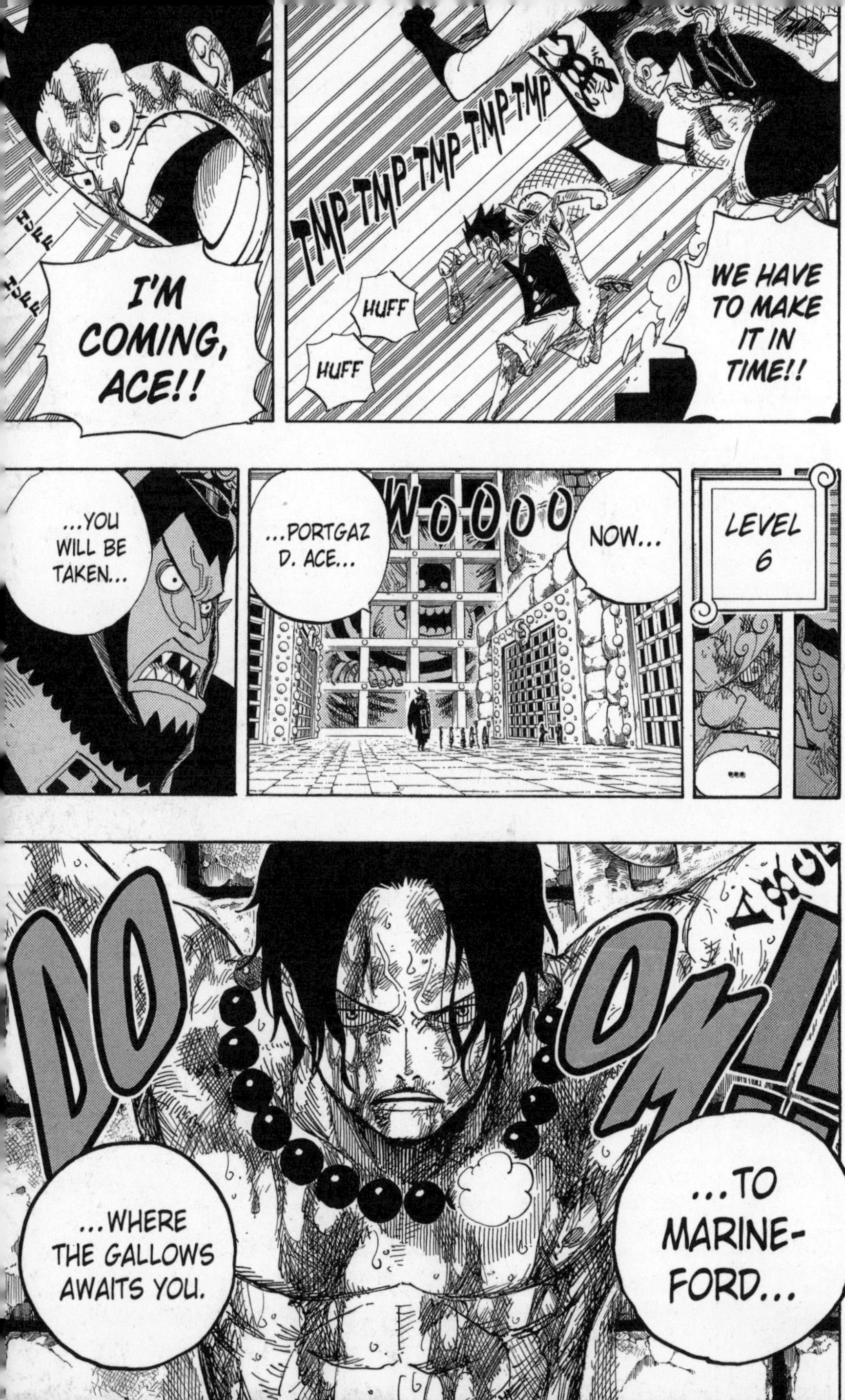
TMP TMP TMP TMP TMP TMP
WE HAVE TO MAKE IT IN TIME!!
HUFF
HUFF
HUFF
HUFF
I'M COMING, ACE!!
LEVEL 6
...
NOW...
WOOOO
...PORTGAZ D. ACE...
...YOU WILL BE TAKEN...
DOOM!
...TO MARINE-FORD...
...WHERE THE GALLOWS AWAITS YOU.

LEVEL 6: INFINITE HELL

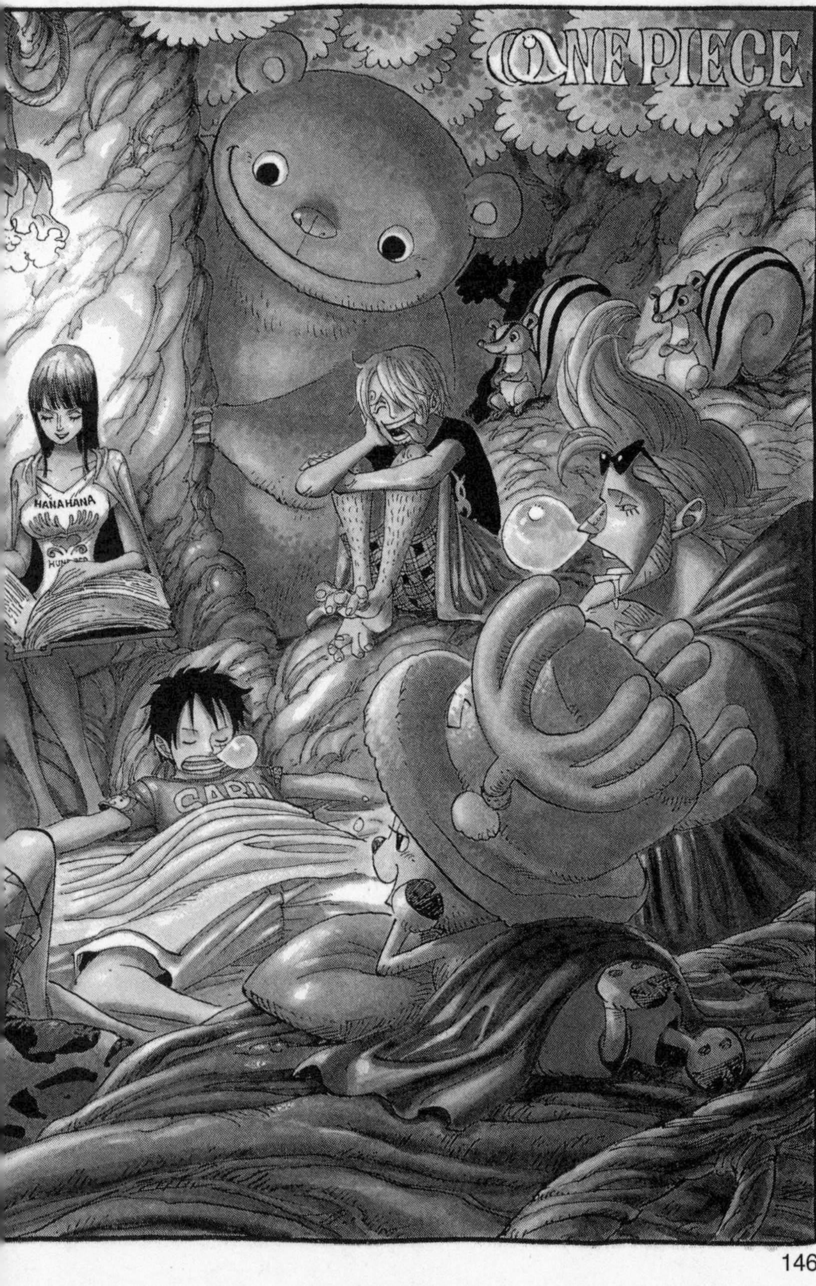
ONE PIECE
HANAHANA

Chapter 540:

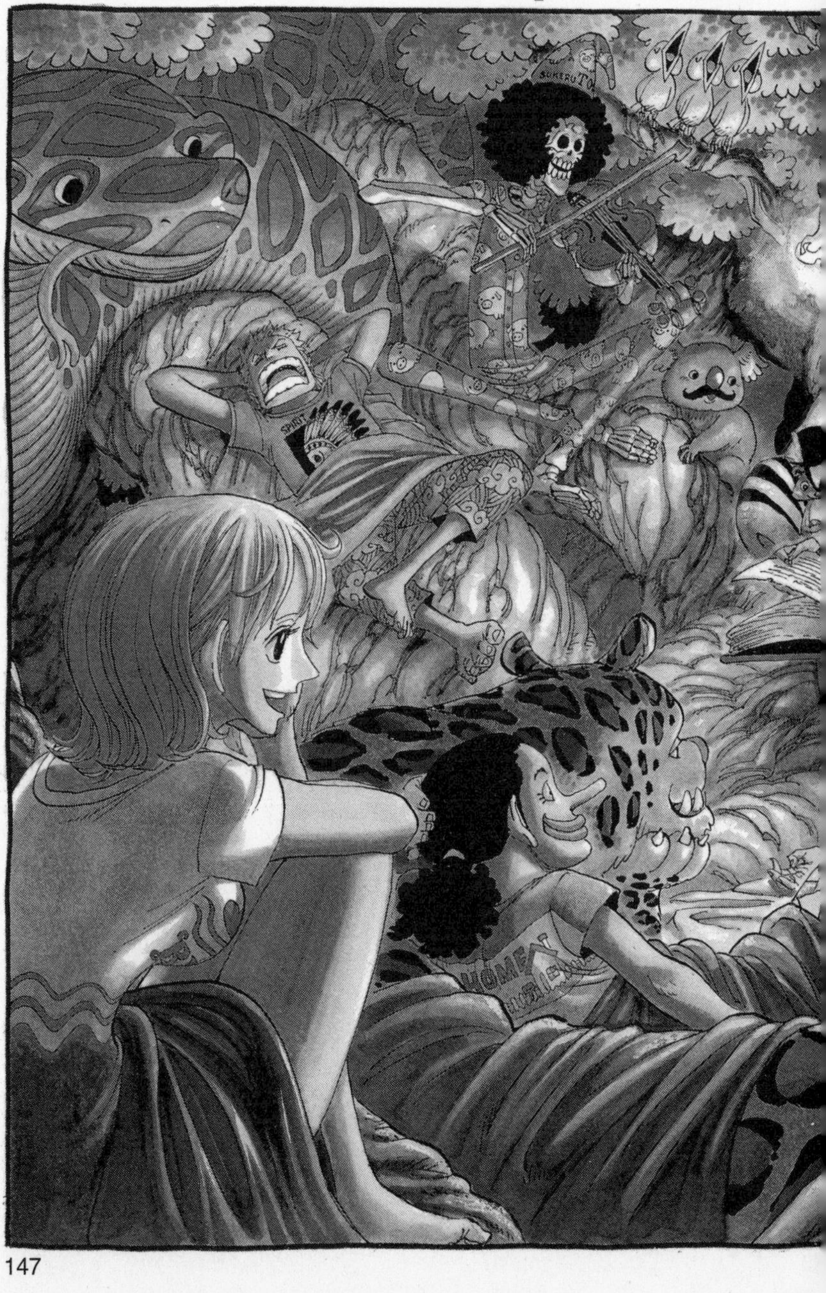
HOME

vol.55

ONE PIECE

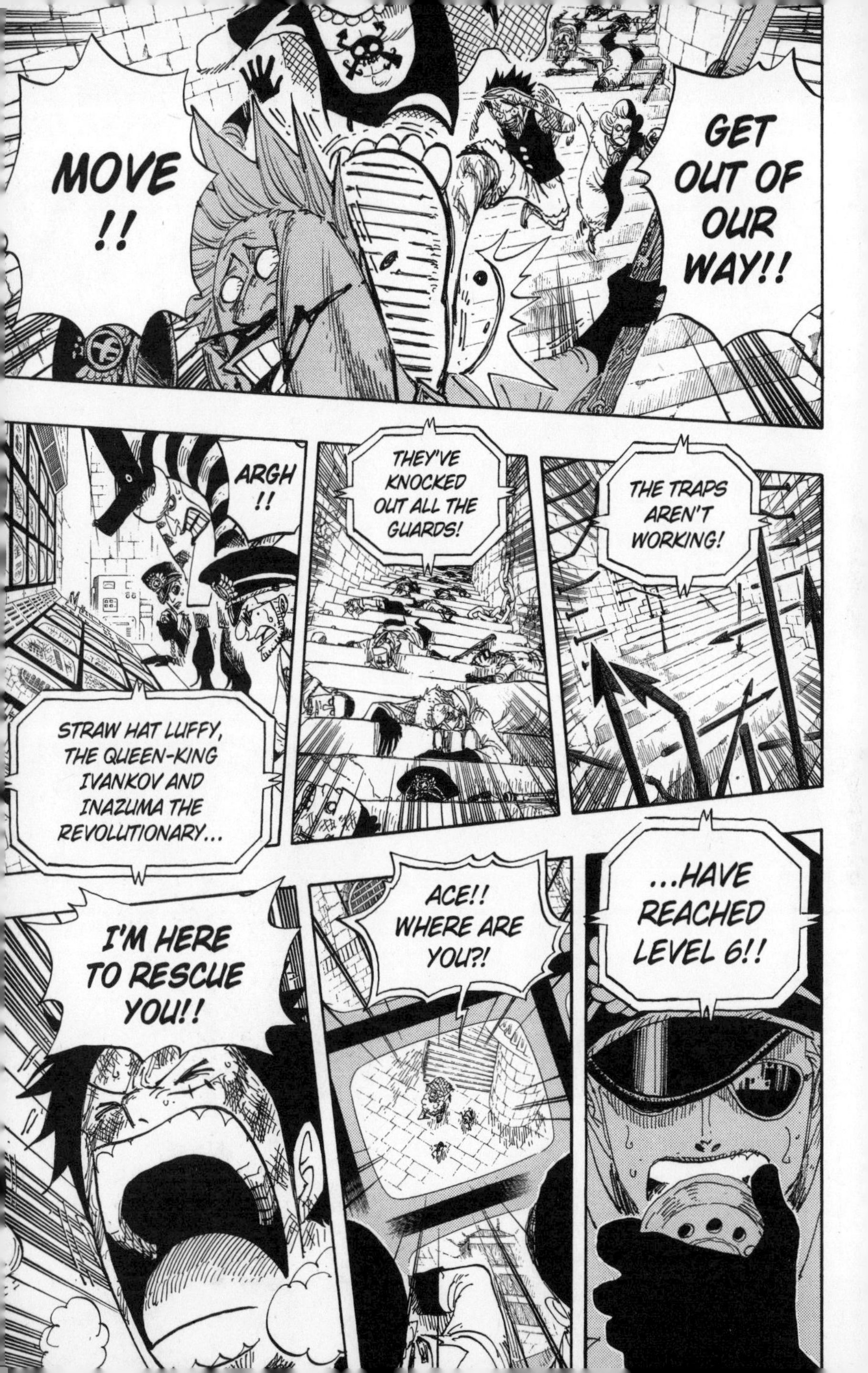
GET OUT OF OUR WAY!!
MOVE !!
THE TRAPS AREN'T WORKING!
THEY'VE KNOCKED OUT ALL THE GUARDS!
ARGH !!
STRAW HAT LUFFY, THE QUEEN-KING IVANKOV AND INAZUMA THE REVOLUTIONARY...
...HAVE REACHED LEVEL 6!!
ACE!! WHERE ARE YOU?!
I'M HERE TO RESCUE YOU!!

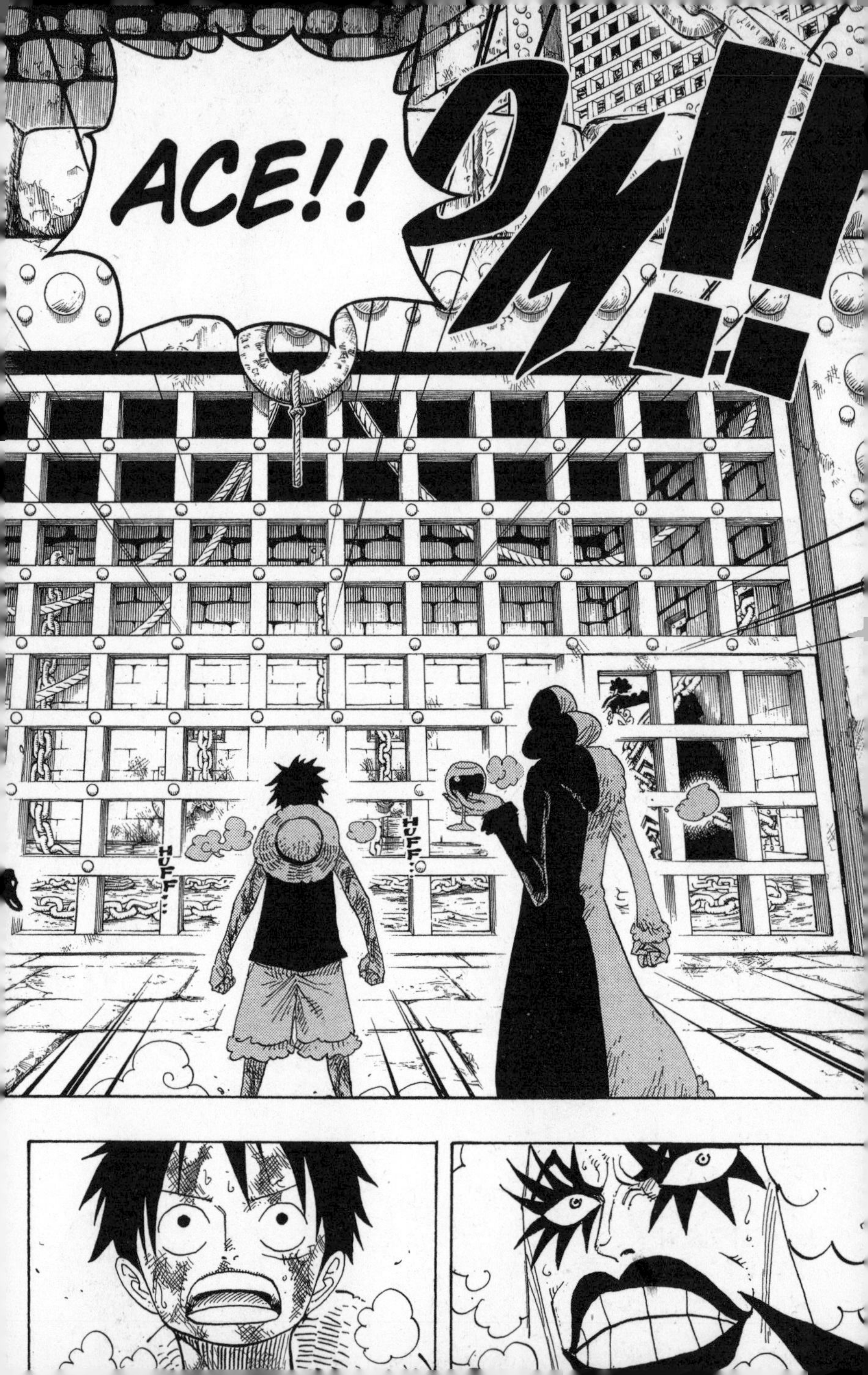
ACE!!
HUFF...
HUFF...

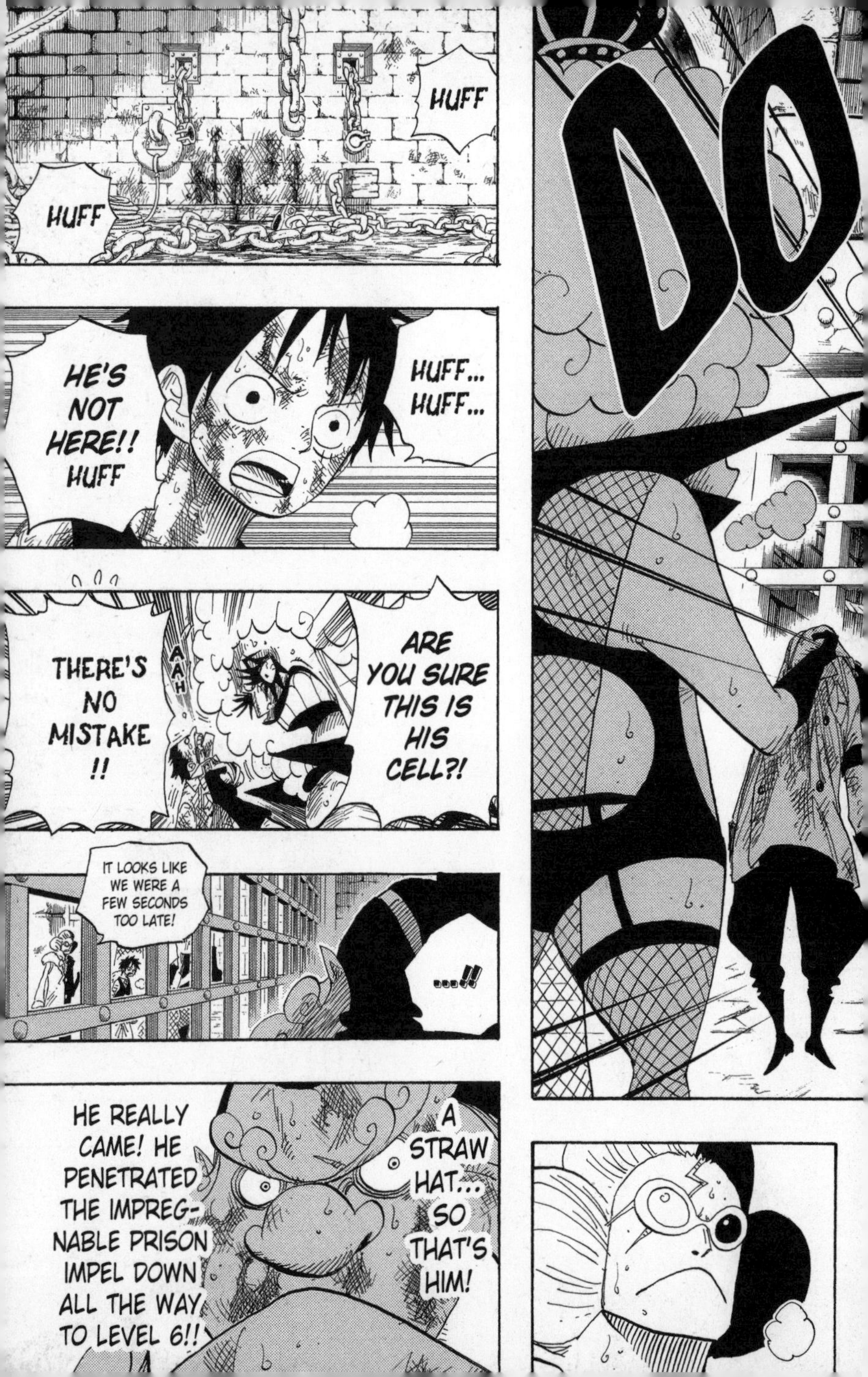
DO
HUFF
HUFF
HUFF... HUFF...
HE'S NOT HERE!! HUFF
ARE YOU SURE THIS IS HIS CELL?!
AAH
THERE'S NO MISTAKE !!
...!!
IT LOOKS LIKE WE WERE A FEW SECONDS TOO LATE!
A STRAW HAT... SO THAT'S HIM!
HE REALLY CAME! HE PENETRATED THE IMPREG-NABLE PRISON IMPEL DOWN ALL THE WAY TO LEVEL 6!!

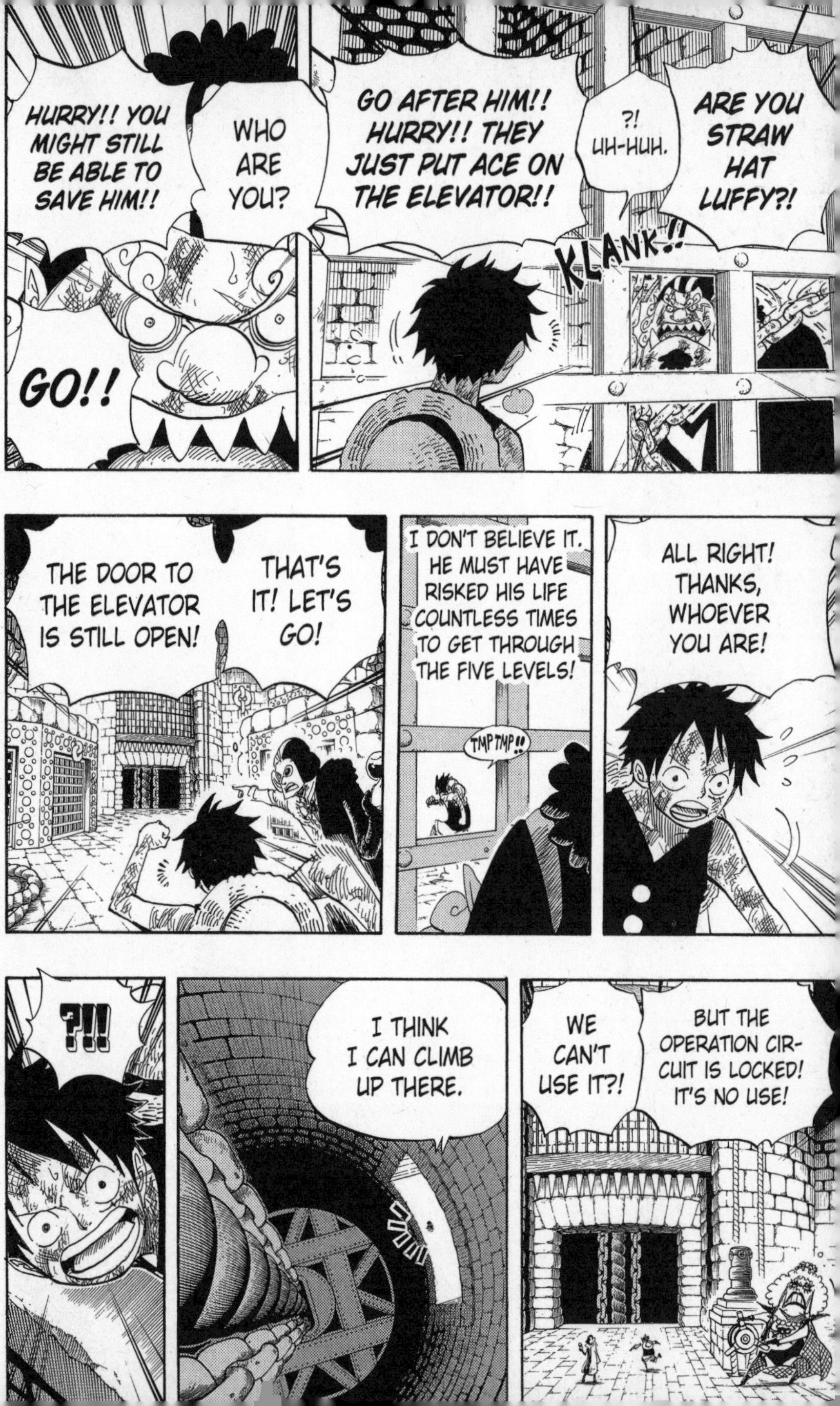
ARE YOU STRAW HAT LUFFY?!
?! UH-HUH.
GO AFTER HIM!! HURRY!! THEY JUST PUT ACE ON THE ELEVATOR!!
KLANK!!
WHO ARE YOU?
HURRY!! YOU MIGHT STILL BE ABLE TO SAVE HIM!!
GO!!
ALL RIGHT! THANKS, WHOEVER YOU ARE!
I DON'T BELIEVE IT. HE MUST HAVE RISKED HIS LIFE COUNTLESS TIMES TO GET THROUGH THE FIVE LEVELS!
TMP TMP!!
THAT'S IT! LET'S GO!
THE DOOR TO THE ELEVATOR IS STILL OPEN!
BUT THE OPERATION CIR-CUIT IS LOCKED! IT'S NO USE!
WE CAN'T USE IT?!
I THINK I CAN CLIMB UP THERE.
?!!

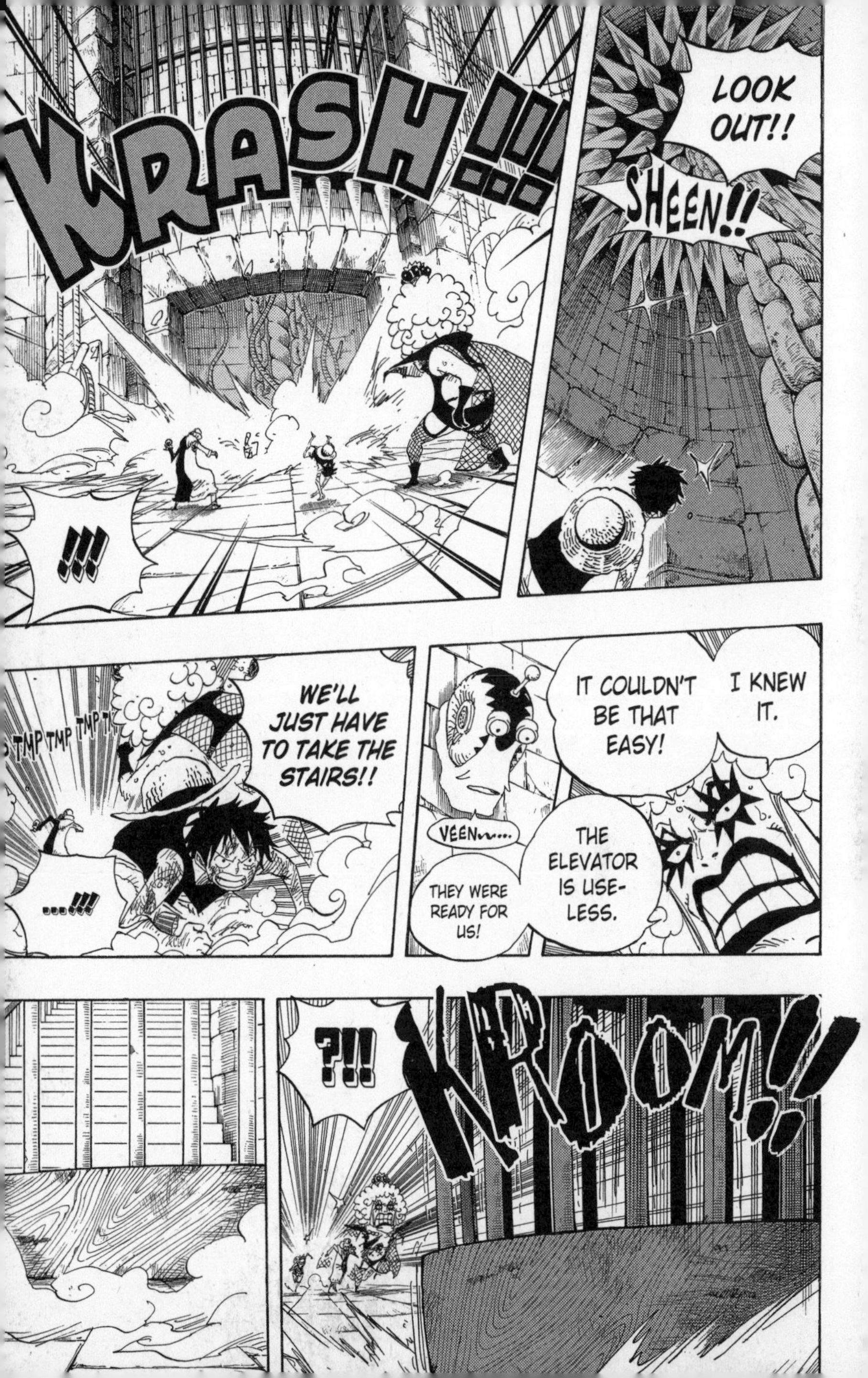
LOOK OUT!!
SHEEN!!
KRASH!!!
!!!
I KNEW IT.
IT COULDN'T BE THAT EASY!
THE ELEVATOR IS USELESS.
VEEN~~...
THEY WERE READY FOR US!
WE'LL JUST HAVE TO TAKE THE STAIRS!!
TMP TMP TMP T
...!!!
?!!
KROOM!!

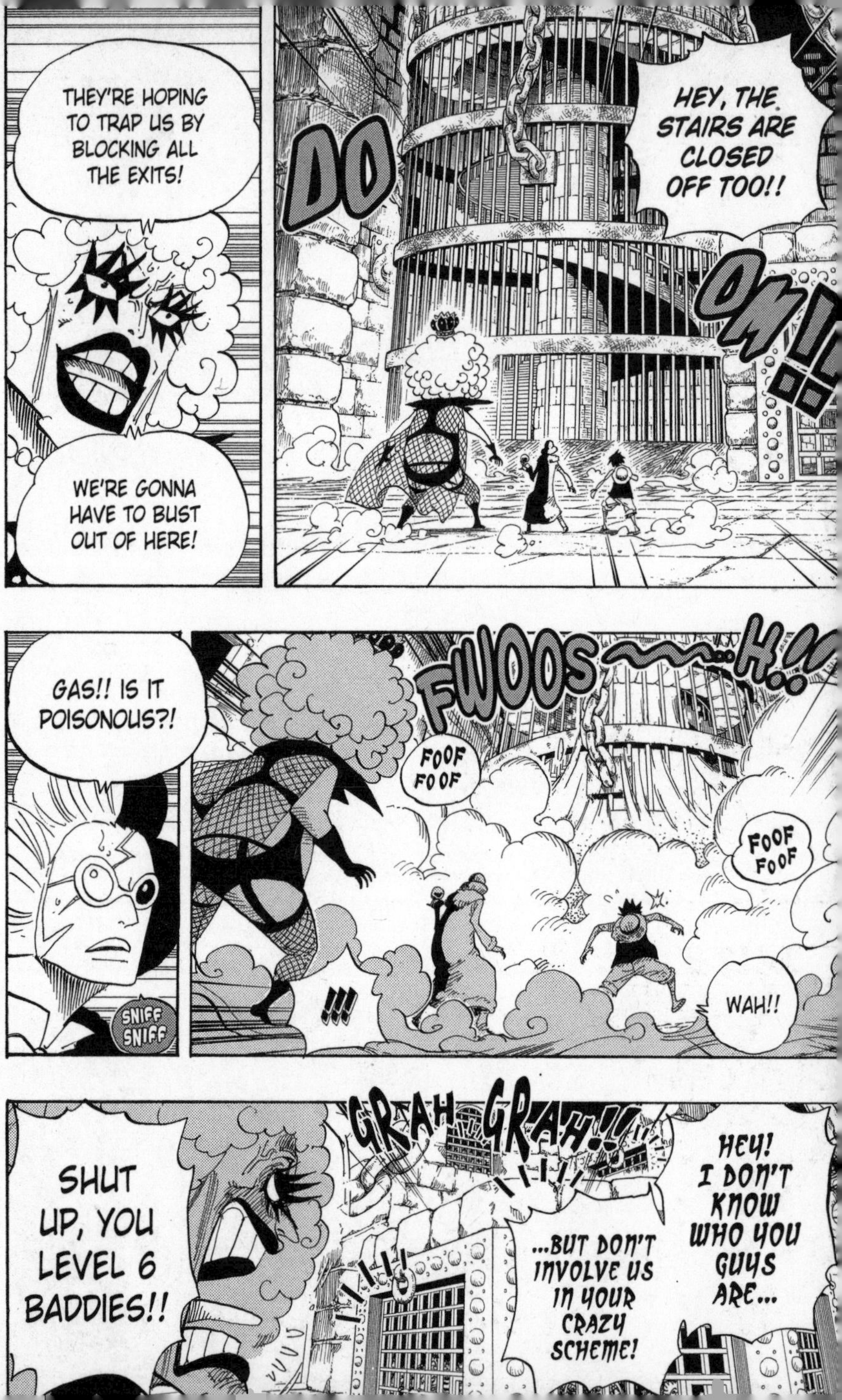
HEY, THE STAIRS ARE CLOSED OFF TOO!!
DO
OM!!
THEY'RE HOPING TO TRAP US BY BLOCKING ALL THE EXITS!
WE'RE GONNA HAVE TO BUST OUT OF HERE!
FWOOS~~H!!
FOOF FOOF
FOOF FOOF
WAH!!
!!!
GAS!! IS IT POISONOUS?!
SNIFF SNIFF
GRAH GRAH!!
HEY! I DON'T KNOW WHO YOU GUYS ARE...
...BUT DON'T INVOLVE US IN YOUR CRAZY SCHEME!
SHUT UP, YOU LEVEL 6 BADDIES!!

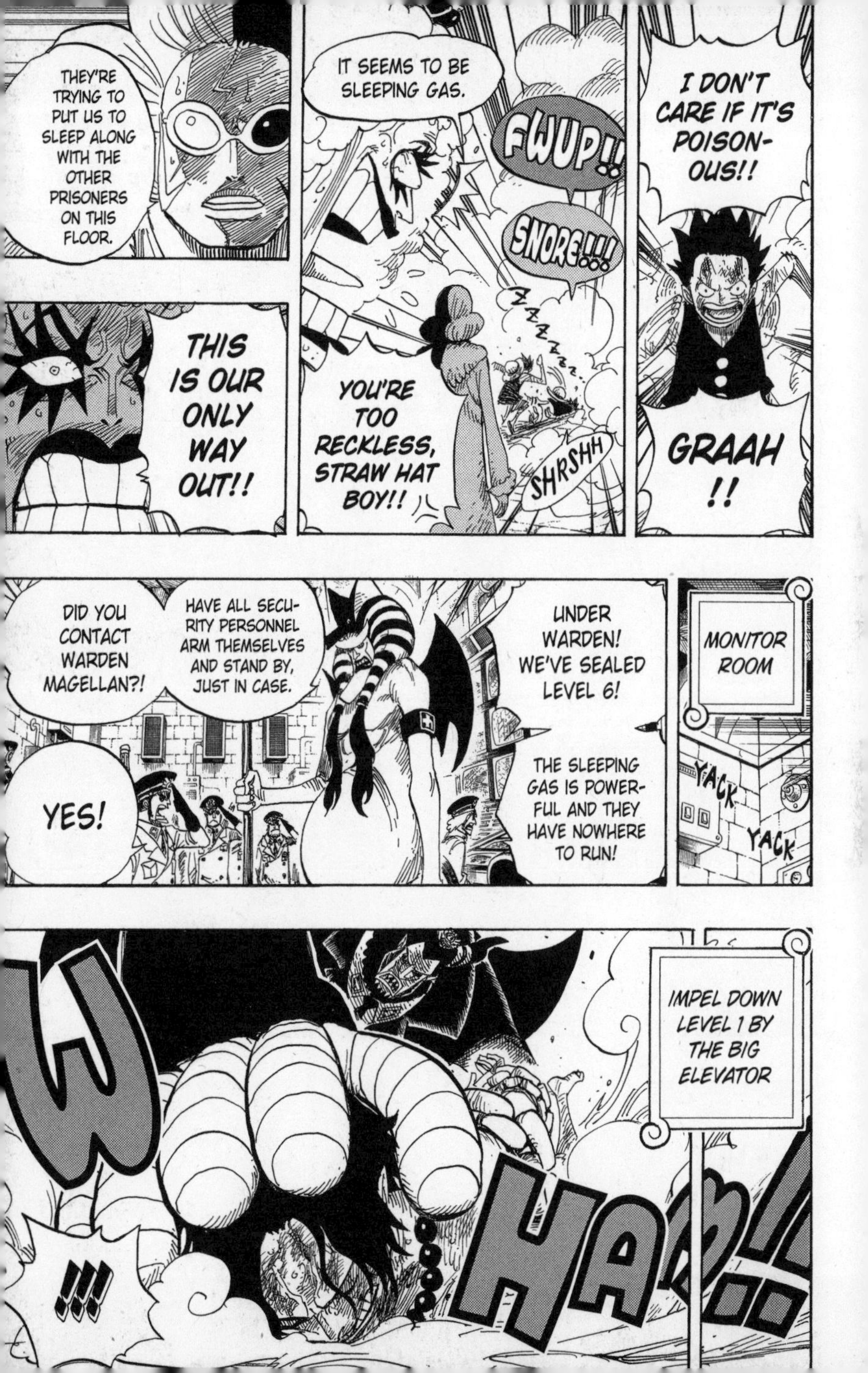
I DON'T CARE IF IT'S POISON-OUS!!
GRAAH!!
IT SEEMS TO BE SLEEPING GAS.
FWUP!!
SNORE!!!
YOU'RE TOO RECKLESS, STRAW HAT BOY!!
SHRSHH
THEY'RE TRYING TO PUT US TO SLEEP ALONG WITH THE OTHER PRISONERS ON THIS FLOOR.
THIS IS OUR ONLY WAY OUT!!
MONITOR ROOM
YACK
YACK
UNDER WARDEN! WE'VE SEALED LEVEL 6!
THE SLEEPING GAS IS POWER-FUL AND THEY HAVE NOWHERE TO RUN!
HAVE ALL SECU-RITY PERSONNEL ARM THEMSELVES AND STAND BY, JUST IN CASE.
DID YOU CONTACT WARDEN MAGELLAN?!
YES!
IMPEL DOWN LEVEL 1 BY THE BIG ELEVATOR
!!!

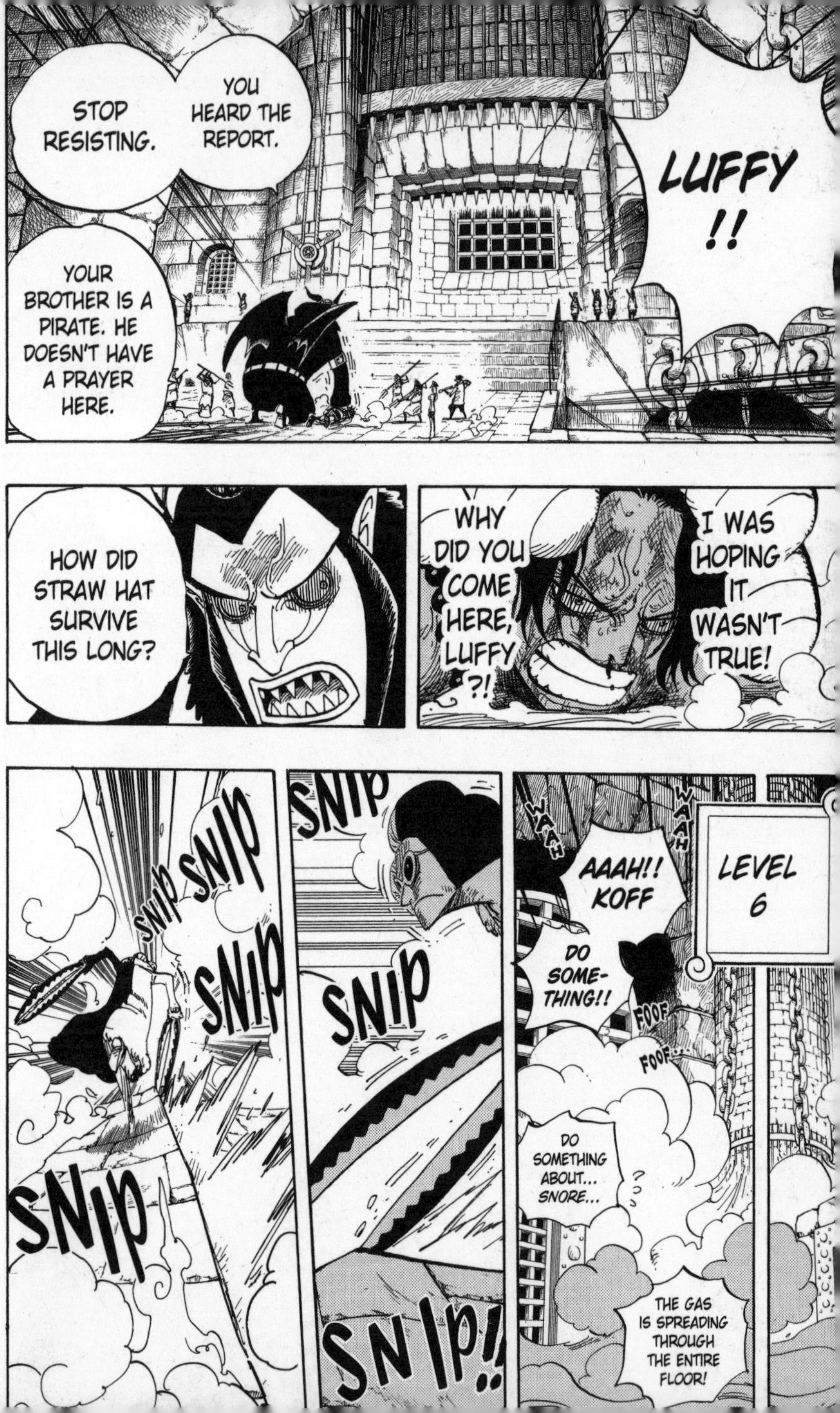
LUFFY!!
YOU HEARD THE REPORT.
STOP RESISTING.
YOUR BROTHER IS A PIRATE. HE DOESN'T HAVE A PRAYER HERE.
I WAS HOPING IT WASN'T TRUE!
WHY DID YOU COME HERE, LUFFY?!
HOW DID STRAW HAT SURVIVE THIS LONG?
LEVEL 6
WAAH
WAAH
AAAH!! KOFF
DO SOME-THING!!
FOOF
FOOF...
DO SOMETHING ABOUT... SNORE...
THE GAS IS SPREADING THROUGH THE ENTIRE FLOOR!
SNIP
SNIP
SNIP!!
SNIP
SNIP
SNIP
SNIP
SNIP

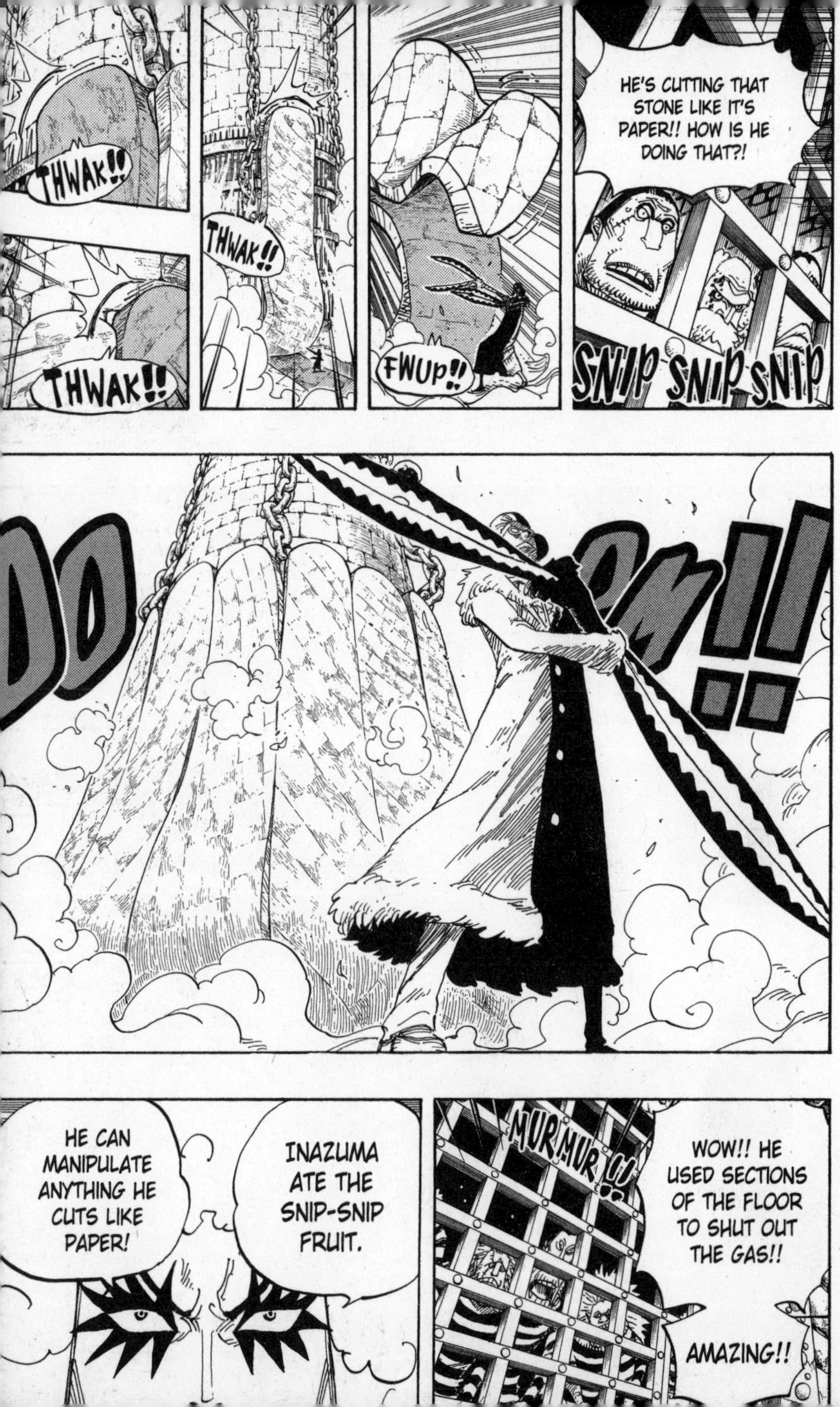
HE'S CUTTING THAT STONE LIKE IT'S PAPER!! HOW IS HE DOING THAT?!
SNIP SNIP SNIP
FWUP!!
THWAK!!
THWAK!!
THWAK!!
DOOM!!
MUR MUR!!
WOW!! HE USED SECTIONS OF THE FLOOR TO SHUT OUT THE GAS!!
AMAZING!!
INAZUMA ATE THE SNIP-SNIP FRUIT.
HE CAN MANIPULATE ANYTHING HE CUTS LIKE PAPER!

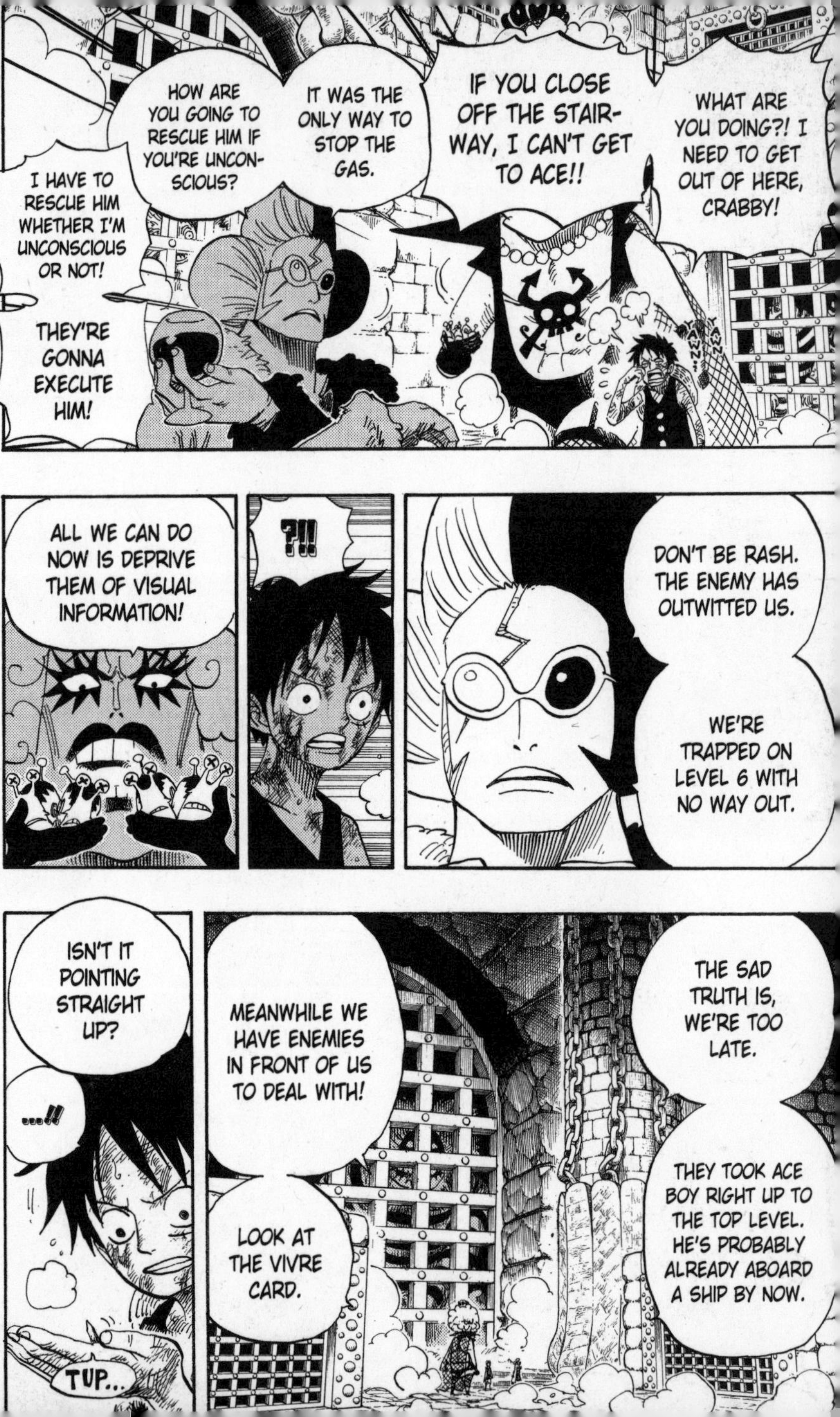
WHAT ARE YOU DOING?! I NEED TO GET OUT OF HERE, CRABBY!
IF YOU CLOSE OFF THE STAIR-WAY, I CAN'T GET TO ACE!!
IT WAS THE ONLY WAY TO STOP THE GAS.
HOW ARE YOU GOING TO RESCUE HIM IF YOU'RE UNCON-SCIOUS?
I HAVE TO RESCUE HIM WHETHER I'M UNCONSCIOUS OR NOT!
THEY'RE GONNA EXECUTE HIM!
DON'T BE RASH. THE ENEMY HAS OUTWITTED US.
WE'RE TRAPPED ON LEVEL 6 WITH NO WAY OUT.
?!!
ALL WE CAN DO NOW IS DEPRIVE THEM OF VISUAL INFORMATION!
THE SAD TRUTH IS, WE'RE TOO LATE.
THEY TOOK ACE BOY RIGHT UP TO THE TOP LEVEL. HE'S PROBABLY ALREADY ABOARD A SHIP BY NOW.
MEANWHILE WE HAVE ENEMIES IN FRONT OF US TO DEAL WITH!
LOOK AT THE VIVRE CARD.
ISN'T IT POINTING STRAIGHT UP?
...!!
TUP...

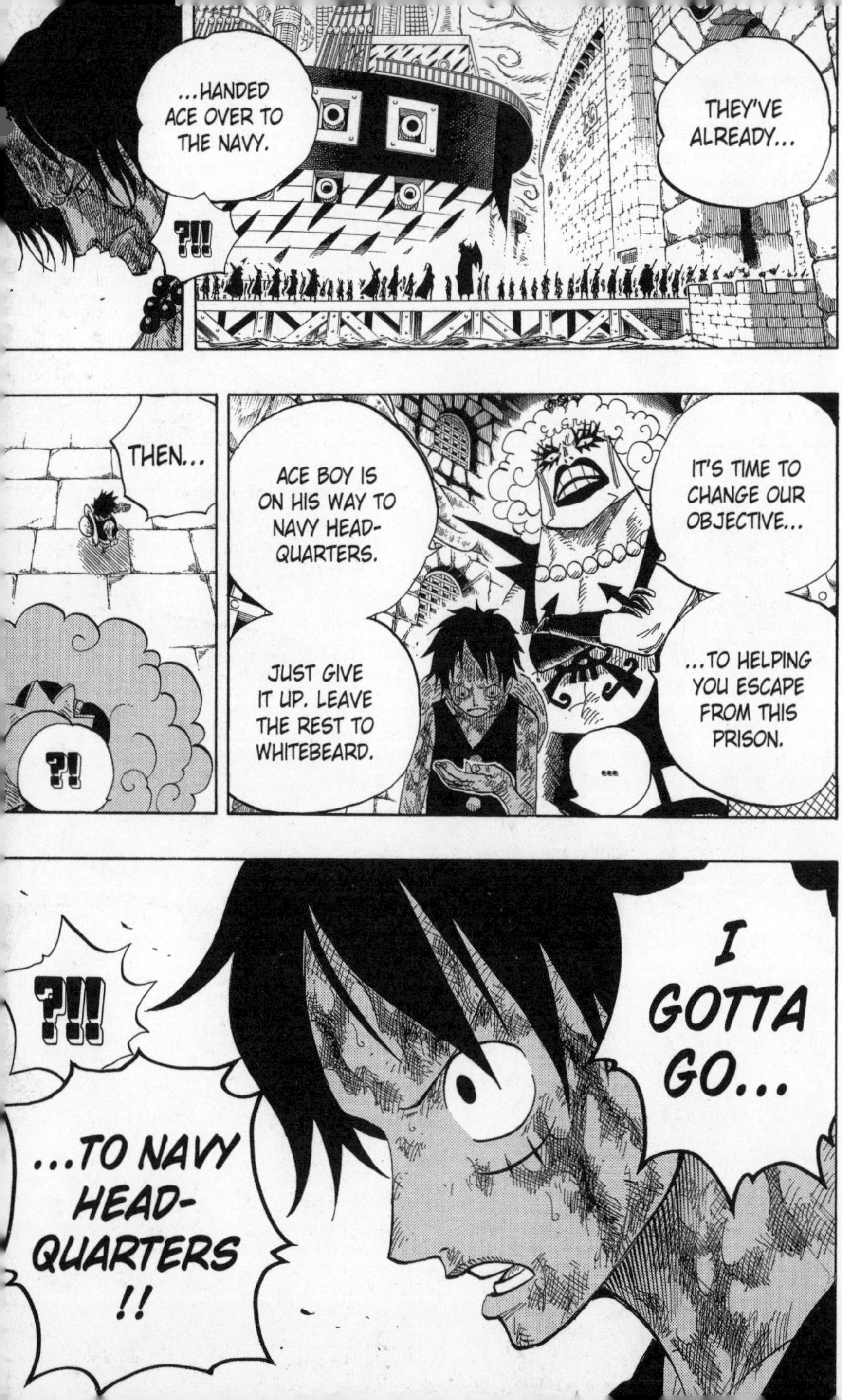
THEY'VE ALREADY...
...HANDED ACE OVER TO THE NAVY.
?!!
IT'S TIME TO CHANGE OUR OBJECTIVE...
...TO HELPING YOU ESCAPE FROM THIS PRISON.
ACE BOY IS ON HIS WAY TO NAVY HEAD-QUARTERS.
JUST GIVE IT UP. LEAVE THE REST TO WHITEBEARD.
...
THEN...
?!
I GOTTA GO...
...TO NAVY HEAD-QUARTERS!!
?!!

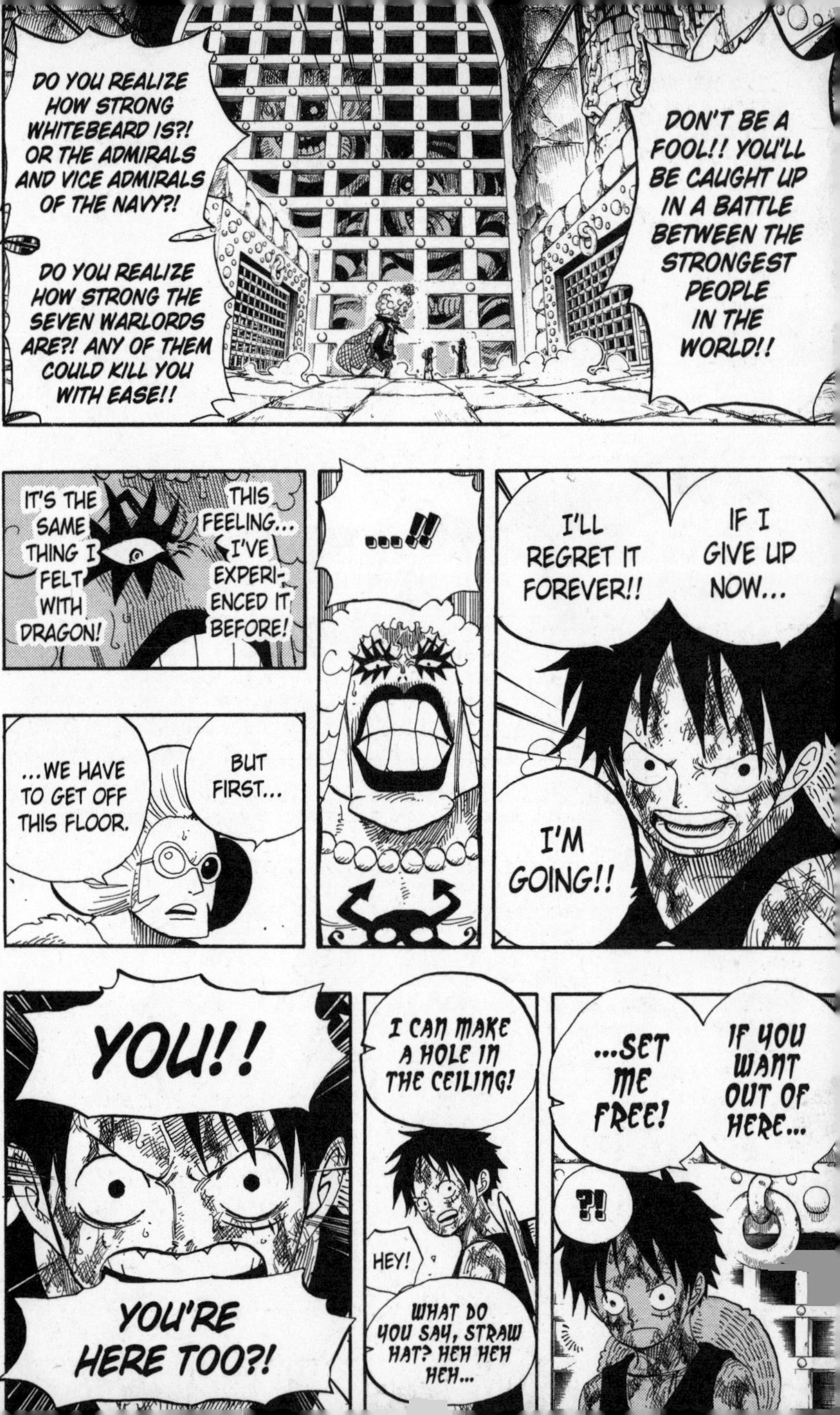
DON'T BE A FOOL!! YOU'LL BE CAUGHT UP IN A BATTLE BETWEEN THE STRONGEST PEOPLE IN THE WORLD!!
DO YOU REALIZE HOW STRONG WHITEBEARD IS?! OR THE ADMIRALS AND VICE ADMIRALS OF THE NAVY?!
DO YOU REALIZE HOW STRONG THE SEVEN WARLORDS ARE?! ANY OF THEM COULD KILL YOU WITH EASE!!
IF I GIVE UP NOW...
I'LL REGRET IT FOREVER!!
I'M GOING!!
...!!
THIS FEELING... I'VE EXPERIENCED IT BEFORE!
IT'S THE SAME THING I FELT WITH DRAGON!
BUT FIRST...
...WE HAVE TO GET OFF THIS FLOOR.
IF YOU WANT OUT OF HERE...
...SET ME FREE!
?!
I CAN MAKE A HOLE IN THE CEILING!
HEY!
WHAT DO YOU SAY, STRAW HAT? HEH HEH HEH...
YOU!!
YOU'RE HERE TOO?!

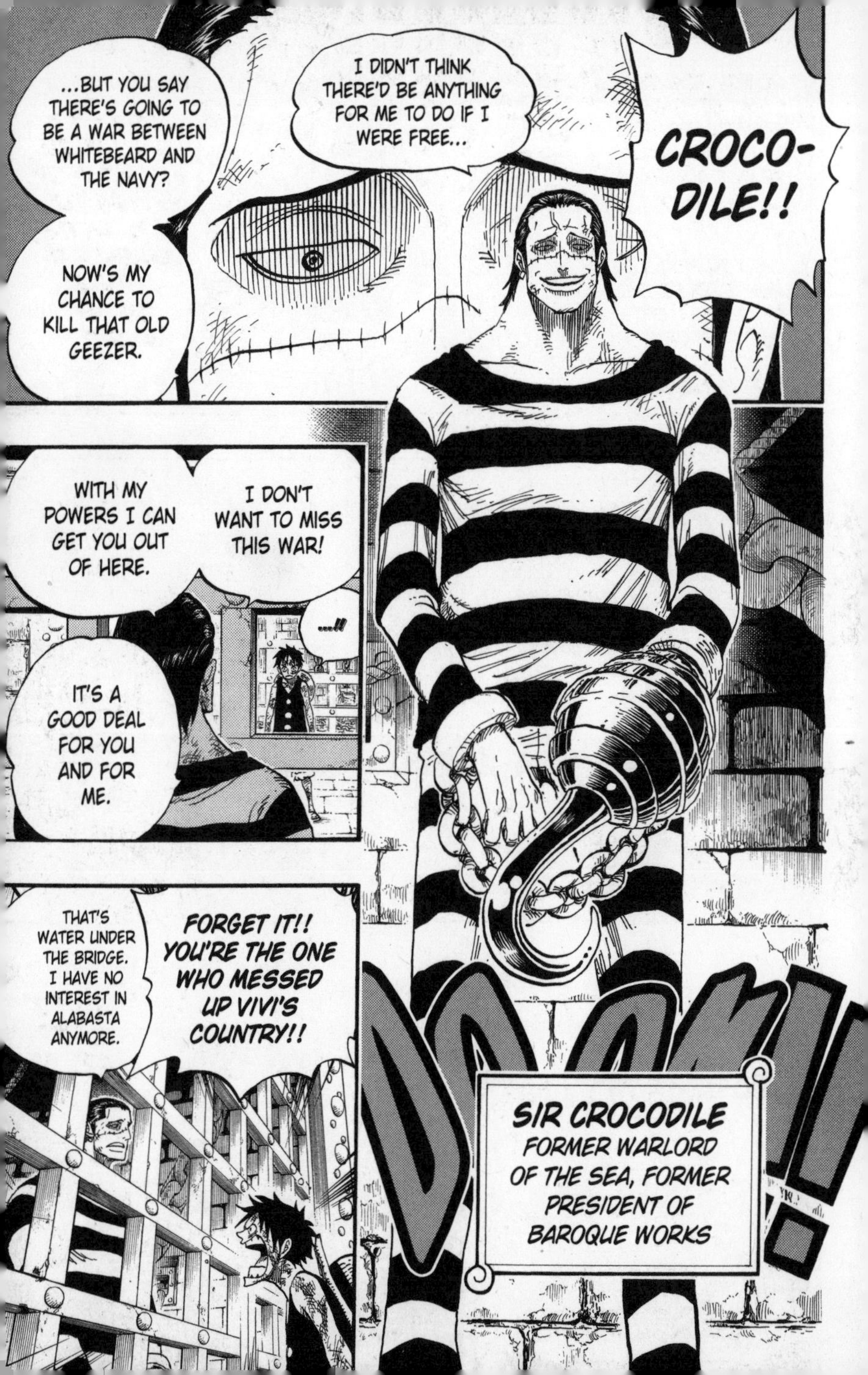
CROCO-DILE!!
DOOM!!
SIR CROCODILE
FORMER WARLORD OF THE SEA, FORMER PRESIDENT OF BAROQUE WORKS
I DIDN'T THINK THERE'D BE ANYTHING FOR ME TO DO IF I WERE FREE...
...BUT YOU SAY THERE'S GOING TO BE A WAR BETWEEN WHITEBEARD AND THE NAVY?
NOW'S MY CHANCE TO KILL THAT OLD GEEZER.
I DON'T WANT TO MISS THIS WAR!
WITH MY POWERS I CAN GET YOU OUT OF HERE.
...!!
IT'S A GOOD DEAL FOR YOU AND FOR ME.
FORGET IT!! YOU'RE THE ONE WHO MESSED UP VIVI'S COUNTRY!!
THAT'S WATER UNDER THE BRIDGE. I HAVE NO INTEREST IN ALABASTA ANYMORE.

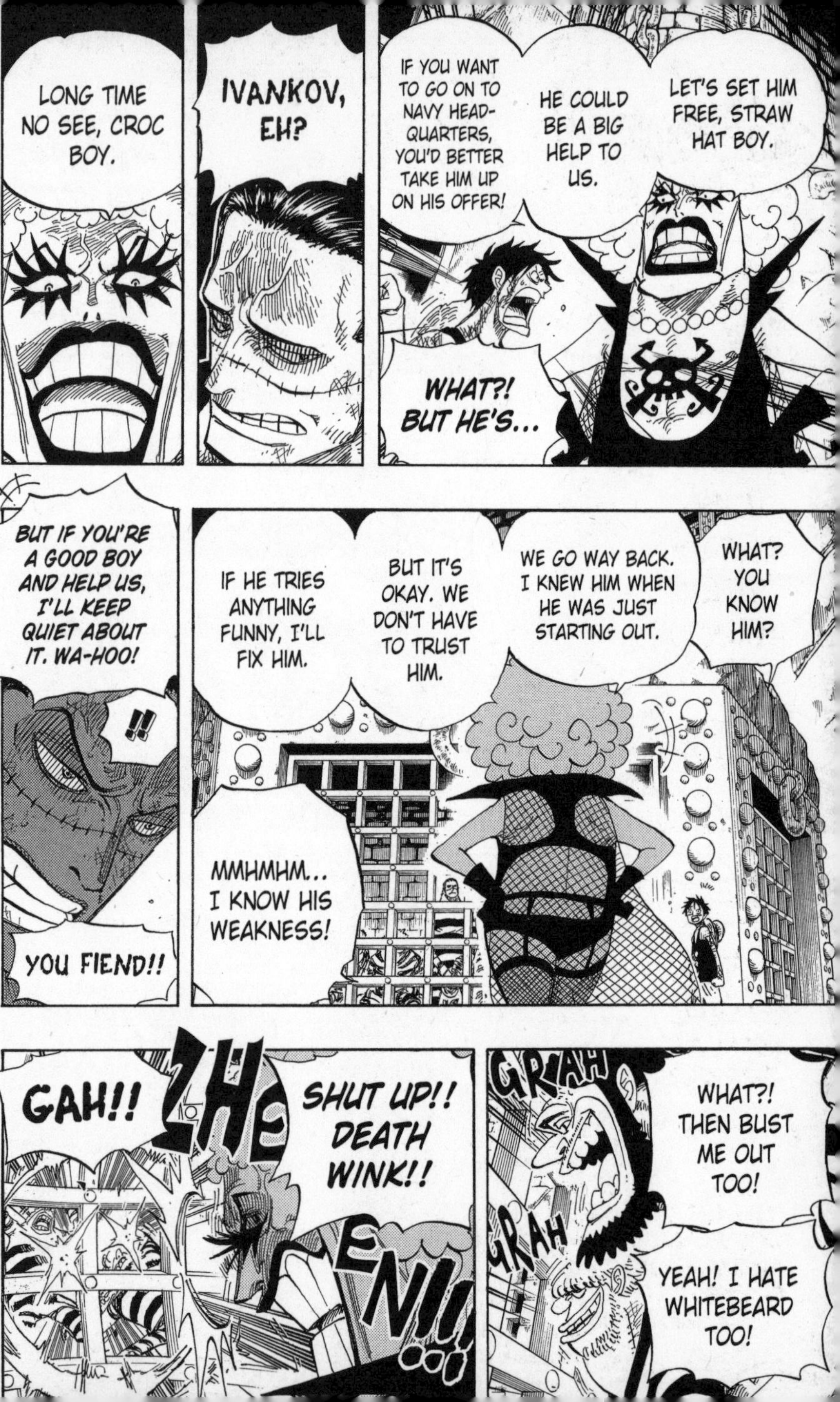
LET'S SET HIM FREE, STRAW HAT BOY.
HE COULD BE A BIG HELP TO US.
IF YOU WANT TO GO ON TO NAVY HEAD-QUARTERS, YOU'D BETTER TAKE HIM UP ON HIS OFFER!
WHAT?! BUT HE'S...
IVANKOV, EH?
LONG TIME NO SEE, CROC BOY.
WHAT? YOU KNOW HIM?
WE GO WAY BACK. I KNEW HIM WHEN HE WAS JUST STARTING OUT.
BUT IT'S OKAY. WE DON'T HAVE TO TRUST HIM.
IF HE TRIES ANYTHING FUNNY, I'LL FIX HIM.
MMHMHM... I KNOW HIS WEAKNESS!
BUT IF YOU'RE A GOOD BOY AND HELP US, I'LL KEEP QUIET ABOUT IT. WA-HOO!
!!
YOU FIEND!!
GRAH
WHAT?! THEN BUST ME OUT TOO!
GRAH
YEAH! I HATE WHITEBEARD TOO!
SHUT UP!! DEATH WINK!!
ZHE
EN!!
GAH!!

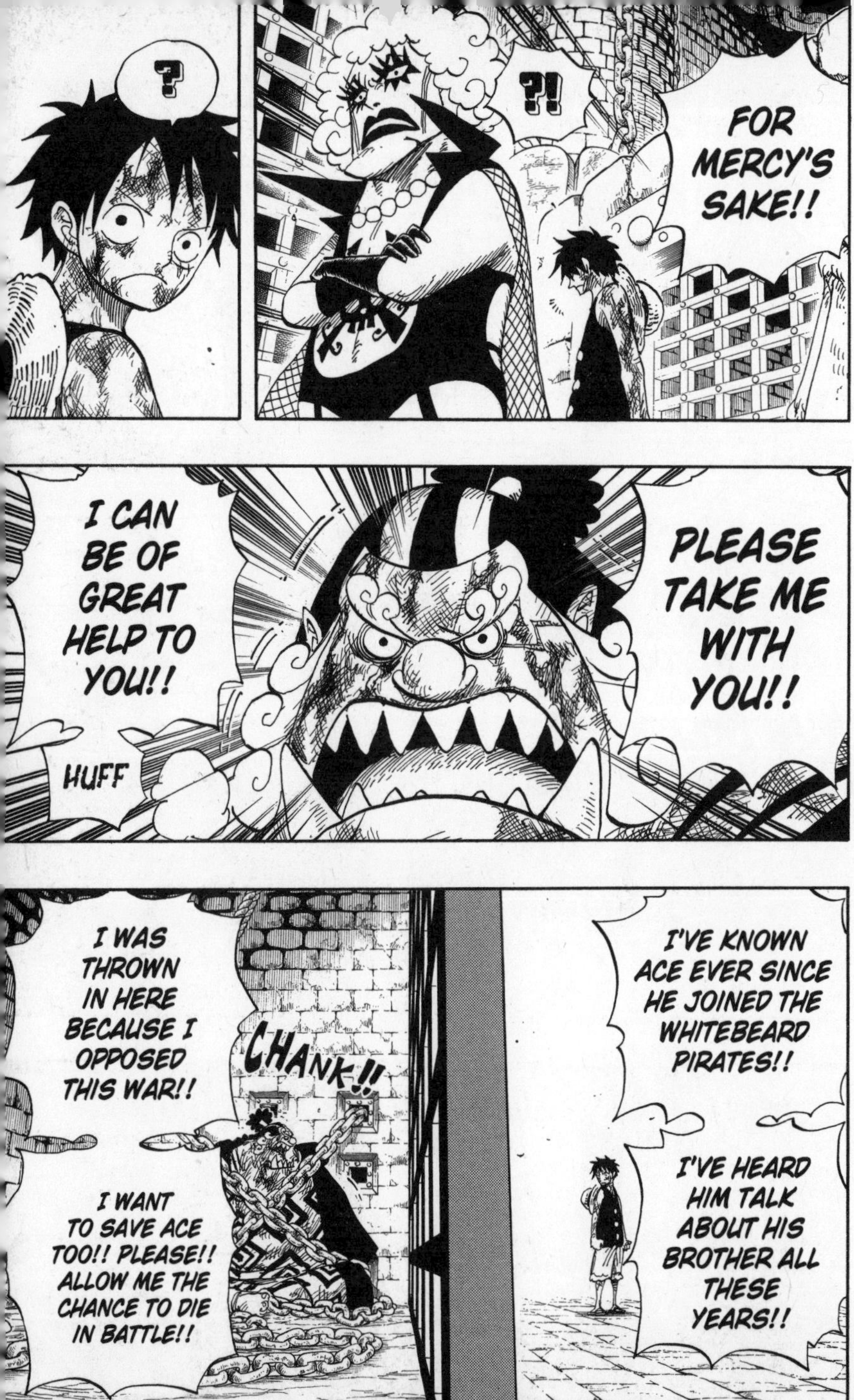
FOR MERCY'S SAKE!!
?!
?
PLEASE TAKE ME WITH YOU!!
I CAN BE OF GREAT HELP TO YOU!!
HUFF
I'VE KNOWN ACE EVER SINCE HE JOINED THE WHITEBEARD PIRATES!!
I'VE HEARD HIM TALK ABOUT HIS BROTHER ALL THESE YEARS!!
I WAS THROWN IN HERE BECAUSE I OPPOSED THIS WAR!!
CHANK!!
I WANT TO SAVE ACE TOO!! PLEASE!! ALLOW ME THE CHANCE TO DIE IN BATTLE!!

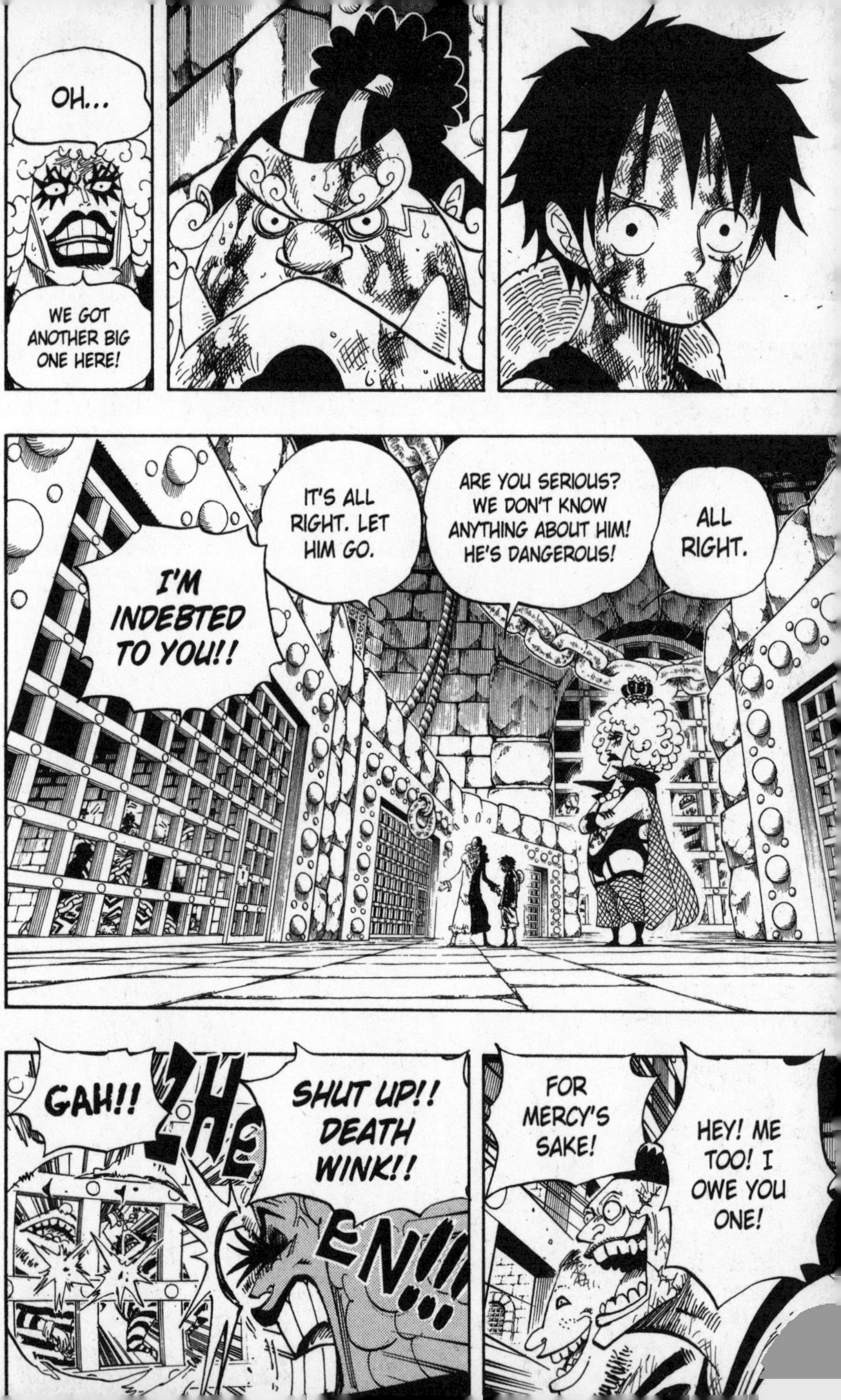
OH...
WE GOT ANOTHER BIG ONE HERE!
ALL RIGHT.
ARE YOU SERIOUS? WE DON'T KNOW ANYTHING ABOUT HIM! HE'S DANGEROUS!
IT'S ALL RIGHT. LET HIM GO.
I'M INDEBTED TO YOU!!
HEY! ME TOO! I OWE YOU ONE!
FOR MERCY'S SAKE!
SHUT UP!! DEATH WINK!!
GAH!!

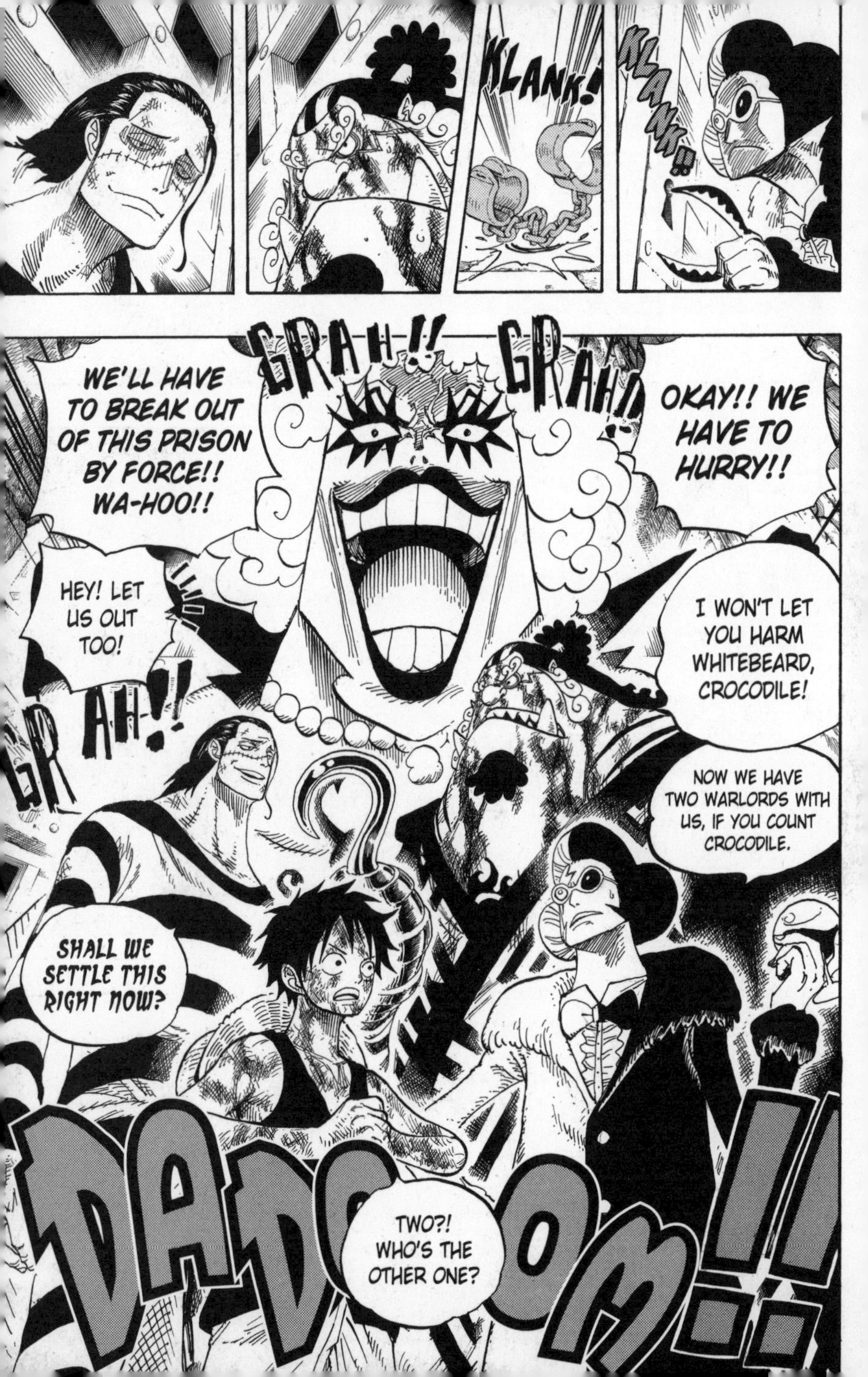
KLANK!!
KLANK!
GRAH!!
OKAY!! WE HAVE TO HURRY!!
GRAH!!
WE'LL HAVE TO BREAK OUT OF THIS PRISON BY FORCE!! WA-HOO!!
I WON'T LET YOU HARM WHITEBEARD, CROCODILE!
HEY! LET US OUT TOO!
GRAH!!
NOW WE HAVE TWO WARLORDS WITH US, IF YOU COUNT CROCODILE.
SHALL WE SETTLE THIS RIGHT NOW?
TWO?! WHO'S THE OTHER ONE?

USOPP'S VOICE ACTOR, KAPPEI YAMAGUCHI!

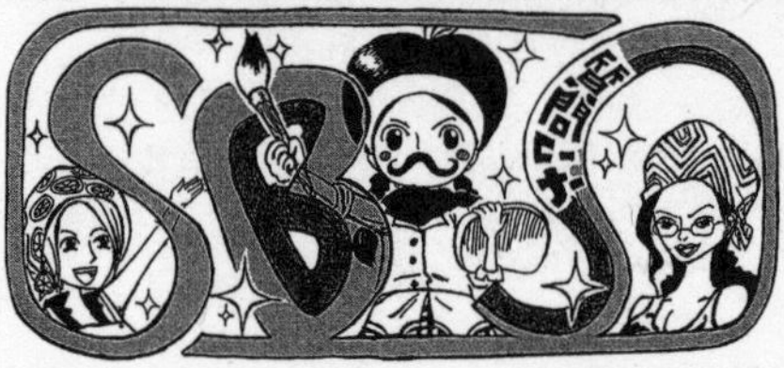
SBS

(Hikonimai Yonaga, China)

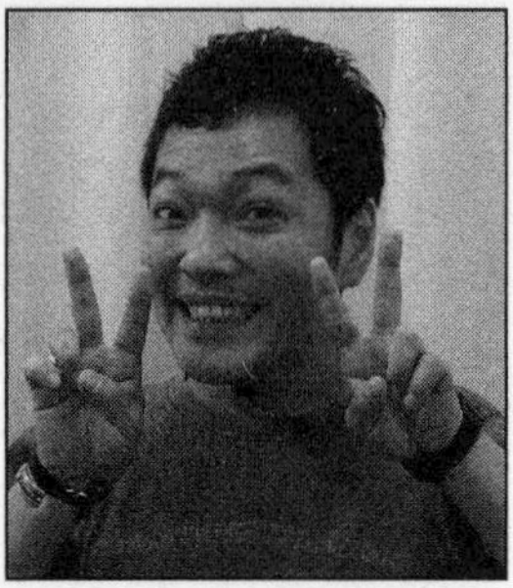

HDYD!! (How do you do?)
This is our 4th Voice Actor Question Corner! 4th! Now let's begin! Our guest today is a popular one! A great actor with loads of experience! Acts younger than his age and is hard to understand! Our brave sniper, Usopp's voice actor! He's actually really famous among other voice actors, Kappei Yamaguchi, in the house!

Oda (O): Here is Kappei. Please introduce yourself.

Kappei (K): The elegant dramatizer! Master Usopp's beautiful voice! Here's Kappei!

O: Why'd you say it like that? Dramatizer? You're just a liar!

K: I'm no liar! I'm a dramatizer!

O: Yeah, sure. Anyway, do you know what SBS is?

K: (S)tart (B)ooking us as your (S)taff Members. ♡

O: I don't want you.

K: That's cruel! Then where am I supposed to go since I don't get to appear in the recent episodes?!

O: Everyone is busy even if they don't have airtime! And your SBS meaning is wrong!

K: Oh, it's wrong? Then how about (S)tart off with (B)eer and (S)tuff. Or how about (S)lurp (B)eer (S)tudiously?!

O: What are you, a bar?! Never mind! You have no intention of guessing right anyway. Now let's begin!

K: Let's smack them down! Yeah!

O: You're getting motivated in the wrong direction!

K: I just figured out what SBS is! (S)lapped (B)usted (S)tupid!

O: Stop it!

The Question Corner with Yamaguchi continues on page 186! ☞

PREVIEW FOR NEXT VOICE ACTOR'S SBS

Next time and the one after that will be these two! Look forward to it!

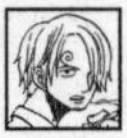 Sanji (Hiroaki Hirata)

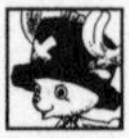 Chopper (Ikue Otani)

Chapter 541:
THE GREATEST EVER

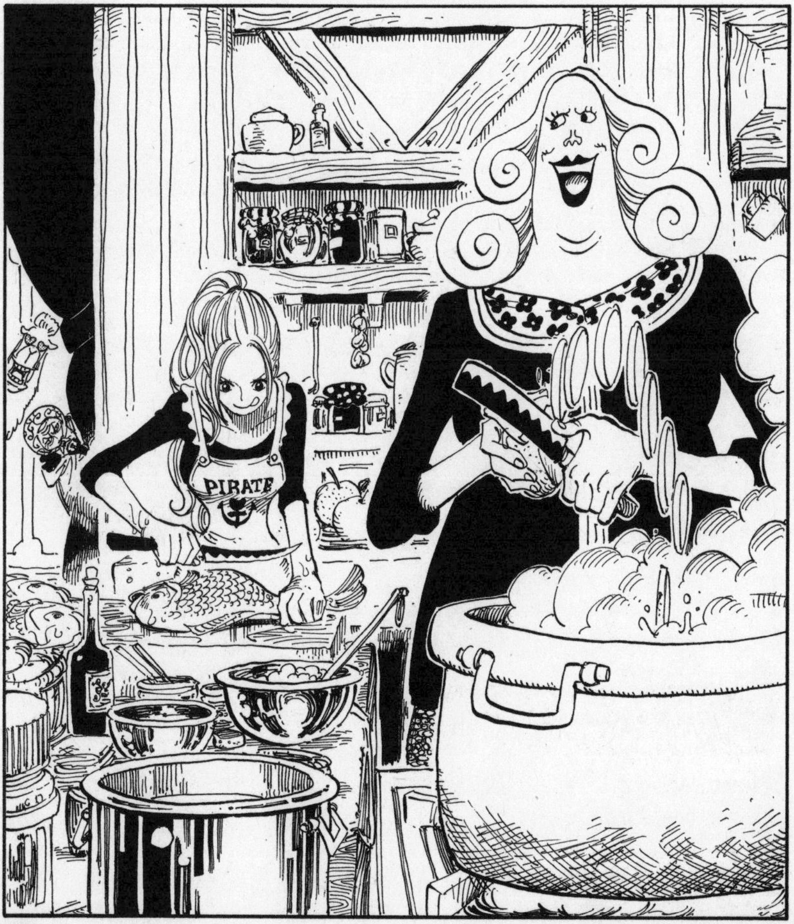
PIRATE

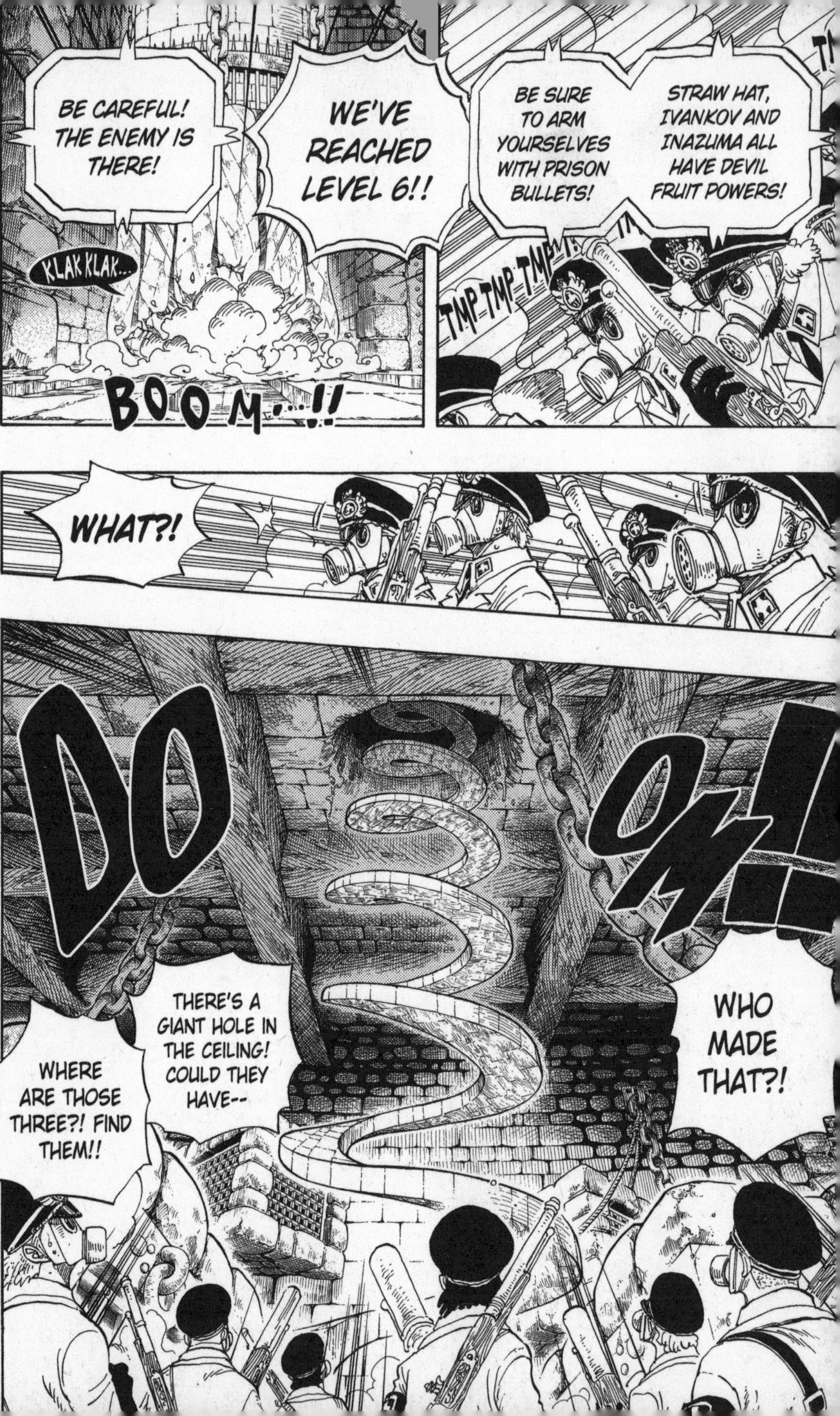
STRAW HAT, IVANKOV AND INAZUMA ALL HAVE DEVIL FRUIT POWERS!
BE SURE TO ARM YOURSELVES WITH PRISON BULLETS!
TMP TMP TMP
WE'VE REACHED LEVEL 6!!
BE CAREFUL! THE ENEMY IS THERE!
KLAK KLAK...
BOOM...!!
WHAT?!
DOOM!!
WHO MADE THAT?!
THERE'S A GIANT HOLE IN THE CEILING! COULD THEY HAVE--
WHERE ARE THOSE THREE?! FIND THEM!!

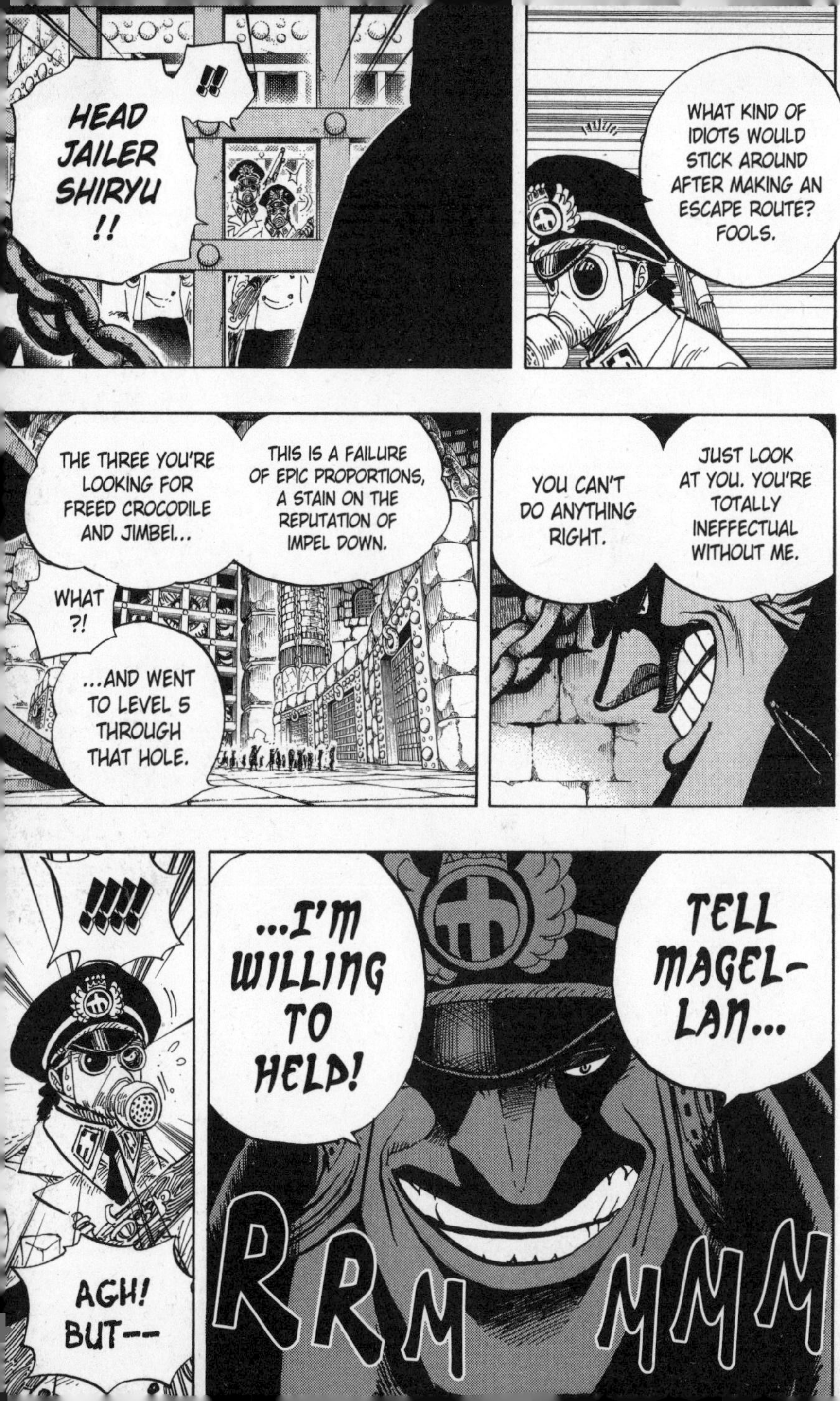
WHAT KIND OF IDIOTS WOULD STICK AROUND AFTER MAKING AN ESCAPE ROUTE? FOOLS.
!!
HEAD JAILER SHIRYU !!
JUST LOOK AT YOU. YOU'RE TOTALLY INEFFECTUAL WITHOUT ME.
YOU CAN'T DO ANYTHING RIGHT.
THIS IS A FAILURE OF EPIC PROPORTIONS, A STAIN ON THE REPUTATION OF IMPEL DOWN.
THE THREE YOU'RE LOOKING FOR FREED CROCODILE AND JIMBEI...
WHAT ?!
...AND WENT TO LEVEL 5 THROUGH THAT HOLE.
TELL MAGEL-LAN...
...I'M WILLING TO HELP!
RRM MMM
!!!!
AGH! BUT--

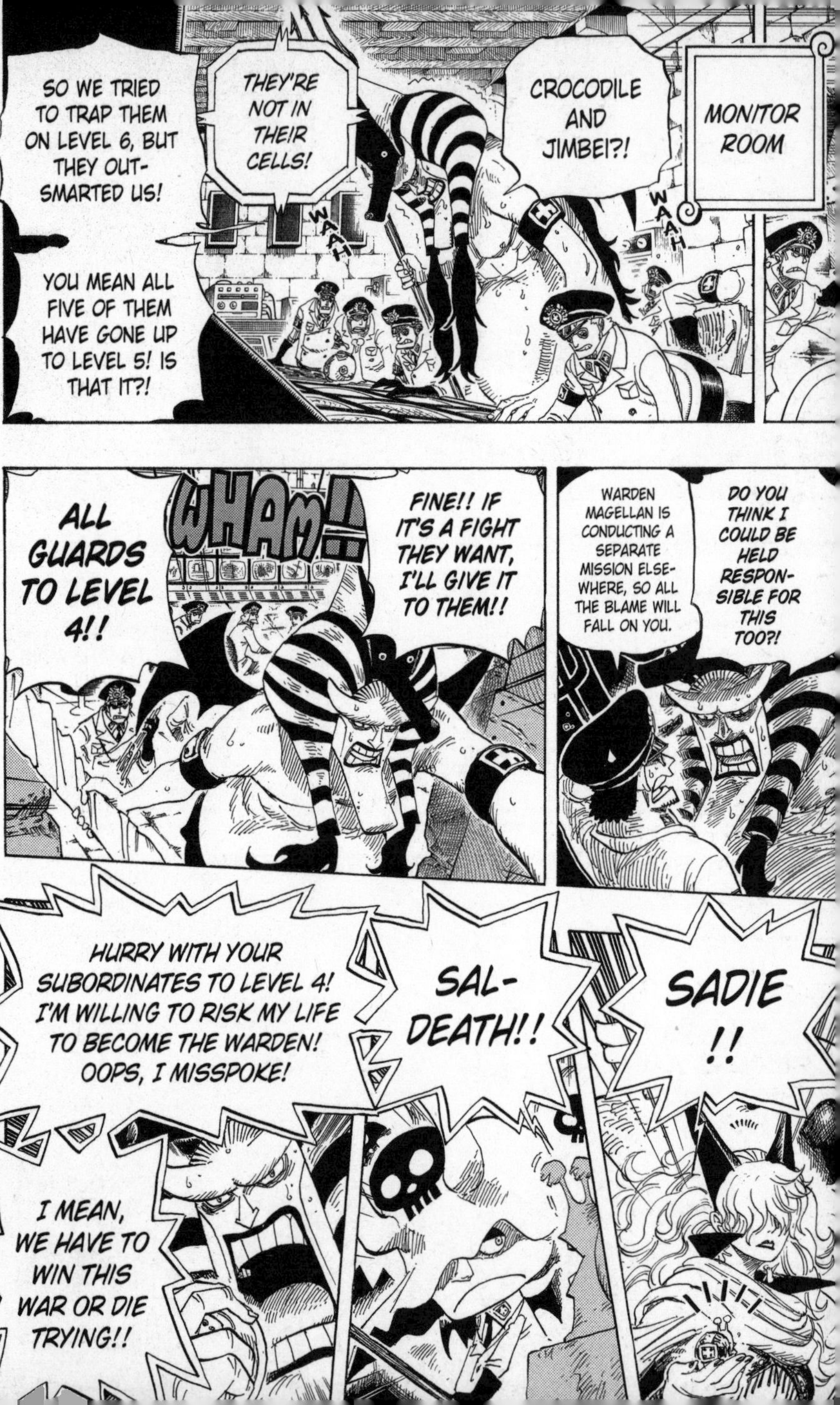
MONITOR ROOM
CROCODILE AND JIMBEI?!
WAAH
THEY'RE NOT IN THEIR CELLS!
WAAH
SO WE TRIED TO TRAP THEM ON LEVEL 6, BUT THEY OUT-SMARTED US!
YOU MEAN ALL FIVE OF THEM HAVE GONE UP TO LEVEL 5! IS THAT IT?!
DO YOU THINK I COULD BE HELD RESPONSIBLE FOR THIS TOO?!
WARDEN MAGELLAN IS CONDUCTING A SEPARATE MISSION ELSE-WHERE, SO ALL THE BLAME WILL FALL ON YOU.
FINE!! IF IT'S A FIGHT THEY WANT, I'LL GIVE IT TO THEM!!
WHAM!!
ALL GUARDS TO LEVEL 4!!
SADIE !!
SAL-DEATH!!
HURRY WITH YOUR SUBORDINATES TO LEVEL 4! I'M WILLING TO RISK MY LIFE TO BECOME THE WARDEN! OOPS, I MISSPOKE!
I MEAN, WE HAVE TO WIN THIS WAR OR DIE TRYING!!

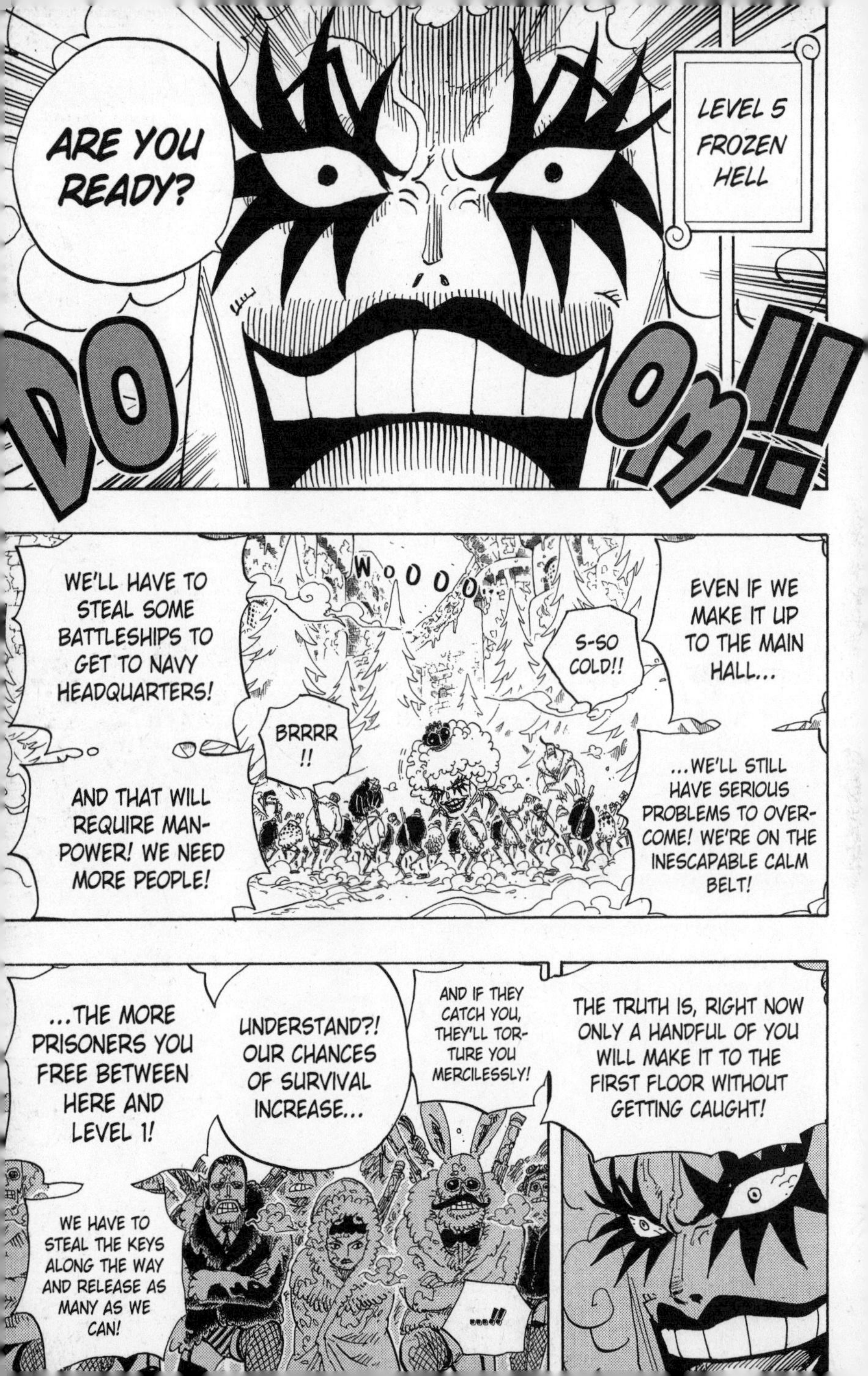
LEVEL 5
FROZEN
HELL
ARE YOU READY?
DOOM!!
EVEN IF WE MAKE IT UP TO THE MAIN HALL...
...WE'LL STILL HAVE SERIOUS PROBLEMS TO OVER-COME! WE'RE ON THE INESCAPABLE CALM BELT!
WOOOO
S-SO COLD!!
BRRRR!!
WE'LL HAVE TO STEAL SOME BATTLESHIPS TO GET TO NAVY HEADQUARTERS!
AND THAT WILL REQUIRE MAN-POWER! WE NEED MORE PEOPLE!
THE TRUTH IS, RIGHT NOW ONLY A HANDFUL OF YOU WILL MAKE IT TO THE FIRST FLOOR WITHOUT GETTING CAUGHT!
AND IF THEY CATCH YOU, THEY'LL TOR-TURE YOU MERCILESSLY!
UNDERSTAND?! OUR CHANCES OF SURVIVAL INCREASE...
...THE MORE PRISONERS YOU FREE BETWEEN HERE AND LEVEL 1!
WE HAVE TO STEAL THE KEYS ALONG THE WAY AND RELEASE AS MANY AS WE CAN!
...!!

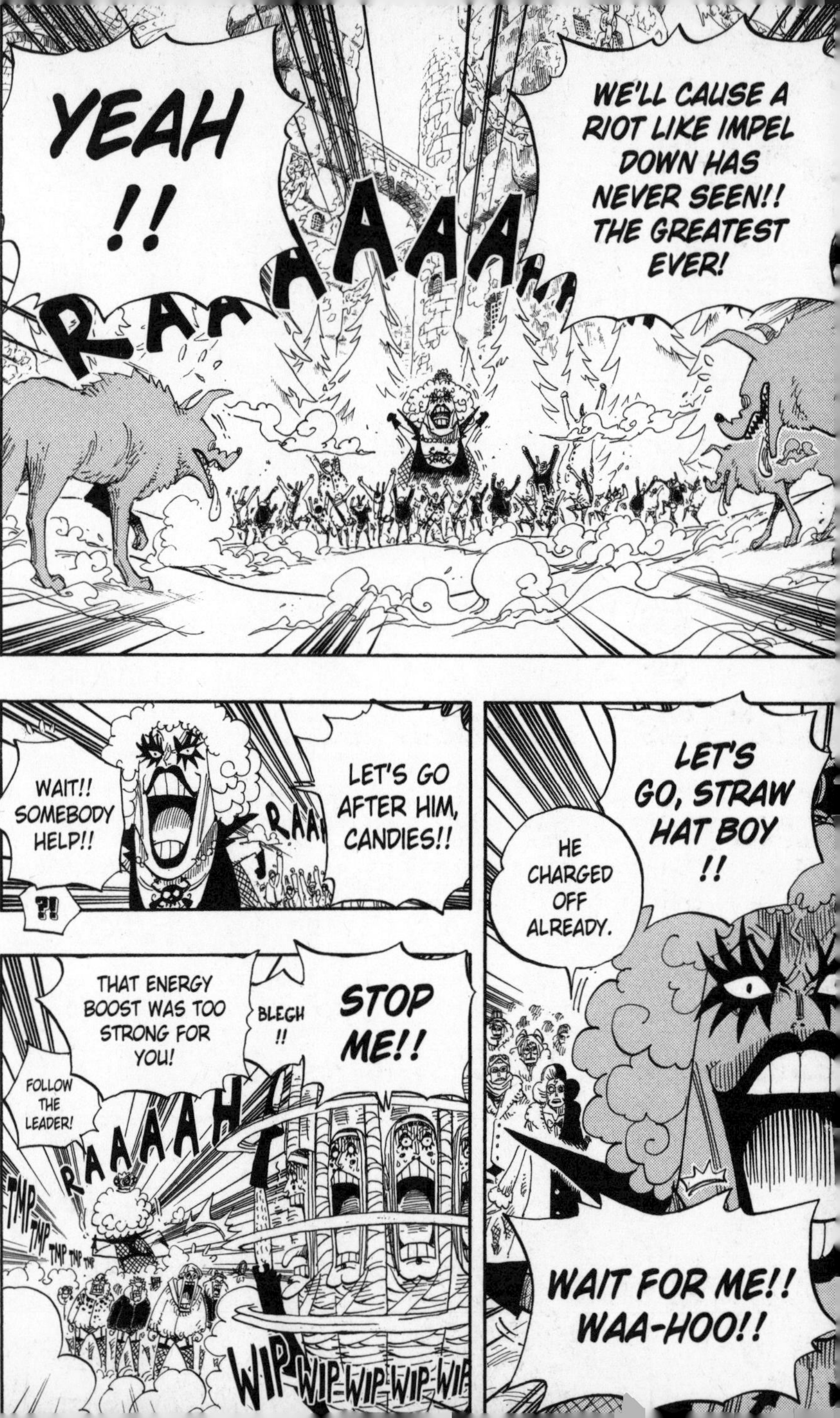
WE'LL CAUSE A RIOT LIKE IMPEL DOWN HAS NEVER SEEN!! THE GREATEST EVER!
YEAH !!
RAAAAAAAAH
LET'S GO, STRAW HAT BOY !!
HE CHARGED OFF ALREADY.
WAIT FOR ME!! WAA-HOO!!
LET'S GO AFTER HIM, CANDIES!!
RAAH
WAIT!! SOMEBODY HELP!!
?!
STOP ME!!
BLEGH !!
THAT ENERGY BOOST WAS TOO STRONG FOR YOU!
FOLLOW THE LEADER!
RAAAAAH
TMP TMP TMP TMP TMP
WIP WIP WIP WIP WIP

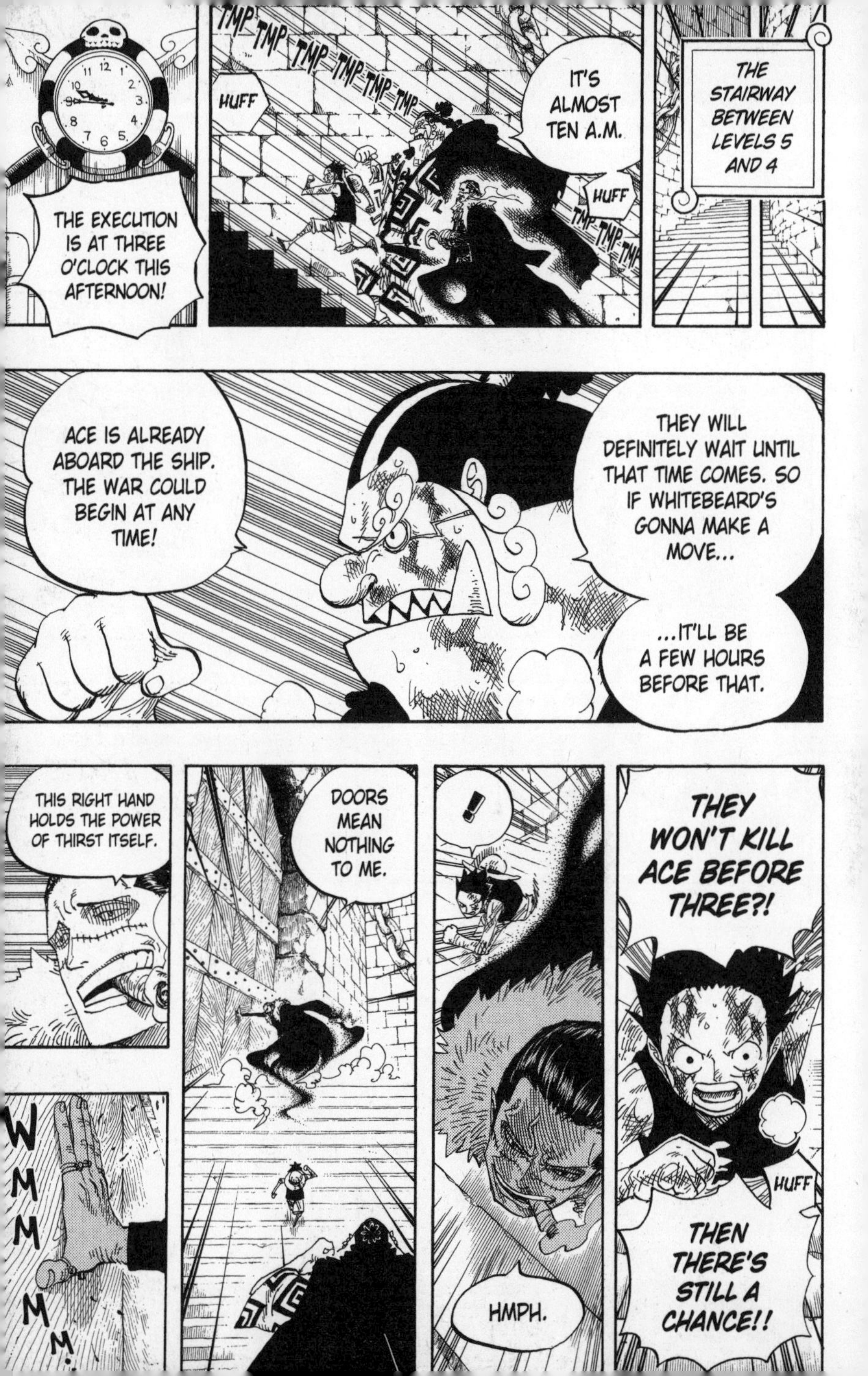
THE STAIRWAY BETWEEN LEVELS 5 AND 4
TMP TMP TMP TMP TMP TMP
IT'S ALMOST TEN A.M.
HUFF
HUFF
TMP TMP TMP
THE EXECUTION IS AT THREE O'CLOCK THIS AFTERNOON!
THEY WILL DEFINITELY WAIT UNTIL THAT TIME COMES. SO IF WHITEBEARD'S GONNA MAKE A MOVE...
...IT'LL BE A FEW HOURS BEFORE THAT.
ACE IS ALREADY ABOARD THE SHIP. THE WAR COULD BEGIN AT ANY TIME!
THEY WON'T KILL ACE BEFORE THREE?!
HUFF
THEN THERE'S STILL A CHANCE!!
!
HMPH.
DOORS MEAN NOTHING TO ME.
THIS RIGHT HAND HOLDS THE POWER OF THIRST ITSELF.
WMMMM

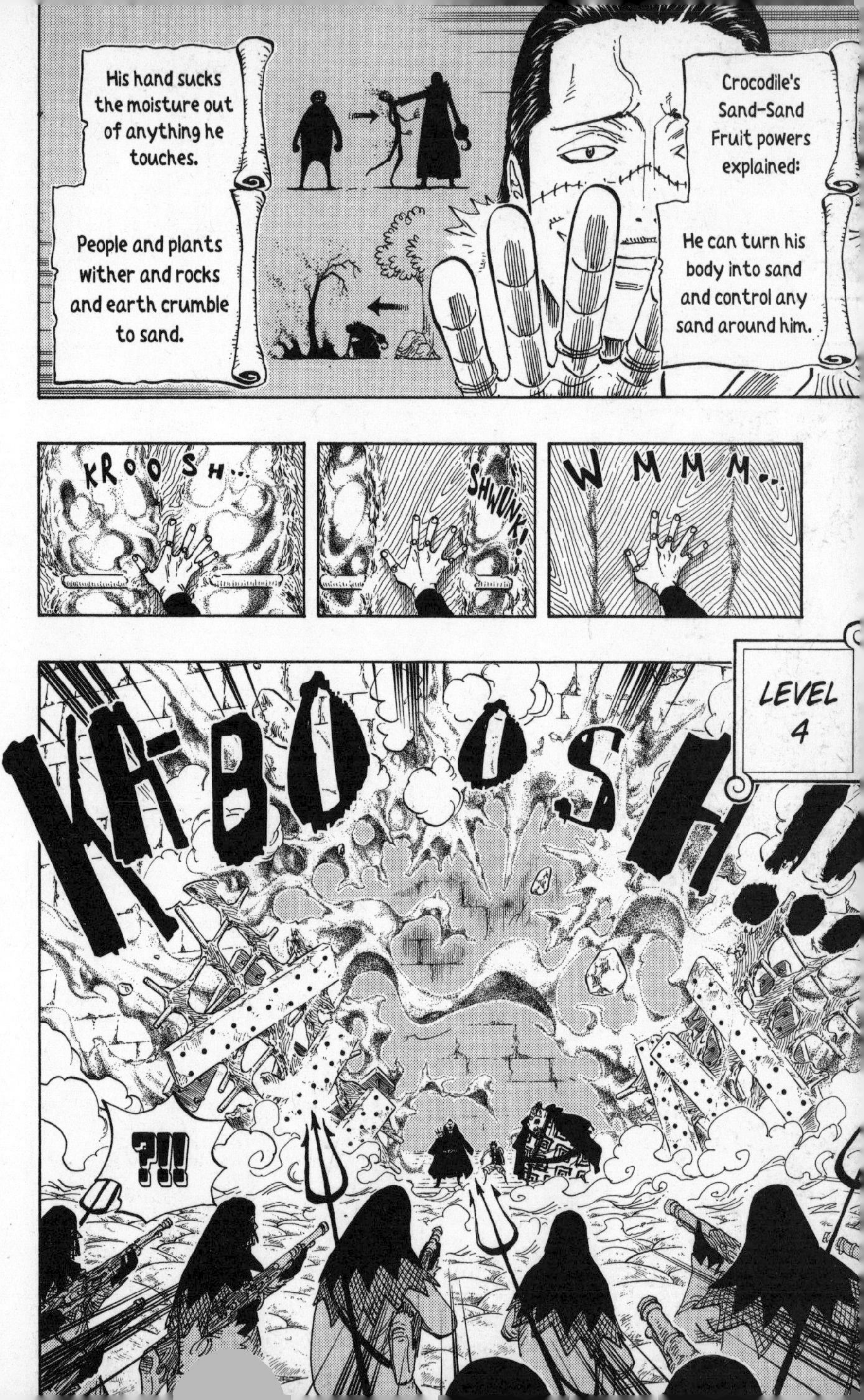
Crocodile's Sand-Sand Fruit powers explained:
He can turn his body into sand and control any sand around him.
His hand sucks the moisture out of anything he touches.
People and plants wither and rocks and earth crumble to sand.
WMMM...
SHWUNK!
KROOSH...
LEVEL 4
KA-BOOSH!!
?!!

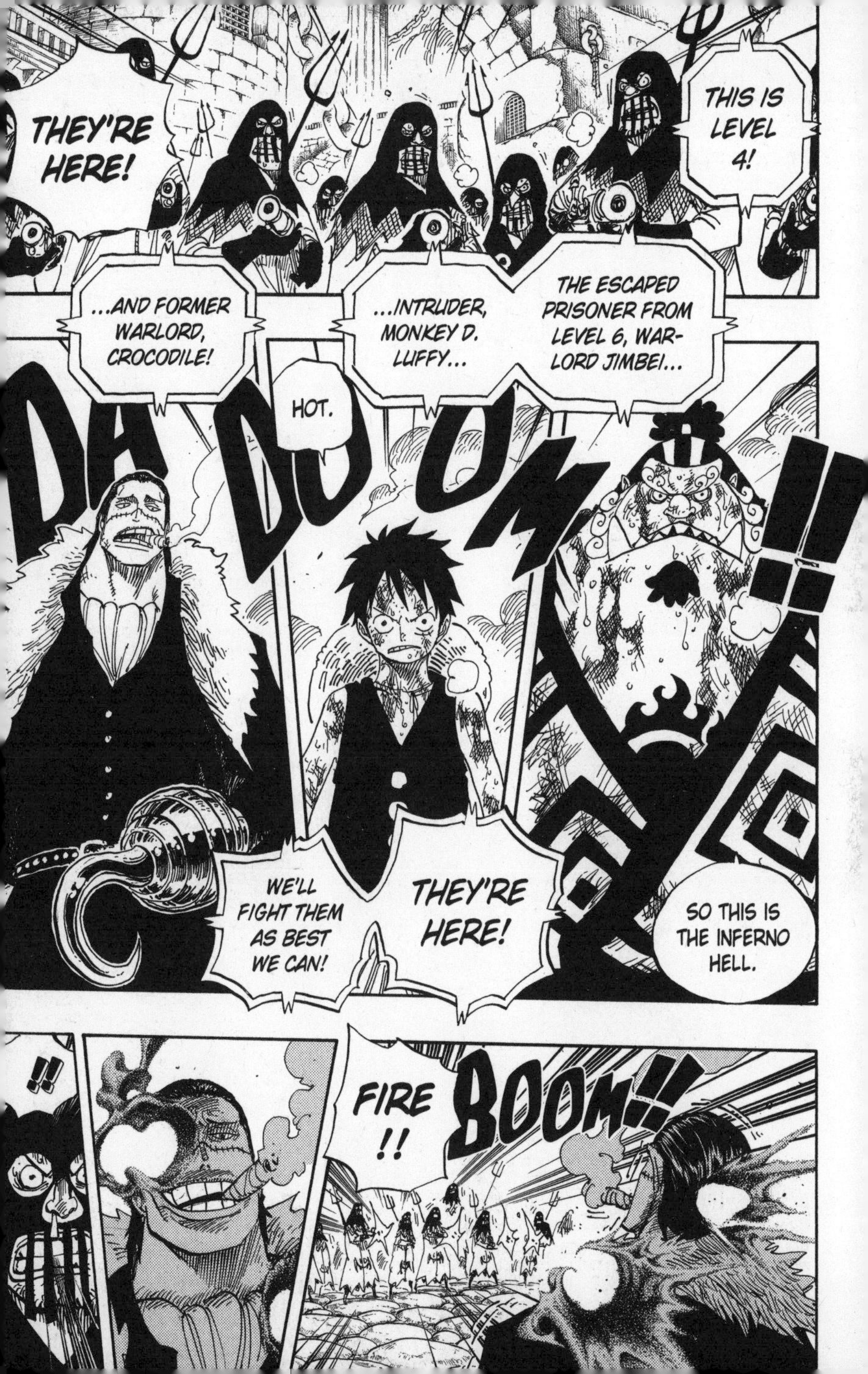
THIS IS LEVEL 4!
THEY'RE HERE!
THE ESCAPED PRISONER FROM LEVEL 6, WAR-LORD JIMBEI...
...INTRUDER, MONKEY D. LUFFY...
...AND FORMER WARLORD, CROCODILE!
DA DO OM!!
SO THIS IS THE INFERNO HELL.
HOT.
THEY'RE HERE!
WE'LL FIGHT THEM AS BEST WE CAN!
BOOM!!
FIRE !!
!!

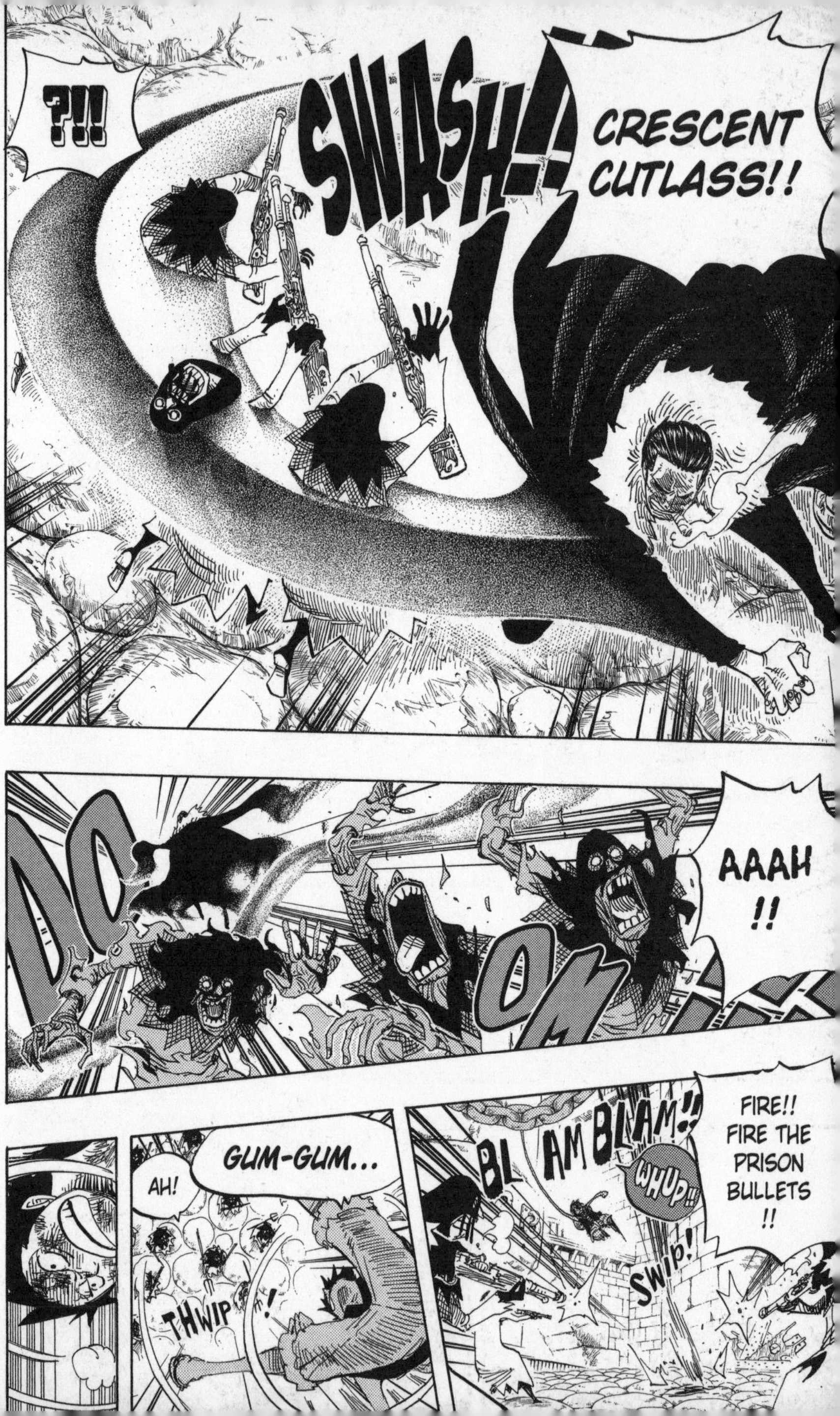
CRESCENT CUTLASS!!
SWASH!!
?!!
AAAH !!
FIRE!! FIRE THE PRISON BULLETS !!
BLAM BLAM!!
WHUP!!
SWIP!
GUM-GUM...
AH!
!
THWIP

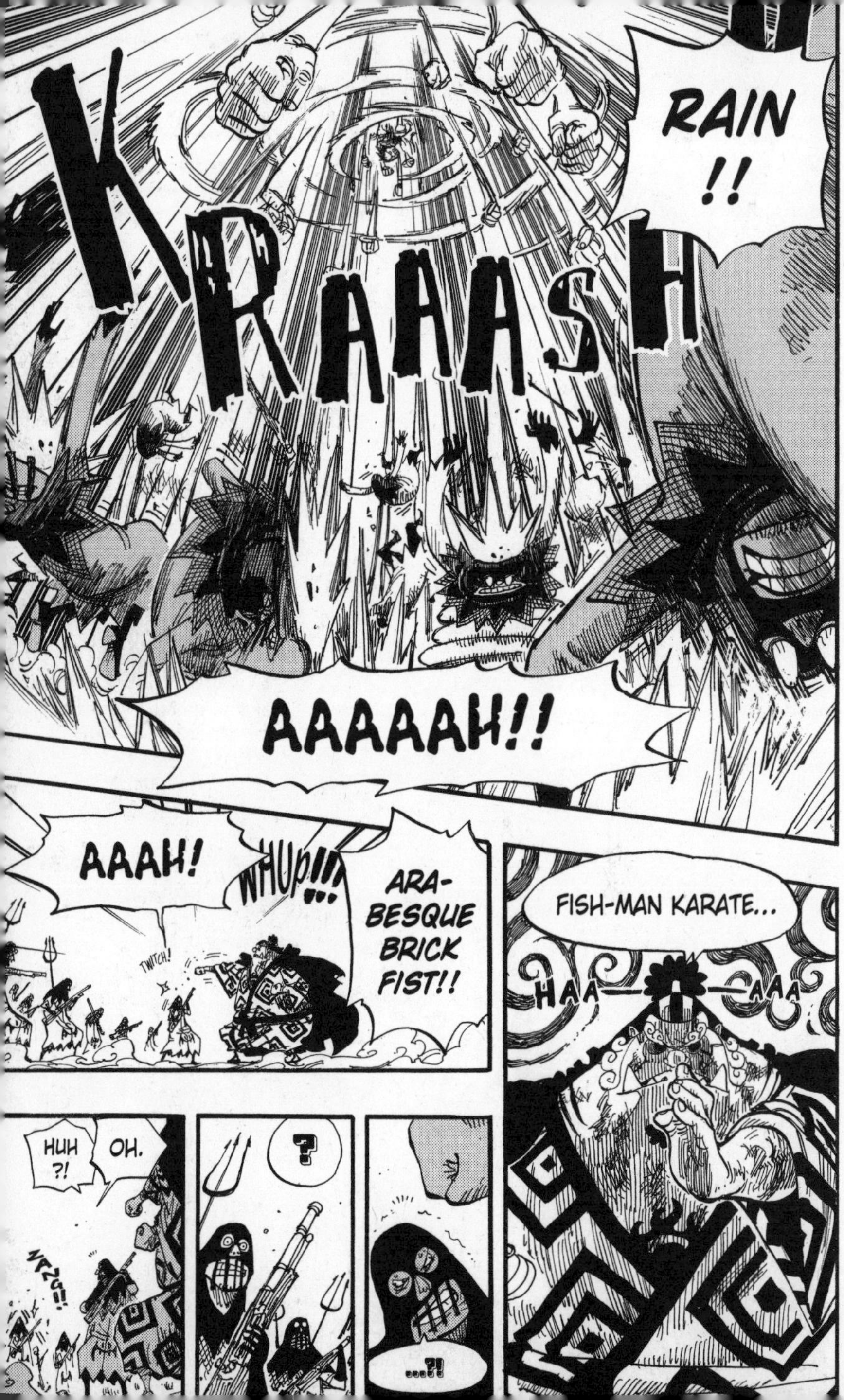
RAIN !!
KRAAASH
AAAAAH!!
FISH-MAN KARATE...
HAA—AAA
ARA-BESQUE BRICK FIST!!
WHUP!!!
AAAH!
TWITCH!
...?!
?
OH.
HUH ?!
ZANG!!

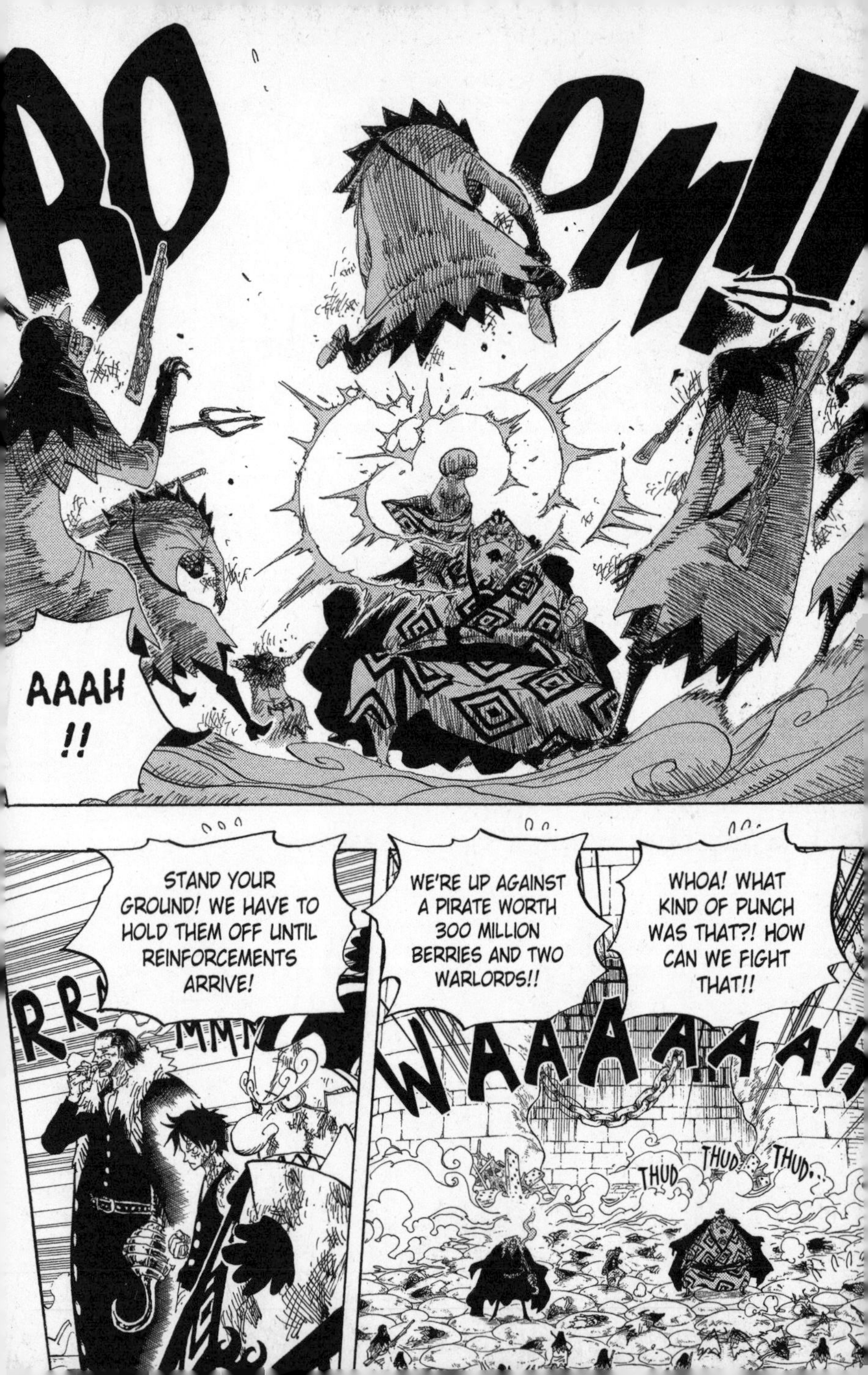
BOOM!!
AAAH!!
WHOA! WHAT KIND OF PUNCH WAS THAT?! HOW CAN WE FIGHT THAT!!
WE'RE UP AGAINST A PIRATE WORTH 300 MILLION BERRIES AND TWO WARLORDS!!
WAAAAAAH
THUD THUD THUD...
STAND YOUR GROUND! WE HAVE TO HOLD THEM OFF UNTIL REINFORCEMENTS ARRIVE!

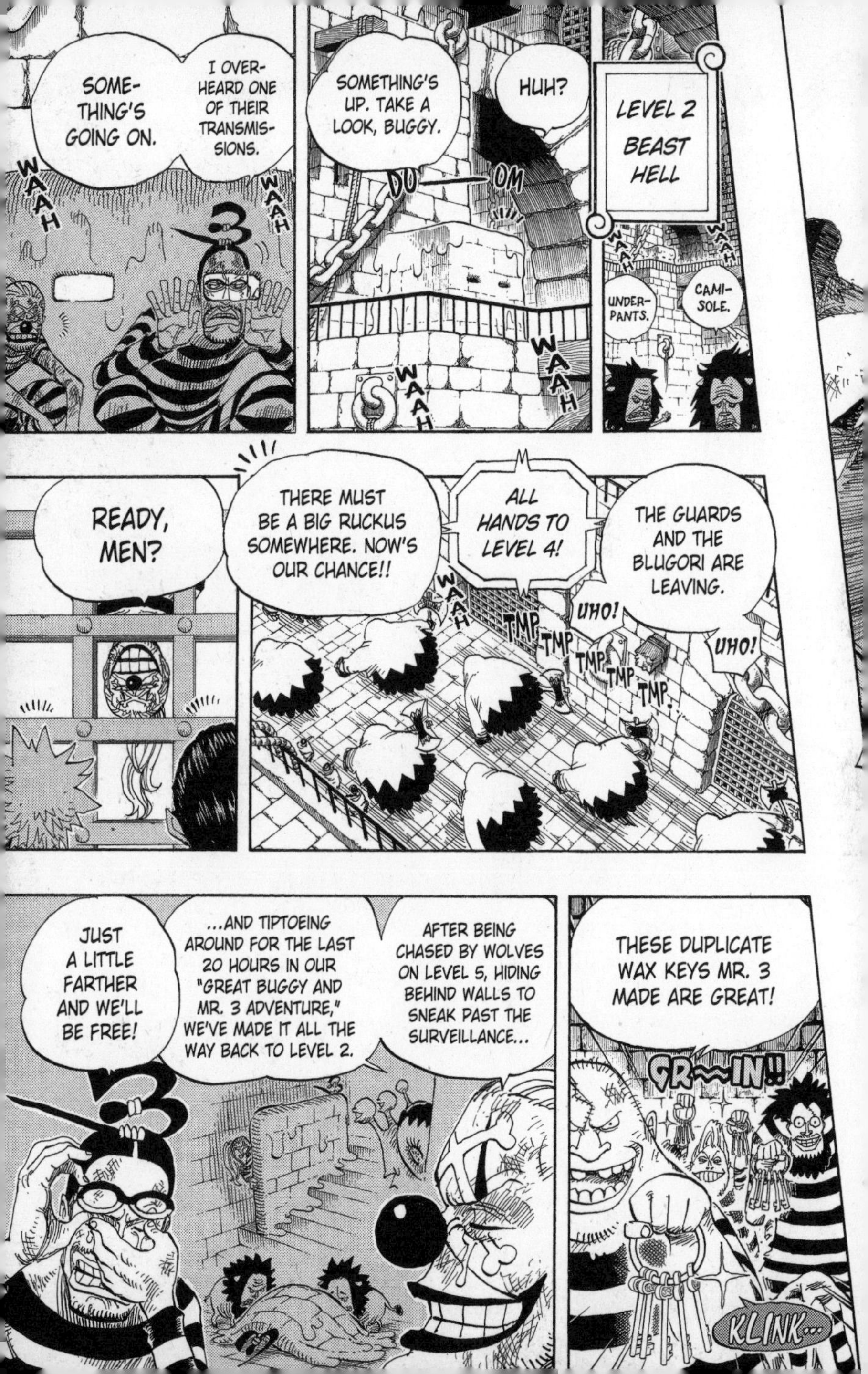
LEVEL 2 BEAST HELL
WAAH
WAAH
CAMI-SOLE.
UNDER-PANTS.
HUH?
SOMETHING'S UP. TAKE A LOOK, BUGGY.
DU—OM
WAAH
WAAH
I OVER-HEARD ONE OF THEIR TRANSMIS-SIONS.
SOME-THING'S GOING ON.
WAAH
WAAH
THE GUARDS AND THE BLUGORI ARE LEAVING.
UHO!
UHO!
ALL HANDS TO LEVEL 4!
TMP TMP TMP TMP TMP
WAAH
THERE MUST BE A BIG RUCKUS SOMEWHERE. NOW'S OUR CHANCE!!
READY, MEN?
THESE DUPLICATE WAX KEYS MR. 3 MADE ARE GREAT!
GR~~IN!!
KLINK...
AFTER BEING CHASED BY WOLVES ON LEVEL 5, HIDING BEHIND WALLS TO SNEAK PAST THE SURVEILLANCE...
...AND TIPTOEING AROUND FOR THE LAST 20 HOURS IN OUR "GREAT BUGGY AND MR. 3 ADVENTURE," WE'VE MADE IT ALL THE WAY BACK TO LEVEL 2.
JUST A LITTLE FARTHER AND WE'LL BE FREE!

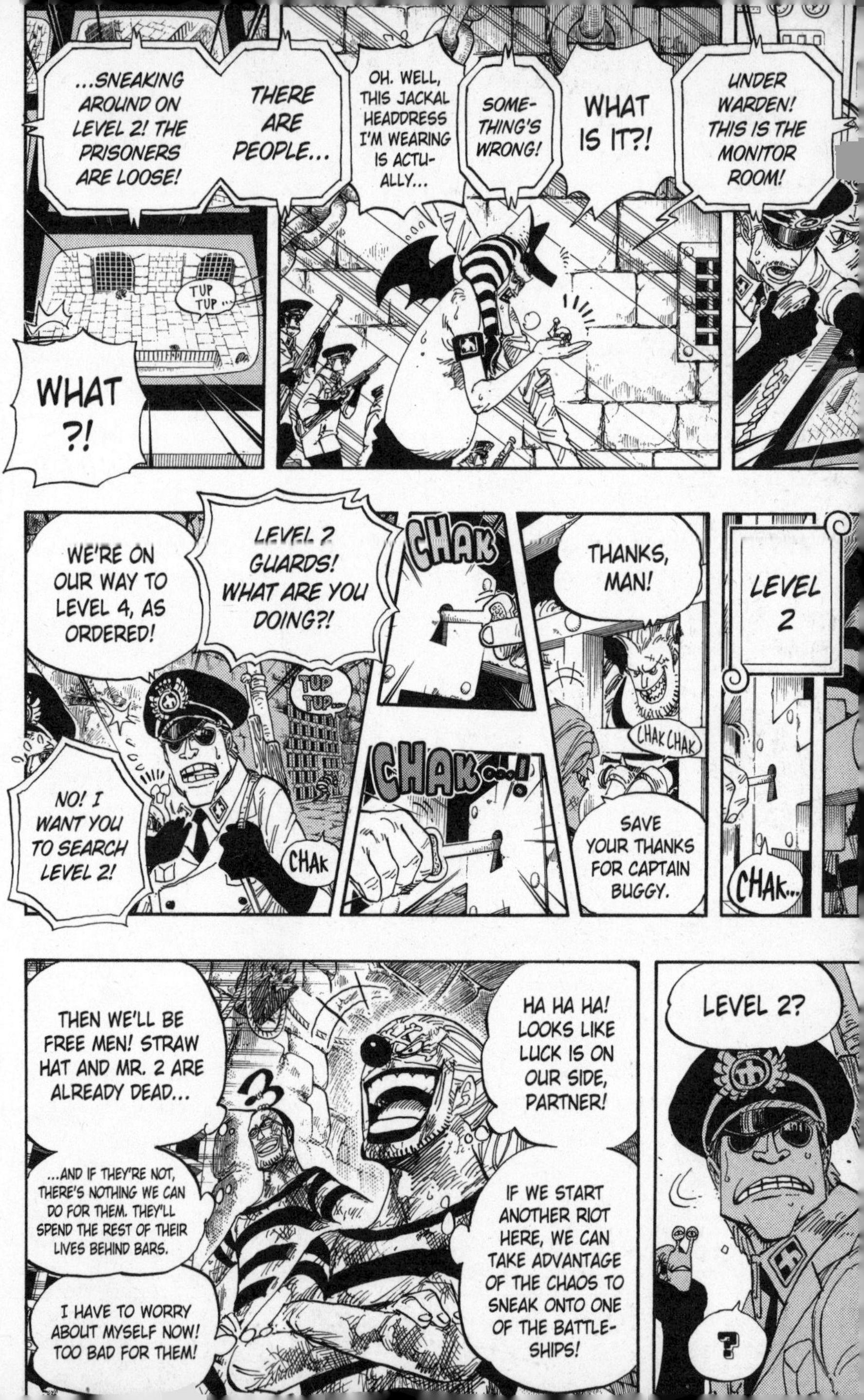
UNDER WARDEN! THIS IS THE MONITOR ROOM!
WHAT IS IT?!
SOME-THING'S WRONG!
OH. WELL, THIS JACKAL HEADDRESS I'M WEARING IS ACTU-ALLY...
THERE ARE PEOPLE...
...SNEAKING AROUND ON LEVEL 2! THE PRISONERS ARE LOOSE!
TUP TUP...
WHAT ?!
LEVEL 2
CHAK...
THANKS, MAN!
CHAK CHAK
SAVE YOUR THANKS FOR CAPTAIN BUGGY.
CHAK
CHAK...!
LEVEL 2 GUARDS! WHAT ARE YOU DOING?!
WE'RE ON OUR WAY TO LEVEL 4, AS ORDERED!
TUP TUP...
NO! I WANT YOU TO SEARCH LEVEL 2!
CHAK
LEVEL 2?
?
HA HA HA! LOOKS LIKE LUCK IS ON OUR SIDE, PARTNER!
THEN WE'LL BE FREE MEN! STRAW HAT AND MR. 2 ARE ALREADY DEAD...
IF WE START ANOTHER RIOT HERE, WE CAN TAKE ADVANTAGE OF THE CHAOS TO SNEAK ONTO ONE OF THE BATTLE-SHIPS!
...AND IF THEY'RE NOT, THERE'S NOTHING WE CAN DO FOR THEM. THEY'LL SPEND THE REST OF THEIR LIVES BEHIND BARS.
I HAVE TO WORRY ABOUT MYSELF NOW! TOO BAD FOR THEM!

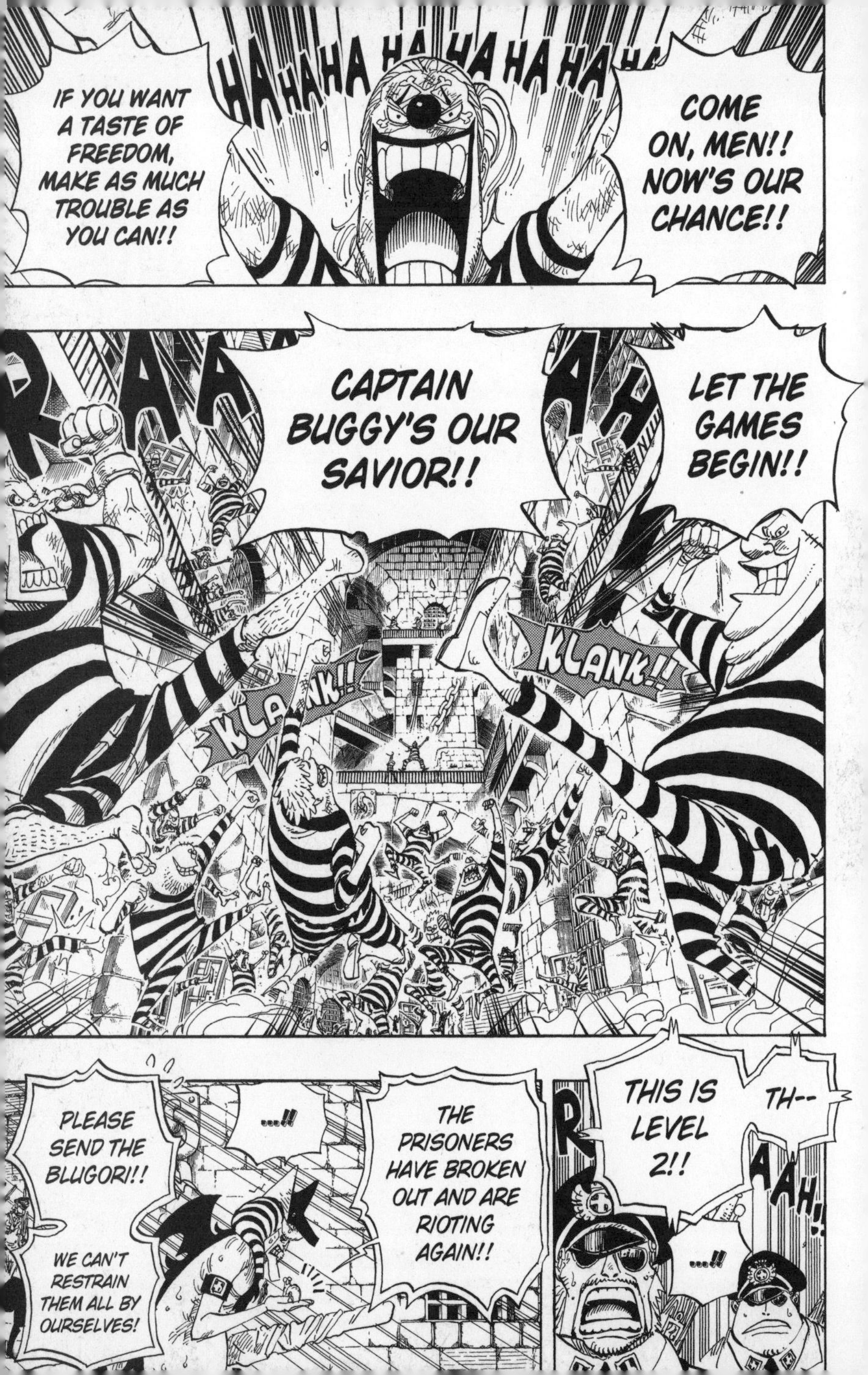
COME ON, MEN!! NOW'S OUR CHANCE!!
IF YOU WANT A TASTE OF FREEDOM, MAKE AS MUCH TROUBLE AS YOU CAN!!
LET THE GAMES BEGIN!!
CAPTAIN BUGGY'S OUR SAVIOR!!
KLANK!!
KLANK!!
TH--
THIS IS LEVEL 2!!
RAAH!!
...!!
THE PRISONERS HAVE BROKEN OUT AND ARE RIOTING AGAIN!!
...!!
PLEASE SEND THE BLUGORI!!
WE CAN'T RESTRAIN THEM ALL BY OURSELVES!

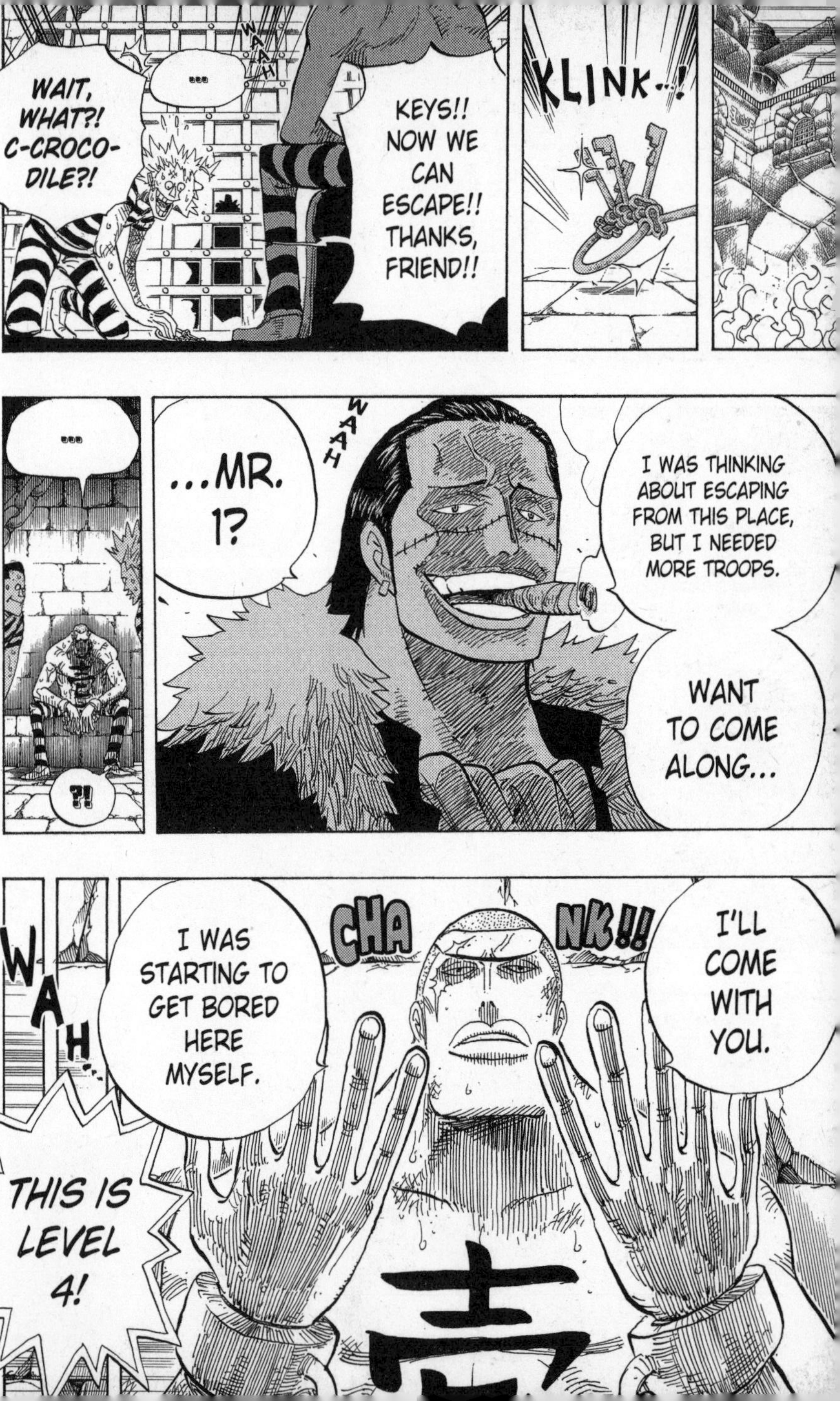
KLINK...!
KEYS!! NOW WE CAN ESCAPE!! THANKS, FRIEND!!
WAAH
...
WAIT, WHAT?! C-CROCODILE?!
I WAS THINKING ABOUT ESCAPING FROM THIS PLACE, BUT I NEEDED MORE TROOPS.
WANT TO COME ALONG...
WAAH
...MR. 1?
...
?!
I'LL COME WITH YOU.
CHANK!!
I WAS STARTING TO GET BORED HERE MYSELF.
WAAH...
THIS IS LEVEL 4!

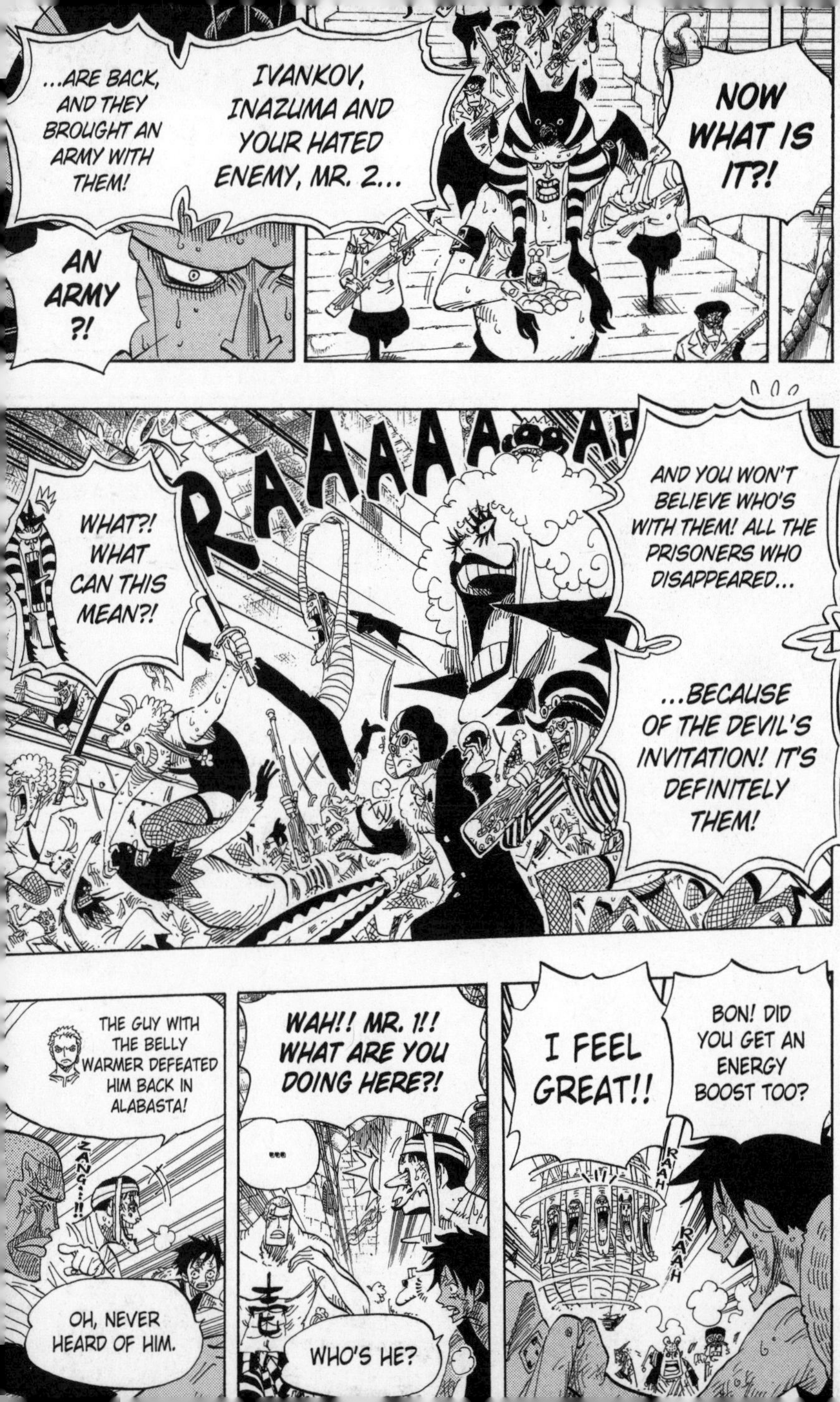
NOW WHAT IS IT?!
IVANKOV, INAZUMA AND YOUR HATED ENEMY, MR. 2...
...ARE BACK, AND THEY BROUGHT AN ARMY WITH THEM!
AN ARMY ?!
AND YOU WON'T BELIEVE WHO'S WITH THEM! ALL THE PRISONERS WHO DISAPPEARED...
RAAAAAAH
...BECAUSE OF THE DEVIL'S INVITATION! IT'S DEFINITELY THEM!
WHAT?! WHAT CAN THIS MEAN?!
BON! DID YOU GET AN ENERGY BOOST TOO?
I FEEL GREAT!!
RAAH
RAAH
WAH!! MR. 1!! WHAT ARE YOU DOING HERE?!
...
WHO'S HE?
THE GUY WITH THE BELLY WARMER DEFEATED HIM BACK IN ALABASTA!
ZANG...!!
OH, NEVER HEARD OF HIM.

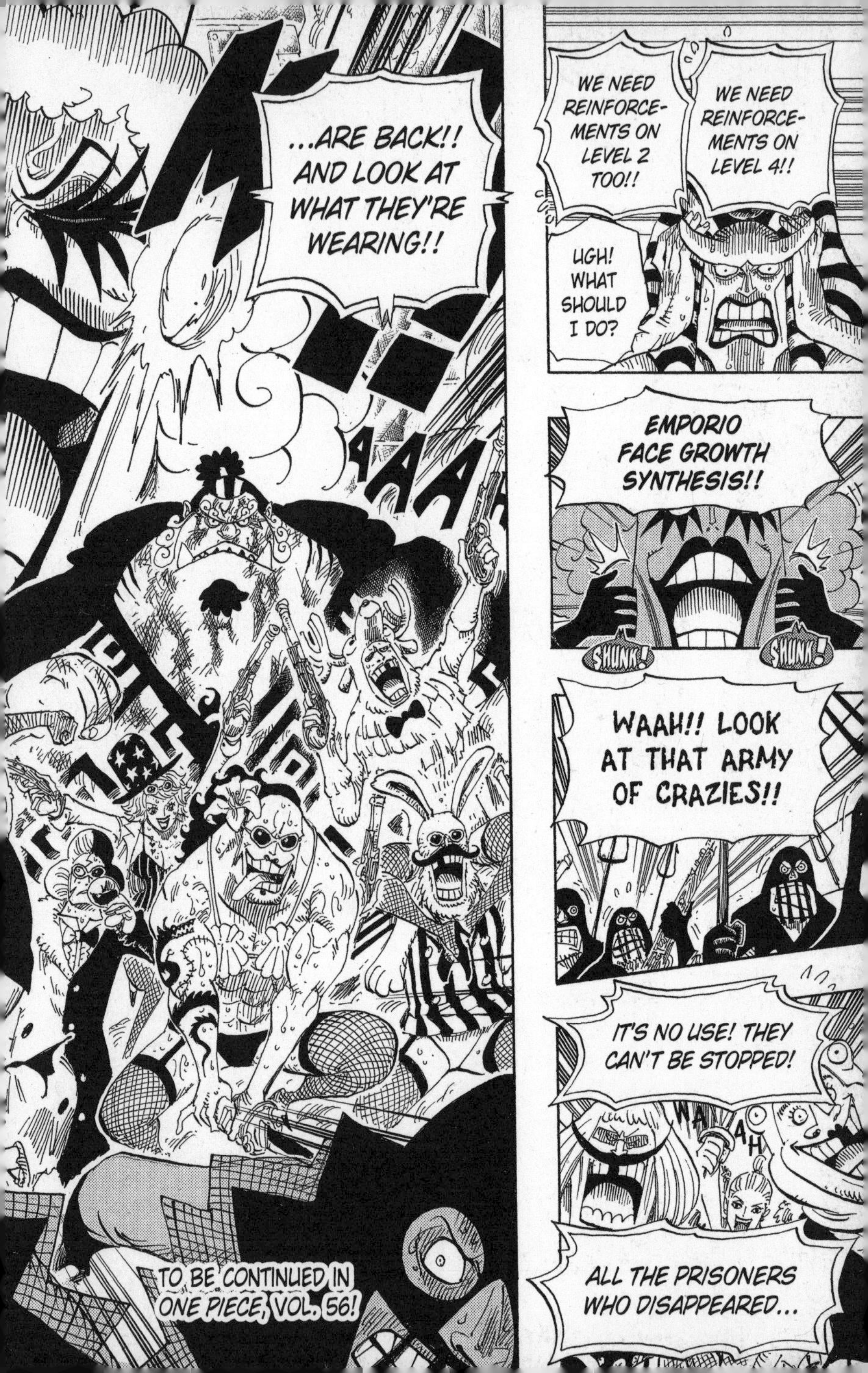
WE NEED REINFORCEMENTS ON LEVEL 4!!
WE NEED REINFORCEMENTS ON LEVEL 2 TOO!!
UGH! WHAT SHOULD I DO?
EMPORIO FACE GROWTH SYNTHESIS!!
SHUNK!
SHUNK!
WAAH!! LOOK AT THAT ARMY OF CRAZIES!!
IT'S NO USE! THEY CAN'T BE STOPPED!
WAAH
ALL THE PRISONERS WHO DISAPPEARED...
...ARE BACK!! AND LOOK AT WHAT THEY'RE WEARING!!
TO BE CONTINUED IN ONE PIECE, VOL. 56!

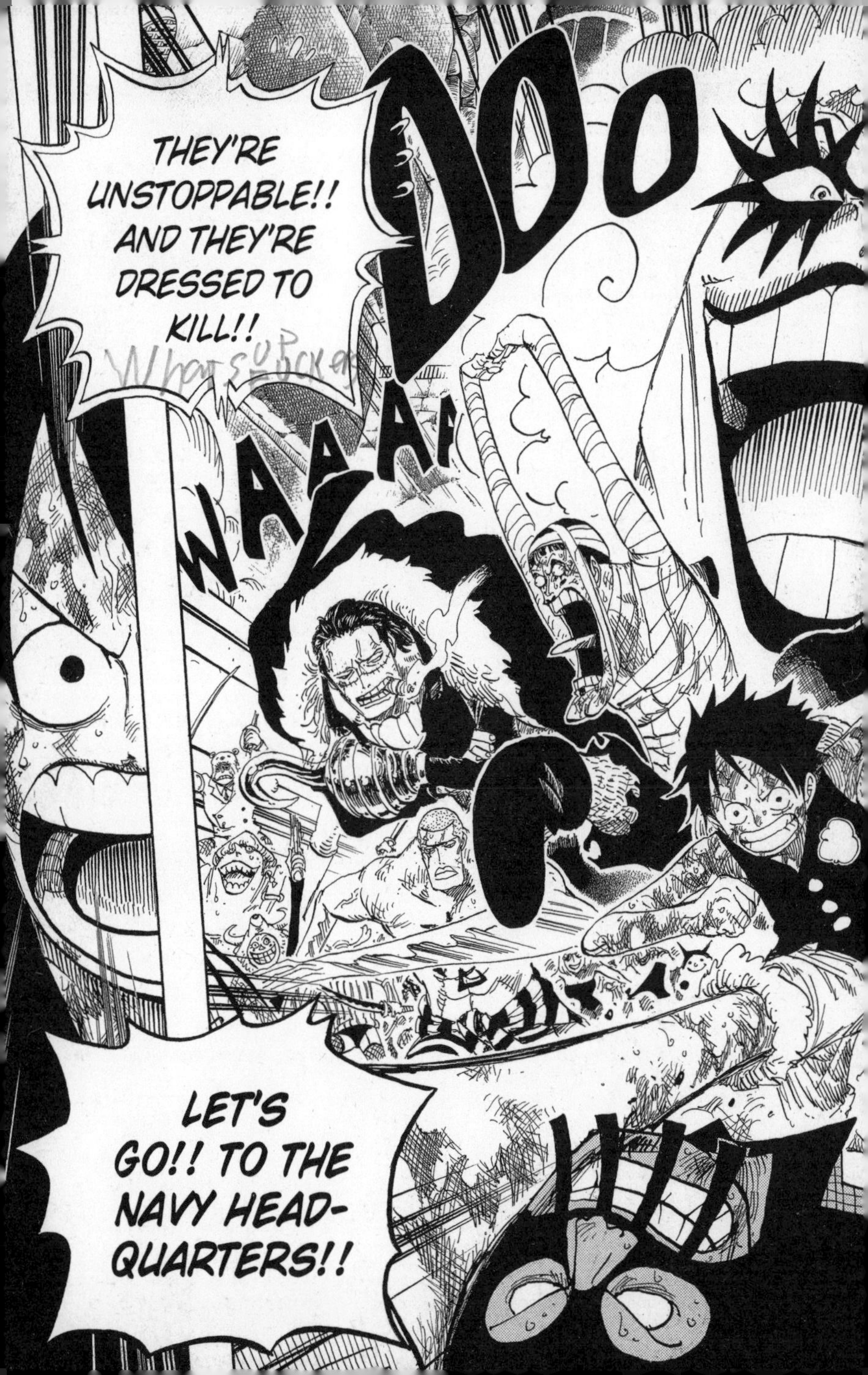
DOO
THEY'RE UNSTOPPABLE!! AND THEY'RE DRESSED TO KILL!!
WAAA
LET'S GO!! TO THE NAVY HEAD-QUARTERS!!

OUR BELOVED SNIPER, KAPPEI YAMAGUCHI!!

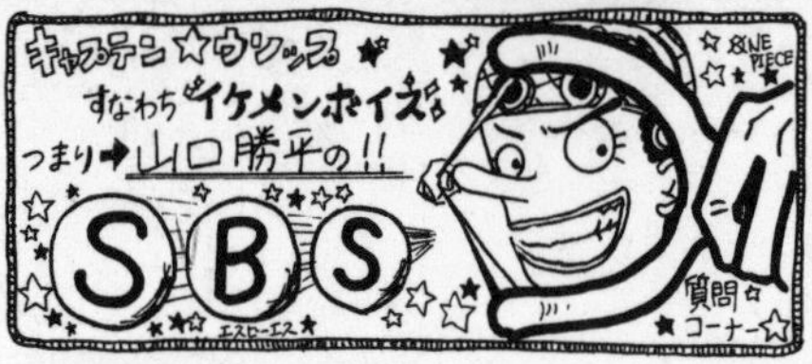
キャプテン☆ウソップ
すなわちイケメンボイズ
つまり➡山口勝平の!!
SBS
エスビーエス
ONE PIECE
質問コーナー
(Shimauma, Ehime Prefecture)

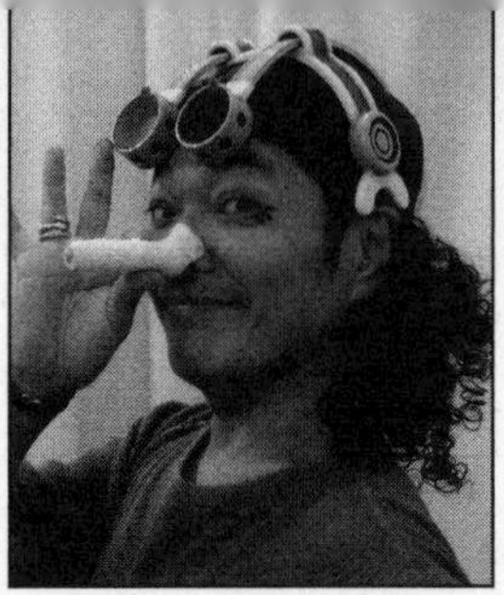

Reader(R): I have a question for you, Kappei Yamaguchi. Which voice actors do you look up to? Please answer seriously. ☆

--Maguko

Kappei(K): Here comes the serious answer: all of the actors who voice the Straw Hat Pirates. Especially Masako Nozawa and Master Kaneta Kimotsuki.

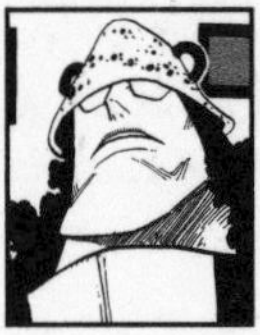

R: Which of Usopp's lines did you have the most trouble with?

--Moko-chan

K: So many! That line about the person who ate the Paw-Paw Fruit! (Looks into the distance) Wait! That's wasn't my line!

R: And can I see your underpants?

K: Sure. Peace! ♡ V! V!

R: Don't you think Kappei of the Yamaguchi seems a bit weird lately?

--Dachshundoria

K: How rude! I've always been weird!

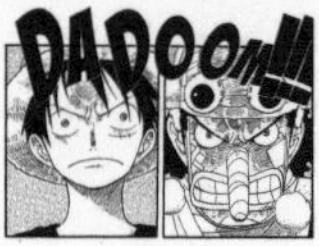
DADOOM!!

R: When Usopp and Luffy had that big fight in Water Seven, did you really duel with Tanaka?

--Silhouette

K: Well, for the sake of realism, we had to. But it was a pretty pathetic fight.

R: What's the difference between a girl and a woman? And which do you prefer?

--Stiff

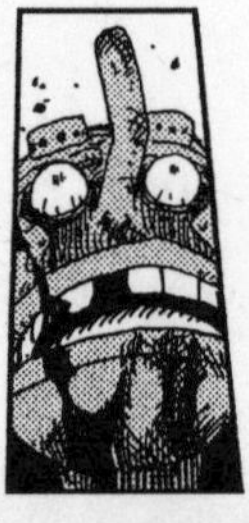

K: Well, I really can't talk about it in a magazine for boys! Tee-hee! ♡

R: I have a question! Who do you like better, Nami or Robin?

--A High School Girl ♡

K: I'll take Kokoro. Blegh!

R: Hello, Mr. Yamaguchi! Here's my question! What's the biggest lie you ever told?

--B'z Fan

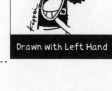

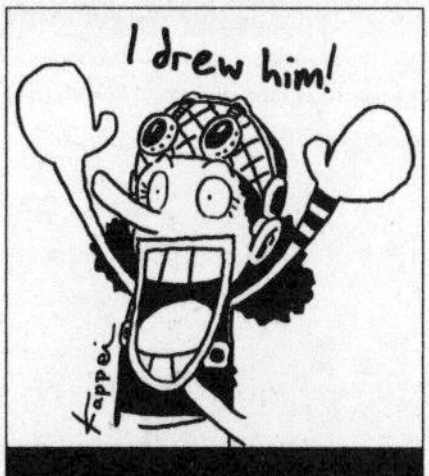
I drew him!
Kappei
Drawn with Left Hand

K: I've never told a lie in my life.♡

R: Hi, Kappei. Please draw Usopp with your left hand.

--Jump Festa 2009 was Fun

K: How's this?

R: Kappei! Turn your back to me, bite the nail of your right thumb, and look over your shoulder…

Sexy pose! ♡

--Bee God

K: I had a picture taken but I was so sexy that the photographer and the camera turned to stone. "Mello-Mello Mellow!"

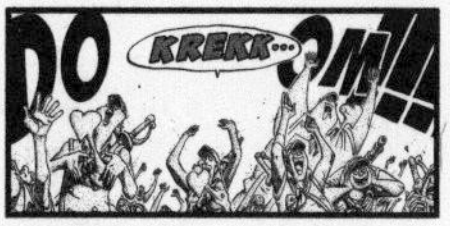
DO
KREKK...
OM!!

R: Hello, there! I have a question, Kappei Yamaguchi! Out of the following, which is most important to you: 1. Scripts 2. Japan 3. Pretty girls

--Demomo

K: I rank them 3, 2 and 1.♡

R: Do voice actors with very distinctive speaking voices get noticed a lot in their private lives? That would be my guess. (Especially the popular ones.) Did it ever happen to you?

--Kanna Miyamura

K: Yeah. But they never notice me when I want them to (when is that?), and they always notice me when I don't want them to (when is that?). The world is a strange place.

R: I love you, Kappei! ♡♡

Eat this! Rotten Egg Star! ☆

--Chan-chan

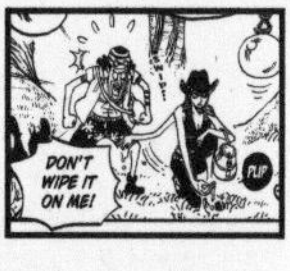
DON'T WIPE IT ON ME!
PLIP

K: Yuck, it's gooey! (Wipes it on Oda)

O: Hey! What are you doing?! It stinks! Geez… Kappei, let's just end it here! But there's one reader who wants to challenge you! Do you accept?

R: Kappei, let's fight a Negative Battle.

--Marron

K: Run!

O: He ran away!! He just does whatever he wants all the time! Wow, he's fast. Oh, he tripped! (Ha!) What?! He took off! He's flying!! How?! Anyway, see you in the next volume! Hey! Kappei!

The Results are in!!
The 4th One Piece Character Popularity Poll

42,116 votes were cast!!

Here are the results of the popularity poll from Issue 49 of Weekly Jump in 2008! Where does your favorite character rank?!

1st Place (7,065 votes) **Monkey D. Luffy**

He left 2nd and 3rd places in the dust!

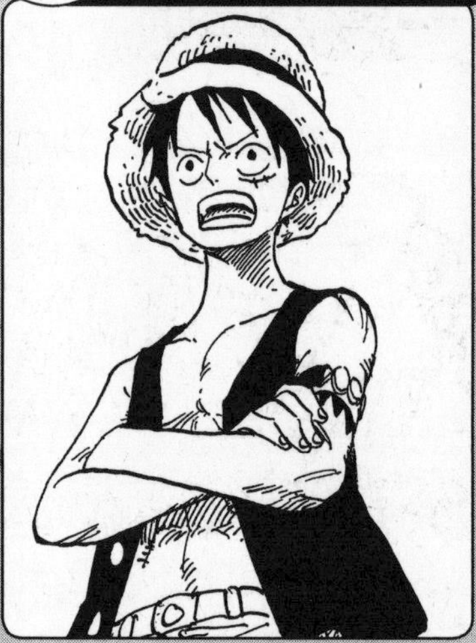

2nd Place (5,645 votes) **Roronoa Zolo**

Received support from people of all ages and genders.

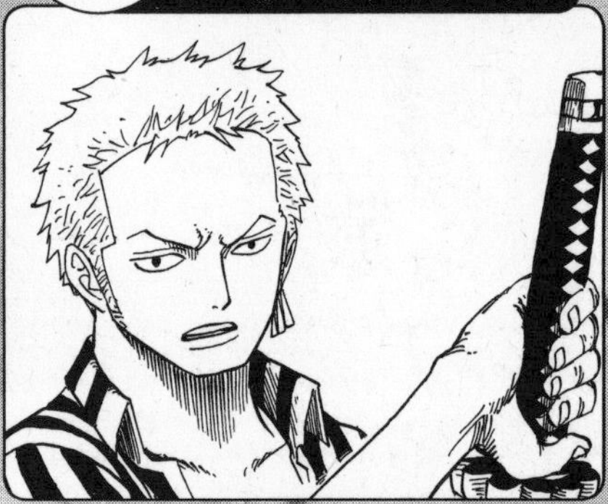

3rd Place (5,547 votes) **Sanji**

The fighting cook made 3rd place!

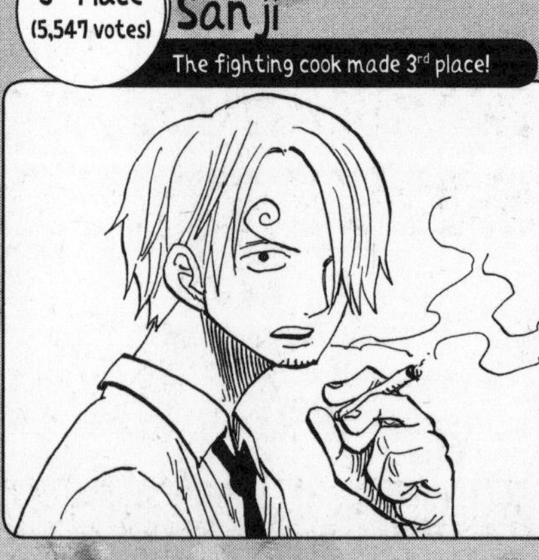

4th Place (3,362 votes) **Tony Tony Chopper**

Everyone keeps saying how cute he is!

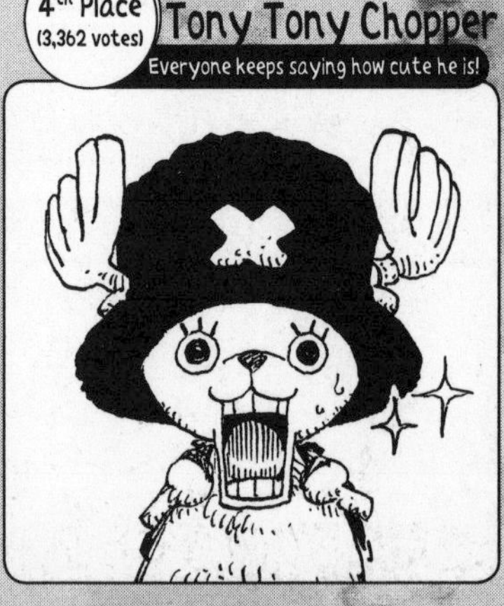

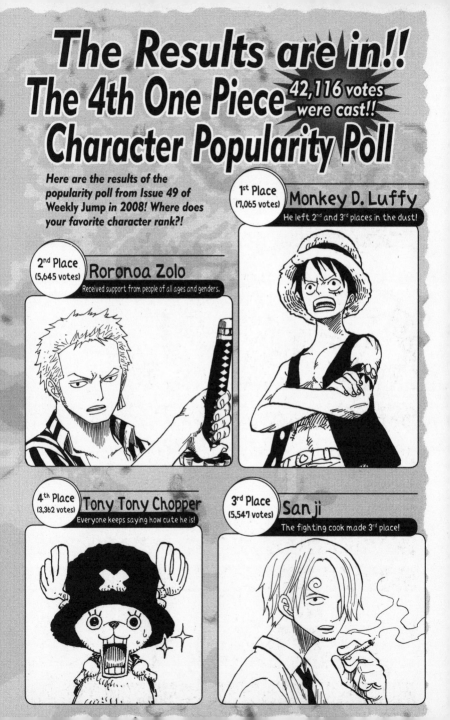

5th place (2,175 votes)
Portgaz D. Ace
Everybody loved him in the battle with Blackbeard!

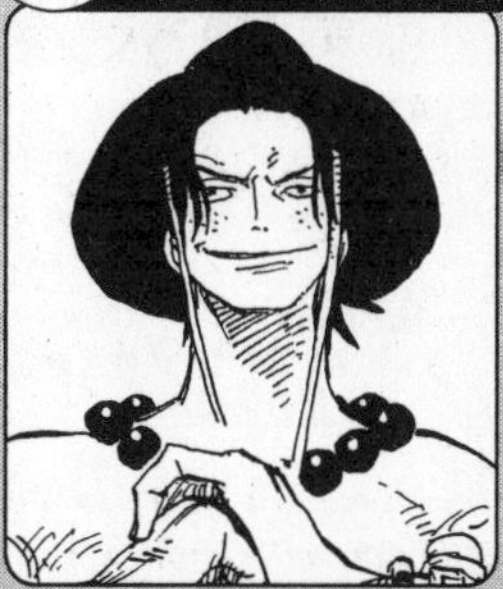

6th place (1,958 votes)
Nami
Highest-ranked female character!

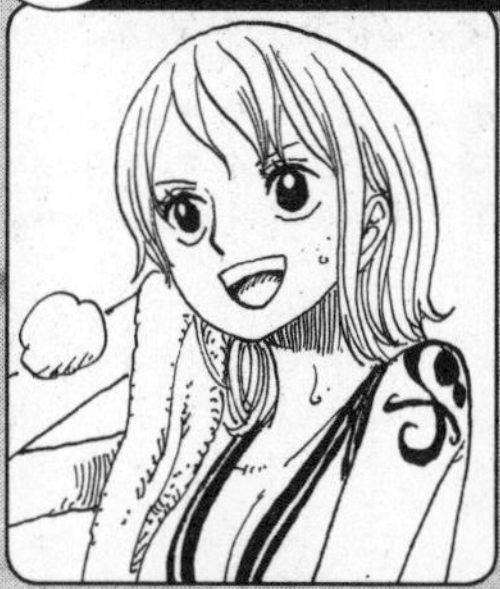

7th place (1,944 votes)
Nico Robin
Received tons of votes from girls!

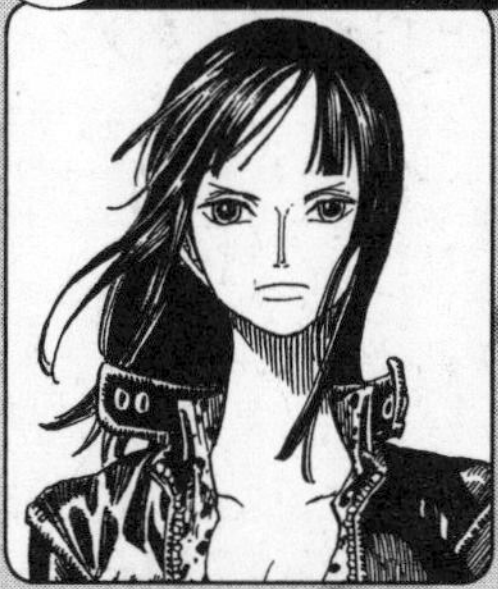

8th place (1,736 votes)
Shanks
Lots of people are waiting for his next appearance.

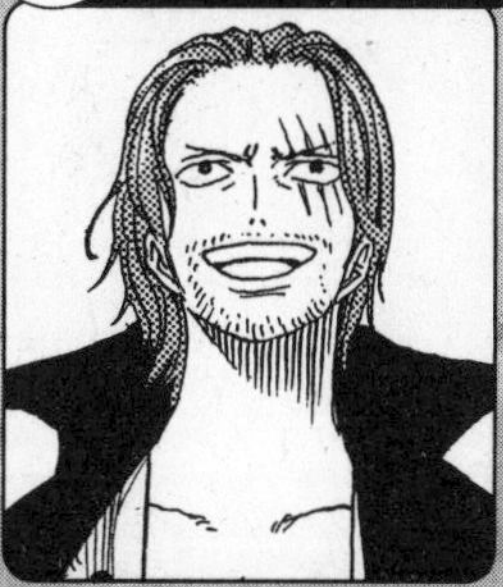

9th place (1,307 votes)
Brook
The newest member of the Straw Hat Pirates makes the top 10!

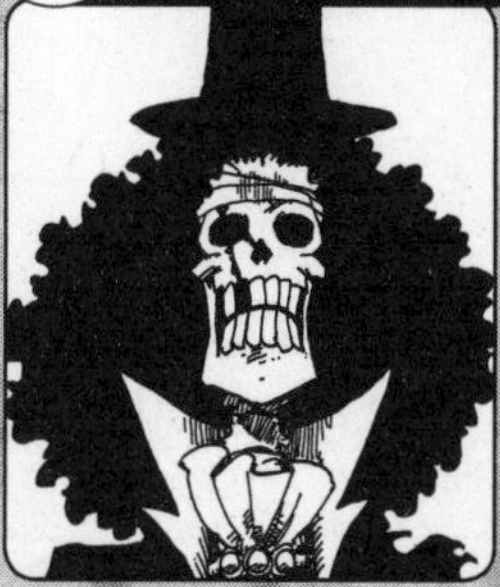

10th place (1,188 votes)
Trafalgar Law
Most popular of the other rookies.

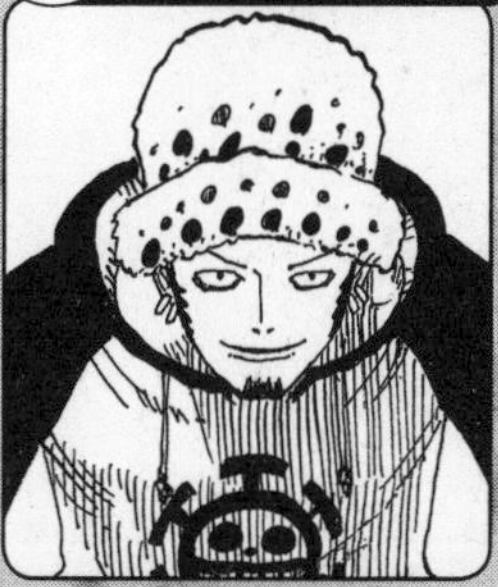

11th place

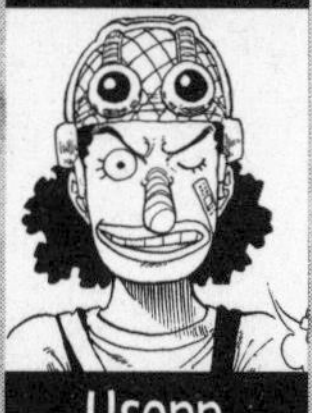

Usopp
(1,043 votes)

12th place

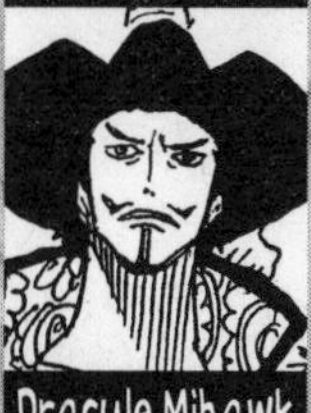

Dracule Mihawk
(743 votes)

13th place

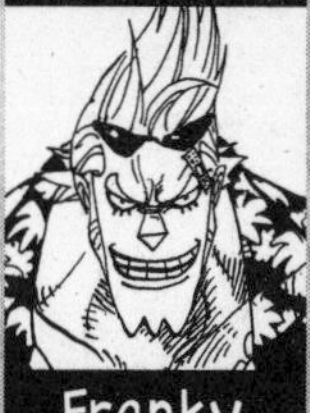

Franky
(715 votes)

14th place

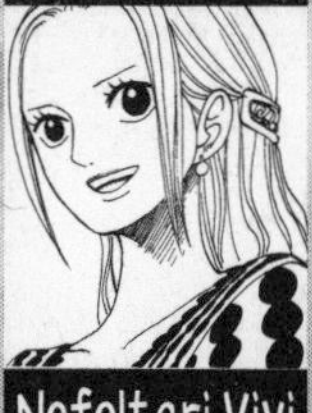

Nefeltari Vivi
(483 votes)

15th place

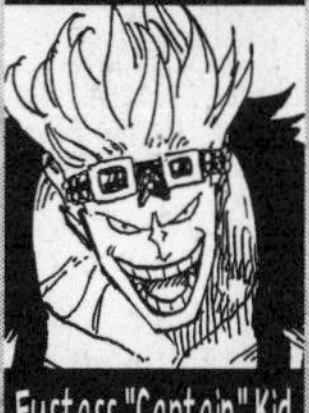

Eustass "Captain" Kid
(357 votes)

16th place

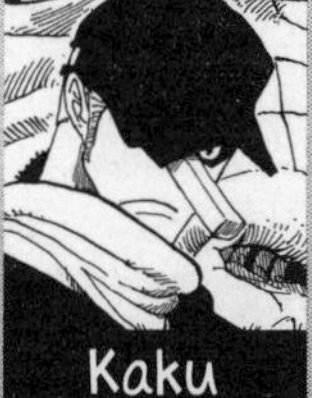

Kaku
(294 votes)

17th place

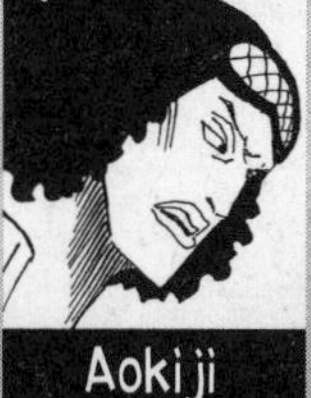

Aokiji
(280 votes)

18th place

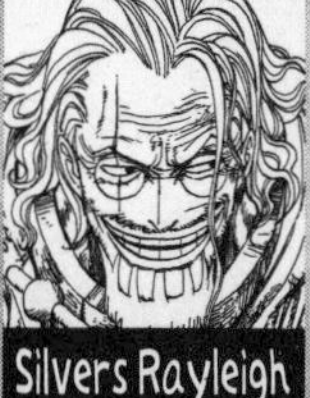

Silvers Rayleigh
(277 votes)

19th place

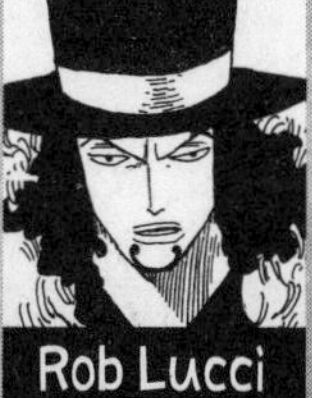

Rob Lucci
(266 votes)

20th place

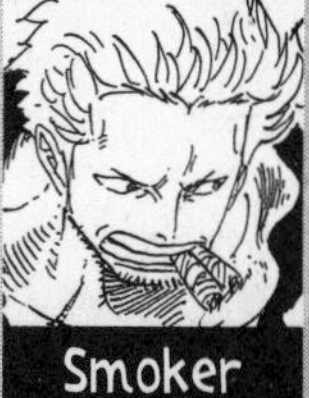

Smoker
(262 votes)

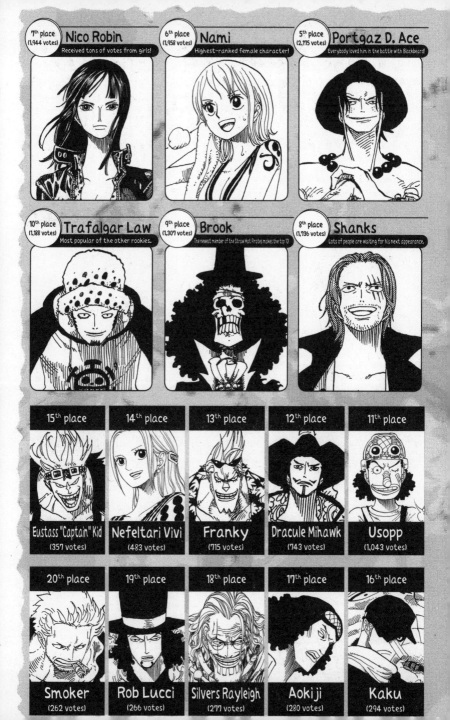

Here are the results from 21st to 122nd!

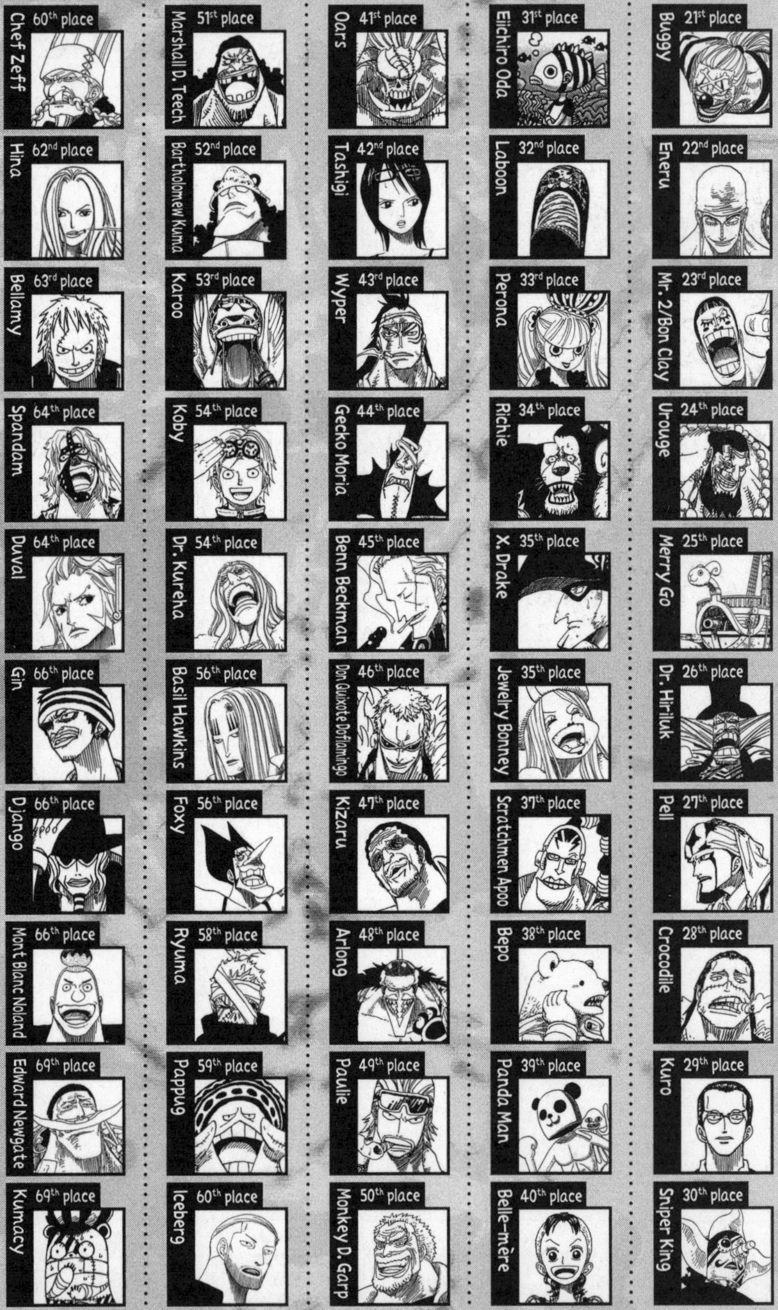

21st place
Buggy
22nd place
Eneru
23rd place
Mr. 2/Bon Clay
24th place
Urouge
25th place
Merry Go
26th place
Dr. Hiriluk
27th place
Pell
28th place
Crocodile
29th place
Kuro
30th place
Sniper King
31st place
Eiichiro Oda
32nd place
Laboon
33rd place
Perona
34th place
Richie
35th place
X. Drake
35th place
Jewelry Bonney
37th place
Scratchmen Apoo
38th place
Bepo
39th place
Panda Man
40th place
Belle-mère
41st place
Oars
42nd place
Tashigi
43rd place
Wyper
44th place
Gecko Moria
45th place
Benn Beckman
46th place
Don Quixote Doflamingo
47th place
Kizaru
48th place
Arlong
49th place
Paulie
50th place
Monkey D. Garp
51st place
Marshall D. Teech
52nd place
Bartholomew Kuma
53rd place
Karoo
54th place
Koby
54th place
Dr. Kureha
56th place
Basil Hawkins
56th place
Foxy
58th place
Ryuma
59th place
Pappug
60th place
Iceberg
60th place
Chef Zeff
62nd place
Hina
63rd place
Bellamy
64th place
Spandam
64th place
Duval
66th place
Gin
66th place
Django
66th place
Mont Blanc Noland
69th place
Edward Newgate
69th place
Kumacy

Results of the 4th One Piece Character Popularity Poll!

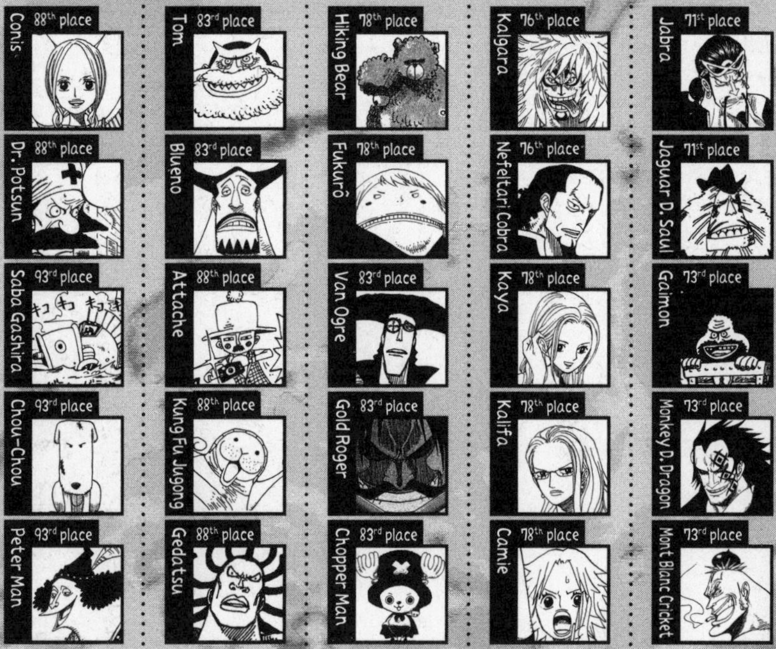

Conis 88th place
Tom 83rd place
Hiking Bear 78th place
Kalgara 76th place
Jabra 71st place
Dr. Potsun 88th place
Blueno 83rd place
Fukurô 78th place
Nefeltari Cobra 76th place
Jaguar D. Saul 71st place
Saba Gashira 93rd place
Attache 88th place
Van Ogre 83rd place
Kaya 78th place
Gaimon 73rd place
Chou-Chou 93rd place
Kung Fu Jugong 88th place
Gold Roger 83rd place
Kalifa 78th place
Monkey D. Dragon 73rd place
Peter Man 93rd place
Gedatsu 88th place
Chopper Man 83rd place
Camie 78th place
Mont Blanc Cricket 73rd place

93rd place

Auction No. 151
Sharinguru
Ms. Valentine's Day
Yokozuna

100th place

Aisa
Absalom
Alvida
Cutty Flam
Killer
Kuina
Krieg
Koza
Ryotsu Kankichi
Lola

110th place

Shriya Bascudo (Animated series only)
Cindry
Jimbei
Tsubaki
Tomato Gang
Higuma
Braham
Bull
Makino
Marumieta
Morgan
Yasopp

122nd place (And under)

Unluckies
Itomimizu
Dog Penguin
Nico Olvia
Kagikko
Kamakiri
Ganfor
Kiwi
Gyaro
Gyoro
Kumadori
Kurapowderman
Clover
Crocus
Kuromarimo
Koshiro
Kokoro
Gonbe
South Bird
Thousand Sunny
Sam
Samurai Batz
Shakky
Shura
Jozu
Johnny
???
Sentomaru
Zolo's shadow
Zolo Milk
Tilestone
Mayumi Tanaka
Onion
Editor Onishi
Master
T-Bone
Transponder Snail
Dr. Vegapunk
Dr. Ratchet (Animated series only)
Dorry
Dalton
Don Krieg
Onion Bear Maria
Nero
Nojiko
Nora
Bagaya
Patchi
Hachi
Hattori
Surprise Zombie
Funkfreed
Lt. Fullbody
Helmeppo
Hocker (Chou-Chou's master)
Porche
Marco
Mikazuki
MIKIO ITOO
Mr. 13
Mr. 3
Mr. 5
Mr. 9
Ms. Doublefinger
Ms. Monday
Straw Hat
Murasaki Guma
Moz
Kappei Yamaguchi
Snowman
Yurusumaji Mask
Yoki
Yosaku
Lassoo
Lafitte
Lil
Doctor who shook hands with Lucci
Luffyzaki
Rockstar
Wapol
Wanze
Nnke

COMING NEXT VOLUME:

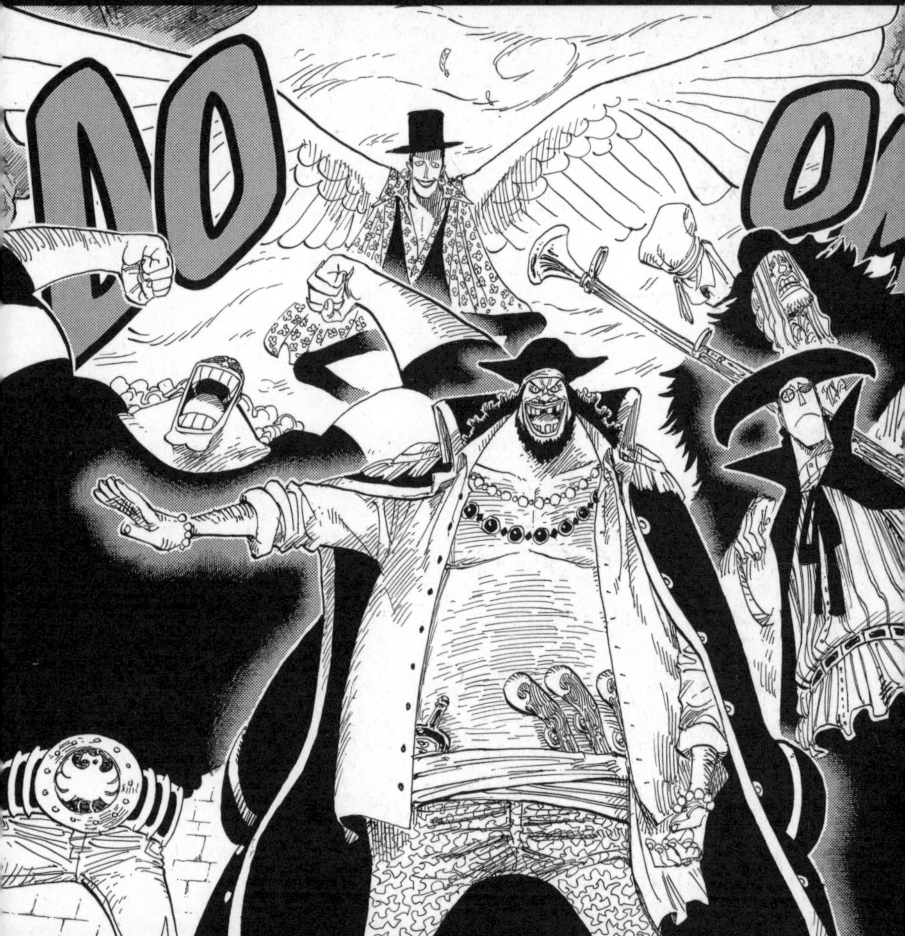
DO
DO

Now that Luffy knows that Ace is headed to Navy Headquarters, he'll have to break out of Impel Down in order to save his brother. He's found some powerful allies in Crocodile and Jimbei, but will it be enough? And when Blackbeard makes his return, will his presence make things even harder for Luffy?

ON SALE NOW!

STORY BY TSUGUMI OHBA
ART BY TAKESHI OBATA

From the creators of *Death Note*

The mystery behind manga making REVEALED!

Average student Moritaka Mashiro enjoys drawing for fun. When his classmate and aspiring writer Akito Takagi discovers his talent, he begs to team up. But what exactly does it take to make it in the manga-publishing world?

Bakuman₀ Vol. 1
ISBN: 978-1-4215-3513-5
$9.99 US / $12.99 CAN *

BLEACH

Story and Art by **Tite Kubo**

TAKING ON THE AFTERLIFE ONE SOUL AT A TIME

Ichigo Kurosaki never asked for the ability to see ghosts—he was born with the gift. When his family is attacked by a Hollow—a malevolent lost soul—Ichigo becomes a Soul Reaper, dedicating his life to protecting the innocent and helping the tortured spirits themselves find peace. Find out why Tite Kubo's Bleach has become an international manga smash-hit!

NARUTO

Story and Art by
Masashi Kishimoto

Naruto is determined to become the greatest ninja ever!

Twelve years ago the Village Hidden in the Leaves was attacked by a fearsome threat. A nine-tailed fox spirit claimed the life of the village leader, the Hokage, and many others. Today, the village is at peace and a troublemaking kid named Naruto is struggling to graduate from Ninja Academy. His goal may be to become the next Hokage, but his true destiny will be much more complicated. The adventure begins now!

WORLD'S BEST SELLING MANGA!

www.shonenjump.com

www.viz.com

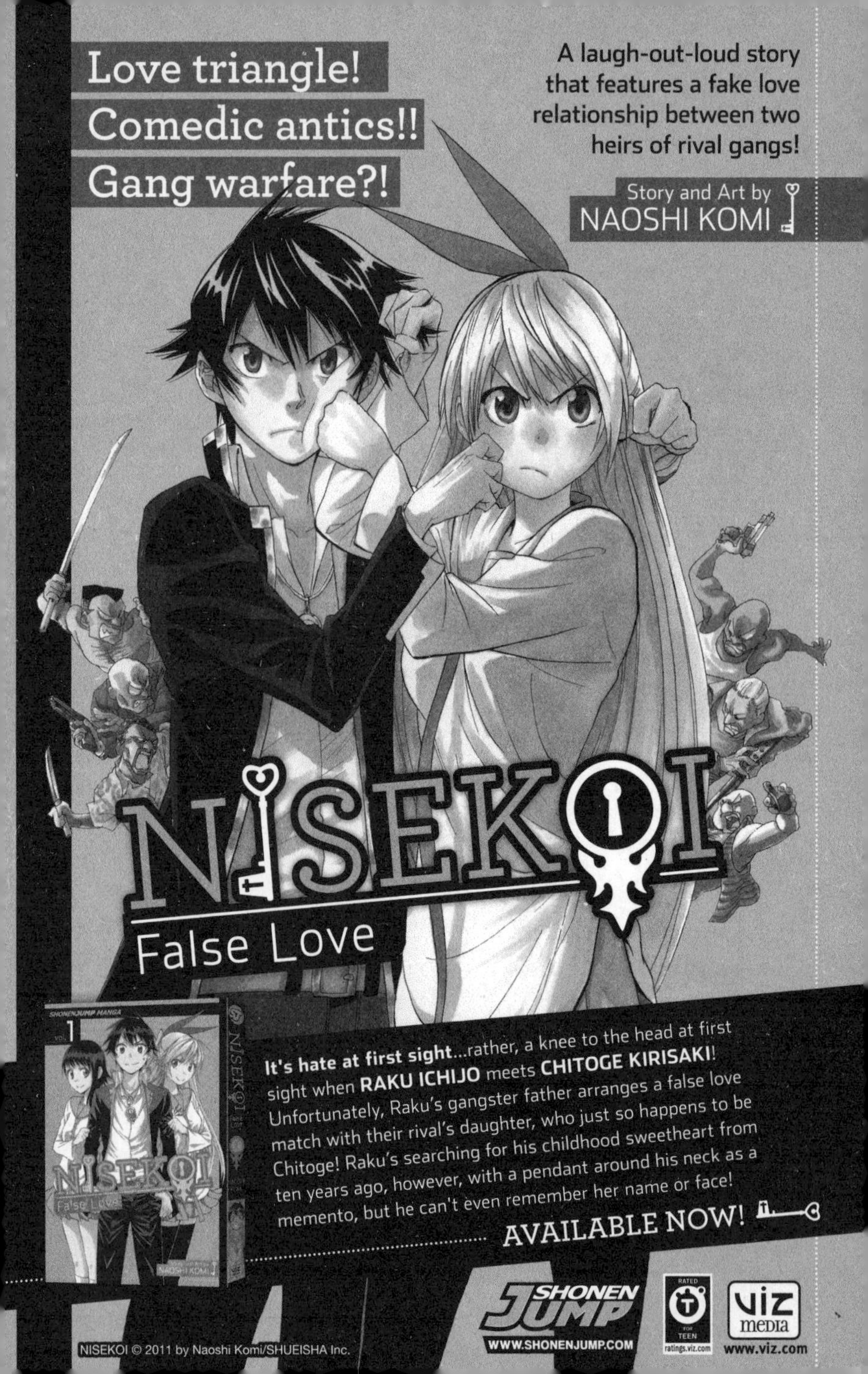
Love triangle!
Comedic antics!!
Gang warfare?!
A laugh-out-loud story that features a fake love relationship between two heirs of rival gangs!
Story and Art by
NAOSHI KOMI
NISEKOI
False Love
SHONENJUMP MANGA
VOL. 1
NISEKOI
False Love
NAOSHI KOMI
It's hate at first sight...rather, a knee to the head at first sight when RAKU ICHIJO meets CHITOGE KIRISAKI! Unfortunately, Raku's gangster father arranges a false love match with their rival's daughter, who just so happens to be Chitoge! Raku's searching for his childhood sweetheart from ten years ago, however, with a pendant around his neck as a memento, but he can't even remember her name or face!
AVAILABLE NOW!
SHONEN JUMP
WWW.SHONENJUMP.COM
RATED T FOR TEEN
ratings.viz.com
viz media
www.viz.com
NISEKOI © 2011 by Naoshi Komi/SHUEISHA Inc.